ONE MAN
AND HIS *Bike*

To Baron von Drais

MIKE CARTER
ONE MAN
AND HIS *Bike*

A 5,000 MILE, LIFE-CHANGING JOURNEY
ROUND THE COAST OF BRITAIN

EBURY
PRESS

3 5 7 9 10 8 6 4

First published in 2011 by Ebury Press, an imprint of Ebury Publishing
A Random House Group company

The Random House Group Limited Reg. No. 954009

Addresses for companies within the Random House Group can be found at
www.randomhouse.co.uk

A CIP catalogue record for this book is available from the British Library

The Random House Group Limited supports The Forest Stewardship
Council (FSC®), the leading international forest certification organisation.
Our books carrying the FSC label are printed on FSC® certified paper. FSC is
the only forest certification scheme endorsed by the leading environmental
organisations, including Greenpeace. Our paper procurement policy can be
found at www.randomhouse.co.uk/environment

Designed and set by seagulls.net

Printed and bound by CPI Group (UK) Ltd, Croydon, CR0 4YY

ISBN 9780091940553

To buy books by your favourite authors and register for offers visit
www.randomhouse.co.uk

Prologue

A fairground booth in Skegness, Lincolnshire.

'I can see you are restless, a free spirit,' says the fortune-teller. 'But soon you will need to go home.'

Chapter 1

'I thought of that while riding my bike.'

Albert Einstein on the Theory of Relativity

'*Eres un imbécil,*' said Simon. '*Eres demasiado viejo para hacer algo como esto.*'

'Eh?' I answered.

'You can't even speak Spanish!' he said.

'I'm learning. Tapes.'

'How long? How long have you been learning?'

'A few months,' I said. This was a lie. It had been a couple of weeks.

'And you're moving to Buenos Aires next month?'

'*Sí.* No going back now.'

He took a sip of his pint. 'Okay. Seeing as we're in a pub, and seeing as you're on your sixth pint, how would you say "I am pissed" in Spanish?'

'Easy. "*Soy un borracho*".'

'That means "I am *a* drunk". In Spanish, there's a distinction between the permanent and the impermanent. Kinda important. Pretty basic.'

Simon turned away to see what was happening in the match on TV. 'Pretty basic,' I muttered under my breath.

'What?' he said.

'Nothing.'

'You've never even been to Buenos Aires,' he said.

'So?'

'Why there?'

'I don't know,' I said. 'I've heard it's a great place to live. Got to be better than here. Is that a good enough reason?'

'Aren't you worried you'll get lonely? Won't you miss Britain, friends?'

'Miss Britain!' I said. 'You kidding me? Have you taken a look around lately?'

We both took a drink of our pints. Silence.

'Got anywhere to live?' Simon said eventually.

'No.'

'Know anybody? Contacts?'

'No.'

'Job lined up?'

I shook my head.

'You're skint. What will you do for money?'

'I'll work in a bar. Be a waiter. Something will come up. It always does.'

'Mike,' said Simon, his voice taking on the concerned tone of a father telling his son that Santa doesn't exist. 'You're 45. Taking off to another country on the other side of the world where you don't speak the language and don't know anybody would be hard at 25. But 45? Madness! Don't you think it's time you stopped, well...'

'Well, what?'

'...running away.'

Chapter 2

'It would not be at all strange if history came to the conclusion that the perfection of the bicycle was the greatest incident of the nineteenth century.'

Anonymous

I pulled up at a red light on the Embankment, on my usual bicycle commute to work.

'*Me llamo Michel*,' said language guru Michel Thomas through my earphones. '*Cómo te llamas?*'

'*Me llamo Mike*,' I said.

'*Todavia quieres hacerlo?*' asked Thomas.

'*No quiero hacerlo ahora*,' I said.

'*Por qué no?*' Thomas asked.

I turned off my iPod.

A woman crossed the road, giving me the look reserved in London for people talking to themselves on bicycles in bad Spanish: fear, contempt.

The lights went green. I pedalled on.

Simon's comments had touched a nerve. Not the bits about being a dreamer or my rubbish Spanish – they were indisputably true – but about running away.

Riding a bicycle is made for thinking. I thought about my life. When I was young, my family had always been on the move: different cities, different houses. By the time I was 11, I'd been to four different schools. I remember being upset about it at first, but losing friends and teachers and a base became so routine that somewhere along the line I must have developed an indifference to everything.

I was 13 when my parents split up. I took to the railways, sleeping on trains and station platforms, sometimes staying away from home for several days at a time. If it wasn't trains, I'd get on my bicycle and just ride for hours and hours. Where I went wasn't important, as long as I was moving.

When my mum died a few years later, I travelled the world, working odd jobs, always looking for the next thing. When my short marriage broke down, I took off on a motorbike. Movement seemed to be my hardwired response when life delivered a blow. It's not hard to see patterns when we look back.

And when I thought about other areas of my life, the same thing kept appearing. Work? Hardly had a full-time job in my life, always freelance, always needing to know the door was unlocked. Relationships? Only had one that was serious. I married her, and look where that got me. I'd never had kids. Homes? Always moving or, if not actually moving, thinking about moving. Security and commitment were fine for other people, just not for me, thank you very much. And for years, all this seemed to work just dandy. Or at least I thought it did.

But I was getting tired. Not just tired of the constant physical movement, but tired of the isolation I'd created for myself, the very thing I'd meticulously cultivated and preserved. The adrenaline rush of being alone, relying solely on my own resources, of not belonging anywhere was, frankly, exhausting.

I stopped at the lights at the north side end Blackfriars Bridge. Every day I came this way and every day I turned left onto New Bridge Street and, 10 minutes later, would arrive at work. As I waited, I looked through the snarled-up traffic to the road opposite, leading east. Queen Victoria Street.

Intuition and instinct are funny things. They're nearly always right and we nearly always ignore them. A thought arrived from nowhere: We live on an island. If I carried on straight, instead of turning left, and followed the Thames out to the sea, as long as I kept the water to my right I would eventually have to arrive back at Blackfriars Bridge, only on the other side of the river. I tried to calculate how far that would be – four or five thousand miles, perhaps – and thought about the places that bike ride would take me: the Northumberland coast; Cape Wrath; the Gower Peninsula; Land's End; through Hull and Edinburgh, Ullapool and Liverpool, Swansea and Portsmouth. And all just by carrying on pedalling up Queen Victoria Street. The simplicity and beauty of the idea made me laugh out loud. The man in the car next to me wound his window up.

I arrived at work. Things had changed a lot at the *Guardian* and *Observer* over the past few years. For one, we'd moved from our tired offices in Farringdon Road to a flash new building overlooking the canal in King's Cross: all glass atriums, and lurid-coloured chairs that looked like giant puckered lips, and 'breakout areas' and 'think-pods', within which we were encouraged to think in the 'blue sky' sense. Old-school hacks stumbled around looking lost, like they'd wandered into a dystopian nightmare.

There were bigger rumblings afoot. The recession was biting. Sales figures were bad. Advertising revenue had plummeted. A cull of staff loomed. There was talk of a ban on freelancers (of which, naturally, I was one). Nobody could see it getting better any time soon. There was an air of restlessness, uncertainty, as there seemed to be in wider society. Was this fuelling the restiveness I was feeling? Was this just the way modern life was? No security? No permanence? People were edgy. Morale was very low.

We went through that day's schedule for the Comment pages. There were six pieces: the MPs' expenses scandal; the news that bankers were to award themselves huge bonuses after being bailed out by the taxpayer to the tune of £80 billion; an analysis of the latest social attitudes survey that revealed 80 per cent of Britons now blamed the poor for being poor, a massive increase from just 20 years earlier; a piece about probable savage public-spending cuts under an increasingly likely-looking Tory government; an editorial on the exponential rise of CCTV; and, finally, a piece about binge drinking and 'broken Britain'.

I met up with my colleague Charlie in the canteen for lunch.

'How are the plans for Argentina going?' he asked.

'Oh, okay.'

'When are you leaving?' he asked.

'Not sure. I'm having second thoughts.'

'Are you mad?' he said. 'Last time I spoke to you, you were full of it. Just going to pack a bag, jump on a plane and see what happened. What's changed?'

'Maybe I'm just getting too old for it all.'

'This country's finished,' he said. 'Look around you. Britain is a toilet.'

'A friend reckons I spend my life running away.'

'He sounds jealous,' Charlie said. 'If I didn't have a family and commitments, I'd be on the next plane out of here. Nobody depends on you. There's nothing keeping you here.'

'Maybe that's part of the problem,' I said. 'So, a year or two in Argentina. Then what?'

'Maybe you'll meet somebody there, settle down…'

'But why would that be any different to doing it here? It's not really about meeting somebody anyway. If that were the case, I'd be on the Internet lying about my height and income. I think it's more about, well… at risk of sounding like a tosser, having roots, belonging somewhere.'

'Belonging?'

'I think so.'

'Tosser.'

'Thank you.'

The truth was, as far as I could fathom, that I really wanted to love Britain. Wanted to love being here. I wanted this to feel like home. I hated the fact that I always thought life would be better if I could be somewhere else – because that never worked out. All this had started to grow in importance in my head since I made the decision to leave.

But Britain was increasingly a hard place to hold much affection for. And things seemed like they were only going to get worse.

I grew up in inner-city areas alongside crime and poverty. But I can't ever remember Britain feeling as squalid as now, as divided, as uncaring, as 'broken'. Could a country have changed so much in such a short time? But as much as I wanted to leave, the very thought felt like an infidelity.

'On the way to work this morning I had an idea. Instead of turning left at Blackfriars Bridge, what would happen if I just kept cycling straight on and followed the coast?'

'You'd get to Middlesbrough,' Charlie said. 'Not quite Buenos Aires.'

'A full circuit of the island. An exotic adventure in my own backyard. The kindness of strangers and all that.'

'There's nothing exotic about moaning Brits. It would be like cycling through the *Daily Mail*. The roads are vile. And as for the kindness of strangers, this is Britain we're talking about.'

'It's not that bad.' I suddenly felt quite protective.

'Remember that old German guy a couple of years back?' Charlie said. 'Cycled round the world for 10 years or something, through Afghanistan, Iraq, the lot. Never had any problems. Arrives off the ferry in Portsmouth, pitches his tent, wakes up the next day and his bike's been nicked.'

'I'm supposed to be leaving in a month's time,' I said. 'I've bought my ticket.'

'I know. Sunshine. Tango. Argentinian women. Adventure. Lucky bastard.'

'But imagine, just riding my bike every day, camping at night, living simply. When I got back in six months, I could always still go to Argentina.'

After work, I cycled through King's Cross, then past the old *Guardian* building in Farringdon Road, all dark now. It was raining hard, the water sitting on the road in oily slicks, reflecting the spectral tungsten glow of the streetlights. In the distance, the skyscrapers of the City burned brightly.

A motorbike flashed past me. Followed by a car. They both screeched to a halt at the lights just before Blackfriars Bridge. A middle-aged man jumped out of the car. Something in his hand glinted, caught in the headlights. The biker jumped off and raised both hands above his head. While the man from the car waved his blade about in wild slashes, a young girl, around seven years old, got out of the passenger seat. She ran towards the biker and, jumping up to reach, started punching him in the helmet, landing one punch each time at the top of her parabola. This was simultaneously so depressing and so funny that I didn't know whether to laugh or cry.

I jumped off my bicycle and let it drop to the ground. My hands were trembling. Calmly, though I'm not sure where the calm came from, I asked the man with the knife whether anything was worth this.

He looked at me with eyes as dead as a fish on a slab. Then he waved his knife at the biker once more, called him a cunt, ushered the girl back to the car and drove off.

'Cheers for that,' said the biker through his open visor. 'That guy was mental. This country's gone mad.' He mounted his bike and rode off into the night.

All was quiet again. I was alone. To my left was Queen Victoria Street. I looked at it. On that grim, wet night, it suddenly seemed as magical as Professor Kirke's wardrobe or the fancy-dress shop's changing room in Mr Benn. A portal.

I got out my phone and sent a text to Simon.

'I'm not going to Buenos Aires,' it read. 'I'm off to Basildon.'

Chapter 3

'[The bicycle] is no longer a beast of steel... no, it is a friend... It is a faithful and powerful ally against one's worst enemies. It is stronger than anxiety, stronger than sadness. It has all the power of hope.'

Maurice Leblanc

Pedalling frantically up and down a towpath in East London in the May rain was not quite how I envisioned my round-Britain bike ride ending. Yet here I was, quite stuck, my *A–Z* not old but completely useless, pinging back and forth like a tin duck in a shooting gallery, unable to make any headway east, all throughways turned into cul-de-sacs by the Olympic machine.

A man about my age cycled towards me on the towpath. I stood in his way, raising a hand. He stopped. He had to, really. My bike, loaded with the amount of gear normally only seen with refugees fleeing a war zone, was completely blocking the towpath. His only other options would have been to ride through the nettles or into the river. London being London, he weighed his alternatives carefully.

'Sorry to stop you,' I said. 'But I'm a bit lost.'

'Where are you going?' he asked.

'Today?' I said. 'Or ultimately?'

Doubtless not expecting to be engaged in matters existential on his morning commute, he steered things towards the purely navigational.

'Now. Where are you going now?'

'Not sure, really. Possibly Burnham-on-Crouch.'

'Possibly?'

'Or maybe Maldon...'

'Where's that?'

'Essex coast,' I said. 'Beyond Chelmsford, I think. Where the salt comes from. I've never been there before. Supposed to be nice.'

'You don't know where you're going?'

'I don't like to plan too much,' I said.

'And you don't have a map?'

'Just my *A to Z*. But it's useless because of all this.' I gestured towards the cranes and the throbbing of heavy plant and driving piles into the ground on the other side of the fence. 'I was going to buy a map when I got out of town. I didn't think I'd need one for Stratford.'

He glanced at the nettles again, and then the river. He needed an explanation.

'You see, I'm going to cycle around the entire coast. I thought that all I had to do was keep the Thames in sight and thereafter the sea on my right and, as we live on an island, I couldn't go wrong. But I lost the Thames shortly after the Blackwall Tunnel, and now here I am.'

'For charity?' he said.

'What?'

'For charity? You doing it for charity?'

'No. Just for me.'

'That's a waste,' he said.

This way of looking at achievement was a new development of the past couple of decades in Britain. Every time somebody did something – climb a mountain, run a marathon, fart the national anthem – it had to be for charity, as if we'd lost the notion that things were worth doing for their own sake. I imagined Scott plaguing his chums for pledges to go towards a penguin hospital, or Hannibal raising money for an elephant rescue centre.

We stood there for a moment. Not only were my actual navigation skills terrible, but my moral compass was shot too, me being so wrapped up in my own existence that I couldn't be arsed to help the needy.

'It's the same distance as London to Calcutta,' I said, feeling the need to inflate myself up.

'London to Calcutta?' he said. 'Are you sure?'

'Yes, the wrinkly nature of the coastline means it's a lot further than you think.'

'Wow,' he said.

'Yes,' I replied.

'Still. Shame.'

We stood there for a moment in awkward silence.

'Follow me,' he said. 'I'll put you on the A11.'

I tried to bump my bike around, but the front wheel slipped in the mud. I tried for a second to arrest the fall, but with the ridiculous amount of weight I'd packed, it was like wrestling a bull steer. The bike fell from under me and came to rest on its side in the mud, me standing over it.

I had ignored the conventional wisdom about taking trial runs with a full load. In fact, the day I'd set off was the first time I'd ridden with luggage – two panniers on the back, two straddling the front wheel, a dry bag full of camping gear bungeed to the rear rack, and a bar bag – in my life.

I am not proud of my lack of planning and foresight, but it's something I've become used to over the years. Some people are planners. Some are not. I'd always been struck by the Ancient epigram: 'Want to give the gods a laugh? Tell them of your plans.'

I'd ignored too the sensible notion that one should get in some serious training miles before a big expedition. The 10 miles I'd cycled since leaving home had felt like riding through treacle. With the weight on the front of the bike, every slight turn of the handlebars had threatened to send me crashing to earth. The rain continued to fall. I thought about the 5,000 miles I still had to cover. My mind wandered to the Aerolineas check-in desk at Heathrow.

We pedalled south together, past fenced-off slip ramps, under rumbling flyovers, weaving between people out walking their dogs. They were always muscular 'fighting dogs' these days – mastiffs, bull terriers, Staffies – with harnesses and studded collars and, according to regular stories in the papers, a taste for baby flesh. It was rare to see anything else now. Every time I saw a poodle or a Labrador or a mongrel, I always felt sorry for it. It must be like they've woken up in some futuristic nightmare, some doggy *Mad Max*. It's a pretty pass when a dog can't sniff another dog's arse without fearing for its life.

The Waterworks River (Oh, that trinity of the world's great waterways: the Ganges, the Euphrates, the Waterworks…) wound its way behind derelict warehouses with broken panes and the dank, musty smell of decay. Reed heads and shopping trolleys broke the water's surface.

'So how long is this trip going to take?' asked the man, over his shoulder. I hadn't bothered to ask his name, of course. I was still in London, after all.

'Not sure,' I said. 'Five months. Six months. It's not a race. I'm just going to see where I end up each day. If I come across somewhere I like, or there's something interesting going on, I'll hang around for a while. You know.'

'I'd love to do something like that one day, though probably Spain or Italy. Somewhere hot. Not this shithole. So, you're going anticlockwise?'

'Looks like it.'

'Why?'

It was a good question. A pity I didn't have a good answer. Every time I went for a loop around Richmond Park, I always went anticlockwise. That didn't seem a sound-enough basis for deciding the direction of this somewhat larger loop though. I needed more substance.

'Ever see those experiments where they show how water goes down the plughole differently in the northern and southern hemispheres?' I said.

'No.'

'Well, if you empty a sink in Australia, the water will always flow clockwise. In Britain, anticlockwise,' I said.

'Why?' The look on his face betrayed the fact that he knew nothing of such weighty and celestial matters. I'd got the keys to Bullshit City.

'It's all to do with magnetic forces and the poles,' I said. 'And the rotation of the earth and hurricanes and all that. It's the natural order of things.'

'What happens on the equator?'

Another fine question.

'The water stays in the sink.'

'For ever?'

'Yes.'

'That doesn't sound right.'

'Look it up.' I hoped he would. I didn't want to be haunted in the future by the voice of Chris Tarrant saying: 'And, for one million pounds, you, East London bloke, said "C: The water doesn't go down." Don't go away, we'll be back after this break…'

Eventually, we came to a ramp with no fences blocking it off, at the top of which was a graffiti-strewn concrete flyover, heavy with trucks and buses. The ride up the ramp made me puff.

'There you go: the A11,' said the man. 'Your gateway to Britain. I bet they're words that have never been used in the same sentence before.'

'Thank you.'

'Good luck,' he replied and, as he cycled off, I'm sure I saw him shake his head. Still, he'd have a good story to tell when he got to work.

I trundled through the Stratford one-way system and then joined the Romford Road, buses squeezing past my wide load in the bus lanes, my eyes scouring the near distance for the potholes that, every time I hit one, threatened to fold my laden steel bike like a wire coat hanger. I noticed how tightly I was gripping the bars, constantly trying to manhandle the bike, fighting it, scared of its weight. It was making my hands and shoulders ache. I was hoping that with practice I'd loosen up. If I didn't, off the bike I'd be walking like Frankenstein's monster for the next few months.

There were plenty of vacant shop units on the Romford Road. Those that were still open for business were mostly Indian restaurants, hairdressers and minicab offices. Outside a grocery shop stood a trestle table full of fruit and vegetables in small clear-plastic bowls. I pulled over.

'How much for the bananas?' I asked the guy standing outside his shop, resplendent in his burgundy salwar kameez. There were six in the bowl.

'Pound,' he said.

'And the grapes?'

'Everything's a pound.'

I asked how he made money, selling his stuff so cheaply.

'No choice,' he said. 'Times are hard. But the supermarkets can't compete with us when we drop our prices so low. They sell their fruit cheap; we go cheaper. They open late; we open later. We're 24 hours now. And so it goes.'

But where could it go after that?

'Must be exhausting,' I said.

'What can you do?' he said. 'That's a pound.'

I stuffed the bananas in my bar bag.

'Anything else?' he asked. 'These plums are good and sweet.'

'I can't carry much,' I said, pointing to my bike.

'Must weigh a ton,' he said.

'Try it,' I said. 'Go on, pick it up.'

He was a big man but, grabbing under the saddle, struggled to lift the bike off the ground.

'What have you got in there!' he laughed.

'Too much. I'm going to have to get rid of some of it.'

I retrieved a banana from the bar bag.

'Do you know where I can get a road atlas round here?' I asked.

'You lost?'

'Not really. I just need a road map. Is there a petrol station nearby?'

'Where you heading?' he asked.

I told him about my trip.

'All the way around Britain!' he said. 'That must be over a thousand miles.'

'More like five thousand.'

'You need some more bananas!' he laughed.

'Nice sales technique.'

'How come you haven't got a map?' he asked.

'This is going to sound stupid, but I thought that I'd be able to keep the water in sight. As long as I could see the Thames and then the sea, I couldn't go wrong. But I haven't seen the water since just past Canary Wharf.'

'Hang on,' he said. 'Keep an eye out. I'll be back in a minute.' He disappeared into his shop, and after a couple of minutes emerged, smiling, clutching a well-thumbed AA Road Atlas of Great Britain.

'Any good? Thought I'd lost it, so I bought a new one, then found out my brother had borrowed it. It's only a couple of years old. Can't imagine much has changed in that time.'

'You sure?'

'I don't need it,' he said, thrusting it at me.

'I'm touched,' I said, and tucked the atlas under a bungee cord on the back rack.

'You're touched all right,' he laughed, tapping his temple. 'Five thousand miles!'

'I'll take those plums as well, please.'

'Pound.'

Through Ilford and Hornchurch the traffic began to thin out a bit, the rain becoming just a light drizzle. A group of pensioners sat waiting for a bus at a stop outside a bank on Hornchurch high street. Without thinking, I waved. The three women waved back, smiling, one of them raising her stick in a friendly salute. What weird disease was this I'd picked up, greeting strangers? Where did I think I was: abroad?

In reality I was past Upminster at the end of the Underground network. I lived at the other end of the District Line. I could have popped on the Tube and got home without having to change trains. This felt like the start of the adventure proper, a feeling only intensified a couple of miles later when I ducked under the M25 and London appeared to stop abruptly and the skies seemed to widen, as if that 117-mile strip of tarmac was keeping the masses constrained like a taut girdle, all its neurotic twitchings hemmed in.

I meandered along the Essex lanes flanked by hawthorn hedgerows, a brisk south-westerly pushing me along. Through North Ockendon, Bulphan and Little Malgraves, even the place names were redolent of a more pastoral world. It was hard to imagine that a few hours before, I had been cycling along the Embankment, with its angry traffic and siren symphony.

I looked at my new map and plotted a route to Basildon. Useful things, maps. The road went through a place called Langdon Hills and I thought I'd test my legs. I mean, Essex is not exactly the Alps. How steep could it be? Oh dear. Within a few minutes I was walking, my feet slipping like a cartoon character on banana skins on the damp road surface as I tried to force the immense weight of my bike and belongings up the hill, stopping every minute or so to wipe the stinging sweat from my eyes.

When I'd set off that morning, I had wondered how long it would be before I had to get off and push. A part of me (the moron part) thought it might be Yorkshire or the Highlands of Scotland. Another part of me (the hopelessly deluded moron part) even imagined that I'd never have to get off and push; that I might circumnavigate the entire island, bum and saddle never parted. And yet here I was, in Essex, just after lunchtime on day one, pushing. But a part of me (the 45-year-old, dodgy-kneed, never-been-cycle-touring-before, packed-far-too-much-stuff part) was glad. At least now I wouldn't have to go through that agonising macho bullshit of killing myself trying to cycle up the steepest hills simply because I didn't want that hill to be *the one*.

I would definitely have to get rid of some gear, though. Maybe even an arm. I mean, who needs two?

In Basildon, I stopped to eat a banana and some plums and looked at the map again. If I was to follow my original plan of sticking strictly to every inch of the coast covered by road, then I now needed to head for Canvey Island, do a loop of that, then on to Southend-on-Sea and beyond to Shoeburyness. But such is the nature of the Essex coastline, with its myriad creeks and marshes and sticky-out bits, to use the technical geographical term, that I would have to come nearly all the way back to just north of Basildon to get around the River Crouch. That would be an out-and-back of some 30-odd miles just to say I'd been to Shoeburyness.

Billy Bragg sang about Shoeburyness in 'Trunk Road to the Sea', but he neglected to say what one might find when one got there. I recalled that in the children's book *Larklight*, Philip Reeve mentioned a 'squalid spot called Shoeburyness'. Thanks, Phil; good enough for me. I only hoped that I wouldn't be haunted in the future by Chris Tarrant sitting opposite me saying: 'And, for one million pounds, Mike, where in Britain can you still see the mile-long remains of a Cold War defence boom designed to trap Soviet submarines? Come on, you'd know it if you'd been there.'

I flicked through the atlas. Now that I could see where the roads went in relation to the coastline, it was clear I'd have to make some decisions about the nature of the ride. It was true that I didn't have a strict timetable for completing the journey, but if I followed every single cul-de-sac to every single headland, I would be on the road for the rest of my life, and possibly some of the next one too.

I opened the pages on the West Coast of Scotland. Some of the peninsulas had no roads at all. And then there were all the islands.

Did they count as part of the British coastline? And how about taking ferries across estuaries? Was that cheating? And bridges?

I'd set off on this journey to see my country, to meet people, not to break any records. This was my journey. I'd use my logic, however inconsistent. If hopping across islands made sense to make progress, I'd do it. If I wanted to go to a particular island just for the hell of it, I'd do it. If there was a ferry, I'd take it. Or not.

I decided to do what I always end up doing: make it up as I go along, see where the road took me. After all, I'd already broken two taboos with barely 30 miles under my wheels: getting off and walking up a hill, and deciding against going to the first headland of the trip. Now I was free to do anything I wanted and it felt liberating.

I looked at the next headland up, a big gnarled thumb of Essex hitching in the North Sea, with Burnham-on-Crouch on the ball joint. There was really only one way on and off that landmass too. But I had to go somewhere, or else I might end up in Basildon for the rest of my life.

The south-westerlies had picked up. If I headed to Burnham, I'd have a tailwind all the way. Going where the wind blew me. I liked that.

If there is ever a place that feels like it's at the end of the road to nowhere, then it's Burnham-on-Crouch. I approached the town, still barrelling along with the wind, under a watery sun with puffball clouds scudding across the sky at breakneck speed. The trees beside the road were being whipped into a frenzied Mexican wave, the mudflats to my right glossed with a patina of mercury. Arthur Ransome and Alfred Hitchcock are both said to have been inspired by the area, the latter for *The Birds* – the attendant vast number of crows squawking their sinister laugh and swooping around me made that easy to see. And it's there that martian invaders stalked across the land towards one of the most dramatic battles of HG Wells' *The War of the Worlds*:

> Then, far away beyond the Crouch, came another, striding over some stunted trees, and then yet another, still farther off, wading deeply through a shiny mudflat that seemed to hang halfway up between sea and sky.

This all seemed to capture that estuarine landscape perfectly: a fantasy playground ripe for children's adventure, underscored by a wild, brooding malevolence.

I wanted to explore Burnham, but first I needed somewhere to sleep. There would be plenty of time to camp on this trip – my budget would see to that – but I thought I'd treat myself, for the first few nights at least, to a nice, comfy bed. Besides, after 65 miles, my backside felt like it had been tenderised with a steak mallet, my thighs like they had been pummelled with a cricket bat. I was assuming, praying, that my journey would get easier.

I saw a sign for a B&B and slipped and slid along a gravel track – not great for a loaded touring bicycle – through a tunnel of trees. At the end was a black-and-white timbered manor house, set in beautiful formal gardens, a riot of colour dissected by symmetric paving, with a gazebo floating on a lake. It was a place to arrive at in a vintage Rolls-Royce trailing horseshoes, not smelly and sweaty and splattered in dead flies.

'Welcome,' said a bouncy woman in her mid-to-late twenties who introduced herself as Kate. 'Come far?'

'London,' I said.

'Blimey,' said Kate.

'I've had the wind,' I said.

'Oh,' said Kate.

A man appeared.

'This is my husband, Ben,' said Kate.

'Welcome,' said Ben. 'Bring your bike inside.'

I looked inside the grand hallway. There was beautiful wooden flooring and expensive-looking rugs, leading to a dark-oak staircase at the bottom of which a bronze Aphrodite held aloft a glass bowl lamp. On a low oak table sat bowls of potpourri and bridal magazines. An exquisite grandfather clock wheezed and clunked asthmatically.

'Are you sure?' I asked. 'My bike's quite clean.' I looked at the Ridgeback. It wasn't clean. It looked as if it had been at Glastonbury. 'I can put some paper under it.'

'Don't worry,' said Kate. 'The floor cleans up well enough. We get all sorts of muck in here.'

She showed me up to my room. I asked how long they'd been there. They did seem very young and, well, normal, to be living in such a big, gorgeous house within commuting distance of London.

'A couple of years,' she said. She told me how she and Ben had been living in London, her working in PR, him in IT. She'd given it up to become a youth worker and Ben retrained as an osteopath. Eventually they'd left the city and bought the manor house, to live the dream. But the sums hadn't added up.

'We started doing weddings to make ends meet,' she said. 'Now that's our main business. The season starts in two weeks and we're booked solid till October.'

'Hard work,' I said.

'Oh, yes,' Kate said. 'Fun, but hard. We try and organise everything ourselves: catering, music, the lot. And I'm pregnant with our second so it's not going to get any easier. Our friends from London are all jealous of us. But Ben and I are often jealous of them, living in the city, normal jobs. It can feel quite isolated here.'

We approached a dark, wood-panelled door.

'This is you: the honeymoon suite,' she said. 'You're the only guest tonight. I warn you, though, we haven't had the time to renovate the bathroom yet. The previous owners had somewhat "interesting" tastes.'

'I couldn't care less what the bathroom looks like,' I said. 'I'm just desperate for a good soak.'

I closed the door, put my panniers down, unpacked them and laid the contents out on the bed. I had to get rid of some stuff. I was exhausted from riding 65 miles on mostly flat roads with a strong tailwind. Weighed down as I was, there's no way I would be able to tackle the upcoming hills, no matter how fit I became.

Looking back now, I can't believe what I'd packed for the trip. Yet when I'd laid it all out at my flat in London, I'd easily managed to justify all items individually. I started to sort my belongings into separate piles.

In the 'non-cycling clothes' pile went: two pairs of jeans (the heaviest fabric there is; one pair that fitted me now and a pair from my slimmer days that I would doubtless need a month from now when I was svelte again); a pair of lightweight hiking trousers (with zip-off legs, thus saving the need for a separate pair of shorts); a presentable jacket (for evenings out); a thick fleece; a micro fleece; four non-cycling T-shirts; two smart shirts (now horribly creased); a pair of smartish shoes (for aforementioned evenings out); a pair of sandals (for quiet nights around the campsite); and a pair of trainers (for walking around the sights). Then there were two pairs of swimming trunks; a dozen pairs of socks, including two pairs of smart silk ones; a dozen pairs of underpants; a pair of long johns; a pair of fleece gloves; and a woolly hat (the latter three items for cold nights in the tent – I wasn't buying into the predicted 'barbecue summer').

On the bike pile went: three cycling tops; two pairs of Lycra shorts; one pair of baggy cycling shorts (to pull on over said Lycra shorts for modesty in cafés, town centres or where there are easily scared children around); one pair of cycling shoes; leg warmers (for non-cyclists, I should explain that these are Lycra tubes worn under cycling shorts and not the Day-Glo woolly variety, packed in case I happened across a 1980s-themed disco night); and arm warmers. I had a warm cycling jacket, a Gore-Tex raincoat, a pair of waterproof overtrousers, a high-visibility gilet (to pull on in low-light conditions), my helmet, Gore-Tex helmet cover, two pairs of sunglasses (I was bound to lose at least one pair), spare sunglasses lenses, two pairs of fingerless cycling mitts, and one pair of long-fingered cycling gloves.

Into the miscellaneous pile went: a guidebook to Britain; three novels; a chunky biography of Che Guevara; a mini dictionary and thesaurus (A mini dictionary and thesaurus! What did I want to look up? Synonyms for steep? More poetic ways to say 'I'm going to have a heart attack'?); a solar recharging system (the optimist in me was still buying into the predicted 'barbecue summer'); various conventional chargers (for when that turned out to be a fiction); a laptop; two box sets of *The Wire* (seasons four and five to watch on those lonely nights in the tent); two cameras (one for back-up); a mobile phone; a headtorch; a radio; a clothesline; a few clothes pegs; a first-aid kit; a Tupperware tumbler; a vacuum flask; a head net for midges; and two pairs of swimming goggles.

In my toiletries bag I had aftershave, moisturiser (a man's gotta take care of his appearance), a big can of shaving gel, and post-ride massage oil (a blend of lavender and citrus), among other things.

Oh, experienced cycle tourists out there, try and control your mirth.

Only that morning it had all seemed essential. Now, feeling my thighs pulsing, it all looked ridiculous.

I resolved to make a pile of things I probably wouldn't need. This was harder than it seemed, because I could easily imagine scenarios when I might need everything. How about meeting that dream woman? I'm going to need the smart jacket and the aftershave. What if I get to the shores of Loch Ness and a strange, prehistoric shape breaks the water's surface and I get my camera and it jams? How about if somebody in the wilds of Wales stops me on a sunny day and says 'The batteries on my wife's home life-support system have packed up. You haven't got a solar recharging system have you?' Okay, that last one is ridiculous. Sunny day? Wales?

But this was exactly why my shed and cupboards at home were full of crap. Because I can always imagine a time when I might need everything. Maybe we should all be forced to stuff our 'essentials' into a few bags and have to push them up a steep hill. It would really focus the mind.

Onto the discarded pile to post home I put a pair of jeans (the fat ones), one pair of swimming trunks, the spare camera and season five of *The Wire*. It was a start. It was going to be mostly flat until Yorkshire after all. I'd eventually find my touring legs and there'd be plenty of time to jettison stuff further on into the trip.

Then I started going through my road atlas, ripping out the coastal pages I needed, numbering them, and throwing away the rest. I was very pleased with myself for this stroke of genius, though I would be in trouble if the shopkeeper on the Romford Road ever wanted his map back.

I went into the bathroom, started running a bath and returned to the bedroom. The room was trashed, my gear spread everywhere like a jumble sale. I looked at my four empty panniers. How had all this stuff fitted into them? I looked at my books. Che was a big man and deserved a big book. But he had La Poderosa, a Norton 500, to help him up the hills. I put him into the reject pile.

I went into the bathroom, turned off the taps and climbed in the tub, sinking into the hot embrace, closing my eyes in ecstasy, the stiffness and tenderness starting to melt away, wallowing in the great feeling of satisfaction after a day of hard labour and fresh air. The bits of me that had been exposed to the elements were tingling, burning, slightly but deliciously. My first day on the road. I'd earned this. I felt like a great athlete resting after a day's heroics. I gently opened my eyes…

'What the…!'

Staring back at me from the ceiling was not a great athlete at all, but a pallid, flabby, middle-aged man, the only bit of him not pasty his bright red face, which was sweating profusely. It was one of the most unattractive things I'd ever seen – and I've spent a lot of time in rugby changing rooms.

I turned onto my side. The entire wall was mirrored too. In fact, now I started looking, I could see that the entire bathroom was mirrored, every surface, including the door. Wherever I turned, all I could see was me. And if I looked beyond my first reflection, there were hundreds of me, stretching into infinity.

Now I understood what Kate had meant by 'interesting tastes'. I wondered how many married sex lives had started in this room, and how many of them had survived the trauma.

I watched me scrub and I watched me wallow. I watched me scratch my arse and I watched me pick my nose. It was no good, the view was too grim to relax. I stood up and watched myself bend over to get the towel (this I accidentally saw from behind: a lifetime's first and, hopefully, a last). Did they have mirrors in Dante's day? If so, I was in the bathroom of his Upper Hell.

I got dressed (chinos, smart shoes, evening jacket, splash of David-off Cool Water, if you're interested) and took the Ridgeback off in the direction of Burnham-on-Crouch some two miles away. Without the luggage, it felt as frisky as a colt, as if at any second it could take off, *ET* fashion.

The church bells were ringing as I pedalled down the high street, passing the Rio, an exquisite, tiny art deco cinema, and then along the wide handsome high street, between the rows of white weatherboard houses draped in wisteria and solid Georgian homes, many with windows formed of stained-glass sailing scenes. It was all as pretty as a cake-tin picture.

On my right, the pavement cut through the base of an octagonal clock tower, with a fish-scale tiled ogee roof, which looked part rocket and part minaret. I pulled over to have a look. At the base was a memorial plaque. 'In memory of Laban Sweeting', it read. And I thought that was quite the loveliest name I had ever heard.

I cut through a narrow street to the seafront and cycled along the promenade. At the end, I came to the art deco splendour of the

Royal Corinthian Yacht Club, designed in 1931 by Joseph Pemberton, which ended up representing Britain at the International Exhibition of Modern Architecture held at the Museum of Modern Art in New York in 1932. With its spiral staircases and brilliant white walls, huge windows with cobalt frames, and a large part of the structure cantilevered beyond the sea defences, it looked as if it could have been blown by the wind all the way from South Beach, Miami.

I'd never been to Burnham before, and I wondered why.

A woman walked past, out with her dog.

'Good evening,' I said. 'Lovely night for a stroll.'

'Isn't it.'

'And what's his name?' I asked, pointing to her West Highland terrier.

'This is Max.'

'Splendid name, Max,' I said, bending down to give him a pat on the head.

Somewhere between London and Burnham, possibly just beyond the M25, I seemed to have morphed into a royal, or a politician on the campaign trail. I would never talk to strangers in London. Or any other city, come to that. I liked it though.

I locked my bike outside the Oyster Smack Inn. There was a group of four men at the bar in an otherwise empty pub. One turned to me.

'Evenan',' he said. He had an accent which, if I'd been pressed, I would have guessed was from somewhere in the West Country, but which I would come to learn was proper rural Essex.

'Evenin',' I said.

'Lovely now, int it?' he said. 'Bit grubby earlier, thou.'

'Aye,' I said. I always said 'aye' when I was in the countryside. It was a ridiculous affectation.

'Is Terry Scott dead?' said one of the others, turning to me.

'Sorry?'

'Terry Scott. Is he dead?'

'Erm... I'm not...'

'You know. Fat bloke. Carry On films, *Terry and June*, Curly-Wurly ads.'

'I think so. Not a hundred per cent but I haven't seen him on telly for a while.'

'Told you,' said the man, turning back to his friends.

I picked up a menu. There was whole roast pigeon, hare cannelloni, monkfish in pancetta, half a dozen Maldon oysters with a red wine vinegar and shallot dressing. I was salivating like Pavlov's dog. I hadn't eaten much all day, aside from the fruit, and it had only just struck me just how ravenous I was, hungrier than I can remember ever being.

'Yes, love,' asked the woman behind the bar.

'Pint of lager, please.'

She poured it and placed it on the counter. I raised it to my lips. The first draught emptied half the glass.

'And could I order some food?'

'Sure, let me get my pad.' She turned round to pick it up from the shelf behind the bar. By the time she'd turned back to me, the pint glass was empty.

'Blimey,' said the woman. 'You're thirsty.'

'Windsor Davies,' said one of the men.

'Sorry?'

'Is Windsor Davies dead?'

'Another pint?' the barmaid broke in.

'Yes please.'

'You know, *Ain't Half Hot Mum*...'

'I'm not sure.'

'There you go, love. And what food can I get you?'

'Always shouting...'

'Can I have the venison burger with extra bacon and cheese, a double portion of chips, some onion rings, deep-fried mushrooms and some garlic bread.'

'Someone's hungry.'

'Welsh. Sang with that little fella...'

'Take a seat. Won't be long.'

'"Whispering Grass"...'

'I think so,' I said.

'Told you,' the man said, looking smugly at his friends.

After the longest 10 minutes of my life, the food arrived, mountains of it. I started on the chips while the woman still had her hand on the plate.

'On holiday?' she asked.

'Sort of. I'm touring on a bicycle.'

'Told you,' she said, turning to the men at the bar.

She didn't elaborate on how she'd come to that conclusion, but I was too busy shovelling onion rings into my mouth to be curious.

I had a pudding, too. A big slab of chocolate cake sitting in a lake of double cream. And for one of the only times in my life, my gluttony was completely unsullied by guilt. My body was like a furnace, the metabolism racing, my stomach like a chick from the nest constantly calling for food. I thought about all my favourite treats now largely proscribed or heavily rationed by the guilt and irrepressible middle-age spread: the wine gums and the biscuits, the Jaffa Cakes and the crisps. I was going to enjoy this trip.

But I'd also somehow got incredibly pissed on three pints of lager, and sat there now, with mouth sagging open, like a man who'd had a stroke.

I went up to pay my bill, fumbling around in my pocket, and then dropped my wallet. I bent down to pick it up but had to grab the bar to stop myself falling over.

'You okay?' said the woman.

'Just tired,' I said.

'Reg Varney,' said one of the men.

'I don't...'

'*On the Buses...*'

And as I stumbled out of the door, all I could hear was 'first person ever to use an ATM machine...'

I don't remember too much about the ride back to the B&B, but I do recall pulling over and talking to some cows in a field.

It took me five minutes to get the key in the door, and another five to climb the stairs, clinging to the banister rail like a man pulling himself up a steep ramp with a rope.

I got into the room, kicked off my shoes and went into the bathroom. Worried about my accuracy in the honeymoon suite, I decided the safest bet was to sit on the toilet, which I did, trousers around my ankles, and soon after I was slumping forwards, with my head in my hands. I awoke two hours later, not quite sure where I was. I lifted my head and, through heavily squinting eyes, gradually focused on the hideous thing staring back at me.

'Arrrraghhhhh!'

Chapter 4

*'Think of bicycles as rideable art
that can just about save the world.'*
Grant Petersen, US bicycle designer

As I hit the road the next morning, the south-westerlies were still keen, the clouds low and ominous. I took a detour back into Burnham, popped into the post office and handed over my parcel. It didn't feel very heavy in my hand. After the gluttony of the previous evening, I calculated that I'd probably made a net gain on weight.

I headed north across the flatlands of the Dengie Peninsula, named after the Daeningas, the Saxons who'd settled the area in the fifth century, sparsely populated due to its isolation. I rode through untamed fields and salt marshes, skirting lonely reaches accompanied by the soundtrack of crows, the skies immense, the grasslands shimmering in the wind, giving the whole landscape a feeling of liquidity. Dengie seemed fabulously onomatopoeic.

Novelist John Fowles has written of the 'vast God-denying skies, the endless grey horizon, the icy north-easterlies of the Dengie flats in winter'. I wouldn't want to be here in winter. Not on a bicycle, anyway.

I meandered along the quiet back lanes, seeing neither cars nor houses, not any sign of human life. Pheasants jumped out from the hedgerows, playing chicken with my front wheel, swifts darted and danced ahead of me like dolphins in the bow wave of a boat. If yesterday had been about escaping from the suffocating confines of London, a mad dash to get somewhere else, then today was about beginning to breathe. Thus I felt, really felt, for the first time on this trip, the miraculous nature of travel by bicycle. How, just by sitting on a saddle and pedalling, in the space of a day I'd managed to transport myself to another world, foot by foot, mile by mile, a sense of journey and progress that's just impossible in a sealed car. There's an Arabic saying that the soul travels at the speed of a camel. I was beginning to understand this.

I rolled through the pretty village of Tillingham, all village green, ancient pubs and white clapboard houses, snoozing under its low, grey blanket.

'By midday they passed through Tillingham,' wrote Wells of the Martians in *The War of the Worlds*, 'which, strangely enough, seemed silent and deserted, save for a few furtive plunderers hunting for food.'

Wells couldn't have picked a better spot for contrasting the collision of two worlds.

A blackboard outside the Cap and Feathers offered four pints for £10 'to beat the credit crunch', while the Fox and Hounds had 'beat the crunch lunches', suggesting an altogether different war of the worlds had started. Even the chapel on the high street was boarded up, a 'for sale' sign poking out above the chest-high weeds, nailed to a peeling board that read: 'Church of the Peculiar People'.

I remembered reading about the Peculiar People, a Christian sect unique to south Essex, founded in the 1830s by John Banyard, a former drunk. They practised a puritanical form of Christianity, eschewing medical care, relying on the healing power of prayer instead. Next door to the chapel was a doctor's surgery. I wondered if the temptation had got too much.

An old boy with wild silvery whiskers was walking past, pushing an empty wheelbarrow.

'What happened to the chapel?' I asked him.

'Dunno,' he said, in that lovely soft rural-Essex accent. 'One day they gorn.'

'Any idea why they were called the Peculiar People?' I asked.

'Religious people awl a bit peculiar, ain't they,' he said. 'Still, make a lovely house. Right next to the doc's. Keep him busy. All you gotta do is put a bit of that Semtex over them walls and it be lovely.'

A few miles further up the road, the grey immense bulk of Bradwell nuclear power station appeared. It looked like sixties planners had built a council estate in the middle of this otherwise empty landscape. It occurred to me that this journey would take me past all of Britain's coastal nuclear stations. And who wouldn't want that on their CV?

I knew Bradwell had been decommissioned just after the turn of the twenty-first century, the first UK station to be closed on a planned basis, and cycled up to it expecting to find dereliction and desertion, nature following its reclamation act. But the large car park was full, the place buzzing, though these days only with people. I stopped and spoke to a security guard, asked him why there were so many people working in a disused plant.

'It's going to take twenty years to decommission. And for the first seven years there'll be no redundancies. The government is still deciding whether to build a new station on the same site, though, so we might all be okay.'

'You local?' I asked.

'Live over there,' he said, pointing across the River Blackwater. 'Mersea Island.'

'Nice commute. This place must be a godsend to the local economy.'

'It is. There isn't much else around work-wise at the moment. But a lot of the locals are against the new station. Mersea Island's only got a causeway that floods linking it to the mainland, so it can't be evacuated in an emergency. They're worried that hot water pouring into the estuary will destroy the fragile ecosystem. The area's prone to flooding – they reckon that the land's sinking about ten inches a century. But a new station would bring jobs. A lot of the people moaning are retired, so they don't have to worry. But this is the real world. You've got to work.'

I asked him about the proposed wind farm I'd read about: 30 giant turbines to be built onshore near Bradwell.

'People don't want that either,' he said. 'Would ruin the landscape, they reckon. I don't know. We've got to do something. Oil's not going to last for ever.'

I cycled down a gravel track. The wind was howling now. Comedy wind, with the kind of sound effects you'd normally associate with BBC radio dramas of people trapped out on the southern ocean. Even the crows were sticking to the trees, now keeping metronomic time with the gusts.

At the end of the track was a small chapel, St Peter-on-the-Wall, standing quite alone on the headland, facing out on the 250 acres of salt marsh and shingle of the Bradwell Cockle Spit nature reserve, carpeted with sea holly and marram grass, rock samphire and sea rocket. It felt like the end of the earth.

The chapel had been built by Saint Cedd in 653AD after he'd sailed down from Lindisfarne to spread Christianity among the godless locals. It is one of the oldest largely intact church buildings in England still in regular use.

There were no other people there. Standing at a certain point, I could see nothing man-made in the entire landscape apart from the chapel; the earth, water, mud and sky bleeding seamlessly into each other. It was easy to imagine myself anywhere in time over the past 1,500 years. It was a raw, elemental place.

I propped my bike against the leeward side of the chapel and entered the empty building, my cycling shoes clip-clopping against the flagstones worn smooth over the centuries. Light streamed in from the windows, set 20 feet above the ground. A few simple wooden benches were laid out. The rough stone walls were unadorned save for a small red cross at the far end depicting Christ and Saint Cedd. At the front was a modern stone altar, inset with three stones, gifts from Lindisfarne, Iona and Lastingham in Yorkshire. On top of the altar was a scattering of shells and pebbles, a few formed into letters to spell 'dad'. I sat on a bench listening to the wind. Time passed. I could have stayed there for ever.

When I did emerge, I stood back from the chapel to take a picture. A white Jack Russell with a half-black head walked into the shot and sat down, staring at me.

'Tizzy, Tizzy, get out of the man's picture,' I heard a woman's voice say.

But Tizzy was having none of it. He just sat there, looking at me, tongue flapping about.

'I'm so sorry,' said the woman. 'He just likes having his picture taken. If you take a shot, then he'll move. You can always delete it later.'

So I did. And Tizzy then went happily on his way, stopping only to cock his leg against my bicycle and then against the chapel. I never did delete that picture.

I had to cycle straight into the wind now, heading west so I could get around the ferryless River Blackwater, a 30-mile ride to reach Mersea Island, just two miles across the mudflats and shifting sands. That was frustrating. But it was something I'd have to get used to on this trip, being physically so close to where I wanted to go but taking hours of toil to get there. It's a mindset that motorised travel has more or less abrogated, where distances and winds and hills are rendered irrelevant by the turn of a key.

I was taking a terrible buffeting, having to stand on the pedals just to make ground. The cars were treating the B-roads like their private racetrack, coming perilously close to me, swooshing round corners, taking the racing line, not remotely aware of the wind and the effect it has on the stability of a heavily laden bicycle.

I'm sure there was no malice involved. Just ignorance. As a cyclist and driver, I can see things from both sides. Maybe one day we'll have a driving test that includes both forms of transport. I'm convinced it would foster much greater understanding among road users.

It didn't help that I was bonking at the same time. Now, I should explain to non-cyclists that I wasn't trying to have sex while pedalling along. That would indeed create a degree of instability, involve a level of dexterity unfamiliar to me since my younger days, and rightly engender a certain amount of antipathy from my fellow road users.

No, the verb 'to bonk' in cycling means to run out of gas, one's natural energy supplies having being depleted by the day's exertions. So common is its usage among cyclists that it's easy to forget that, for non-cyclists, it means something else altogether. Maybe they could incorporate it in the written part of the new driving test. Clear up any misunderstandings. It's a great pity they never made *Carry On Cycling*.

Starving, and still unused to the amount of food I would have to consume constantly throughout long days in the saddle, I pulled into a garage, popped my bike against the wall, and joined the queue.

'Any fuel, love?' the woman asked the guy in front of me. 'Number four? You got a BP card?'

'Any fuel, love?' she asked me.

'Just these,' I said, holding out a jumbo-sized packet of fig rolls.

'One pound fifty,' she said. 'You got a BP card?'

'It's my fuel,' I said.

I thought this quite clever, and granted myself the indulgence of a little chuckle. The woman would have needed to know that I was on a bicycle to join in the joke. In retrospect, she obviously didn't.

'That's nice,' she said. 'One pound fifty.'

'Because I don't need petrol. This. Is. My. Fuel. Biscuits.'

'Next,' the woman said. 'Any fuel, love?'

I took my fig rolls outside and, beside the window where the woman was on the till, hoovered the entire packet, one biscuit after another, shovelling them into my mouth, crumbs cascading down my shirt. After I'd finished, I mounted my bike and waved at the woman, pointing to my Ridgeback, then to my mouth.

She turned back to the next customer.

I was desperate to reach Maldon. Not so much because of its unique spot in literature as the place where the first great epic poem in English, *The Battle of Maldon*, was written. Nor, indeed, because it's home to the largest surviving fleet of nineteenth-century Thames sailing barges, those wooden vessels whose flat bottoms made them perfectly adapted to those shallow creeks and estuaries, a dozen or so of which lined the quayside. No, lovely as Maldon was, the only thing that interested me that day was the fact that it lay at the head of the River Blackwater and, having battled for the last 20 miles into a strong south-westerly headwind, after it I could head east. Such is the solipsism of the long-distance cyclist.

Now on a starboard tack, I flew along the B1026. If I'd packed a spinnaker, I'd have flown it. Hills just flattened out, my legs getting into a steady high tempo; I effortlessly clocked 25mph, flying through a village called Tolleshunt D'Arcy and, while still trying to imagine what the origin of that name might be, hit Salcott-cum-Virley and gave up.

One of the things I find about cycling is that flying before the wind always feels like the natural state of things, how things should always be, as close to perfection and harmony with the world as it's possible to get, the elements (wind, muscle) combining to speed you on your way.

I am a terrible golfer, but when I hit a rare good shot – clean, crisp, straight – instead of acknowledging it as the fluke it was, it always feels like the 'real' me, a perfection of alignment, a confluence of mind and muscle that, if found once, could, given application (and talent), be found every time. Every duff shot that inevitably follows is an aberration, an injustice.

Well, that's how I've always felt about the wind and cycling. Tailwinds I deserve. Headwinds I do not. Most people learn about the injustices of the universe when they're children. But a strong headwind? I just want to lie on the floor, stamping my arms and legs on the ground, going 'waaaah, waaaah, 'snot fair…'

I gybed, and headed across the Strood, an exposed Roman causeway that bolts Mersea, the UK's most easterly inhabited island, five marooned square miles of salt marshes, creeks and mud, to the mainland. The causeway still glistened from its last tidal soaking and this, combined with the wind now whistling across my starboard beam and the traffic trying to squeeze past me on the narrow road, made for tricky riding. I jumped on the pavement and, more than once, the wind, catching the large surface area of my luggage, blew me into the wooden fence, which I'd hang onto for dear life.

I watched the gusts sweep across the surface of the Strood channel, pricking up the water like hairs on a scared cat's back, and between them released my grip on the fence, pedalled like fury, then hung on like grim death again. You don't get that in a car.

I rode past caravan parks and retirement homes and houses where little signs on home-made boards advertised manure for sale, or pleaded for the return of a lost dog, sad little eyes staring back at me from blown-up photographs. There was nearly always a reward offered. One was for £750! How we English love our dogs. I tried to keep a mental rogues' gallery of all the assorted dogs and kittens and where they lived, in case I should come across any strays. But then I imagined myself careering across the countryside with panniers full of mewling furballs, and abandoned the idea.

I passed a convex mirror standing opposite a driveway and gave myself a little wave as I flashed by. I had started doing this earlier that day and it had already become a habit. It felt like the equivalent of a montage sequence in a movie, an indication of the passing of time. There I am! Look at me! Moving! Cycling round Britain! Helloooooo! But then again, this could just be what happens to a man with too much time on his hands sitting on a bicycle all day.

I arrived in the tiny town of West Mersea. A couple of miles across the Blackwater was Bradwell nuclear power station, brooding, terrifying. I remembered what the security guard had said regarding the evacuation of Mersea in the event of an accident. Thinking about the causeway, the scenario was chilling.

On the front, between the land and the muddy creeks, was an area of marshy grassland. On it, with mooring lines tethered into the earth, were dozens of houseboats, floating on the grass, marooned, like those trawlers on the dried-out Aral Sea. When I say boats, I use the term in its loosest sense. For many looked like sheds that had been nailed to a hull, or had ramshackle cabins that comprised fence panels, mismatched doors and double-glazed windows of every shape and architectural idiom, as if the owners had ram-raided their local reclamation yard, grabbed what they could before the police arrived, and made the best of their looted booty.

It was a bit early for me to tackle the fabled Mersea native oysters, sprats and clams raked from the nearby creeks that are served up by the island's two seafood institutions, the West Mersea Oyster Bar and the Company Shed, both housed in plank-board shacks that looked like village community centres. Besides, I wasn't sure about the cycling nutritional value of shellfish, and the combination of getting a dodgy clam while wearing Lycra bib shorts with no immediate access to a lavatory would not be a happy one.

So I plumped for an outside table at a café on the corner of the high street, watercolours of Mersea seascapes festooning the walls. A group of four well-fed and ruddy-faced middle-aged men in rugby shirts and deck shoes sat at the next table drinking beer. Three young mums rocking strollers sat chatting at the table next to them. I ordered a cappuccino and a blueberry muffin and, after eating that in three mouthfuls, ordered another.

'Hungry?' asked the young waiter as he brought me my second muffin.

'I'm cycling,' I said to him. 'Need the energy.'

'How far have you come?'

'From London.'

'With all that gear!' he said pointing to my bike.

'I'm on a long trip.' I told him where I was heading.

'Amazing,' he said, and his eyes flashed with envy. 'I'd love to do that. Think of all the incredible places you'll see.'

'I've seen some pretty amazing things already,' I said. 'I never knew this coastline was so beautiful.'

'Not bad, is it?' he said. 'Could never live anywhere else.'

I asked him what it was like living on an island that periodically got cut off from the mainland. It seemed such a weird anachronism in the twenty-first century, where busy councils and engineering departments saw every obstacle that nature created as a problem to be solved.

He told me that the debate about improving the causeway rumbled on. How they've been told that by raising it just a few feet, they would never be cut off again.

'But to be honest, most of us like being cut off,' he said. 'It's part of the Mersea character, the sense of strangeness living on an island brings. It feels like things happen here just that little bit slower than in the outside world. Nobody wants to lose that.'

I picked up the café's copy of that day's *Guardian*. The Speaker, Michael Martin, had finally quit over his handling of the parliamentary expenses scandal. On the Comment pages, where I usually worked, a headline thundered: 'The Speaker exits with revolution in the air. I say, bring it on.' I read on:

> Voters share a sense of revulsion that has no recent precedent…When the nation loathes not this individual or even that political party, but the entire governing class – yearning to throw out the whole lot of them … Power should belong to us all… We demand a full statement of our rights, in a language and a style any of us could understand… Fundamental rights are ours unconditionally, because we are all in charge… (©Guardian News & Media Ltd 2009)

This made me smile. Three days earlier, I had been at my desk at the *Guardian*'s Comment pages, working as a subeditor on pieces like this, getting stirred up by the rhetoric, corroded by the perceived injustices done to the country by the political classes, as I had done for many years, seeing the same pieces and the same arguments trotted out year after year, the same outrages, the same accusations, and nothing ever changing. Revolution in the air? Real, meaningful change? It would be like turkeys voting for Christmas.

The waiter came back out of the café, placed a couple of bowls of chips in front of the ruddy-faced men, three coffees for the young mums, then swung by my table.

'There you go,' he said, plonking another muffin down in front of me. 'On the house. You'll need it.' Now that felt like a revolutionary act.

On the way out of town, I tried to find a shop selling bananas. Everywhere seemed closed. I stopped to ask an elderly woman pushing a walking frame. Behind her was an estate agent's, weeks of mail piled up beyond the glass door.

'Most of the shops are closed on Wednesdays now,' she said.

'Tradition?' I asked.

'This depression,' she said. 'It's not worth them opening.'

At the eastern end of Mersea, I scanned the beach for a likely spot where the foot ferry to Brightlingsea might make landfall. I only had 10 minutes to make the next service, and a long wait if I missed it. I asked two female walkers with Ordnance Survey maps if they knew where it landed. With great authority they sent me off to the north, pedalling along a dirt track atop a high earthen sea wall, overgrown with brambles which ripped at my legs; my panniers, chain and wheels collected assorted foliage as I went.

After five minutes I stopped and, looking back, could see the ferry heading for the beach, to the exact point where I'd started. Frantically executing a nine-point turn in the brambles (the bike still being too heavy to lift easily), and cursing people with the dangerous combination of maps, authority and a terrible sense of direction, I proceeded to deracinate the fragile Essex littoral some more, all the while shouting frantically at the boat in the distance, now sitting on the beach, ramp down, like a tiny landing craft. 'I'm coming, I'm coming…'

Above the boat's landing spot was a steep flight of rickety wooden steps, down which I manhandled the bike, bashing my left calf with the pedal, drawing more blood, which sent profanities ringing out, and then a dash of around 200 metres across soft sand, through which I tried to ride, fell off, then tried to push, which was impossible.

'I'm com… I'm com…' I gasped.

Gathering my fast-diminishing strength, I lifted the bike's dead weight and proceeded, my feet sinking in the sand, my back arched backwards, like a groom carrying the world's fattest bride, until I reached the ferry.

'No need to rush,' the young ferryman said. 'We'd have waited. Looks like you're the only one.'

This was my first ferry of the trip. I'd been excited about it, imagining the serenity of sitting there, as noble as a pharaoh, crossing one of the great bodies of water (the Colne might not be the Nile, but it's all relative), fingers trailing in the water, breathing lungfuls of the salty brine, licking the crust off my sweaty lips, watching land slip away, closing a chapter, with new land rising to greet me, promising delicious new prospects for adventure.

Instead, I sat on the boat, exhausted, bleeding, exfoliating the bike of brambles and dandelions and trying to get the sand out of my derailleur.

There were whitecaps in the middle of the grey, boiling channel and the flat-bottomed boat was making heavy weather of it. Then the engine died.

'We've been having a few problems with it,' the ferryman confessed. 'I'll have to radio for help.'

We sat there for 15 minutes, flopping around like a dead flatfish, my bike beginning to roll, my stomach beginning to churn. By the time the rescue boat reached us and towed us into Brightlingsea, and the little ramp was lowered so the invasion of the next peninsula could begin, I felt like I'd been to war. I staggered with the bike along the jetty, went around the corner, found a litter bin, and deposited there the remains of three blueberry muffins, two bananas and one jumbo-sized packet of fig rolls.

I followed the rolling contours of the B1027 and then, in Jaywick, there it was: the sea in all its immensity! Such is the estuarine nature of the Essex coastline that in two days and nearly 130 miles since leaving London, I hadn't actually seen the proper sea: that is, 180 degrees of nothing but ocean. It felt deeply comforting to think that this vast presence would now, more or less, be my constant companion for the next 5,000 miles.

But if I felt happy to see Jaywick, it looked as if Jaywick hadn't felt happy about much in a long time. In the early 1980s, the American writer Paul Theroux, in *The Kingdom by the Sea*, an account of his journey around the British coast, had compared the town to 'a seaside slum in Argentina or Mexico', its run-down demeanor making it seem like it had been the victim of 'war or weather'.

Not much seemed to have changed in the intervening 30 years. Many of the roads were hideously cratered, like bombed runways, the holes filled with fetid, muddy water. Some of the houses – little more than shacks, frayed and peeling – looked like another North Sea blast would render them into dust. It was shocking to come across such a place in modern Britain.

According to my guidebook, Jaywick had been built as a resort for working-class Londoners in the 1930s, with the houses poorly constructed and meant only for holiday use. As time passed, more and more people moved into the town permanently. Investment, partly due to Jaywick's low-lying situation in a high-risk flood zone, was never forthcoming. It was now one of the most deprived communities in the country in terms of unemployment, crime and health. I thought about all those British dreams of moving or retiring to the seaside, and how many of those dreams ended there. And I thought about the budget deficit and the spending cuts and the austerity to come. The only solace for Jaywick, I supposed, is that it didn't look as if it could get much worse.

I pedalled next door to Clacton, along a cycle path high above the beach, the chill onshore wind making me stop and pull on my warm cycling jacket. A couple of brave children ran into the brown surf, their squeals drifting up to meet me.

In cars parked facing the sea, under the low, grey ceiling, pensioners sat. Mostly couples, one usually asleep, the other staring out into the vastness, sipping absent-mindedly from a plastic mug, as if the answers lay somewhere past the horizon. Some of the cars had just one pensioner, never asleep, always just staring out to sea.

Looking down on the pier, I could see that the fair was still shaking off its winter ennui. A couple of rides were moving, garish lightbulbs of red and green penetrating the gloom, the tinny, jangly music drifting up to blend with the children's squeals from the beach. The rest of the rides were still under wraps, draped in stained white tarps, like exotic birds put away for the night.

And then a few miles on to Frinton-on-Sea, dotted with the art deco houses and apartment blocks of architect Oliver Hill, built between 1934 and 1935 and occupying a broad, cliff-top grassland.

With its flat roofs, terraces, portholes and ship deck guardrails, this new seaside architecture was meant to evoke the then fashionable transatlantic liners. And stunning it was too. It was as different from Jaywick as it's possible to imagine.

Frinton has a reputation for being somewhat staid (the town's first pub only opened in 2000) and a gerontologist's dream – not helped by the old music-hall joke: 'Harwich for the continent, Frinton for the incontinent!' – but I dare say it doesn't mind too much. The pensioners I saw all seemed to be dressed for golf or sailing, and looked infinitely healthier and happier than their counterparts in Clacton and Jaywick. For some reason, the three places, lined up side by side on the coast just seven miles apart, reminded me of the *Frost Report* sketch featuring John Cleese, Ronnie Barker and Ronnie Corbett, which starts with a posh Cleese saying 'I look down on him...' and proceeds to Corbett's classic line: 'I know my place.'

It was to the backwaters of Walton-on-the-Naze that I headed next, naze being the Norse word for promontory. I was looking for a man named Tony Haggis, whose splendid name was sadly unmatched by the run-down industrial estate in which I'd been told I could find him. And there he was, waving at me, all blue fisherman's smock, close grey stubble, mahogany tan and a pair of cool shades. He looked like a middle-aged guitar legend.

'How did you cut your legs?' he asked.

'Bit of bother getting to the Brightlingsea ferry,' I said. 'It's a long story.'

He unlocked a rusty chain-link gate and we walked down a ramp and onto a narrow jetty, at the end of which was a small blue wooden boat. He clambered in.

'We've got to hurry to catch the tide,' he said. 'Hand me your stuff.'

I released my camping bag from its bungee and cargo-net restraints, then unhooked each of the four panniers and the bar bag, swinging each one across the water to the outstretched hand of Tony, who was balanced brilliantly on the small rocking vessel like all good boatmen.

'Now your bike,' he said. I felt like I was handing over a child. Tony reached out and, one-handed, grabbed the bike and laid it in the bottom of the boat.

'Now you,' he said.

The jetty was slippery with algae, matters not helped by my cycling cleats. I went to step off, then thought better of it, instead sitting down and shuffling myself into the boat like a dog rubbing his backside on the carpet, before landing on top of my luggage and almost falling overboard. Dignity didn't come into it.

Tony fired up the outboard and we were off, putt-putting between the mudflats and the bright mooring buoys and the beached boats listing perilously.

I asked Tony about his life there. Walton born and bred, for over 30 years (he was 58) he'd fished those backwaters and the North Sea for bass, cod and dogfish (like his father before him), before a back injury made that impossible. So he'd swapped commercial fishing for a more serene life running wildlife boat trips around the 7,000 acres of the Naze Site of Special Scientific Interest on the *Karina*, a former Trinity House ship's lifeboat. He was now in his eleventh year.

'And there she is!' he said, pointing to a larger, blue-hulled vessel at anchor some 100 yards ahead.

After a second bike and luggage transfer, we slipped out of the narrow creek and into the wider Hamford Water.

'This is where Arthur Ransome set *Secret Water*,' Tony told me. 'You can just see it, can't you?'

Indeed I could. Little fingers of water branched out like jungle reaches into the thick samphire. On a muddy bank stood black-backed gulls. From the sea lavender, a skylark rose high into the sky, singing constantly, before plunging to the ground and starting all over again. A dozen redshanks attacked a marsh harrier as it got too close to their nests.

Every boat that passed, exchanged greetings. 'Hey Tony, how's it going?', 'Great day, eh, Tony?' 'See you in the pub tonight, Tony?' I felt a sharp pang of envy for this man: for the relationship he had with the natural world and his knowledge of it; for his 'office' in the middle of it all; for his place in a community.

'Hey, Mike, look,' Tony said. 'There's a halo around the sun.'

'What's that mean?' I asked, like a wide-eyed naïf at the feet of a sage.

'It means good weather's coming,' he said. 'Or maybe bad.'

He winked and let out a little laugh.

Tony killed the engine and we sat there in the slack water, perfectly still apart from the gentle, almost imperceptible, rocking of the boat. The silence was immense. My skin felt like a giant sponge, soaking it all in. London seemed a million miles away.

A squadron of oystercatchers flew past, low, in tight formation, a couple peeling off the back before rejoining the group, all the while making their usual racket. 'I reckon the Red Arrows learn to fly by watching them,' said Tony.

Tony told me some more about his life. In 1985, he'd become the skipper of the *Ross Revenge*, Radio Caroline's 1,000-ton trawler anchored 15 miles off Walton. And the month before I met him he'd been seen on cinema screens across the world playing Emma Thompson's boatman in *The Boat That Rocked*, a comedy about Caroline's heyday.

'Wild times,' he said. 'I'd go back tomorrow if it was still illegal.'

He'd also worked as a volunteer for Greenpeace aboard their ocean-going tug *Solo* taking part in seal surveys on the Scottish West Coast and many other actions over the years. In winter, when few tourists are around wanting to explore the creeks, he took off travelling: India, North Africa, South America.

He had also cycled half the British coastline, from Walton up to Cape Wrath.

'I loved that,' he said. 'What freedom! What a coastline! Now I've met you, I'm jealous. I'm going to have to do the other half.' I had no doubt that he would.

Tony started the engine and we motored off, rounding an island where a line of old barges sat on the beach, an attempt to defy nature's inevitable reclamation of the eastern seaboard.

'That's Horsey Island,' Tony said. 'They breed horses there.'

After the halo conversation, I wasn't sure whether he was joking or not.

'Seriously, Arabs. Ah, there they are…' he said, pointing off the port bow.

I followed his finger. On a mudflat, about 100 yards away, were around 50 seals, greys and commons, their backs rust red so that, from a distance, they looked like garden slugs.

'The red comes from the iron oxide of the salt marshes,' Tony said. 'It's unique to this area.'

We got as close as Tony was willing to go. One or two inquisitive doe-eyed heads bobbed up by the boat, like silken Labradors, and then slipped quietly under. On the mudflat, two large bull grey seals squared up, chests puffed out, making an unearthly din, sending the juveniles scurrying and wobbling into the water.

I had left London wondering whether it was possible to have an exotic adventure in my own backyard. And here I was, only 70 miles away as the crow flies, in the middle of a landscape as weird as any I'd ever seen, watching these huge, magnificent beasts in the wild.

'Where are you off to next?' Tony asked.

'I'm going to head there tonight,' I said, pointing towards Harwich, some five miles distant, over which, from the opposite bank, the serried cranes of Felixstowe loomed like H.G. Wells' mechanical monsters about to annihilate the good burghers of Essex's last town.

'That's about 15 miles by road,' he said. 'It's getting dark. I'll take you.'

'No, I couldn't...'

'No arguments,' he said. 'Always like to help a fellow traveller.'

And so Tony nosed the *Karina* towards the open sea and soon we were out in the big swells, my panniers flying all over the boat, my bike rolling back and forth on the wooden planks like a gimbal, me unable to corral them because both hands were hanging on to the *Karina*'s handrail for dear life. We dodged between the huge, silent container ships and ferries bursting out of the gloom, lights ablaze. Icy water exploded over the gunwales, soaking me. I licked the delicious salt crust from my lips. For the second time in a day I was on a boat being tossed around. But this time I didn't feel sick, I just felt stupidly, ridiculously happy. Was this an adventure? No doubt.

Chapter 5

'The bicycle is the perfect transducer to match man's metabolic energy to the impedance of locomotion. Equipped with this tool, man outstrips the efficiency of not only all machines but all other animals as well.'

Ivan Illich, *Energy and Equity*

As I cycled through Harwich the next morning, it seemed as if a nice crowd had lined the cobbled streets to wave me off. Then a policewoman stepped out and told me I needed to get off my bike and push. The roads were closed.

'What's going on?' I asked.

'We're mayor-making,' she said, as if that would explain everything.

Around the corner came a procession. At its head was a grey-bearded fellow in tricorne hat, scarlet frock coat and black pantaloons. In his hand was a large brass bell, which he rang with great enthusiasm while proclaiming many things, none of which I could hear. This was because beside him was a portly man, dressed in a splendid purple tartan kilt and sporran, with a Glengarry on his head worn at a jaunty angle, blowing loudly on the bagpipes. I couldn't readily identify the tune he was playing, but I was pretty sure its origins were not in Essex. Behind them was a woman in white gloves, crimson robe and mayoral chains, a chap dressed like Black Rod, complete with mace, and, behind them, a long snaking line of people in gowns.

I asked the woman next to me what was going on.

'It's an old Harwich custom going back to the Middle Ages,' she told me, 'when we elect a new mayor.'

'What about the bagpiper?'

'No idea,' she said. 'The best bit's coming up, though.'

The dignitaries disappeared into the Guildhall and moments later a window opened above the street. 'Catch a kitchel if you can!' cried the mayor, who then proceeded to throw cakes to the excited crowd of children who'd gathered below the window, arms outstretched in joyous expectation, grabbing at the buns raining down.

'It used to be a Christmas thing,' the woman said. 'When children used to visit their godparents and ask for their blessing, which they'd receive along with a small cake called a God's kitchel.'

'What's that got to do with the mayor, and May?'

'Not sure,' she said.

A cake landed near my feet. I picked it up, unwrapped it and took a bite. A long-distance cyclist doesn't miss a fuelling opportunity.

'Delicious,' I said to the woman. 'Like a hot-cross bun.'

'They,' she said sternly, 'are meant for the children.'

I left Harwich and headed west along the B1352, past fields of golden rape, the road dipping and climbing, giving occasional views out across the River Stour. There had been a ferry at Harwich that I could have taken across to Felixstowe, but I preferred to take the long inland detour, to get around the bridgeless rivers Stour, Orwell and Deben, before rejoining the Suffolk coast at Orford. The weather was fine, if still a little grey, the winds had dropped, and my belly was full of free cakes stolen from the mouths of children. All was well with the world.

Mistley, a handsome town of Georgian houses on the banks of the Stour, was no stranger to controversy. Back in the seventeenth century, when the people of Harwich were innocently throwing their buns, the people of Mistley got their kicks watching Matthew Hopkins, the Witchfinder General – who claimed to hold the Devil's own list of all the witches in England – put hundreds of benighted women through 'swimming' tests in the Stour, their ability to swim being somewhat compromised by the fact their arms and legs had been tied together. He was by all accounts a bit of a Renaissance witchfinder, though. Not for him the barbarity of burning alive those unfortunate lonely crones with a penchant for cats. This wasn't the dark ages: hanging was his chosen method of execution.

Hopkins would have struggled to find a spot to dunk witches in Mistley on the day I passed through. The entire river and mudflats were covered in swans, hundreds of them. It was a quite magnificent sight.

Not everybody seemed to share my enthusiasm, though. In the high street, there was a local newspaper billboard outside a shop. 'Swan Wars!' it read. I went in, bought a copy and retired to a bench on the riverbank to read it. After swan numbers had increased vastly in recent years, some residents were accusing a local swan charity of overfeeding them. 'They shit all over the place,' one resident, who'd declined to give his name, was quoted as saying. 'Those feeding them should get bloody ASBOs.'

A defender of the swans, also unwilling to be named, accused incomers from London of orchestrating the campaign. 'They have little knowledge of rural matters. Now they're joining the local council to try and pass by-laws. They turn up and think they can poke their noses in, when the swans have been here for hundreds of years.'

Tucked away on page nine were the latest revelations from the MPs' expenses scandal, sandwiched between stories about a stolen lawn mower and a missing dog. Opposite was a picture spread of local children taking part in a fancy-dress competition to raise money for their school. One had gone as a swan, which, given the circumstances, could have been seen as a tad inflammatory.

Local newspapers are dying on their arse in Britain. Some forecasts predict that half will fold in the next five years – victims of the collapse in advertising revenue, the rise of freesheets, the growth of the Internet, and the rapacious acquisition of them by multinational media organisations. I know nothing ever stays the same, especially in these accelerated times, but to me local papers are one of the real joys of travel in Britain: a window into the soul of communities, with all their idiosyncrasies and dirty laundry on display; where a battle over swan shit is far more important than a Westminster row about a duck house.

Ipswich, the county town of Suffolk, may be ranked only the 168th biggest metropolis in the UK, but after a week or so of riding through the sparsely populated countryside of the Essex marshlands it felt like Mexico City.

I rode through the centre, past the docklands developments of flash apartments and gentrified warehouses. Every time I looked over my shoulder before changing lanes, there was a car tight on my wheel. I felt harassed, like a sheep being marshalled by collies.

Queues of cars lined up to get into the shopping centre car parks, people staring grimly at the bumper in front of them, windows up, sealed off from the world. People walked along the street clutching armfuls of shopping bags. I rode past streets of tightly packed terraced houses. I heard my first police sirens since London. There were car horns, shouting, banging. The cacophonous rumblings of urban life had supplanted the birdsong. The world had been photoshopped from glorious Technicolor to grey. It felt aggressive, crowded. Yet I'm sure Ipswich is neither, particularly.

William Wordsworth, that great advocate of the restorative powers of the natural world, had been convinced of the toxicity of conurbations. Yet this was only partly down to the smoke and congestion and slums he encountered. For he thought cities damaged our very souls, creating anxiety about our place in the social hierarchy, jealousy at the status and success of others, a need to puff ourselves up in the eyes of strangers, and a relentless drive to acquire new things that promised happiness and fulfilment but ultimately left us feeling empty. Cities, Wordsworth thought, made meaningful human relationships difficult.

'One thought baffled my understanding,' he wrote, of London, in *The Prelude*:

> *'...how men lived*
> *[As] next-door neighbours, as we say, yet still*
> *Strangers, and knowing not each the other's name...*
> *How oft, amid those overflowing streets,*
> *Have I gone forwards with the crowd, and said*
> *Unto myself, 'The face of every one*
> *That passes by me is a mystery!''*

Something had happened to me. The carapace that protected me from the mayhem and aggression in London seemed to be dissolving. A memory came to me of standing on the platform of my railway station, fighting to get into a carriage, my fellow commuters regarding each other with suspicion, contempt even, 'the face of every one that passes by me is a mystery'.

And I was in Ipswich! Population: 120,000! The thought of ever trying to settle back into my life in London sent a shiver up my spine.

I rode out of Ipswich. In the distance I could see a church spire, poking out of a cluster of trees. I headed for it. I felt suddenly tired, and churchyards, when you're on the road, offer a very singular form of sanctuary.

I pushed my bike through the little gate, and wheeled it along a line of rowans. A rabbit, startled, bounded off, its white tail enabling me to follow its progress down the hill. I propped my bike against the last rowan and lay down in the long grass, between Elizabeth and Edgar Warren and Abraham and Susannah Pinner, whose plots suggested they had been long forgotten. I could hear the crows again, and a nightingale. With the sibilant hiss of the traffic on the A12 in the background, I fell into a deep, dreamless sleep.

When I awoke, an hour later, a spider had made steady progress building a web between the toe of my left shoe and a fractured urn celebrating the life of Mr and Mrs Warren.

I rode into Woodbridge at the head of the River Deben, and along its high street, with its old shire hall and Georgian, Regency and Tudor houses in pastel shades, all strung together by a web of red, blue and white bunting.

In the middle of the high street was a big shop unit of white-washed windows; on the red fascia panel above, the familiar name of Woolworths. Between 27 December 2008 and 6 January 2009, all 807 Woolies stores in Britain had closed, and 27,000 people had lost their jobs. I'd already seen a few on the trip, but I still hadn't got used to the idea that Woolworths was no more. And the huge gap it left in the high streets of Britain always looked like an act of Stalinesque revisionism, something that had been an ever-present entity suddenly airbrushed away.

Opposite Woolworths, a young girl, maybe 15, was playing a guitar and singing a tormented song about lacking confidence. She looked self-conscious to the point of mortification, unable or unwilling to meet the eyes of passers-by, perhaps driven by the idea that she would one day be famous and here was a story to enliven a memoir. She had a soulful voice, not unlike Alanis Morissette, and I popped a pound into her cap. She nodded thank you, but didn't look up from the pavement.

I pedalled down to the waterfront, and sat on a bench next to the sixteenth-century tide mill, one of only two in the UK still working, and the oldest. The sun was shining now, flashing diamonds on the surface on the Deben, the dazzling white clapboard walls of the tide mill almost too painful to look at.

'Come far?' a man asked. I'd been amazed how many people had stopped to ask me this question. Forget cute dogs, it would seem that a loaded touring bicycle was the ultimate icebreaker. I wasn't sure whether it was connected to our friend H.G. Wells' assertion that 'every time I see an adult on a bicycle, I no longer despair for the future of the human race', or something else.

Psychologists might say it's to do with attachment. The great majority of us first learn to ride as a child, the bicycle a type of 'transitional object', taking us away to really explore the bigger world for the first time out of the sight of our parents, our first real taste of independence and freedom. It's the symbolic moment when horizons broaden, possibilities open up; you are moving under your own power, controlling where you want to go. It wouldn't be too much of a stretch to imagine that as adults we would always cherish a thing that had given us such a formative experience.

'From London originally,' I told the man. 'I'm cycling around the whole coastline.'

'Wow, you are living my dream.' Obviously an enthusiast, his eyes were ablaze with a mixture of joy and envy and yearning. 'I'm planning to cycle all of Europe in five years' time when I retire,' he said.

He fired questions at me, about what I'd seen, whether I was enjoying it, about the gear I was carrying, about the relative merits of 600cc or 700cc wheels.

And then, because the bicycle had brought us together, and we were now in a dialogue, I could ask him questions about himself that would have been unthinkable had I just been sitting on that bench without a bike.

I found out he was from the Midlands. That he was visiting his elderly parents, who lived locally. That he worked as an engineer, but redundancies were a worry and he was just hoping to make it to the finish line in five years' time. That he was divorced, with two grown-up children who had both moved to London after graduating. That he didn't worry about his daughter, who had settled down and married a nice man. But he did worry about his son, who didn't like his job and always seemed troubled on the phone. That he didn't much like football, but enjoyed cricket and sailing. That his favourite bird was the skylark. 'What a song!'

And after about an hour, I left him. And although I would never see him again, I felt as though he would never be a stranger to me; his face, in my memory, never a mystery.

I picked up the Suffolk Coastal Cycle Route 41, along glorious narrow lanes, skirting Rendlesham Forest. I passed fields of free-range pigs, saying hello to them as I wheeled along. A hare bolted across the road. I said hello to him, too. The roads were quiet, almost traffic-free; the only noise the sound of my tyres and the gentle whirr of the chain running over the ring and sprocket. In the middle of the road up ahead was a pheasant, inert. I was getting used to seeing the daily carnage now – Mrs Tiggywinkle, Peter Rabbit, Tufty the squirrel – fluffy bundles battered and bloodied, like somebody had gone berserk with a baseball bat at a petting zoo.

As I approached, the pheasant lifted its head briefly, limply, before flopping it down again on the tarmac. I could see the vivid red seeping through its feathers. I stopped, kneeled down beside the bird, reached across and put my hands around its neck. But I didn't know what to do. I'd never killed anything in my life, beyond the odd wasp. I twisted a bit, with no great enthusiasm. The pheasant looked up at me with imploring eyes, if a pheasant can have such an expression. I pulled a bit, yanked a bit, but succeeded only in delivering something akin to a shiatsu massage. The bird let out a pathetic cluck. I went back to my bike, got my Leatherman, flicked out the saw, held it to the bird's neck, flicked the saw back into its slot, went looking for a large rock, found one, held it over the bird's head, put the rock back where I'd found it. By now the pheasant was in more danger of dying of old age.

I decided I'd run it over. I was, after all, carrying the weight of a small car. I took a long run-up, to get up speed, aiming at the neck. There was a little bump. I looked around. The pheasant looked up at me. A Land Rover pick-up came around the corner and hit the pheasant. There was a loud valedictory cluck, and an explosion of blood and feathers. I had triumphed only in making that poor bird's final earthly existence a misery.

I was reunited with the sea at Orford, with its twelfth-century castle built by Henry II and a fine medieval church dominating the skyline. Across on the shingle spit, a candy-striped lighthouse stood bold against the now perfect blue sky.

The quayside rang out with posh London accents. Like many of the towns along the Suffolk coast, Orford had become a magnet for affluent Londoners seeking second homes, with Southwold, some 20 miles to the north, now having the distinction of being the least affordable town in Suffolk.

Boden catalogue families were busy catching crabs from the harbour walls. Two young boys with floppy blond hair shrieked with a mixture of fear and delight as they tried, and failed, to scoop one of the captured crustaceans into a plastic bucket. Their father, in the London weekend uniform of deck shoes, chino shorts and rugby shirt, took charge and tried to pick up the crab himself, but he was obviously as terrified as his boys.

Out on the water, Mirror dinghies were racing towards a buoy, their red sails looking like thorns gliding through quicksilver. 'Mummy, mummy,' said a little girl in clipped tones. 'Why is daddy last again?'

'Because he's useless,' said the woman.

I passed the vast, white dome of Sizewell, really quite quickly, and then took a swift lap of lovely Dunwich, crumbling slowly but inexorably into the sea. It was getting dark now, and with 80 miles on the clock for the day, I was looking forward to stopping for the night.

I rode into Southwold, past its lighthouse, which looked bizarre, built as it had been in the late nineteenth century in the middle of town to prevent it being swept away by the long-shore erosion that's doing for Dunwich. Southwold high street had delicatessens selling high-priced organic and free-range produce, and little cafés and restaurants advertising prices on blackboards that would suggest the town was not only the least affordable in Suffolk, but possibly the entire world.

I pitched up at the town's only campsite, right on the seafront. I hadn't booked, naturally, because I hadn't known I would end up here. But scanning the field, and seeing the kind of scene normally associated with tented refugee villages in Africa, I was beginning to think this might have been a mistake. This sense was only further heightened when I saw the sign saying 'site full'.

The door to the camp office was locked. I walked around to the window. There was a man behind it counting a large wad of money. I rapped gently. He looked up, appearing rather annoyed to be disturbed.

'Hello,' I mouthed through the glass.

'Full,' he mouthed back, and crossed his arms back and forth.

I wanted to ask him where the next nearest campsite might be. But when I rapped on the glass again he just ignored me. I looked at all the organised people, the planners, sitting outside their tents in the gloaming, reading by headtorch, or cooking on little barbecues, the smell of sizzling sausages and chicken finding my nose like I was one of the kids in the Bisto advert, me on the outside of the fence, looking in, thinking what a smug bunch of bastards they all were.

I rode back though the town, the streetlights all on now, warm puddles of light on the pavements emanating from the cafés and restaurants. I stopped and asked a woman if she knew of a campsite nearby, but she was up from London for the weekend and didn't know the area. The next woman I asked seemed to think there was a site in Kessingland, 10 miles away.

'But on May bank holiday weekend, you might struggle,' she said.

'Is it a bank holiday?' I asked. Truth was, I really had no idea it was a weekend, let alone a bank holiday.

She looked at me like I was from Mars.

And so in that moonless, pitch-black night, I hared up the A12 like a time-triallist, head down, lorries and coaches flying past me, the draught from their bulk buffeting me, threatening to send me flying off the road.

The sign for Kessingland came into view and shortly after a little picture of a caravan and a tent on a brown sign. It was like seeing an oasis shimmering in a desert. I followed a dirt track and eventually came to a cluster of lights, which were being attacked by vast swarms of assorted strange and exotic insects that only seem to live on campsites.

The couple on reception were lovely, as welcoming as if I were a long-lost son.

The site was a member of the Camping and Caravanning Club. 'It's seven pounds forty-nine for the night,' the man said. 'As you've got a one-man tent and are on a bicycle, the C&C classes you as a backpacker, see. We're always obliged to try and accommodate a backpacker, even when we're full, which we are.' I liked that, like giving alms was to Muslims.

By the feeble light of my headtorch, and attended by a swirling cluster of flying exotica, I put up my tent, then headed back up the dirt track, desperate as always for food, walking along a line of trees, their outline just discernible in the dark. From within the trees came the usual night rustles of the countryside. Then came a terrifying guttural roar, like some diabolical beast was stalking me. I stopped dead in my tracks, my heart pounding. I walked on a few paces. Then the noise came again, this time attended by a screeching rising to a crescendo, as if some act of terrible brutality was occurring somewhere nearby.

Then it went deathly quiet again. I picked up the pace, feeling like the backpackers in *An American Werewolf in London*. I decided that I must be hallucinating. I'd covered 90 miles that day and hadn't eaten since lunchtime. That must have been it.

At the top of the drive was a pub. I walked in. It was not unlike the Slaughtered Lamb in the aforementioned film, in that the four men sitting at the bar all turned slowly to look at me in choreographed unison.

'Pint, please,' I asked the guy behind the bar. 'And a whisky.' After that walk, I felt like I needed a chaser. 'Any food left?'

'Only that,' he said, pointing to a manky-looking pie sitting quite alone and unloved in a hot cabinet on the bar. 'But I wouldn't eat it.'

By that stage I would have eaten my own foot. I looked at my foot, imagined how that might taste after a long, sweaty day in the saddle. Then looked at the pie. It was a close call.

'I'll take it.'

'Might be all right if you cover it in ketchup,' he said.

It wasn't. The pie was the most disgusting thing I'd ever eaten: dry, full of congealed gravy and gristle and, quite probably, botulism. The ketchup didn't help much. But every crumb was picked from the plate.

I then proceeded to eat two bags of Scampi Fries, two packets of Bacon Fries, four bags of salt and vinegar crisps (the only flavour they had) and half a dozen packets of salted peanuts, in the process revealing that the woman on the cardboard sheet was not in fact fully naked but wearing a tiny red thong, her hands arranged in front of her breasts. I didn't even know that they still made those displays.

The four men at the bar were trying not to stare, but they were obviously unused to seeing such a weird creature blown into their pub late at night and trying to give himself a salt-induced coronary.

'Hungry, eh?' said the barman.

'You could say that. Tell me,' I said, 'erm… do you ever hear strange noises at night round here?'

'What kind of noises?' he said.

'Oh, erm… big cat type noises?'

He looked at the four men. They looked back at him. I thought I saw a flicker of something between them.

'Never,' said the barman. 'You heard them noises? Might have been a fox, I suppose. Or a badger, maybe. Badger makes strange sounds.'

'Badger?'

'Maybe,' he said.

I was feeling a little braver on the walk back in the dark. This might have had something to do with the fact that all was now deathly quiet. More likely it was the whisky.

But that night I had the strangest dream. In it, I had gone to sleep in my tent in quietest Suffolk and awoken, still in my tent, transported to the middle of the jungle, surrounded by roaring lions, macaws and monkeys screeching.

Now properly awake, and rubbing the sleep from my eyes, I was pondering the significance of it all when I heard an unearthly sound, like a pack of hyenas laughing. It could not have been badgers, even if they'd just been told the funniest joke in the world.

I struggled, blinking, out of my tent.

A woman from the next-door caravan shouted over: 'Like a brew, love?'

'Very kind.' A pause. 'Did you hear those noises?'

'Noises?'

'Erm, well… I stuttered, rapidly losing confidence in my sanity, 'cuckoos… blackbirds… lions.'

'Africa Alive!' she said.

'Eh?'

'Safari park. Next door. We're taking the kids later. Sugar?'
'Two, please.'

The smell of bacon cooking drifted over the hedge bordering the campsite. I walked towards it and peered through a gap. In the field next door it was total gridlock, with hundreds if not thousands of cars. At the top of the paddock, a snake of vehicles queued patiently to get in. It was just like the closing shot in *Field of Dreams*.

I walked through the gap and then through another hedge into the adjacent field. There were stalls as far as the eye could see, and piles of assorted crap: the Great British Car Boot Sale. I was quickly disabused of any idea I had that here was a field of dreams, unless your dreams involve five lighters for a quid, cheap socks, pirate DVDs or pushbikes the provenance of which probably shouldn't be scrutinised too closely.

I had an idea. I went back to my tent, sorted through my stuff and put a few things into one of the panniers. Then I walked back to the field and approached a guy standing by a trestle table full of dog-eared paperbacks, a Ker-Plunk and what looked like bits of a lorry's diesel engine. He had a large tattoo of a dragon on his forearm.

'Want some stuff?' I asked him.

'What kind of stuff?' he said, in a Welsh accent, turning his head and looking over both shoulders.

I opened my pannier, pulled out the items, laid them on the end of the table. There was a novel, the mini dictionary and thesaurus, two T-shirts, one smart shirt, four pairs of underpants (clearly not new), four pairs of socks (ditto), a small bottle of yellow liquid, and series four of *The Wire*.

'Snide is it?' he asked, picking up the box set.

'Pukka,' I said. I don't think I'd ever used the word before, but it seemed appropriate.

'What's this?' he asked, holding up the tube of yellow liquid like it was a urine sample.

'Post-ride massage oil,' I said.

'Post what?'

'You use it to give yourself a massage after you've been riding.'

'Oh.'

'It's good.'

'I don't want the kecks or socks,' he said. 'But I'll take the rest. How much?'

'Nothing,' I said.

'Nothing?'

'You'll be doing me a favour. I'm trying to lose weight.'

'Lose weight?'

'From my bike, see. I'm having to carry all this stuff.'

'Ahh. That's what you meant by having a massage after you've been riding.'

'Of course.'

'I'd have sold it as something else. Could have been done on trade descriptions,' he said, chuckling to himself. 'Let me buy you a bacon butty.'

'Deal.'

I packed away my stuff. It felt great that the bags were getting slightly less stuffed, easier to organise. There was a feeling of liberation too about giving stuff away. The thought of it had felt bad, but the feeling afterwards was marvellous.

I popped in to say goodbye to the lovely couple on the desk. There was a selection of leaflets on the counter advertising local attractions. One had a picture of a chapel on the front, under the headline 'The Shrine of Our Lady of Walsingham'. I remembered reading about Walsingham years before. 'England's Nazareth,' they call themselves, a magnet for pilgrims from all over the world. I'd thought it sounded fascinating, but had never really known where it was. I read on. 'Whether you come as a pilgrim or tourist, a believer or explorer, we hope you find peace and God's blessing as you reflect on life.' Well, I was a tourist and explorer at least, and without series four of *The Wire* to reflect on, I might give life a shot. I put the flyer in my bar bag.

Another leaflet had a picture of a bespectacled man in a bush-man hat paddling a canoe. 'Bushcraft trails on remote reaches of the Norfolk Broads,' it said. 'Learn to build your own shelter, make a fire and get close to nature.'

That sounded good to me. I've lived in cities all my life, but I was beginning to feel in my bones how calm and happy I felt away from them.

I called the number. Mark, the Canoe Man, could accommodate me the next day and would meet me by the River Bure in

Coltishall. I pedalled away from Kessingland knowing where I was going that day, and that, sometimes, was a nice feeling too.

I followed the coast road up to Lowestoft, officially the most easterly town in Britain. And if that were not enough, also the birthplace of Benjamin Britten and the guy who played DS Ted Roach in *The Bill*. What more could a place ask for? It was lovely as I cycled through, baking under a hot sun, a row of tall Victorian terraced guesthouses with names like 'The Coventry' and 'The Longshore' facing out over the golden sands, where families played beach cricket and old people sat staring out to sea.

Through Great Yarmouth, with banks of giant wind turbines spinning furiously but noiselessly offshore, then to Caister-on-Sea, where I headed inland, mercifully away from the strong headwind of the coast, across the flatlands of the Broads.

I took a room at the King's Head in Coltishall, right next to my rendezvous point for Mark, and, it being only mid-afternoon, wondered what I could do to fill the rest of the day. From somewhere in the distance, I heard a steam train whistle, and I asked the woman behind the bar where it had come from.

'That's the Bure Valley Railway. Starts just up the road in Wroxham,' she said.

I cycled the few miles to the station and bought a ticket. The woman in the station shop and café, mobbed with excited young children buying jelly snakes and pestering their parents for Thomas the Tank Engine stuff, kindly said I could leave my bicycle in the café's kitchen, propped up between the gallon jars of cooking oil and the sacks of spuds.

'Should I put a lock on it?' I asked.

'Why?' she replied.

We might not have much industry left in Britain. We might not have an empire any more. We might all be terrified for our jobs and pensions. We might top all kinds of indices involving obesity and teenage pregnancies. But, my God, are we good at preserved and miniature railways, or heritage lines as they are collectively known. At the last count there were well over 100 of them, and the number is growing all the time, with over 6 million passengers carried a year. I'm not sure there's another country in the world where people love their old trains as much as we do.

The train was waved off by an elderly man in a Victorian frock coat and peaked cap, with a large green flag and a whistle that, as he was standing right next to my open window, nearly burst my eardrums. The narrow-gauge engine hissed into life, expelling great huffs and puffs as we picked up speed.

I shared my little carriage with a middle-aged couple, both as animated and excited as children. Outside the window, people waved frantically as we passed, and we waved back. That was a strange phenomenon. We wave, almost instinctively, at a train on a preserved line, like we're one great big happy family, but not at the 08.32 Guildford to Waterloo. Yet many of our preserved trains were presumably, back in the day, pulling the 08.32 Guildford to Waterloo, or its equivalent, and I'd bet my old Ian Allan spotter's book that nobody waved at them then. Curious.

'It's coming up soon,' said the man in front of me to his wife, positioning himself at the open window, camera in hand, poised. 'I wonder what it will be.'

The thing that was exercising him was the passing loop and the chance to see what locomotive was pulling the service running in the opposite direction.

'It's the *Blickling Hall*!' he exclaimed loudly, as if he'd displaced the water in his bathtub and hit upon a rather exciting discovery. 'Fantastic.'

The *Blickling Hall* went on its way to Wroxham. The man sat down again on the wooden bench, and turned to his wife. 'Fantastic.'

'Fantastic,' she said.

'Fantastic,' he said again.

The next afternoon Mark Wilkinson was waiting for me in the car park of the King's Head. Behind him was Mr Darcy, who had just emerged from the River Bure and, although undeniably as handsome as his literary counterpart, as a spaniel was doubtless much smellier.

We loaded the gear into the canoe. Then I put my bike and the rest of my stuff into Mark's van.

'Will I need my tent?' I asked him.

'No need for tents,' he said.

We pushed off, Mark in the stern, me in the bow, Mr Darcy in the stern, then in the bow, then in the Bure.

'How are you in a canoe?' Mark asked.

'Okay, I think,' I said. I'd done a bit of canoeing and kayaking and knew how unstable they could feel. But I'd never shared a canoe with a soaking-wet Duracell spaniel before. I expected to join him in the river at some stage.

We paddled past the point where the ubiquitous Broads cruisers couldn't navigate and into the dark, narrow, jungle reaches, canopied by alder and willow and elder bushes with delicate white clusters of flowers, where the sounds of Africa Alive! would have been more congruous than the English birdsong that accompanied us.

'Listen. Hear that chaffinch?' asked Mark. 'And that one's a Cetti's warbler. Quite rare in Britain, but not in Norfolk.'

It all just sounded like noise to me. Lovely noise, but noise all the same. And how could anybody, from this wall of sound, distinguish one note from the next? I was frustrated that one man's ears could be attuned so much better than another's.

'I guess I hear it every day. Those birds all have different accents to me. It's like the difference between a Geordie and a Cornishman, or somebody from Wales. Listen…'

There was an explosive *chee, chippi-chippi-chippi*.

'That's the Cetti's,' Mark said.

Then another song, identical, from the opposite bank, bursting out of a clump of yellow flag irises.

'Cetti's?' I said.

'Blackbird,' said Mark. 'They're excellent mimics.'

We had to portage the canoe over an ancient and derelict lock, dripping with algae of the most verdant hue, then we turned a corner into a straight section, not a sound save for the birdsong, the gentle splish-splosh of the paddles and Mr Darcy's excited panting. Time seemed to freeze. A pair of swans with a clutch of cygnets took exception to Mr Darcy, and paddled furiously up to the boat, honking loudly. Mr Darcy just sat on the prow, cocked his head haughtily in the air and ignored them. I'd never seen a swan dissed with such aplomb before.

In the distance, a bittern boomed. I just heard the boom. Mark added the bittern bit. Half obscured by the reeds stood a grey heron, with its prehistoric head, transfixed, ready to stab with its dagger-like bill. 'They're called hansers round here,' said Mark. 'Some reckon the name heron comes from the old name hernshaw, which had all kinds of dialect interpretations. Hamlet says: "I am but mad north-north-west; when the wind is southerly, I know a hawk from a handsaw." So handsaw was one interpretation, and hanser was the Fens'.'

The sun was just beginning its descent, the high puffball clouds all oranges and lemons, the whole scene like a Florentine painting.

Suddenly, we were engulfed by clouds of mayfly, flitting delicately around us like thousands of will-o'-the-wisps.

'I've never seen so many as we've got this year,' Mark said, as the fat lips of a chub broke the surface and sucked up one of the waterlogged sprites.

As we slipped silently along, Mark told me how overnight camping trips on the Broads had previously been impossible because of the lack of campsites. But he had built up relationships with the various landowners and authorities and they'd given him permission to wild camp.

'They told me we couldn't leave any trace of our presence behind,' he said. 'I told them, "Don't worry, that's exactly the point."'

We beached the canoe and went ashore, hurrying to set up camp in the fading light. We hadn't seen another human being for hours. It felt like we could be deep in the Everglades. I sank almost to my knees in the mud. Mr Darcy was busy transforming himself from a white to a brown dog.

Mark threw me a bit of old plastic sheeting and some lengths of frayed rope. 'You need to build your shelter,' he said, as if he were simply asking me to tie my shoelaces. 'And rain and wind is forecast, so make it strong. Don't forget you'll want a sloping roof. You'll find some decent saplings for supports over there.'

I looked at the materials. I would have had about as much chance making the Hadron Collider from them. I found a few saplings, stuck them in the ground, tied the sheeting to them with the bits of old string and tensioned one side. The structure swayed in the breeze, then fell over.

'Why don't you go and get some wood for the fire,' Mark said. 'I'll sort out the shelters.'

Mr Darcy and I squelched our way through the swamp. Every time I picked up a stick, Mr Darcy looked at me imploringly. I threw one. It flew into a bank of nettles. Mr Darcy followed the stick, emerging seconds later without the stick, but rubbing his nose frantically on the ground, pausing only to sneeze violently.

'That's too damp,' said Mark, on my return, pointing to the wood I was cradling in my arms. 'Look. It's green.'

Mr Darcy sneezed at my feet, rubbing his nose with his paws. 'What happened to him?' Mark asked.

I'd failed to build a shelter, I'd gathered useless wood, and now I'd brutalised Mark's dog. I wondered if they'd ever find my body out here.

'Dunno,' I replied.

Mark found some dry wood and got the fire started. The air was thick with the delicious fug of wood smoke and filled with the sound of crackling logs.

He handed me a large knife and an even larger fish.

'Normally we catch our supper, but it's the close season so I have to buy it. Know how to gut and prepare a fish?' he said.

'No.' I felt like a terrible disappointment.

He deftly inserted the knife in front of the anal fin, cut up along the belly, split the flesh, scraped out the contents, scored behind the gills, and then several times along the back.

'You can do the other one while I go and find more wood.'

By the time Mark returned, I was covered in fish shit and guts, the poor creature looking as it had been juggled by Freddy Krueger. If it had been *The Generation Game*, I'd have been the black-sheep uncle in the comedy suit.

'You can have that one,' Mark said.

We sat down to eat, the rain now gently splattering against the sheeting, Mark popping the cork from a bottle of wine, the two sounds that are surely – after wood crackling on an open fire – the finest on the planet.

From somewhere in the dark, an owl hooted. I felt an intense sense of calm.

I asked Mark how long he'd been paddling the Broads. Only a few years, he'd said. Born in London, he was married at 21, had kids, and sold pensions for the next 20 years. 'Then I had my midlife crisis,' he laughed.

'I felt something was missing. So I started working with the Scouts, learning bushcraft and how to paddle a canoe. That felt like the real me.' Then, around 40, he couldn't ignore the voice any longer and set up his own company offering wilderness experiences on the Broads. It ultimately cost him his marriage, but he seemed to be at peace.

'It's not such a bad office, is it?' he said. 'Sure beats my last one, anyway.'

We talked and drank long into the night, stinking of fish guts and wood smoke, swapping stories around the fire, laughing, listening to the rain and the night.

I eventually crawled under my narrow tunnel of a shelter, now being buffeted by the wind and lashed by the heavy rain, the sheet inches from my face, grateful that it was Mark and not me who'd built it. With an owl lullaby, I fell into the deepest sleep imaginable.

At lunchtime next day, I phoned the Shrine of Our Lady of Walsingham. 'We'd be delighted to have you,' said a lovely-sounding woman called Venetia. 'Tonight, after the liturgy, there's a torchlit procession. You're most welcome to take part.'

I headed cross-country, zig-zagging along all the tiny back lanes, through comatose little villages. There were enormous churches everywhere, which looked more like the cathedrals of France than the type of small parish churches one might have expected. It was hard to imagine there had ever been enough people living in this remote part of England to fill them. The elaborate buildings had skyrocket spires and huge flying buttresses and were often in the middle of nowhere, surrounded only by barley fields, the nearest building another vast church a few fields away.

Norfolk has over 650 medieval churches, the highest concentration in the world, built to service the armies of agricultural workers who flocked to Norfolk in the prosperous Middle Ages. The Great Plague and the Industrial Revolution did for the rural population, but the structures remained, inspiring John Betjeman to write: 'Norfolk would not be Norfolk without a church tower on the horizon or round a corner up a lane. When a church has been pulled down, the county seems empty or is like a necklace with a jewel missing.'

The church of St Michael the Archangel at Booton (population 100) was perhaps the most extraordinary and eccentric of them all, with slender twin towers soaring over the East Anglian landscape and a central pinnacle that looked like a minaret. I propped my bike against the flint wall and went for a closer look. Inside, dramatic wooden angels held up the roof, while the delicately-coloured stained-glass windows showed the usual assortment of angels, but also musicians with long flowing hair and pretty female faces. The whole thing had prompted the architect Edwin Lutyens to call the church 'naughty, but built in the right spirit'.

I rode through Little Snoring and then Great Snoring and, of course, couldn't pass up the opportunity to take a photo of myself apparently asleep under the village sign. How the villagers must laugh most days when they look out of their windows and see such sparkling originality.

I pitched up in Walsingham, which is actually two conjoined villages, Little and Great Walsingham, and Venetia met me at the Shrine of Our Lady. 'There's something I have to tell you,' she said, gravely.

What? Christ has returned?

'The Vodafone signal's down.'

She showed me along a corridor, at the end of which was a statue of a bishop with a sword through his head, and up a narrow staircase to my room.

'You're staying in the same block as the visiting priests,' said Venetia.

The walls of my room were covered with crucifixes and prints of scenes from the Bible. In the corner was a shower unit, into which I climbed, after I'd ascertained that there was no minibar.

There was a knock at the door. I turned off the water, grabbed a towel too small to fit fully around my waist and opened the door. There stood a bishop in full regalia.

'Bishop Lindsay Urwin,' he said with a slight antipodean twang as he extended his hand.

'Hello,' I said, shaking with my left, seeing as the thumb and fore-finger of my right were desperately trying to keep my towel together.

For some reason I get quite intimidated by members of the clergy (especially if they're wearing a fancy hat and I'm wearing a tea towel). It's as though I feel spiritually naked in front of them. So to be actually naked was quite the trip.

And thus it was that I decided then was the perfect time to tell the bishop (his holiness, I think I called him) that I didn't believe in God. 'At least I don't think so, I mean, I think there must be something, some reason for everything, I can't believe it's just a random sequence of events, that we're just here on this rock. I mean, where did the rock come from, eh? I can't believe it was made by a man with a white beard, but there's too much that can't be explained...' And on and on.

'I just came to welcome you and invite you to join me for dinner,' said Bishop Lindsay. 'Shall we say 6 p.m.?'

'Great,' I said.

We met for dinner in the refectory. The orange squash was dispensed into chunky plastic beakers, the burger and chips served on chunky plastic plates. We walked through the crowded room. It was full of pilgrims, maybe 200 people, mostly silver-haired, but sprinkled with some younger people too. Most, that evening, seemed to have Liverpool accents. They all greeted the bishop as we passed. 'Hello farder,' they said, nodding reverentially before him.

We found a table in the corner. I asked the bishop what had brought him to Britain and to Walsingham. He'd left Melbourne as a young man to go travelling, he told me, ending up in London. He was working in a bar one day when a customer said to him: 'I fucking hate priests.'

'That was it,' he said. 'I knew right then that I wanted to become a priest. I can't explain why.'

Ordained as a priest in 1981, aged 25, he'd progressed quickly. In 2008, he was asked to become the Administrator of the Shrine of Our Lady of Walsingham. 'It was too good an opportunity to miss,' he said.

The bishop told me that north European Christians have been coming to Walsingham for nearly 1,000 years, ever since the Virgin Mary appeared in a vision to Lady Richeldis de Faverches, a Saxon noblewoman, and bade her to build a replica of the Nazareth house where the Angel Gabriel had asked Mary to become the mother of Jesus. 'All who seek me there will find succour,' Mary had said in her visitation.

It became known as the Holy House and pilgrims flocked to it until, in 1538, on the orders of Henry VIII, it, along with the abbey, was destroyed, and the pilgrimages stopped for nearly 400 years, leading to the Elizabethan poetic lament:

Weep Weep O Walsingham,
Whose dayes are nights,
Blessings turned to blasphemies,
Holy deeds to despites
Sinne is where our Ladye sate,
Heaven turned is to helle;
Satan sitthe where our Lord did swaye,
Walsingham O farewell!

It wasn't until 1931 that the shrine was rebuilt and the pilgrimages resumed.

'And are you coming to the liturgy this evening?' he asked, his eyes all kindly and beatific. 'And the procession afterwards? It's a journey with others on a winding path. Quite a metaphor for life.'

I said I'd love to.

The Shrine Church was packed with pilgrims, each holding a candle contained in a cardboard cone, which gave them the look of holding radioactive popcorn. To the rear of the church was the Holy House, built to the exact measurements of the original Saxon shrine, where pilgrims end their journeys. In the main chapel, huge arrangements of lilies and roses cascaded down from ornate red-brick pillars. Dotted around the chamber were the carved, painted tombs of various bishops and Crusaders and, to the left of the altar-piece, a feretory containing an arm bone and some of the blood of St Vincent of Saragossa, roasted alive on a gridiron by the Roman Emperor Diocletian in 304AD for refusing to deny the Gospel. It was quite a place. For rural Norfolk. For anywhere.

The procession of clergy arrived, an incense bearer swirling thick, sweet smoke, Bishop Lindsay bringing up the rear. They reached the altar.

'There's something I have to tell you,' said the bishop, gravely. 'The Vodafone signal's down.'

Huge laughter.

'But please switch off your phones anyway,' he continued. 'Once, I was getting to the main part of my sermon, and I said "And the Lord is calling you" and somebody's phone went off.'

More laughter. Then a hush. Bishop Lindsay read from Corinthians. 'For we are the aroma of Christ to God among those who are being saved and among those who are perishing, to one a fragrance from death to death, to the other a fragrance from life to life. Who is sufficient for these things?'

He was a great speaker, funny and charismatic, and the congregation clearly adored him.

At the end, he said: 'Now, together we process.'

The procession left the shrine, at the head the bishop and the incense bearer, swirling cumuli of thick smoke now eddying in the cool breeze. Behind them came the pilgrims, all still carrying their candles, now glowing bright in the twilight. Two pilgrims were carrying a large statue of the Virgin Mary on their shoulders.

With 'Ave Maria' booming out of the garden speakers, the procession wound its way along the serpentine path, twisting and turning and cutting back on itself, so that the snake of pilgrims could greet each other in passing time and again, a look of reverie on their faces. Between the lavender and the roses they wound, past the campanula and agapanthus and quivering grasses, and under the Calvary Hill, with its three crosses, every so often raising their candles in unison, chanting: 'Ave, ave, ave Maria.'

The benediction followed the procession and afterwards the pilgrims started to drift off. I found the bishop.

'Thanks for letting me come.'

'A pleasure,' he said, and repeated the words I'd read in the leaflet. 'Pilgrims or tourists, believers or explorers, all are welcome here.'

'What happens now?' I asked, thinking there might be further devotional activities.

'We go to the pub,' said the bishop.

The Bull Inn was full of pilgrims, many of whom seemed to be very thirsty after all that processing.

We took a table in the corner, with another six or seven priests, together with the bishop all still in their vestments. The bishop asked me if I wanted an Abbot's. This could get confusing. I scanned the bar. At least they didn't sell Bishop's Finger. The landlord was probably in his forties but looked 25, the spit of Johnny Rotten, dressed all in white, like a dandy, the very antithesis of the archetypal rural landlord.

'You still watering down your beer?' asked the bishop.

'You still watering down your sermons?' said the landlord, in a Rotten-like drawl. 'And paying for your pint from the collection tin?'

There was a roar of laughter.

The night wore on, the Abbot's and the bishop and the priests. The pilgrims were still working hard trying to slake their thirsts. The room was hot, raucous. I caught snatches of conversations. About football, theology, horseracing.

'Remember when the bishop was on Ali G?' one priest asked another.

'I remember that,' I said. 'Was that you?'

'Alas, yes,' said the bishop, holding his head in his hand.

'It was ranked second in Channel 4's '100 Greatest Funny Moments',' said the priest, proudly.

With another priest, he then went through the sketch.

'Remember when Ali G asked whether God was a man or a woman, and Lindsay said neither.

'"God was a ladyboy then, aiii," Ali G said. Remember?'

Oh yes, they all laughed.

'Then he asked what God had ever done, and Lindsay said "made the world". He made the world? "Look, I can only tell you what I believe, man."'

'Man!'

More laughter.

'"But was Mary really a virgin?"'

'"I believe she was a virgin. Then she found herself pregnant and asked herself 'How can this be?'"'

'Aiii, me also know girls like that,' said one of the priests doing a piss-poor Ali G impression. 'Usually dem drunk.'

Lindsay just sat there sipping his pint, looking sheepish, taking it all in great spirit.

Time ticked on. Things started to get a bit blurry.

'Where was that restaurant in Rome?' one priest said to another. 'Oh, you know, close to where St Cecilia is buried?'

'St Cecilia? Are you sure you don't mean St Genesius?'

'We had the scallops.'

'That was definitely Genesius.'

I was now in an episode of *Father Ted*.

By 2 a.m., things were still going strong. Alas, I was not. The room was spinning.

'I have to go,' I said to the bishop.

'Would you mind putting Father Brian to bed?' one of the priests said.

Father Brian, a visiting priest on a pilgrimage, was slumped on the bench, like somebody had sucked out his skeleton.

'Sure,' I said.

And so endeth the night, with me walking around Walsingham in the dark, drunk as a lord, my right arm tucked under the armpit of Father Brian in his vestments, drunk as a priest.

'Where do you live?' I asked.

Nothing.

'Hey, Father, where are you staying?' I asked again.

Father Brian raised his head for a second.

'I don't know,' he said.

Chapter 6

I rejoined the coast at Wells-next-the-Sea, which should technically now be called Wells-a-mile-from-the-Sea as a result of the silting up of its estuary. It was a very pretty town, with large, elegant Georgian houses surrounding a large green ringed by lime trees. Many of the town's houses had 'for sale' signs outside.

A woman strolled past, out walking her dog.

'You've got a lot of stuff, duck,' she said. I love being called duck. 'Going far?'

I asked why so many houses were for sale.

'They call this place Wealth-next-the Sea or Chelsea-on-Sea,' she said. 'People from London buying all the houses for second homes. One good thing about this recession is that they're all having to sell. Maybe local people might be able to afford to live here again one day.' She said all this with a certain relish, as well she might.

I continued along the coast road, past Holkham Bay and, in the distance offshore, the nature reserve of Scolt Head Island, whose salt marshes are said to be the finest in the UK. As I hit the north-west corner of East Anglia and started heading south, the vast expanse of the Wash came into view. The sun was out now, and the temperature soaring, with only the faintest breath of wind. The world felt freshly open, infinite, the sky vast, concave almost, like I was looking at it through a fisheye lens. Ragged little blobs of white dotted the blue canvas.

I rode through the thick woods surrounding Sandringham House, the sunlight penetrating the dense canopy in pinpricks, making the road look like batik cloth. I was lost, looking for a campsite I thought was near. I pulled over, removed my helmet, clipped it onto the handlebars, looked at the map, realised my mistake and cycled on.

Something was very different, but it took me a couple of minutes to realise what it was. For the first time in my adult life, I was riding without a helmet. And it felt not only glorious, but ever so slightly deviant too. It wasn't that it opened and lightened things up, in the way riding a motorcycle without a helmet does, because of course cycle helmets are just light plastic lids that perch on top of the head. But it felt liberating in a way I could not fully explain.

Who cared if I wore a helmet or not? Not the law. Only the lobby groups, paid to get into sanctimonious tizzies about such issues. I pulled over again, took the helmet from the handlebars and clipped it to the rear rack. I would hardly wear it again on the trip.

I eventually found the campsite. I wished I hadn't. I was already beginning to get an instinctive feel for whether a site was likely to be any good, and that one screamed armpit. For a start, there were signs up everywhere, listing at length the proscribed activities. No music. No entry to the site after 10 p.m. No dogs. No open fires. No ball games. No washing of clothes in the sinks. No cycling on site. No clotheslines. Pitches must be vacated by 9 a.m. Please control your children.

At least they'd said please.

I had come to realise that the quality of a campsite is usually inversely related to the number of signs that are on display. Don't ask me what that's all about.

I thought about how signs and instructions have proliferated in all areas of British life in recent times. All the taped-loop messages on public transport – please remember to take all your personal belongings with you; stand clear of the closing doors; the one on the Tube in the summer which advises you to carry water because hot weather can make you more thirsty; all the safety instructions pinned on the walls; the yellow lines on the platforms to warn you that getting too close to a speeding train may be injurious to your health.

And the signs everywhere which tell you that wet floors might be slippery and coffee may be hot and closed-circuit TV operates in this area, as do pickpockets, and don't park here, or there, but you can park there between 10 and 12 Monday to Friday, and we've got cameras watching this too, so don't say you weren't warned. Smoking is very bad for you, as is too much alcohol, and don't eat too much fat or sugar or too many carrots, because carrots can give you cancer (this week anyway), but broccoli is great, but only if it's steamed, and Ever Wondered What Would Happen To Your Family If You Died Suddenly?

And I know I'm getting older and therefore acquiring, apart from hairy ears, a certain exasperation at the world, but I reckon that when you constantly tell people what to do and how to behave, they invariably start acting like fuckwits, incapable of behaving sensibly and responsibly. If we're being watched all the time, nagged, isn't it logical to assume that we'd adopt the idea that we're inherently stupid? What would happen if we had a national 'No Sign Day', instead of a 'No Smoking Day'? Would we all fall under trains, leave our bags on the bus, burn ourselves with coffee or park in the middle of the street? I propose that we would not.

Witness the experiments in Holland where they removed all street furniture such as traffic lights, signs, kerbs and white lines. Did chaos ensue? On the contrary. When people had to think for themselves, cooperate and communicate with each other, safety improved and accident numbers fell.

So, the signs should have had me performing a U-turn, but it was getting dark and I was tired. I went to the check-in. The thin-lipped woman behind the counter regarded me with suspicion.

'Yes?' she said.

'How much is it for a one-man tent?'

'Have you booked?' she said.

'No. Are you full?'

'Does it look like we're full?'

I looked out of the window. It didn't look full at all. It looked positively unfull.

'No,' I said.

'Well, why ask?' she said.

'Sorry,' I said, suddenly feeling about seven years old.

'Fifteen pounds a night. No mains. Off the site by 9 a.m.'

The most expensive site I'd stayed at so far had cost eight pounds. And it had been lovely. I considered sharing this information with her, telling her I could almost get a B&B for that price. But looking into her angry eyes, I thought I'd probably be murdered. Battered to death with a sign, most likely.

'Great,' I said, for I am nothing if not gutless. 'Do you have the Internet?'

'Eight pounds an hour,' she said.

'Blimey, that's expensive,' I said involuntarily.

Her eyes narrowed into slits. 'No one's forcing you.'

'No, erm… Anywhere I can charge my phone?'

She looked at me like I'd just asked if I could have a peek up her skirt, then rolled her eyes.

'If you have to. There,' she said, pointing to a socket in the wall of the check-in. 'Pound.'

'A pound!'

'Electricity's not free,' she said.

'Can I plug my laptop in there too?'

'Another pound.'

She reminded me of Mr Fiddler, the money-grabbing campsite owner in *Carry On Camping*, where every response to Sid Boggle's enquiries about amenities invoked the answer: 'A pound.' I suppose the fact that in the 40 years since that film was made campsite inflation had stagnated should have been some consolation. And the fact that Sid (played by Sid James) and his mate Bernie Lugg had had the added bonus of meeting Babs and Fanny, and seeing the former's bikini top ping off during an exercise session, must have made the extra investments seem worthwhile. I looked out again at the forlorn, near-deserted field. There would be no Fanny or Babs, of that I was certain.

I handed over my £15, headed outside, jumped on my bike. There was an angry rap on the window. I looked back. The woman was pointing to the No Cycling sign. I dismounted and started pushing, but as soon as I was out of sight behind the shower block I got back on my bike again. If this was a war, I knew I'd lose. But I would go down fighting.

I passed a few caravans. They all had big satellite dishes flying from the roof or extendable aerials puncturing the canopy of trees. From inside, spectral blue light pulsated. I could see the silhouettes of heads not moving much.

I found a spot in a far corner, out of sight of the thin-lipped woman, unbungeed my tent bag, the boggy ground squelching under my feet. This activity alerted the local mosquitoes, of which there were whole squadrons. It's a pity mosquitoes can't read signs.

I started putting the tent up in a great hurry, the mozzies attacking every inch of exposed flesh, bringing up, almost instantaneously, great red welts which begged to be scratched but which, because my hands were full of poles and guy lines, would have to wait.

I went for a shower, scratching furiously on the way. The shower block was predictably dire, exposed wiring hanging from the ceiling like entrails, dead insects plastered everywhere, ancient cobwebs in the corners, shower doors broken, curtains either half hanging off their rails or missing altogether. And there were signs everywhere: clean the cubicle after use; caution – hot water; no food preparation; no clothes washing (in case one had forgotten). I emptied my wash bag, tipped my dirty clothes into the sink, stuffed a sock into the plugless plughole, held down the tap (it was of course one of those taps that needed to be held down because otherwise there would need to be a sign that read: please turn off the tap after use because otherwise the water will keep coming out of it). The water was not hot, despite the kindly caution, but no matter: I was chalking up another little victory, and that had to be preferable to going crazy with a gun. But only just.

I undressed, went into a shower cubicle, the only one with a curtain. I pressed the metal button on the wall. Nothing. I pressed again. Still nothing. I went into the cubicle next door. Same thing. I wrapped my towel around my waist, put on a T-shirt, and then walked right back across the site to the office. The woman rolled her eyes.

'What?' she said.

'The showers are broken.'

'Did you put any money in the meter?'

'Money?'

'Yes. Hot water's not free.'

'How much?' I asked, but I already knew the answer.

I went back to my tent, grabbed a pound, went back to the shower block, put the coin in the meter, which began to click, then entered the cubicle and pressed the button. A trickle of water gurgled out of the nozzle, like I was been urinated on by a man with prostate issues. It wasn't warm like urine, though. It was as cold as a mountain brook. I soaped up. The water stopped. I pressed the button again. Nothing. I came out of the shower, looked at the meter. The clicking had stopped.

I walked across the shower block covered in soap, filled the sink next to my washing with water and rinsed myself off, scratching at the angry welts. Was I being punished for something? Cycling without a helmet perhaps? I finished my washing. It seemed like a hollow victory now.

As I walked back to my tent, 'I Kissed A Girl' by Katy Perry boomed out from behind a hedge. I peered over. A family of five had arrived. Dad was busy putting up the tent, a huge starfish-shaped construction, with rooms leading off a vast central chamber. The music was coming from the stereo of the car, whose four doors were flung open to maximise the family's listening pleasure. The children were all singing at the top of their lungs. 'I kissed a girl just to try it. I hope my boyfriend don't mind it.' Mum laughed as she cracked a Foster's.

I went back to my tent, and hung my travel washing line between a tent loop and a tree, pegging my wet pants and socks to the line. I then crawled into my tent and found the bite cream.

'I Kissed A Girl' started up again. It was obviously the family's holiday song. Katy was still tormented about her boyfriend finding out about her sapphic adventures, her head so confused, but adamant that while it felt so wrong, it also felt so right.

I drifted off to sleep.

'Hello!' I heard a voice bark outside. I climbed out of my sleeping bag and half unzipped the flap, poking my head out in the manner of a mole emerging from a hole.

The thin-lipped woman was standing over me.

'What's this,' she asked, pointing to my pants.

'Eh?'

'Did you wash your clothes in the sink?'

'No.'

'Did you wash your clothes in the sink?'

The battle was lost.

'Yes.'

'Can't you read?' she said. 'There's bloody great signs up every-where.'

'Sorry. I'd run out of pants.'

'Is that my problem?'

'No, it isn't.'

'Take it down.'

'Sorry.'

'And if I have to come over again, you'll have to go.'

'Sorry.'

'Did you read the sign that says pitches must be vacated by 9 a.m.?'

'Yes, I saw that one.'

'Good,' she said, and walked off. I watched her go, past the hedge beyond which the family was enjoying its holiday. Katy Perry abruptly stopped, and I felt the slightest twinge of affection towards the old trout.

Into the immediate silence that followed came the words: 'Can't you read?'

With no desire to cause the campsite owner any further distress, I was gone by 8 a.m. the next day, skirting The Wash with my wash, now at least twice its dry weight.

One of the joys of hitting the road early with nothing in your belly was imagining the breakfast that awaited you. Some mornings, when the will and the masochism were strong, I'd pass café after café, inhaling the delicious greasy aroma, delaying the moment, maybe clocking up 10 or 20 miles of dribbling anticipation, my mind going through the various configurations of the artery-choking fat feast that awaited me. Would it be double bacon today? Black pudding? Chips or beans? Would I manage to eat the molten-hot tomato for the first time in my life?

In the end, I lasted less than 10 miles that morning, pulling up at a café in King's Lynn. I ordered the Gut Buster, which, according to the menu, contained at least half a whole pig – including the kidneys – fried eggs, bubble, a mountain of chips, and crusty bread and butter. None of which would do anything to lighten my load.

But dry clothes would so, bagging a table on the pavement, I draped my wet socks and underpants on my bike's top tube and handlebars, where they hung limply.

A guy in a vest brought over my Gut Buster. It certainly looked like it did what it said on the tin. By the look of the guy, it was his favourite start to the day too.

'Doing your washing?' he said, putting down the plate and a big mug of tea the colour of a Manila envelope, into which I emptied half the sugar dispenser.

'Aye,' I replied. For I figured King's Lynn still technically counted as the countryside.

A man at the next table asked where I was headed and I told him Lincolnshire.

'Bandit country,' he said. 'This is where you leave civilisation. Funny lot next door.'

That made me smile. It reminded me of all those trips abroad when, crossing a land border, one is invariably told of the dangers and iniquities that await you in the strange and foreign land next door. Of course, the people are inevitably as normal and pleasant as in the country you've just left, but it demonstrates how strongly the perceptions of 'otherness' are hardwired into us, even on the border badlands of Norfolk and Lincolnshire.

I finished my breakfast – apart from the tomato – and strolled along the main shopping street in the bright morning sunshine, saying good morning to random strangers as if I were a Christian missionary.

I popped into a bookstore and bought a guide to British birds. This also did nothing to lighten my load, but I was frustrated seeing the most extraordinary creatures flitting around me every day and not knowing what they were. It felt rude, like sharing a long journey with a group of people you grow to love and never asking their names.

I rode along the arrow-straight back lanes across the flat, featureless Fens, the vastness of The Wash unseen beyond the swaying corn, but nonetheless present and imposing. H.V. Morton had written of this landscape in *In Search of England*:

A man who loves the rounded contour of the West Country is at first inclined to dislike the flat monotony of the Lincolnshire Fens. His eye looks round vainly for landmarks; there is nothing on which to focus... Gradually, however, the peculiar atmosphere of the country grips the imagination. The slightest eminence becomes important; a windmill or a tall tree occupies the eye, and the flight of the birds is marvellous against the sky. As in all flat countries, the clouds billow splendidly against the rim of the earth, and you find the greatest beauty in the changing heavens.

The traffic was light in numbers but heavy in character, the only vehicles I saw mostly smartly turned-out juggernauts with banks of spotlights above their cabs and Dutch plates, on their way to deliver their consignments of flowers.

I had learned on my trip thus far that left-hand drive vehicles were by far the biggest hazard to cyclists, being able from their driving position to gauge exactly their distance from you and thus coming much closer than right-hand drive vehicles, who tended to overcompensate and give you much more room. (The only other consistency I noticed was that people with St George's flags flying from their cars also tended to give you less room. Thankfully, the left-hand drive/St George's flag combo was rare). But Dutch flower trucks were the exception. They always seemed to pass slowly, widely and respectfully. I couldn't work out whether this was a trait of the famously bike-loving Dutch, or whether the oft-touted idea that you'll never meet a nasty gardener, soothed and mellowed as they are by their relationship with nature, had somehow permeated the cabs. Maybe it was a combination of the two. Whatever, Dutch flower lorry drivers, I salute you. Maybe, as an experiment, we should all place troughs of geraniums on our parcel shelves, and see what happens to the accident statistics.

In the middle of the village of Long Sutton, next to a church boasting the country's highest and oldest wooden spire, a large crowd had gathered. I stopped to have a look. It appeared to be an auction, and the man at the centre, with his florid complexion, cream linen suit and stripy tie, all topped off by a rather fine panama and a gavel clutched in his right hand, looked like he should be selling off Fabergé eggs or vintage Bugattis. But when I looked more closely, the precious lots on the floor consisted of rusty lawnmowers, rickety stepladders covered in paint, lengths of rotting timber, bags of old nails, rusty boxes and an old camping chair.

'Anybody know what these are for?' asked the man in the hat, holding up a knot of rubber tubing. 'No? Well, what am I bid? 10p?'

Somebody did indeed bid 10p. It was enough to secure the treasure.

'Now, anybody know what this is?' pointing to a small white plastic box that had wires sticking out of it.

'Maybe it's a bomb,' shouted somebody, to general laughter. 'Them Arcada lot.'

'Reckon it's a dehumidifier,' somebody shouted from the back.

'Ah, a dehumidifier,' said the auctioneer. 'It can dehumidify you. What am I bid? 50p? They're all the rage in Chelsea.'

Beside me, two women were engaged in conversation.

'Did you hear that Karen's lost an eye?' said one. It was rude to eavesdrop, but my need to know how Karen came to lose her eye was overwhelming.

'How?' asked her friend.

'Geoff's dog jumped up at her to say hello. Knocked her eye clean out.'

'Really?'

'Honest. Hanging on by it thread it were.'

'Blimey,' I said.

'You know Karen?' the woman said.

'No,' I said.

'Oh.'

On the pavement to the side of the crowd, a middle-aged woman sat on a sofa. It was quite threadbare and covered in the stains of a long and noble service. A large Rottweiler was sitting beside her, drooling in the heat, adding considerably to the distressed appearance of the furniture.

Feeling fatigued by the heat, I asked her if I could join her.

'Help yourself, darlin',' she said, with a cockney twang. I sat down next to the dog, who said nothing, but whom the woman introduced to me as Bess. Bess seemed supremely indifferent to me, which, after hearing about Karen, suited me just fine.

'Just bought the sofa,' she said. 'Fiver. Didn't want to spend that much on it. It's just a piece of old shit really, but I can't resist a bargain and Bess can sleep on it.'

Was this sale a regular event in Long Sutton, I asked.

'Every week. Rain or shine. It's a tradition. The old farmers go mad for the old tools and stuff. Gawd, we love our tat in this country.'

'You don't sound as if you're from round here,' I said.

'Nah. Islington. Lived here ten years.'

'Like it?' I asked,

'Not really,' she said, but didn't elaborate, as we sat in companionable silence, watching a bit of old tarpaulin go for 5p, Bess's tongue lolling in and out in rhythmic time.

'I miss the big city,' she said, finally.

'Really?' I said.

'Never thought I would. Came here to follow a man. That was a mistake. Now I'm stuck here. Could never afford to move back to London now.'

I rode across Holbeach Marsh, along long straight lanes, unflanked by hedgerows, that seemed to float, like dykes, above the endless fields on either side. On the horizon was the odd tree, but that was it. Most of the fields had young crops in them, but I was clueless as to what they might be. I felt as sad about this as I did not knowing about the birds. If the crops looked like they did when they landed on my plate, then of course things would have been different. I felt slightly ashamed of my ignorance.

At the edge of a field, I noticed a row of cars with Polish and Lithuanian number plates. In the distance, in the field, I could make out heads bobbing up and down in the crop. There was a house on the far side of the lane, and I asked the guy working in his garden about the people in the field.

'Eastern Europeans mostly now,' he said. 'But the cast list changes. One year it'll be all Thais, the next Filipinos. When we had the Chinese here, they used to sit in my garden having their lunch because they thought it was a park. They were smashing girls, though. So polite and cheerful.'

I wanted to go and talk to the workers, but was afraid of the ruthless gangmasters who, according to my imagination fuelled by lurid tabloid tales, kept their charges chained to their beds at night and would slit the throat of anybody asking questions. But I figured that if immigration were to launch a raid on remotest Lincolnshire, it probably wouldn't be undertaken by an overweight middle-aged man in Lycra shorts on a bicycle. I hoped the gangmasters would at least take this into consideration before cutting my throat.

I pushed my bike along the rutted track that bisected the field, towards a group of men having a smoke.

'Hello,' I said.

'You lost?' said one, aged in his early twenties, in an east European accent.

I told him I wasn't lost, just wanted to chat, find out what they were up to. 'What are you picking?'

He looked at the crop. Then looked back at me. It was as if I'd asked what the giant orange thing emitting warmth from the sky was called.

'Peonies,' he said. 'Of course.'

'I thought so,' I said. 'But peonies can look so different.'

'Not really,' he said.

I stared at the flowers for a while. Now I was standing there, I didn't really know what I wanted to talk to them about.

'I'm Mike,' I said.

'Armesto,' he said.

'Where are you from?'

'Lithuania,' Armesto said. 'From the middle.'

'I've been to Lithuania,' I said, and then mentioned a city I'd visited, Kaunas.

'I'm not far from there,' he said.

'Ever visited the Devil Museum?'

'No,' he said.

'Or the Museum of Lithuanian Pharmacy?'

'No.'

'Or the museum that's in total darkness and you have to feel your way around it?'

'No. Are you sure they have these things in Kaunas?'

'Of course. They're famous.' Though I did, at that moment, recall being the only person in both the Devil Museum and the Museum of Lithuanian Pharmacy, whose curator looked somewhat shocked to see anybody after I'd awoken him from his slumber in a chair. As to whether I'd been the only person in the museum in total darkness that you had to feel your way around, it was impossible to say.

'Never heard of them,' Armesto said.

'You should go. They're great,' I said. This was a lie. They'd been shit.

'So, where's everybody from?' I asked, pointing to the field.

'Poles and Lithuanians working here mostly at the moment,' Armesto said. 'And a few Thais.'

I looked at the heads bobbing up and down. It looked like back-breaking work. Several Oriental-looking women were wearing coolie hats. I guessed those were the Thais. I'm quite perceptive like that.

'How long have you been here?' I asked him.

'Nine months.'

'How are you finding the locals?' I asked. I'd been reading in the local papers that there'd been some tension between the pickers and the locals in Lincolnshire.

'They're fine as long as you try and speak English,' he said. 'If you can't, they can get angry.'

'I read that locals were upset that imported labour was stealing all the work,' I said.

'They will not do this work. And if they do, they won't work hard. They cause trouble. The bosses prefer us because we are not afraid of hard work. What can you do? It's not our fault.'

'Are you worried about the recession, about what might happen if jobs get harder to come by, whether the English might get more hostile towards you?'

'Why should we worry? We are in the EU. We are entitled to be here. If the work dried up here, we are happy to go somewhere else where the work is. This is not my home. This is just my work.'

I warmed to that young Lithuanian man, admired his spirit. But I also saw in that field the essence of modern labour – mobile, hard-working, few rights, dispensable – and thought that if a time machine could have taken me back to the same field in feudal England I'd be hearing much the same story, but with different accents. Wat Tyler would be turning in his grave. But then, protest was what had taken him to his grave in the first place. So much for progress.

Armesto asked me where I was going.

'Wow,' he said. 'You are lucky. This is a beautiful country.'

'Yes, it is,' I said, and I actually meant it. 'And I am.' I held out my hand and he shook it with a meaty farm labourer's handshake that nearly broke my fingers.

'*Ardievas*,' I said, for that was goodbye in Lithuanian.

'*Sudie*,' he said, for that was really goodbye in Lithuanian.

'*Ardievas*,' Armesto said, 'is Latvian. We don't like the Latvians. Strange people.'

I skirted the south side of The Wash, leaning into the crosswinds as if I was cycling in italics, crossing railway lines with semaphore signals and old-fashioned gates manned by men in uniforms. I then pointed the Ridgeback north. Gadzooks! Curses to Boreas, Greek god of the north wind. Legend has it that Boreas resides in a cave on Mount Haemus. But he spends his summers holidaying in Lincolnshire. Must do. Because he's out there, every single day, blowing a fury, tormenting the mortals. Great for the windmills, of which there were many; terrible for northbound cyclists, of which there seemed to be only one.

I tacked and gybed in the quiet back lanes, northbound progress agonisingly slow, having to stand on the pedals again to make headway. There was little cover to disturb the wind's progress. I passed through a chain of villages with enigmatic names: Leverton Outgate, Leake Hurn's End, Old Leake, Wrangle Lowgate. A traction engine came clanking and hissing by, the smoke from the stack ripping behind it in the wind, my nostrils momentarily filled with that delicious smell of burning coal and steam. That is surely one of the many, many joys of being out in the world on a bicycle: the fragrances that come with the package as you pass by – a woman's perfume, tobacco smoke, a whiff of lavender or the tang of rape, a freshly creosoted fence, a roast dinner.

At Friskney, I stopped to watch a cricket match on the green, where they had dispensed with the bails and all manner of debris blew across the pitch. I guessed they'd grown used to playing in such conditions, the ball swinging like a banana and, depending on which end he was standing, a ball hit high from the batsman either going backwards or flying over the ropes for six.

Some local kids walked past, wearing hooded tops, hands in pockets. Wearing the same garb in London, they'd have carried a malevolent air. I was going to say hello to them but they beat me to it.

'All right, mate?' they all said in unison.

By the time I got to Friskney Eaudyke (I'm not making this up!), the wind had got even worse. I made a decision to get on the busy A52. It may not have been any more sheltered from the wind, but at least it was straight. The followers of the Greek god of caravans were out worshipping in force, as were the trucks, coming so close to me on the two-lane highway that I breathed in instinctively every time I heard one approach. By the side of the road were signs telling motorists how many fatal accidents there had been that year – a lot! – and in the distance at the end of a long straight a speed camera with a neon display. '66 mph. Slow down!' the sign flashed. Then '58mph. Thank you!' it beamed. '5mph. Thank you!' it flashed as I approached. I knew my speed because my speedo told me. And now the whole of the A52 knew. Bloody signs.

A few miles from Skegness, things got worse when I smashed into a pothole, rattling my spine and buckling my back wheel, the ping and release of tension like a girdle popping. Pedalling, with the wheel jamming against the brake blocks, was now even harder. That worried me, but the shaven-headed man standing by his white van at the side of the road up ahead, staring at me psychotically, worried me more. Had he heard me scream 'arseholes' at the gods and the potholes as he'd passed and assumed it was aimed at him?

As I neared, at 5mph, I could see he had his hands behind his back. Just as I reached him, he started to bring his hands into view – a knife? a baseball bat? Instead he held out a bottle of mineral water. 'Keep going,' he said, as if I were hauling myself up Mont Ventoux in red polka dots. I almost burst into tears at the sheer kindness of it.

I arrived in Skegness in the early evening, too late for the bike shops to still be open. As pedalling was almost impossible with the buckled wheel, I had no choice but to stay in 'the Blackpool of the East Coast' for the night and try to get the bike fixed in the morning.

Finding a B&B wasn't difficult. Finding a house that wasn't a B&B would have been more of a challenge. From one guesthouse,

I could hear 'YMCA' blasting out, and could see residents in the bar doing the dance. I decided against that one.

Most of the red-brick semi-detached guesthouses had little canopies over the big picture windows draped in lace curtains that made them look like hairdressing salons. The front gardens were concreted over and signs advertised off-street parking, licensed bar, all en suite, and tea- and coffee-making facilities. They were all obviously fighting for attention, but they all curiously offered exactly the same amenities. 'Family-run' seemed to be a big draw.

Just down the street was a semi whose front garden collection of garden gnomes and cartwheels suggested an altogether more sedate experience than dancing with one's fellow guests. That suited me fine.

I went up to my single room. The TV was on a platform above the bed connected to the wall by a long metal arm. The bedspread was pink and polyester. The tissues on the bedside table were in a Tesco's own brand basics box put inside a wooden box covered in pink lace.

There's something about single rooms: they carry an indelible sadness. At least as the sole occupant of a double bed, you can imagine the other person's just popped down the shops or is in the bathroom or that your solitude is just a temporary state of affairs. But with a single bed, there's no escaping the fact that it's just you. And somehow, a single bed in a holiday town carried extra pathos. I tried to imagine who'd come to Skegness on holiday on their own, and soon I was imagining widows and widowers, returning on autopilot, year after year, to the scene of great former happiness, too late to try somewhere new.

I had made myself sad, the first time I had really felt sad since leaving London. Maybe it was the loneliness of being on your own when you're surrounded by people, in the same way that you can sit alone on a mountain top and not feel remotely lonely, whereas find yourself in the middle of a city surrounded by people and you can feel totally isolated.

I went into the bathroom and looked in the mirror. The Lincolnshire wind had given me the ravaged appearance of a polar explorer. I couldn't decide whether I looked rugged or like somebody with third-degree burns. I had another look: definitely the burns.

I washed and went downstairs. The woman running the B&B asked if everything was okay with the room.

'Great.'

Then the words tumbled out.

'I'm not on my own, you know,' I said.

'Somebody else joining you?' she said. 'You can't have two people in a single.'

'No, I am on my own,' I said. 'Here. I mean, right now. But I'm not "on my own", as it were. I don't have to be on my own.'

'Whatever you say, duck,' she said.

'I just don't want you thinking I don't have any friends.'

'I wasn't,' she said. 'None of my business.'

I walked towards the front door. If she hadn't been thinking that I didn't have any friends, she surely was now.

I went out into the soft light of early evening. The hurricane-like winds were still in full force. If I wasn't totally excited, then I was curious for the opportunity, unplanned and serendipitous, to explore the fleshpots of Skegness, a place with which I'd never previously had the pleasure to meet and, had it not been for the wheel of (mis)fortune, would more than likely never have done.

I walked up a side street, known locally as 'Chip Pan Alley' on account of the fact that nearly every shop was a chippy. Chip wrappers and fast food cartons were being tossed around in the chill wind. The only notable exceptions to the fast-food shops were the big, whitewashed windows with a red fascia where Woolies used to be, and a little shop selling baby dolls that looked horrifically human, most of whom seemed to have some dreadful skin disease, together with teddy-bear mods on Lambrettas and gnomes riding geese.

It seemed that every second person was riding a mobility scooter, silently weaving through the crowd, the whole scene like some choreographed dance. Some of the riders were old, but most weren't: just middle-aged or sometimes even young, but all hugely overweight. This seemed to be a recent phenomenon in Britain: a growing number of people getting so fat they could no longer walk. On Roman Bank there were a couple of mobility scooter shops, just like car showrooms, rows of gleaming scooters lined up outside in every conceivable colour and spec. Outside the pubs and restaurants, more mobility scooters lined up, like they were waiting for valet parking.

I found a bike shop, shuttered up. A sign in the window said it was open at 9 a.m. the following day. I went into a bar. It was cavernous. The music was booming out of unseen speakers, being accompanied by videos on screens that appeared whichever way I turned my head. After the recitals of birdsong, and the peace of the road, this felt a monstrous intrusion, like my deaf aid had been turned up. I felt irritated by it. I ordered a pint and took it to a table. I picked up the menu. The words giant, extra, huge and double dotted the laminated page.

I finished my pint and walked along the road to an Indian restaurant. Among the mobility scooters parked outside was a red Ferrari with the number plate RAJ 1. The restaurant was in an imposing building, a grand hotel in the British seaside's heyday. On the wall of the large dining area, a former ballroom of pillars and vaulted ceilings, was a giant screen showing a Bollywood movie, but the space was full of the ghosts of afternoon dances and cream teas. A waiter came over. He was Albanian, called Sokol, from near the Macedonian border, and had been here ten years. We talked about Albania for a while.

I asked him why he'd chosen Skegness.

'Construction,' he said. 'That's my trade. There were jobs here but they're all closed now.'

He wanted to move to London. 'For the money.'

'Many Albanians in Skegness?' I asked.

'Around twenty,' he said.

I asked him if he liked it here.

'People are friendly,' he said. 'Boston is a bit rough.' He'd worked in Greece and Italy, but found the Italians hard work.

He'd spoken not a word of English when he arrived. I told him how impressive his English was now.

'It's nothing,' he said.

I ordered a Cobra. Took a sip. Closed my eyes. Next thing I knew, Sokol was shaking my shoulder gently, pointing to the balti sizzling in front of me.

The next morning I wheeled my bike into town. It was nine o'clock and already people were sitting outside the pubs in the warm morning air, eating fish and chips and pie and mash and nursing pints of lager. Holidays were surely invented so we could tear up the rule book: eating and drinking whatever we like, when we like, whether it's Christmas morning or the departure lounge at Gatwick before midday. If there is a more sublime, deviant pleasure than drinking booze first thing in the morning when you're on holiday, I have yet to find it.

I took the Ridgeback into the shop. It was a lovely old-fashioned bike shop, with rows of machines waiting for attention, children's bikes in lurid colours, walls full of bells and stabilisers, the floor a jumbled mess of bike bits, all suffused with the smell of rubber and lubricant. Much as I love the bike porn of modern bicycle shops in big cities – and my, how they've taken off in the past few years: those sanitised emporia of eye-wateringly expensive carbon frames, and energy gels and high-end Italian groupsets – there's nothing quite like the innocence of an old-fashioned bike shop to transport you back to that magical moment when you got your first wheels and suddenly the world to explore became a much bigger place.

I remembered when my parents took me to get my first bike. I must have been seven. It was a second-hand shop, run by a Polish émigré called Gustav with wild grey hair and thick black eyebrows that looked like slugs. All the kids of the better-off parents had brand-new Choppers. But those flashy, impractical machines with the tiny front wheel and the ape-hanger bars held no attraction for me. I wanted a bike that could take me places.

I'd walked along the rows of bikes, running my fingers along the steel frames, feeling that something magical was happening, but not knowing exactly what. Then I saw it: a bike that had been lovingly resprayed cobalt blue by Gustav. It had rubber grips on the drop handlebars and a smart steel crest on the head tube. On the right-hand side of the down tube was a little lever, with its middle cut out to save weight. Every other bike just disappeared. I knew what it was to fall in love. That night, I propped the bike against the side of my bed and slept with my arm draped over its crossbar.

The man came out from behind the counter and looked over the Ridgeback. 'Now, what seems to be the problem?' he said, like a kindly doctor talking to a child.

'I've got a bit of a backlog,' he said, pointing towards the row of injured bikes. 'But I could have it done by the end of the day. Any good?'

Perfect, I said, but the minute I said it I felt somewhat trapped. It felt odd after so much continual movement to be stuck somewhere. I went into the public toilet in the car park of the Co-op. I had to put backspin on a 20p to get it to let me in through the turnstiles. At the urinal, I was flanked by two men. Both simultaneously spat into their respective bowls. I don't know why men do this, but do it we do.

'Well, that weren't 20 pee's worth,' said the man to my left in a Yorkshire accent, shaking his old chap with his hand. I was praying that he was addressing the man to my right, whom I hoped was his friend, because there are certain rules of public toilet etiquette, in London at least, which say that under no circumstances are you to attempt small talk with strangers in a public convenience when you've got your tackle out. It's just not allowed.

'In Bridlington it's 50p,' said the man to my right.

'Noooo,' said the man to my left.

'But that's nothing,' continued the man to my right. 'In London, that wealthy bloke who got in with Diana, he's got a business and he charges a pound. A pound!'

'Chuffin' ridiculous!' said the man to my left.

Chuffin', I said to myself. It was lovely that people really used that word outside sitcoms and soap operas.

We all finished up and went outside. The two men said cheerio and went their separate ways. Strangers talking at the urinal. It must be the North.

I walked back towards the sea. I now had a whole day to kill in Skegness with no idea what I might do. I looked at the people enjoying their boozy breakfasts. That was one option, but I didn't really feel like I was on holiday. No, I would have to be more inventive than that.

I crossed the road running along the seafront and stopped by the large grey statue of Skeggy's iconic Jolly Fisherman, prancing in perpetuity.

If ever a town rose to fame on the back of a poster and a slogan, then it's Skegness. John Hassall drew the picture for the poster in 1908, commissioned by the Great Northern Railway Company. The 'Skegness Is So Bracing' slogan was thought to be the brainchild of an unknown member of the railway's staff.

Hassall and I had something in common: we'd both only visited Skegness once. Him in 1936, when he was granted the Freedom of the Foreshore. 'The reality of Skegness has eclipsed all my anticipations,' he'd said at his acceptance speech. 'It is even more bracing than I had been led to expect.' A piece of diplomacy par excellence.

I looked at the statue. It didn't look too jolly to me, seeming somehow to miss the essence of the original poster. Whoever had sculpted it had made him look like he'd just taken a sniper's bullet, like Robert Capa's falling soldier.

I sat on a bench on the concrete promenade. Giant seagulls perched menacingly on the iron railings, waiting for the day's first chip mugging.

Offshore, giant wind turbines whirled silently and furiously. On the wide sandy beach, donkeys plodded up and down, squealing children astride them. Families huddled behind stripy windbreaks. Children built sandcastles, or buried a parent up to their neck. Granddads sat in striped deckchairs with rolled-up trousers reading the *Daily Express* or the *Racing Post*. It was like I'd slipped back to the 1950s, and it all felt rather comforting. At the same time the giant turbines spoke of a future that in the 1950s would have seemed as absurd as science fiction.

On the billboard outside the nearby Embassy Theatre, some of the season's visiting attractions were listed: Roy Chubby Brown; One Night in Vegas; Sally Morgan, Psychic to the Stars; and the International Meccano Show. The roster seemed as timeless as the beach scene.

I entered the fairground. It was still early, so the bingo callers were calling to mostly empty pews. Shooting galleries, test-your-punch boxing balls and assorted sideshows played their tinny jingles and flashed their lights to nobody. On the waltzer, the two male teenage operators, fags hanging languidly out of the corner of their mouths, lavished all their spinning attention on two teenage girls, who screamed with pleasure and fear and adolescent longing.

I walked up to a booth.

'Can I help you, love?' said a dark-haired woman in her fifties, sitting on the Hillbilly Shooting Range next door.

'I'm looking for the fortune-teller,' I said, pointing to the booth.

'Darn varmint,' came a tinny voice from the range.

'That's me,' she said. 'One palm, both palms, or everything with tarot thrown in?'

'Everything,' I said.

'Yee-ha! Ya cotton-pickin' knucklehead,' came the voice.

'Follow me,' said the woman.

We sat down.

'First things first,' she said. 'Can I tell you everything?'

There was a question. It was all baloney, of course, but still...

'Darn varmint,' came the voice.

'Hang on,' she said, getting up and shutting the door tight.

'Tell me everything,' I said, but not with any great conviction. 'Unless there's a 37 bus with my name on it this afternoon.'

She grabbed my right hand and turned it over. 'Not this afternoon,' she said with a warm smile.

On the wall were dozens of photographs of the fortune-teller with the smiling celebrities she'd read for over the years. Some of them were dead now, or in *Holby City*. One in particular had had a somewhat bizarre ending. I wondered whether he'd said 'everything' and whether the fortune-teller had flagged up the perils of trying to adjust roof aerials in strong winds.

'I can see that you always tell the truth, even if you think it will offend someone,' she said.

'That's true,' I said. Even though the truth was the opposite, but I didn't want to offend her.

'Who's Sean?' she asked.

'I don't know anybody called Sean,' I would have said, if I'd been the man she thought I was.

'Oh, Sean! That's spooky,' I said.

'You have to confront him.'

'I will. I will.'

'I can see that transport's very important to you at the moment,' she said. 'What are you driving?'

'A bicycle.'

'Oh, never mind,' she said, sounding disappointed. 'You're about to sign something that will make you financially better off, but read the small print carefully.'

'I will.'

'I can see you're a free spirit and happy and that's not going to change,' she said. 'But really soon, I'm seeing next year, you're going to need to find a base, a place to call a proper home, somewhere to close the door behind you on the world. That's a strong reading: you really need a place to call home, somewhere you feel you belong.'

That was weird. But not as weird as what came next.

'Who's the grey-haired lady? Lovely smile.'

Ah, yes, don't we all know a dead grey-haired lady?

'I'm feeling great sorrow. What's the anniversary today?' she asked.

I looked down at my watch. It was the first of June. My mum, grey hair, lovely smile, had died on the first of June. My heart felt like it was going to burst out of my chest. I could barely breathe. I looked up. The fortune-teller was smiling at me.

'My mum,' I said, quietly. 'She died twenty-two years ago today. I'd forgotten...'

'She's here with us now.'

I could feel tears welling in my eyes.

'It's her that pushes you.'

The first drop ran down my cheek.

'I know,' I said. 'She's a pain...'

'A nice pain, though,' said the fortune-teller.

I walked back onto the seafront in a daze, my mind racing with what had just happened. The familiar feeling of wanting to get away, anywhere, gripped me with renewed intensity. I saw a double-decker bus whose destination board read 'Butlins'. Before I'd thought about it, I'd hopped on, climbed the stairs and sat down at the front.

As the bus ran along the seafront, I thought about what the fortune-teller had said and also back to what Simon had said about me always running away.

'All of us, from cradle to grave,' the psychologist John Bowlby wrote, 'are happiest when life is organised as a series of excursions, long or short, from the secure base provided by our attachment figures.' Bowlby's 'secure base' was not a physical place, per se, more an internal representation of the world.

Again, I thought back to my childhood, the constant moving, the endless hellos and goodbyes, my parents divorcing. My mum got cancer the following year. Lumpectomy. Remission. Radiation treatment. Remission. Chemo. Remission. Chemo again. This had been the punctuation of my adolescence. Cancer was like a cat playing with a mouse, unwilling to kill it yet not letting it go.

That was really when the travelling started for me with a vengeance – the train travel, the long-distance cycling – and I started running, too, for hours at a time. This was the late seventies, before the jogging craze, and everybody thought I was some mad, lunatic child as I'd pull on my pumps and run 10 or 15 miles. But however I travelled, and wherever I went, it never felt far enough. Home was always a bittersweet place waiting for me at the end.

I had just turned 23 when my mum finally died – technically I was a man, but I didn't feel like one. The house was sold, and my childhood belongings put into boxes and stored in various attics to gather dust. The fortune-teller was right in that I'd been a free spirit ever since. But it wasn't a freedom I would ever have chosen.

From the top deck of the bus, Butlins hove into view. I hadn't been to a Butlins since happy holidays spent there as a child. At the middle of the complex, I could see a huge, white, tented structure, like a mini-Millennium Dome, held up by minaret-like spikes. Surrounding this centrepiece was a small city of odd-shaped buildings and chalets.

I bought a day ticket to the camp and picked up a brochure. In it was advertised Skegness Butlins' new holistic spa centre. Get them! The word massage leapt off the page. The bike was having some TLC, and after 611 miles getting here from London, my legs needed some too.

I walked through the camp. Every other building seemed to be offering fast food of some description, the air a mad miasmic fug of doughnuts and chips and fried chicken.

There were a lot of replica football shirts on display; mainly South and West Yorkshire teams – Leeds United, Bradford, Barnsley, the two Sheffields. Some people may look down their noses at it, but I love the tradition of wearing your colours on holiday: it seems to say something primal about our need for tribal belonging.

I walked through the Skyline Pavilion, an unholy cacophony of competing noise – auditions for an *X Factor*-style show on one stage; cartoon dinosaurs singing and dancing to a rapt audience of toddlers on another; banks and banks of slot machines and video games in all places in between; all around children raced and shrieked. I popped into Reds, the main auditorium. On stage, the Redcoats were performing 'Agadoo', the few kids clustered at their feet clumsily trying to nail the moves. The male Redcoats were goading the 'smelly girls'; the female Redcoats the 'stinky boys'. A gender-based dancing competition ensued. The 'smelly girls' won, though it must have been a tough call to make, seeing as all the kids seemed to just flail their arms and legs around randomly as if they were drunk.

I walked into the Yacht Club. I guessed this was Skegness Butlins' poshest restaurant, with a maître d' and pot plants and framed pictures of sailing scenes on the walls. It looked like a cross between a motorway service station and a smart joint in the Hamptons. Mobility scooters glided noiselessly past the windows.

The young girl behind the buffet counter was from Hungary. This was her first summer at Butlins, her first summer away from home. She dispensed the pork chops and curry, coronation chicken, and sausages in tomato sauce.

'What do you think of Butlins?' I asked her.

'I never see anything like this before,' she said. 'I tell my family about this place, but they not believe me.'

'Good?' I asked.

'Very good,' she said. 'People very happy here. Good people.'

We were interrupted by a voice from a microphone. I turned around. A Redcoat was standing by a table.

'Ladies and gentlemen, June is sixty-two today,' he said. The music started and the dining room burst into singing Happy Birthday to June, followed by three cheers.

While everyone seemed to be having a good time at Butlins, it was, in truth, making me feel a little sad. This was no doubt partly connected to the strange encounter with the fortune-teller, but also because some voice inside was telling me that whereas once I belonged here, now I definitely did not. This was no longer my tribe. I sacrificed that membership when I decided I wanted something else, something 'better'. And that's the thing about leaving: you can never, ever find your way back.

I walked back through the pavilion – people smiled and said hello, which still felt weird, wrong somehow – and out the other side to the spa centre. Butlins may be trying to change too, reinvent, modernise, whatever that means, but judging by the queues for the fairground rides and the total absence of punters in the hydrotherapy suite, rainforest showers and crystal steam room, not everybody shared their vision of progress.

My therapist led me past Balinese stone Buddhas to a darkened treatment room lined with mahogany panels and complete with piped whale sounds.

'My name is Sian,' said the therapist.

I thought back to the fortune-teller. Sian. Sean! What's in a vowel? I must confront her.

'Tell me if this is hurting,' she said, massaging my thighs, tender from the road.

'No, that's great,' I grimaced. I was going to see the fortune-teller for a refund afterwards.

Sian was from Chesterfield. She was 18, and wanted to work on the cruise ships at some stage for the money and the chance to see the world.

'Don't go away for too long,' I said.

'Oh, no, I couldn't,' she said, in a mellifluous Derbyshire accent that sounded like it might have been further honey-glazed in massage college. 'I love it here. People are so friendly. It's my home. I'm just going to apply some hot coconut oil with mango into your back.'

And as she rubbed the concoction into my road-jarred shoulders and I drifted into half-sleep, all I could hear were the voices of Janice and Ray, the perpetually disgruntled Yorkshire couple from *The Catherine Tate Show*. 'Whale music. Coconut oil. With mango! In Skegness! The dirty bastards.'

I headed back to Skegness. My bike was ready. One new spoke, a trued wheel, a tightening of cables, some lube, and all for a tenner. I stopped off at my B&B, told them I'd be staying another night and then rode off south, following the coastline, across Croft Marsh.

At the end of the tracks I came to the National Nature Reserve of Gibraltar Point, 1,000 acres of salt marsh, shingle ridges and mudflats overlooking the huge intertidal embayment of The Wash.

I got off my bike and started pushing it across the wooden board-walk that traversed the reserve. The grasses were bursting with bird-song. The skylarks I recognised. The others I did not.

I came to the beach. There was nobody around, just miles of empty sand. I propped the bike against a fence, took off my shoes, walked onto the sand and found a spot against a dune and lay down. I felt serenely calm, helped no doubt by the massage, but primarily by being reunited with my bicycle, now fully restored and fit for adventures; I hadn't fully grasped until I had been parted from it just how much I had come to feel part of it, and it me. This is tricky to explain to non-cyclists.

I looked over at my bike and smiled. The light was fading now, the sky immense, stretched and curved. I saw those skies every day in that part of the world, but they still took my breath away, still always made me feel very, very small.

Chapter 7

*'Bicycling is the nearest approximation
I know to the flight of birds. The airplane simply
carries a man on its back like an obedient
Pegasus; it gives him no wings of his own.'*
Louis J. Helle Jnr

It felt good to be on the road again. Even after such a short time of not moving, or rather not being able to go, I could feel my mood grow tenser, as if the blood that usually flowed to my muscles instead went to my brain, when the exhausting thinking and analysing and reflecting would kick in. Daily life on a long-distance bike trip seemed to be reduced to the core constituents: physical effort, food for fuel, finding shelter. Simple. Blissful.

Just after Butlins, where the tinny jangle of fairground music and the shrieking of excited children drifted over the road, the National Cycle Network's Route 12 took a right down to the shore-line and through a world as different from Butlins as it was possible to imagine.

Here were beaches, deserted save for the odd early morning dog-walker, fringing a flat, marshy landscape, lonely and beautiful. The roads were deserted too, my breath, the wheels and the crows the only sounds. I passed Anderby Creek, Moggs Eye, Marsh Yard; all names worthy of Abel Magwitch.

At Sandilands, the cycle route took me along the concrete promenade, only the occasional walker out, past a long row of beach huts, most in rainbow colours, but some drab and peeling and faded, like diseased teeth in an otherwise glittering set. The hut names gave less-than-subtle clues as to the prevailing weather here: 'Dambreezi'; 'Windrush'; 'Canute 2'. I loved that last one. In this area of high coastal erosion, it made me wonder what had happened to 'Canute 1'.

A brisk, cold onshore wind was gathering strength, blowing flecks of fine sand across the prom and onto my sweaty skin, so when I rubbed my face it felt like sandpaper.

By the time I got to Mablethorpe, the sky was the colour of a battleship and the wind was blowing a fury, churning and whipping the grey sea into a bubbling maelstrom. A few hardy souls sat on the benches looking out to sea, wrapped up that June day, the older women with transparent plastic scarves covering their heads.

I'd done 15 miles that morning on empty and was ready for breakfast, but Mablethorpe seemed to be closed. I rode along the prom, past the deserted crazy golf and the children's fairground rides cocooned tightly in their drab tarps. Right at the end of the prom there was a café, its bright lights burning into the gloom like something from an Edward Hopper painting.

I went in. It was empty save for the two women and a man behind the counter. The two women wore name badges: Josie and Liz. The man, who wore chef's fatigues, did not.

I ordered two bacon sandwiches. And a bowl of chips.

'Hungry, love?' said Liz.

'It's all the cycling,' I said. 'Quiet, isn't it. Is this normal for June?'

'Hope not,' said Liz. 'We only opened for business this morning.'

'Snackattack's going to be famous,' said Josie.

'It's not Snackattack!' said Liz. 'It's Snack Shack.'

'I keep saying that,' said Josie. 'Don't know what's going on in me 'ead.' The two women dissolved into laughter, with the unself-conscious excitement of a pair of schoolgirls setting out on a great adventure together.

'I didn't sleep last night, I were so nervous,' said Josie. 'For weeks I've been dreaming that I've been taking a pig for a walk or being chased by chickens.' They started laughing again.

Josie was Liz's mother-in-law, but they looked to be similar ages, a pair of young-looking glamourpusses fizzing with energy. The cook, whose name was Bob, was Josie's son, and married to Liz.

Outside the big picture window, the frame filled entirely with sea and sand, a pair of mobility scooters pulled up silently, each piloted by an elderly woman wearing a heavy woollen coat, hands swathed in thick gloves.

'Eh up,' said Liz. 'Action stations.'

'The old ladies go around in packs on them scooters,' Josie said. 'Some are souped up. Bloody fly they do. Mablethorpe's Hells Angels.'

Josie went outside to take the orders.

I asked Liz whether she was from the area.

She said they'd only been there 10 years. They were townies who had come to the coast for some peace.

'We're still seen as outsiders, probably always will be. Every year we have big parties up at the house. Fancy dress. Last year it were Rocky Horror Show. We invite the neighbours but they never come.'

Josie came back in: 'Two teas and scones, Bob love.'

'There's a woman walks her pig on the beach down there,' Liz said. 'Next time I see her I'll bring my Lamb Chops down.'

Lamb Chops?

'Farmer gave me three lambs which I was going to have slaughtered,' said Bob, from the kitchen. 'But now I have three pet sheep.' He cocked his thumb in the direction of Liz and rolled his eyes.

'I'm no *Good Life*, me,' said Liz. 'No Felicity Kendal.'

'Oh, no,' said Josie, 'can't be killing Lamb Chops.'

I finished my food and went to leave.

'See them beach huts outside,' said Josie. 'We bought them too. Twelve of 'em. Gonna do 'em up and rent 'em out. Next time you come for a visit, we'll be rich.'

'Dream on,' said Liz.

'You got to dream,' said Josie.

'Always look for something to better yourself,' said Liz.

My bike was hemmed in by the mobility scooters.

'Sorry, love,' said the first old lady, executing a perfect three-point turn one-handed in the narrow space, the other hand being occupied by a scone oozing jam and cream.

They were Rose and June, from Yorkshire, and they spent a couple of months each year in their caravans in Mablethorpe.

I asked them about the scooters and wondered what people did before they were available.

'Just sat indoors if they had nobody to push them in a wheelchair,' said June. 'Plenty of old folk seem happy staying in. My husband breeds canaries, doesn't like going out any more.'

'But they've changed our lives,' said June. 'We're never in. Go all over. Couldn't be without it now.' And with that they went scooting off, waving. 'Ta ta, love, be careful on that bike.'

The grey blanket enveloping the world was going nowhere that day. It just sat there, pressing down, making me feel tired and listless. I pulled over, got my sunglasses out of my bar bag and changed the dark lenses for the yellow, light-enhancing ones. And voila! All of a sudden I could have been cycling alongside the Indian Ocean under a cloudless sky. Okay, I may have looked like Bono, but you can't have everything. I made a point to contact the Department of Health on my return, to suggest they stop prescribing antidepressants or CBT and just give everybody happy glasses instead. I could patent the idea. Next time I visited Snack Shack, we'd all be rich.

Cleethorpes immediately scuppered any thoughts that I'd found a universal cure for melancholy. No happy glasses could work their magic there. It was grim beyond imagination on that grey day with that biting wind. Half of the shops on the seafront were shuttered up and adorned with graffiti. Many of the pubs were boarded up, the peeling 'for sale' signs suggesting that grand reopenings were not imminent. This was by no means unique to Cleethorpes – a vast number of pubs all over Britain were closing down – but somehow the sight of closed places of entertainment and enjoyment in a holiday resort carried extra pathos.

I went into the public toilets on the front. The mirrors on the wall above the sink were sheet metal, scratched to buggery with names and profanities and crude hairy balls and spurting cocks. Besides them were posters in bomb-proof cases advertising HIV and addiction helplines and advice for the safe use of needles. There were slotted boxes for the depositing of said needles. In the cubicles were security tags and labels, presumably ripped off stolen clothes, and the detritus of drug use: silver foil, discarded needles.

I went into a chippy. 'Is that roe?' I asked the woman behind the counter, pointing at a round thing in the cabinet the colour of MDF.

'Rure,' she said. 'What's rure?'

That was odd. They'd definitely sold roe in Skeggy's Chip Pan Alley, just 50 miles away. I'd seen it.

'Cod's eggs,' I said.

'Oh, no,' she said. 'People won't eat cod round here. Haddock fishing area, you see. Grimsby, up road.'

'Is there still a haddock fleet in Grimsby?'

'Not any more,' she said.

I took my haddock and chips and pushed my bike back to a bench on the seafront. I dug out my guidebook and looked up Grimsby. There were over 500 trawlers operating out of the port in the 1950s, making it the largest and busiest fishing port in the world, it said. As a result of the cod wars with Iceland, and over-fishing, and the British fishing industry going the way of mining and agriculture and so much else, the number had declined. Today, there were just 12 fishing boats left in Grimsby.

The guidebook went on. Today, around 500 food-related companies are based there, including giants such as Findus and Young's, bringing in frozen fish by lorry from all over Europe for processing.

It seemed perverse to me that freighting fish the length of Europe and even further afield made more economic sense than popping out to sea to catch it. That idea, of course, would entail some kind of sustainable fishing plan, which wouldn't, you'd think, be beyond the wit of man.

People who know about these things gently assure me that the reason I can't understand the ways of the modern business world is because I am a moron. And they may be right. But still, it all seems wrong. How can an island nation be in a position where it imports its fish? I know, I know. I'm just a moron.

I looked down at my haddock. Who knows where that had been caught? And when?

In Grimsby there were giant murals painted on the end walls of terraces, like those of the Falls or Shanklin roads, except instead of hooded men or crossed Armalites, there were trawlers and haddock and fishermen doing heroic deeds in the big swells of the North Sea. Above all this rose the huge 200-foot Italianate spike of the Dock Tower, built in 1852 when Grimsby was booming, based on the design of the Palazzo Pubblico in Siena. It looked utterly out of place now. In the distance, beyond the town, along the bank of the Humber, I could see the sulphurous smoke of the chemical complexes of Immingham, backlit by the flames. It looked as if Hades was on the horizon.

Heavy rain was falling now, being blown almost horizontally by the frigid wind coming off the sea, which cut through my skin and whistled through my bones. The roads were greasy. People shuffled along the pavements, heads bowed against the blow. I had once been in the Siberian city of Irkutsk, in the depths of winter, a bleak place 3,500 miles east of Moscow, 2,300 miles west of the Pacific and south of nowhere. People there looked grey and beaten, swollen with misery. Grimsby that day reminded me of Irkutsk.

I decided against going to the National Heritage Fishing Centre, a museum dedicated to the days when Grimsby was the busiest fishing port in the world. Instead, I propped my bike up against a wall and went into a pub, ordering a large Scotch to fight the damp chill. It was early afternoon in midweek, yet the pub was full of men, young and old, who sat and drank in a sepulchral silence befitting a mausoleum.

On the bar was a copy of the *Grimsby Telegraph*. The splash carried the headline 'Unemployment soars to 12-year high'. The reporter had spoken to the local Jobcentre Plus, who'd said that they constantly had vacancies for cleaners and care assistants, but that local people were not interested. 'They have to become more flexible about the type of work they are willing to do,' a spokesman had said.

Sharing the front page was a story about the ongoing dispute at Total's Lindsey refinery just up the road in Immingham, where nearly 900 workers had been sacked after going on strike in protest over claims that Total were importing cheap foreign labour. A picture accompanying the story showed pickets with placards denouncing 'greedy bosses'. One read 'British jobs for British workers'. It was a statement terrifying in its implications, and doubtless the man holding it would join me in the class for morons who failed to understand the modern business world. But it was easy to understand the fear and anger.

I sensed that the man sitting at a bar stool a few yards away was staring at me. I looked up at him. He must have been about my age. His face was gnarled and jowly, his nose bulbous, thread veins running down it and spreading to his cheeks like red rivulets running through shattered porcelain. His shirt was undone to the waist, his huge gut rippling out of it and tumbling over his trousers like a glacier.

He drew his lips back into a smile, revealing just four tombstone teeth hanging from the upper gum and three poking up from the lower. Then he stuck up his thumb.

'You all right, mate?' he said.

'Grand. You?'

He took a slurp of his pint, hand shaking, and then put it back on the bar.

'Aye, fucking grand,' he said, sticking his thumb up once more.

With a tailwind, I flew along the south bank of the Humber in the driving rain, the spray from the passing chemical tankers soaking me but making not a jot of difference to how wet I was. That's liberating on a bike: when you're so wet you can't get any wetter. After a while you stop worrying about it and relax into your discomfort until it disappears, which it always does.

The chemical plants stood like mini sci-fi cities on the riverbank, with giant pipes and rocket launch pads and so many chimneys reaching into the sky that from a distance they looked like a forest of denuded sequoias. They may not make it into tourist brochures, but there was something magnificent about those living, breathing, flame-belching behemoths.

Around the Goxhill headland and suddenly, across the wheat fields, there were the twin supports of the Humber Bridge, for nearly two decades after it opened in 1981 the world's longest single-span suspension bridge.

I freewheeled down the steep slip road and then climbed onto the bridge itself. After a relatively flat trip so far, the climb onto the bridge felt like an alpine ascent. I knew that the Humber marked the end of the flatlands, and that somewhere beyond the water the Wolds of Yorkshire were waiting. I'd hoped that my legs would be feeling pretty strong by now, but alas: they weren't.

Up onto the great parabola of concrete and steel, suspended in the sky, the whole structure bouncing from the traffic, as if there was an invisible hulking monster stomping along behind me.

If the small ferry crossings seemed to mark small endings and beginnings, new paragraphs if you like, I always felt when I left London that the county borders and the big bridges would feel like significant milestones on the journey, the ending and beginning of chapters. And so it felt that day, three weeks after leaving London, high above the Humber.

I was cycling next to the railings on the shared pedestrian/bike walkway. From the saddle, my head several feet above the railings, it felt like I was flying through space, the mudflats of the Humber far, far below, ships ghosting along underneath me, Immingham in the distance wearing its nicotine-stained bonnet. As I wobbled along, the thought occurred that if my bars clipped the railings, just inches to my right, I could easily be pitchpoled straight over the bars and out into space. But far from making me afraid, this just made me laugh out loud.

Halfway across, I stopped to take a picture of the view. On the railing was a plate carrying the phone number of the Samaritans. Next to it, tied to the railings with string, was a dried and shrivelled bunch of long-dead flowers, the heads hanging limply over cellophane now dirty from the fumes.

Stopping at a traffic light in Hull, I saw one of the city's famous cream telephone boxes. Kingston-upon-Hull had been the only area of the UK not under the Post Office monopoly, with telephones being under the control of the council. So, in the name of civic identity, the phone boxes were painted cream and the crown omitted.

This made me think about the role a town's 'colours' play in identity. When I was a kid, whenever we drove down from Birmingham to London to see relatives, the game we played was always the first person to spot a red bus. I can still remember how exciting that was. Ditto the deep-green buses of Liverpool, the maroon of Glasgow or the orange of Manchester. There was always a frenzy to see a Brummie blue-and-cream bus on our return home. The sighting of one always made me feel as if I were home proper, as reassuring after an adventure into a land marked 'here be monsters' as a comfort blanket.

Since buses were deregulated in the mid-1980s, colours change when franchise holders do, or when a marketing department's got the fidgets. I know I'm a reactionary old fart now, but this makes me more than a little glum. I'd recently been back to Brum and seen that most of the buses were now painted in the red, purple and white of National Express. A little bit of me seemed to die, another connection with my childhood severed.

But are these things important in the grand scheme of things? I'd say that they are. Because where does it end? The colours of your football club's shirts changing on the whim of a new owner, in the same way that the stadiums are now renamed after the sponsors? Whole towns renamed after corporations? We're already seeing schools go down that road. In a world where everything can change overnight at the whim of a boardroom, I'd argue that it's things like football stadiums and bus colours that can give us an implicit stability when everything else is mutable, liable to change or disappear overnight. But such is the modern world. It doesn't mean that I can't feel sad about it, though.

For the record, in Hull, many of the buses were painted in Stagecoach's corporate colours of blue, white, orange and red. Pre-privatisation, I believe Hull was a royal blue and white kinda place.

After negotiating Hull's Byzantine one-way system, I was finally out the other side, into the immutable open countryside and the arrow-straight lonely lanes through Stone Creek and Sunk Island.

A handwritten sign on a post by a farm said 'camping', and I was directed by the farmer to a little field at the back of his house, with a basic shower room converted from an old breeze-block shed with a heavy steel door that banged in the wind. There were no signs up anywhere, though, so it felt just dandy.

In the rapidly fading light and still pouring rain, I pitched the tent, shoved my panniers into the porch and was just about to follow them in when I saw that the occupant of the only other tent on the site was heading across the field my way.

'How do,' he called, when about 20 yards away. 'Saw you arrive on the bike. Come far?'

I told him what I was up to. I kept it brief, trying to talk in a manner that I hoped suggested I was not being rude, just not in the market for a long and meaningful. I eyed my panniers, now snuggled up under canvas. I also knew that somewhere in those bags were a couple of baguettes, some honey-roast ham and a slab of Boursin.

'How marvellous,' he said. 'What a great adventure you're on.'

The rain was sheeting down now and it was almost dark.

'And you?' I asked. I looked over at his tent. There was no sign of a car. 'How are you travelling?'

He pointed down at his feet and shuffled them backwards and forwards.

'On those. Walking round the coast of Britain. Not all in one go. Doing the leg from Berwick to King's Lynn this time.'

'David,' he said, and held out his hand. He wore little clear-plastic spectacles. Beyond them were deep blue eyes that sparkled like sapphires.

He was 62 and lived in Bury St Edmunds. When on his walks he got up at 6 a.m. every day and hit the road, never knowing where he would end up that evening. Sometimes he would find a campsite, sometimes he would just rough it in a field.

'I just love walking,' he said. 'Being in nature. It makes me happy. Done five thousand miles in the last five years, with only one blister in that time. Land's End to John O'Groats, most of the major British trails.

'These,' he continued, pointing to his well-worn boots, 'have cost me about 10p a mile.'

He said something about a wife that suggested to me that she was dead, but no, she was alive.

'She doesn't like camping. Lets me get on with it. We've been married thirty-eight years. I call her once a week just to let her know I'm alive. I picked a good 'un.'

David's enthusiasm for the nomadic life oozed out of him; he seemed so alive and engaged with the world around him. But didn't he ever get lonely?

'Lonely? Good God, no,' he said. 'Haven't got the time to be lonely. There's so much to see, so many birds and animals and amazing views. I meet dog-walkers along the beaches, and there are always very interesting people to meet if you're prepared to introduce yourself. I think the important thing is that I quite like my own company, am happy to be on my own, chattering away to myself. People must sometimes think I'm a right nutter.'

A young hare hopped up to us, as calm as you like, and just sat there by our feet for a few seconds.

'That's funny,' said David. 'Hares are usually such skittish animals.'

As if the hare suddenly realised what it was, it bolted at full tilt away from us, flying across the grass and then into the green wheat a couple of hundred yards away.

'I used to cycle a fair bit too,' David continued. 'Took part in marathon club rides. Did 246 miles in twelve hours once.' Nothing he said sounded boastful in the slightest.

We'd been talking for about half an hour. I'd completely forgotten about the food awaiting me just inches away.

I thought of the people I knew in London in their thirties and forties who say how much they detest their jobs and are bored, who self-medicate with booze and drugs and seek their thrills on mini-breaks at five-star hotels in obscure European cities, eating expensively. There never seemed to be any real passion in their voices when recounting their adventures. And here was David, in his sixties, wandering alone, sleeping in a one-man tent in fields, eyes on fire with it all as if he'd just acquired the power of sight.

I wondered what this meant for my generation, many of whom seemed to have lost their appetite for simple pleasures; living in a world full of choice that has brought not happiness but a bitterness for the things they don't have.

'Good to meet you,' he said. 'I'm off to bed. Up at dawn. Going to try and get over the bridge by tomorrow night.'

He took out a piece of paper, scribbled a number on it. 'That's me,' he said, 'if you're ever in Bury St Edmunds.' Next to the number, as an aide-memoire, he'd written: 'The old man walking around Britain.'

And with that he was off, walking across the field in the rain, turning just once to say 'Be happy, Mike' with a wave of the hand, and I watched him all the way as he got into his tent and zipped up the flap.

Next morning the rain was still falling and the winds had swung around from due easterlies to north-easterlies, carrying with them even more of a chill. As a cyclist, it's the first thing you try and work out when you pop your head out of the tent in the morning: the direction of the wind, and its strength; to find out whether you will be riding with tormentors or angels.

The north-easterlies would blow me down to the end of Spurn Head, which I'd wanted to visit since ever seeing it on a TV programme. It's one of the most extraordinary features of the British coastline: a great narrow anteater snout of sand and shingle banks held together by marram grass and seabuckthorn stretching out three and a half miles into the Humber Estuary.

But the strength of the headwind, which was now gusting around 25mph, would make the return ride up the narrow spit agonisingly hard work. Decisions. You wouldn't think twice about doing it in a car, but when you've only got your legs for an engine, it's a whole different calculation. I pulled out a coin. Heads for Spurn; tails for missing it out. Heads. Bollocks. Best of three. Heads. Double bollocks.

I flew along the spit, travelling at 20mph with my feet off the pedals, my bike taking horrendous hits from the concrete paving slabs forming the single track road that had shifted and sunk over time, leaving kerb-like edges that brought rattles to my teeth and sickening thuds to my rims. To my left, huge spumes of water from the North Sea broke high over the sandbanks. To my right, the glassy Humber; the two bits of water separated only by 50 metres, the sea seemingly furious that this fragile piece of land was defying it.

The track was dusted in sand, too, blown this way and that, sometimes pooling in unseen gullies into which my front wheel would sink and the bike would abruptly stop, and I'd find myself on the ground.

About halfway along the spit, I noticed a Tiger Moth caterpillar making its way across my bow. I managed to swerve and to avoid it, but looking ahead saw that the entire track was carpeted with them, bright orange beasts with black backs and white hair sticking up like they'd been plugged into the mains. Some were losing their precarious grip on the road in the wind and pitchpoling and rolling like tumbleweed. Some rolled under my tyres, I regret to say.

In the spiky seabuckthorn bushes hung white woven nests, like lace doilies, where some of caterpillars were already cocooned for the next stage of their journey. The bushes looked like they'd been decorated for Christmas.

The lifeboat station at Spurn Point was, outside London, the UK's only permanently manned one – the journey down the spit making any other arrangement impractical.

There was a cluster of houses, a small village really, the white woodwork peeling and weather-beaten and the brickwork distressed. Outside each house was a child's bike, lying on its side, the place had the feel of an American Midwest town circa 1950.

I really wanted to talk to the crewmen about their life in that remote place. But then I saw something that seemed much more interesting. It was a sign that said 'Café'.

I ordered the Belly Buster breakfast. I asked the woman behind the counter how long she'd lived there.

'Twenty years now.'

The windows rattled violently in the panes. Outside, two enormous herring gulls were being tossed around like spindrift.

Also behind the counter was a girl, aged around 14, putting various bits of pig into a huge pan, sizzling and spitting.

'Your daughter?' I asked. She nodded and smiled.

'How is it for kids living so far away from anywhere?' I asked, for it really did feel like we were floating in the middle of the sea.

'They love it when they're young, but when they're this age,' she said, cocking a thumb in the direction of the girl, 'they hate you for bringing them here. Then they go. But they tend to come back. This place gets under your skin. My eldest two are in the forces now. When they come back from Iraq, they come down here to clear their heads. We get cut off on spring tides when there's a sea behind it. It never feels more remote than when that happens.'

I finished my breakfast and went back out into the maelstrom. The lifeboat men were sheltering from the wind behind a shed.

'How's business?' I asked one of them.

'Really quiet this year,' he said. 'It's cos of the recession. There's a lot less ships operating. A few years ago, there'd be a constant line of ships queuing to get into the Humber, to Grimsby, Goole, Immingham and Hull. You could stand here and watch 'em offshore, going up and down the coast, day and night. Not now. It's strange for us. I mean, we're here to save lives, so it's good that there's less lives been lost. But it's not good to have all this time on our hands.'

A couple of kids ran past chasing a football.

'It's great for them here, though. They can't get into trouble. Well, kids would get into trouble in an empty room. But we're away from all the drugs here, all the stuff that goes on in the towns. They can have proper childhoods, running wild, playing in nature.'

'See them bikes outside the houses,' he continued. 'People think they're the kids' bikes, but they're not. When the siren goes we race on them to the end of the pier where the boat is. That's why they're always lying there. Nobody would dare touch 'em. Record for getting to sea from the siren is just under four minutes.'

It took me almost an hour to get back up the spit, what with the wind and the sand traps and the carpet of caterpillars that I did my best to avoid.

But at least the afternoon was dry, the road flat, dipping in and out of resorts like Withernsea, which seemed down at heel, and Hornsea, which did not. The one thing that all the towns had in common, though, was the smell of chips as I pedalled through. A blind cyclist would have a tale to tell on a journey around Britain's coast.

And all afternoon I could see, in the far distance, at the end of the long sweep of Bridlington Bay, the immense cliffs of Flamborough Head, the first real cliffs of the trip. For another great joy of long-distance cycle touring is the way you get to see and feel how a country is put together, how the geographical parts of the jigsaw fit. 'It is by riding a bicycle that you learn the contours of a country best, since you have to sweat up the hills and can coast down them,' wrote Ernest Hemingway. 'You have no such accurate remembrance of a country you have driven through as you gain by riding a bicycle.'

Quite so, Ernest. Thank you. There hadn't been too much sweating up hills so far, but the brooding presence of Flamborough and the Wolds, and the North York Moors beyond was a reminder that that was all about to change.

At a caravan park in Hornsea, I stopped and said hello to an elderly man drinking tea on the deck of his static home.

'You cumpin', on t'pushbike?' he asked, in a broad and lovely Yorkshire accent that could have sold me anything.

'Aye,' I replied, in a piss-poor Yorkshire accent. I don't know why I do that.

I told him about my trip.

'For charity?'

'For the hell of it,' I said.

'Well fancy that. Good luck to ya, love.' I loved the way older Yorkshiremen called other men love.

'Want a cuppa?'

He disappeared, came back with a mug of steaming tea, handed it down to me over the railings.

'Fancy that, eh?' he said again.

It was late afternoon by now. I was beginning to think about stopping for the night.

'Do they allow camping here?'

'They stopped it. Bloody bastards. You can cump in my garden though if you like. That'll upset them, the bastards.'

With no great desire to upset 'the bastards', whoever they may have been, I asked him if he knew any campsites nearby.

'Aye, happen there's one oop in Atwick, love,' the place being pronounced like the room at the top of a house.

Three lads came by on scooters. They'd obviously taken the baffle out of the exhausts. The noise was like being stuck in a metal bin with a swarm of bluebottles.

'Bastards,' the man said. 'Day and bloody night they're up and down here, seventy miles per hour. No bloody respect these days.'

I rode on the three miles to Atwick, turned right up a steep narrow metalled track following a sign for camping, and stopped just before the track disappeared into space over the cliffs. It was the kind of road from which Wile E. Coyote would plummet as Road Runner whipped out his Acme jetpack.

I knocked on the door of a caravan which bore a sign saying 'Site office'. The caravan was about 20 yards away from the edge of the cliffs. I waited a few seconds. There weren't many signs up. In fact, the only other one I could see read 'stay away from the edge'. That one seemed fair enough. I knocked again.

'Hang on, hang on,' came a muffled voice from within.

The door opened.

''Ow do,' said the man. He was wearing only a vest and a pair of underpants, both once white back in the day, but now the colour of a corpse.

'What's happened there?' I asked, pointing to the road to oblivion.

'Cliffs are crumbling, erosion,' he said. 'When I came here fourteen year ago, it were a long walk to the edge, now look.'

'Is it safe?' I said.

'Long as you don't fall off,' he said. This, I had to admit, contained some sound logic.

'How much for the night?' I asked.

'I can't take any money when I'm naked,' he replied. This, too, must have contained some sound logic, though I was struggling to see it. 'Come and see me tomorrow morning.'

His faith in there being a tomorrow morning was reassuring, but a wiser businessman would surely have got the money up front on such a campsite.

I pushed my bike along the edge. The cliffs had great bite marks in them. Most of the concrete caravan plots nearest the edge had been abandoned, yet some vans stubbornly remained. I looked over the edge. On the beach some 200 feet below, mixed in with lumps of fallen cliff, was the debris from smashed caravans: bits of old carpet, wood panelling, and whole slabs of aluminium wall. The sea was churning, licking at the cliffs. It was at once both terrifying and magnificent to see nature so brutal and unsentimental up close.

About 50 yards back from the cliff edge there was a solitary bush, being battered by the wind. I pitched my tent next to it and looped the guy ropes around the trunk. I had visions of waking up in the middle of the night hanging in mid-air, the only thing saving me from crashing 200 feet into the surf below a small bush and a lightweight guy rope. There was really only one thing for me to do.

'Large Scotch, please,' I said to the barmaid in the pub in Atwick village. I followed this with several more.

By the time I got back to the site, it was pitch black. I found my tent, then paced the distance to the cliff edge, listening to the sough and the fury below. It didn't seem like 50 yards now, the darkness somehow intensifying the unseen maelstrom below. I walked back, checked the guy ropes on the bush, climbed into my tent and, despite the large quantities of Scotch, lay there awake for most of the night, listening to the North Sea eating Yorkshire.

On cue, next day the land started to rise, heading into the Wolds and the Carrs. My calves and thighs started to burn with the effort. My breath grew shorter. The fields were brilliant with rape, dazzling under the morning sun. From time to time, I passed dead crows that had been ghoulishly strung up by their wings with wire, like black angels, to deter other potential avian miscreants hell-bent on crop munching. The crows still alive squawked their contempt.

I continued up the hill. There's something masochistic about enjoying them as a cyclist, as many do. I think this comes from the fact that it's a temporary pain – your lungs feel like they're going to explode, your heart and thighs likewise. But you'll look up, and see the top, and you know that the pain will end soon, you've just got to keep going and you'll reach that point eventually where things will stop hurting and you will soon be riding along the flat or downhill as if nothing happened, stronger for the experience. Maybe, deep down, cyclists know that hills, and the temporary pain and struggle they involve, are a fantastic metaphor for life. It's shit when you're struggling. But the pain will end. It always does. There's always a summit. You've just got to keep going.

At the top of a large climb, I stopped and looked back. England behind me was flat as far as the eye could see: a vast plain. I could see the Humber, like a slug's silvery trail, the proboscis of Spurn and the yellow angry cotton balls sitting over Immingham. If my legs were grumbling about the new workload, my spirits weren't: H.V. Morton might have found great beauty in the flatlands, but for me, buckles and folds and creases provide a much more powerful aesthetic, with depth and perspective.

After another long, gradual rise, I approached the brow of a hill. A sign said 3.0% and I thought how cautious these supposedly tough Yorkshire folk were to flag up such a piddly gradient. But I had misread: there was no decimal point. The road simply disappeared beneath me, in a straight line down, like a ski jump. Yorkshire hills didn't seem to bother with anything as poncey as bends to soften the gradient and I could imagine the response to my whining: 'Straight oop, straight down. What dus thee want bends for, saft lad?'

After my speedometer showed 40mph I stopped looking at it. The weight of my luggage was like Thomas the Tank Engine's naughty coaches pushing me faster and faster. I pulled hard on the brakes, but all I got for my trouble was aching wrists and a hideous squealing that sounded worse than fornicating foxes. Luckily, there was a long run-off at the bottom, and I stopped soon after to prise my fingers off the handlebars, one by one. In the space of little more than a mile, I had come to two conclusions. One, you could shove the buckles and the folds and the creases, and the depth and the perspective, and all that rubbish; I was already pining for Lincolnshire. And, two, I would need to get rid of a lot more stuff.

I looked at my watch. This was something I hadn't really done much of since leaving London. But this was one of the rare occasions when I'd made a prior appointment. I'd arranged to meet a chap named Jay at the railway station in Scarborough. Jay was a ranger for the North York Moors National Park, and he'd kindly agreed to cycle with me from Scarborough to Whitby.

Now, Scarborough seemed to be the perfect town for bikes. But you would ideally need an engine, built as it is up the side of a cliff. Undeterred by the obvious gravitational aspects, the council had fully embraced the bicycle, plastering bike lanes everywhere. But I'm surprised all the paint hadn't just run off when wet and pooled at the bottom.

I followed a bike lane, looking for signs for the station, and found myself sucked down a hill so steep that it would need ropes and crampons to renegotiate. Before I knew it, I was at the bottom, cycling along the front.

'Where's the train station?' I asked a man.

'Up there,' he said, pointing to the sun.

Just along the front was one of the town's cliff railways. I had a crisis of morality. Would it be cheating? Of course. Did I care? My head said yes. But my legs were shouting the loudest. And anyway, riding back up the Alpe Scarborough would probably make me late for Jay. I also figured that as long as I wasn't making forward progress, it wasn't really cheating. It's amazing how one can justify things to oneself to avoid pain.

As the old railway clanked up the cliff, I surveyed the scene before me. I hadn't been to Scarborough for over 30 years, and it seemed not to have changed one jot. Basking in the sunshine that day, with its stately Victorian terraces following the undulations of the cliff-top and castle looming proprietorially over it, and with gig rowers in the harbour below, it had a timelessness that gladdened the soul. I couldn't help but feel that if Scarborough had been on the Amalfi coast, Frank Sinatra would have sung a song about it.

Jay was waiting for me when I got to the station. We were soon weaving through the backstreets and parks of the town, following the signs for National Cycle Network Route 1, of which the Scarborough to Whitby section is part. And not just any old part either, for it is one of the jewels in the NCN. Nearly all off-road, it follows the track bed of the former railway line that once linked Whitby to Scarborough, opening in 1885 and bringing thousands of day trippers and holidaymakers to this previously remote and inaccessible stretch of coast. It had been a true miracle of Victorian engineering, needing 60 bridges and two viaducts to carry its 18 miles of track.

The line had never been profitable, and when Richard Beeching sat down in the early 1960s with a brief to shut loss-making services, this line was earmarked for closure. The last train ran in 1965.

Soon we were clear of Scarborough and cycling under a canopy of hawthorn and silver birch, sheltered from the wind, its sibilant hiss the only reminder of its presence. Occasionally we'd emerge from the tunnel of trees and pass through the platforms of honeystoned former stations, all now lovingly turned into homes, often with the station clock still in situ, as were the semaphore signals now set at stop in perpetuity. I longed to live in one of those dwellings.

The first half of the line was a gradual climb up to the summit at Ravenscar, and trackside markers had the incline rising at 4 and 5 per cent. Even on a bicycle it was work, and I could imagine the sound and fury of a steam engine hauling a rake of laden coaches up there. It must have been quite a spectacle.

From time to time the trees would part momentarily and we'd be given a tantalising glimpse of the sea, now far below us, before the curtains closed once more.

As a lover of railways, I never thought I could forgive Beeching for his vandalism and the superb engineering his cuts squandered, not to mention the impact it had on communities. But as we made our way along the magnificent trail, I found myself perfidiously saying a silent thank you to the old hatchet man.

As we climbed, I asked Jay about his job. Part of it involved cycling the trails and inspecting the bridleways and reporting back on jobs the maintenance crews would need to come out to do.

'That's some job you've got,' I said.

'I'm very lucky,' he replied.

We didn't talk much, but it was lovely to be riding alongside somebody, if only for a short while. For although I find solo cycling a joy, I think there's nothing finer than sharing a ride with a friend. There's something about the joint witnessing of the world that gives the experience a sense of permanence.

We stopped just past a stone bridge, ancient soot trails still smudged on its arch. Jay dismounted and checked the repair work on a trackside fence. He sniffed the air. 'Fox, not long come through,' he said.

I sniffed the air too, but could smell nothing.

At Ravenscar, the track was expelled from the shelter of the trees and suddenly we were flying 600 feet above the sea, the wind ferocious, to the north the three-mile-wide sweep of Robin Hood's Bay, flecked with whitecaps. It was a truly magnificent scene.

'Do you know about Ravenscar?' Jay asked me.

I said that I didn't.

'The resort that never was,' he said. 'I'll show you.'

Jay explained that in 1895, now that the railway had helped spark the birth of the seaside holiday, the Peak Estate Company had hoped to capitalise by buying up all the land in this remote spot, with dreams of turning it into a smart, upmarket holiday resort. There were to be houses, shops, hotels, formal gardens and a marine esplanade running along the cliff-top.

To prepare for the new town, 300 men made roads and installed a mains water supply. The land had been divided into 1,500 building plots and offered for sale.

They even built Station Square along with the Station Hotel as a grand entrance to the resort from the railway.

'What went wrong?'

'Just about everything really,' Jay said. 'For a start, because Ravenscar is so high and exposed, there's no shelter from this wind, which batters it most days of the year. And then there's the small matter of it being 600 feet down to the beach. And even if trippers made it down to the beach, they would have found no sand, only rocks. It was sheer folly.'

Unsurprisingly, only a handful of plots were ever sold and the Peak Estate Company went into liquidation in the early 1900s.

In Station Square today, the old Station Hotel remains alone, standing defiantly over a century on, still looking as if it is waiting to burst into life, where porters in stiff collars and ridiculous moustaches might run out at the sound of a train whistle.

Jay and I rode our bikes along the now grassed-over streets, complete with kerbstones. He stopped and pointed to something on the ground. It was an iron manhole cover. 'They even built the sewers,' Jay said.

We passed the rooftops of the old smuggler's port of Robin Hood's Bay, rode around a final headland, and were soon entering Whitby, cycling across the lovely old railway viaduct high above the River Esk, the brooding and menacing ruins of the old abbey sitting above the town.

After saying farewell to Jay, I found myself a B&B and went through my stuff. Into a pile went my remaining pair of jeans, both remaining novels, my guide to British birds (nice idea but way too heavy), my solar battery recharger, the smart evening jacket, half my stock of pants and socks, my waterproof trousers (I'd not worn them at all in the rain), and my helmet cover (ditto). Like the last time I'd shed gear back in Suffolk, it felt liberating to have fewer possessions, and not just for the weight loss. Life seems less complicated somehow when you only have one pair of trousers – a phrase I'd have put on my gravestone if it didn't sound quite so weird.

Then, wearing my only pair of trousers, I went off to explore. I went to the museum, high on the hill, which was lovely: stuff in dusty old cases with typewritten notes of explanation on sepia-tinged card that curled at the corners, and fossils of dinosaurs on the wall, alongside stuffed aardvarks and puffins. There were displays celebrating Whitby's whaling heritage, with nice model whaling ships, and a room devoted to the life of the town's most famous son, Captain James Cook. Whitby's museum felt like it should be in a, well, a museum. Even the ancient curators looked like they were from Central Casting. I loved it.

I walked along the front by the harbour. There was the usual cavalcade of mobility scooters in the soft early-evening light, joined by gaggles of pale Goths eating ice cream and comparing piercings, and families eating fish and chips from newspaper wrappings, being eyed by unfeasibly large herring gulls. I don't know why the herring gulls don't just waddle into the chippies and demand food. They're so big and menacing-looking these days, who'd be brave enough to deny them?

There were fossil shops and shops selling gear for Goths (what was it with that Whitby Goth thing?), and a tour bus powered by steam, whose shrill whistle sliced through the air and mixed with the cry of the gulls.

In the visitor centre I saw a leaflet for Heritage Harry Collett's ghost walks. There was one starting in 15 minutes' time, commencing from the Whalebone Arch on West Cliff.

By the time I got there, a large crowd of excited schoolchildren, around nine or ten years old, were clustered around a figure dressed in a black cape and black top hat.

'Would you like to join us?' said Heritage Harry, for I was guessing it was him.

'Please.'

The schoolchildren seemed entirely indifferent to me, seeing as they were in the process of being scared witless by Harry.

'You've all got to go "Wooooooooooo" and wave at that hotel,' he said. 'If somebody comes to the window and waves back, that means they're okay. If they don't wave, it means they're a zombie!'

The children all went 'Wooooooooooo'. An elderly man came to the window to see what the fuss was about, to be greeted by 30 children waving up at him. He grumpily pulled a face and didn't wave back.

'Zombie,' said a little boy.

'Must be,' said the little girl next to him. 'Do you think there are zombies in Melton Mowbray?'

'Reckon.'

'Oh.'

But if the kids were indifferent to me, the four teachers accompanying them eyed me with a little suspicion. I didn't really blame them. I suppose in twenty-first-century Britain, a middle-aged man on his own joining in a ghost tour with a group of 30 schoolchildren was bound to elicit some raised eyebrows. They subtly positioned themselves between their charges and me.

We moved on. Outside the Royal Hotel, where Bram Stoker started his seven-year labour that would produce one of the most famous Gothic novels in history (ah, the Goth mystery produces a lead), Harry pointed to the steps leading up to the ruined abbey on the East Cliff.

'Anybody know who ran up those 199 steps?' he asked.

'Lord Voldemort?' said a little boy.

'Count Dracula!' said Harry. 'Who one dark and stormy night came ashore from the wreck of the Russian ship *Demeter* in the shape of an immense black dog.'

'Dracula!' said a little girl, her mouth flapping open and shut like a fish.

'Ha, ha, ha, ha, ha, ha, ha,' said Harry in bloodcurdling fashion.

The teachers seemed to have forgotten about me now. They looked as scared as the children.

Harry led his charges like the Pied Piper, all swirling cape, through Whitby's narrow alleys and snickets, stopping to point out the house where the Witches of Whitby had lived with their cats, the spot where a bankrupt man had hanged himself, where the ghost of the one-armed lighthouse keeper could still be seen, and where a horseman had been decapitated by a low branch. Whitby must have been the unluckiest town on the planet.

'Occasionally, people think they see a football rolling down the hill, but when they look more closely, they see that it's a head,' said Harry. 'Ha, ha, ha, ha, ha, ha, ha.'

The children looked terrified and exhilarated. I imagined that there wouldn't be a peaceful night's sleep in the dorm later on.

'Now,' said Harry. 'Anybody know what a Hand of Glory is?'

A hand shot up at the back. I shouldn't have done it, but I couldn't resist. The competitiveness of the classroom never leaves you.

'Yes?' said Harry.

'Well,' I began, 'criminals back in the day would cut off the hand of an executed man while he was hanging from the gallows. They used to carry it around with them, as they thought it would bring them immunity against getting caught.' I finished with a smile and a nod, which coming from a smartarse 10-year-old is one thing, from a 45-year-old quite another.

'Been to the museum, have we sir?' asked Harry.

I nodded, shamefully.

'Well, what you might not have read is that sometimes those hands come back to life, all green and mouldy, and they slither across the floor, reaching for your neck...'

Harry looked at me the whole time he was imparting this information.

The tour ended and in the dark I climbed the 199 steps up to the derelict abbey, the holes where the windows once sat looking like the empty sockets of a skull. Up there, high on the cliff, overlooking the oily black North Sea, I propped myself against a ruined wall, keeping a sharp lookout for mouldy slithering hands.

I wouldn't have been remotely surprised if a giant black dog had bounded up the steps. But instead a couple of Goths ghosted up, a boy and girl in their late teens or early twenties, pale-faced and pierced, long black leather coats, faces frozen into an attitude of perpetual miserableness.

They were from Birmingham. We chatted. They were lovely, on their first holiday together.

'Why Whitby?' I asked them.

'Whitby is like Disneyland for Goths,' the girl said.

'How come?'

'Dunno, really. Just is.'

Soon after, they disappeared around the other side of the wall, from where, a few minutes later, I could hear giggling and smell the sweet incense of marijuana.

Chapter 8

*'Nothing compares to the simple
pleasure of a bike ride.'*
John F. Kennedy

I huffed and puffed up and down the sharp hills north of Whitby, surrounded by open fields, curious cows and small parish churches. At one such church at the top of a brutal hill, a gravestone next to the road read 'died suddenly'. Cycling, no doubt, I thought. Soon after, I passed the poster-girl village of Staithes, tumbling down its ravine into the sea like a cataract of red bricks.

But something felt different, like the feeling you get that something unseen yet remarkable lies around the corner. Maybe it's the connectedness with the world, to its atmosphere, its temperament, that travelling by bicycle brings that enables cyclists to sense change as surely as a barometer does.

I passed a hulking, belching, grey factory, whose sign told me it was the Cleveland Potash plant. Underneath that sign hung another. That one read: 'Boulby Underground Laboratory for Dark Matter Research – searching for the missing mass of the universe.' Who'd have thought you'd be looking for it on the A174 just outside Staithes?

And then bam! Suddenly I was in another world. From the top of a hill, the industrial North-East lay smoking before me. I looked north, following the grand sweep of Tees Bay, at its centre Middlesbrough, sitting under a yellow cloud entirely of its own making. The sight was amazing, if amazing's the right word. For it reminded me of those lithographs you see of the Black Country at the height of the Industrial Revolution, where the landscape is covered in chimneys all belching forth smoke and creating a perpetual twilight. People from Teesside are called Smoggies, I'm told, and it wasn't hard to see why, the whole stretch of coast looking as if it was smouldering, having being damped down after a huge fire.

I approached Middlesbrough on busy dual carriageways, taking the hits to my rims from the drain covers in the gutter to avoid swerving into the traffic. I saw a sign for a bike route (it's incredible how attuned one's eyes become to those little blue signs with red panels after a while, like a hawk spotting a field mouse from on high), which took me away from the main road and wound through a large estate. Half the houses had breeze blocks for windows, while many of the occupied ones had cardboard for panes. On every wall seemed to be scrawled graffiti. On a central area of grass and mud and broken glass stood tall metal poles, on top of which perched CCTV cameras surrounded by diadems of razor wire. Two children ran around a playground where short links of chain hung from otherwise empty frames.

The bike lane ducked along back alleys and through areas of head-high weeds, where the path was covered in glass and bags of set cement. Branches from trees had been pulled down across the track, so I had to get off and duck down while pushing my bike under them. Soon, the bike lane was impassable, covered by a sprawling dump of old mattresses, the charred remains of cars and scooters, and split bin bags spewing forth food waste and shitty nappies like gruesome cornucopias. Children played there, too.

I turned back, wanting to get away. How was it possible, in one of the richest countries in the world, that people still had to live in such squalor? It didn't bear thinking about what would happen to those people in any upcoming 'age of austerity'. Although, like Jaywick, it didn't look as if it could get much worse.

I found my way back onto the dual carriageway. A chap came alongside on his bike and introduced himself as Terry.

'You look like you're on a long trip,' he said.

'I just got lost in that estate back there,' I said.

'Lucky you've still got your wheels,' Terry said. 'Where you off to now?'

'Just north,' I said.

'Me too,' Terry said. 'On my commute home.'

We rode together, taking the bike lanes that weaved between the scrap-metal yards and the industrial units. We paid our 60p and rode the transporter bridge, one of only two left working in Britain – the other one being in Newport, South Wales – its bright yellow gondola swinging us across the Tees. Then we rode past Graythorp, where the vast hulks of several US warships were being sliced up. Their arrival had been held up, subject to civil action taken by residents worried about the toxicity of the vessels and the potential harm to public health. But they'd come anyway.

Away from Middlesbrough, we found some beautiful quiet country lanes.

'Long commute?'

'No,' Terry said. 'I live back by the Tranny. I'm just helping you to find your way.'

We carried on, mile after mile, chatting. Terry told me he worked as a welder making mechanical diggers. A few weeks ago his shifts had been cut right back.

'Everybody's pretty nervous round here.'

We passed a sign for Trimdon, from whose social club Tony Blair had made his post-election victory appearance in 1997, sitting as it does in his former constituency of Sedgefield. Everything had seemed possible back then.

'What do people here think of Blair?' I asked Terry.

'Betrayed, mostly,' he said. 'Did you pass the Corus steel plant in Redcar? Rumour is that's next to shut.'

We headed about another five miles up the road.

'Where you staying tonight?' asked Terry.

'Thought I'd find a B&B. I'm not really in the mood for camping.'

'I'll find you one.'

'There's no need.'

'I'd like to help.'

Using my Boy Scout sense of the sun, it appeared we now headed east and then, shortly after that, south. After riding around the outskirts of Hartlepool, we emerged on the coast at Seaton Carew, a town that sounded familiar. A road sign on the seafront read 'Middlesbrough, 10 miles'. I looked at my speedo. We'd covered 50 miles since the transporter bridge.

Terry came with me from door to door while I tried to find somewhere to stay. A small part of me still had that vestige of London suspicion. Who is this bloke? What does he want? But that vestige was shrinking all the time.

A door opened. Standing there was a man in his sixties with a white goatee beard and a large dangly earring hanging from his left ear. Crawling up the corridor behind him was a large, brown, ancient dog, limping badly.

'This is Connie,' he said, pointing to the dog. 'Fell off the sea wall. Destroyed her back legs. Ain't as agile as she once was. But then again, who is?'

I said goodbye to Terry, and followed the man and Connie along the corridor. He pointed at the breakfast room, said I should leave my bike in there. He grabbed half my luggage and started to climb the stairs. Connie watched us go with sadness and memories in her eyes.

'What's your name?' the man asked.

'Mike.'

'Well, Mick…' I liked it when people called me Mick. That's what I was called in Birmingham before I left for London and decided London was no place for Micks. '…we're a working-man's hotel. Lads stay here during week and go home to their wives on Friday. Friday breakfast is bloody miserable, I tell you. Dinner's six quid, with pudding, mind. Cans of lager are a pound from the fridge. Help yourself.'

We walked up four flights of steep stairs. He opened a little door that had been cut off in the top right-hand corner to fit the slope of the roof. In the room was a single bed, which he proceeded to sit on after putting my bags on the floor. He was breathing heavily. I told him I'd be knackered too if I hadn't just cycled from London.

'London! Me dad were on the Jarrow March. Can't imagine young people marching like that today, can you? Went with me uncle. The uncle decided to stay in London after, like, but me dad borrowed a bike and cycled back to Middlesbrough. Imagine! Took him best part of a day and a night. But it were an old, knackered bike, not like yours. How long's it taken you then?'

'A month.'

'Oh. Still, can't imagine young people marching for work today.'

He stood up, went over to the little window, beckoned me over.

'See the beach down there? That's where John Darwin went off paddling his canoe into Tees Bay.'

'John Darwin?'

'Aye. You know. The Canoe Man.'

The only Canoe Man I had in my head was Mark back in Norfolk, paddling blissfully among the backwaters of the Broads with Mr Darcy.

'Faked his own death. Turned up in Panama. Wife were in on it, but kids weren't. Did it for the insurance. Was in all the papers.'

Now I remembered why Seaton Carew had a familiar ring.

'I were part of the rescue team out there looking for him,' the man said. 'Imagine. Doing that to your family just for the money.'

'Unbelievable,' I said. But it really wasn't any more.

'Not excusing him, but people are getting desperate. Times were good a few year back. Got a big mortgage. Banks falling over themselves to lend us money. Me and the missus were living the dream. Not any more. Hardly any guests now.

'We've had enough. Put the place on the market last year, but didn't even get a viewing. It's worth half what we paid for it. I just want to retire. But we're stuck.

'I've got a German mate in Fuerteventura. You been? Lovely place. Met him when we went on holiday a few year ago. Recently, I told him I wanted to move there to retire. He said to me: "You'd need to get a job, else you'd be an alcoholic within a month." Well, I said to him: "What's the problem with that?" I just want to sit in the sun and get pissed. I might only have five or ten year left.'

He shook his head and gently stroked his chin. We both stood at the window, staring out at the tankers at anchor far off the beach.

The Durham coast road took me through former pit villages, such as Blackhall Colliery and Horden. Their names were as evocative and familiar to me as those obscure little Scottish towns whose location I knew not, but whose names, thanks to *Final Score* on a Saturday, would be with me for ever. But in the case of these pit villages, it was their role in the 1980s miners' strike that had brought them via the TV into my living room.

In Blackhall, by the side of the road, stood a pair of big pit wheels, painted black and half sunk into a red-brick dais, the whole thing as pristine and well-looked-after as a freshly occupied grave. Beyond the wheels stood rows of terraced houses, all festooned with satellite dishes like a bloom of fungus.

On that weekday afternoon in Blackhall, young women, most looking little more than teenagers, pushed prams along the main street. Behind them skulked young men in beanie hats and T-shirts with the arms cut off. Most looked depressed. Many were quite overweight. I know from personal experience how the two can be inextricably connected.

There was a brass plaque on the brickwork surrounding the pit wheel. 'Presented by Blackhall Settlement Renewal Initiative,' it read. 'For those who worked and those who died at Blackhall Pit. A small token of respect we bring for men who gave their ALL. Opened 1913. Closed 1981.'

Beside the memorial, the grass was neatly cut, edged by a little black fence. Through the wheel, framed by the spokes, I could see a house, its windows boarded up with plywood. The Durham miners had been some of the nation's most solid backers of the strike. It looked like they and their families had paid a terrible price.

In Horden, the streets ran steeply down the hill towards the sea. At the end of one of them I could glimpse the bright-red stand of the villages football club. It wasnt difficult to imagine what a community like this would have been like not so many years ago, with its pit and football team and sense of permanence and place in the world. Like nearly every town I'd cycled through, there were the boarded-up pubs.

In the town of Easington Colliery, I cycled along the main street, deserted at midday, and followed a track across a large expanse of grass, and then up a steep little incline, every few yards marked by a little plaque denoting a memorable year in the town pit's history. From up high, looking back over the town in one direction and out across the North Sea in the other, I could see how the houses had once clustered around the pit head, now just a big void, airbrushed from the picture.

'Come far?' asked an old man, out walking with his friend and a black and white dog, who looked like he had a bit of lurcher in him and ran frantically around and around in circles, barking at nothing in particular. The man introduced himself as George, 'but people call me Geordie'. His mate was Jimmy.

'And what do they call you?' I asked.

'Jimmy,' he said.

'And that's Keano,' Geordie said. 'Named after Roy Keane. Just as mad, like.'

'Did you work there?' I asked, pointing down the hill at the empty space.

'Aye,' Geordie said. 'Started down the pit Monday. Turned 14 the Tuesday. Ye bugger!'

This was an expression I'd started to hear since I crossed from Yorkshire into Durham, tagged onto the end of sentences, like an exclamation mark.

Keano flew off down the hill towards the sea and dived into some deep scrub. Although he was out of sight, it was easy to follow his progress with his running commentary.

I asked them about their ghost town I'd cycled through, and all the Durham former mining towns before that.

'Aye, it's very sad, all the drug problems and closed shops, like,' said Geordie. 'Nee jobs now. Loads getting laid off at Nissan and Caterpillar. Cars getting pinched, loads of burglaries. Asylum-seekers moving in. Everybody used to know each other, but the council now moves problem families here. There's a sign up in Durham prison, no lie: it says if anybody needs a house they should move to Easington. Ye bugger!'

We sat there in silence for a while, the only noise the birds and the sound of the waves crashing on the beach far below. It was a stunning, tranquil place, the purple heather carpeting the down slope, the sea an impossible cobalt, over which Geordie and Jimmy stared out, lost in their memories, no doubt, of Stakhanovite toil with shovel and pick, of colliery bands, of dances with their best girls, of...

'See who that Ronaldo slept with?' said Geordie.

'Who?'

'Paris Hilton. Lucky bugger.'

'Why aye, man, she's no good without her make-up.'

'Hadaway, man. She's bonny. But it's all just memories to me now.' They both laughed.

Fascinating as Ronaldo's sex life was, I was more interested in hearing about the pit.

Geordie told me how the coalfield ran out under the North Sea for six miles, how there were tons and tons of coal left untapped when the pit was closed in 1993.

One of the marker plaques I'd passed had mentioned an explosion in May 1951. I asked them about it.

'I were here when they found him,' said Jimmy.

'Who?'

'John. John Ellison. My best pal. In three bits, poor bugger. Nineteen he were. I had a broken wrist, else I'd have been down there too. The pit alarm siren went off that night, hanging over whole village for hours. Eerie it were. I can still hear it to this day.'

Keano seemed anxious to go, but I wanted to ask Geordie and Jimmy whether they missed it.

'Miss it? I've got arthritis and me lungs are shot. The work were back-breaking and dangerous. It were all black and filthy up here. The beach was disgusting. Do I miss what we had on top?' said Geordie, pointing to the town. 'Aye. But I don't miss going underground. And I'm glad young people don't have to do it. But I wish they'd find 'em something to do, cos it's heartbreaking to see them young men with nothing. Ye bugger!'

It was a beautiful bright June day, and Sunderland, a place I'd never been to in my life – a fact that hadn't hindered me creating a mental image of dirt and pollution and decay – sat there under a cloudless blue sky looking as handsome as any seaside city I'd seen in the world. On a large swathe of well-kept seafront grassland, men played football, couples canoodled and Frisbees slipped through the air. Beyond was a stunning beach, and beyond that an RAF Nimrod was making low, sweeping runs over a glassy sea. I suddenly felt the need to communicate all this to a work colleague of mine from Sunderland who now lived in London, as if wanting to atone for my prejudices.

'Hi, Rory.'

'Mike! How's it going? Can't chat. Bit busy at work.'

'I'm in Sunderland.'

'Great.'

'It's lovely.'

'Okay.'

'Reminds me of Bondi Beach.'

'Bondi?'

'Yes. Who'd have thought it?'

'Look, I've got to...'

'People playing on the grass, swimming...'

'Mike...'

'There's a plane...'

Just at that moment, a man emerged up the steps in front of me, walking as if he'd recently been struck on the head with a large rock. In his right hand was a pint glass, half full, the amber contents sloshing around.

He fixed his gaze on me, squinting for focus.

'What you fookin' looking at?' he said.

He then sat on a wall, continuing to stare at me, before keeling slowly backwards like a scuba diver from a boat, disappearing from view completely, accompanied by the sound of breaking glass and the exclamation 'Fook.'

'Now that sounds like Sunderland,' said Rory on the other end of the phone.

At the mouth of the Tyne I was surprised to find that somebody had stolen Newcastle. Who knew that the city was 10 miles inland? Well, apart from people from Newcastle and anybody with a brain. I don't mean that the two things are mutually exclusive or anything.

Having crossed major waterways on this trip by boat and bridge, I decided to take the deep tunnel under the Tyne near South Shields, the place where I'd expected Newcastle to be.

I stepped onto the old wooden escalator; to describe it as travelling at a snail's pace would be to do a grave injustice to gastropods. It was steep too, and disappeared off into the bowels of the earth seemingly for ever, and to keep my bike from careering downwards I had to lean forward and clamp the brakes tight, as well as wedging my foot under the rear wheel, so that my hands, wrists and foot were presently in agony. The escalator whirred and progressed, inching its way down. I looked towards the bottom. If I lost control of the bike it would rapidly reach terminal velocity, and only be identifiable from the crumpled mess at the bottom by its serial number.

I started to compile my all-time best West Brom XI, as I tend to do when I'm stuck in a stressful situation and I want time to pass quickly. I sometimes find this a useful technique when I'm actually watching West Brom, too. But it was no good. The pain started to shoot up my arms and spread across my shoulders. The rear wheel was trying to get over my foot, so it felt as if it were in a vice.

After 16 hours, or thereabouts, I stepped off the escalator feeling like a man who'd been attacked with a baseball bat. To my right, a set of doors slid open and a man emerged with a bicycle.

'Why didn't you take the lift?' he asked.

We rode through the tunnel together. His name was Sean. Sean? The psychic had told me I must confront a Sean. But this Sean seemed far too nice to engineer a confrontation with just to appease a Skegness fortune-teller. No disrespect, o wise woman.

Somewhere under the Tyne, my odometer clicked over from 999 to 1,000 miles. Soon we were deep in conversation. Sean told me about his job as a civil servant, about his teacher wife, about the area.

We talked about commuting by bike. I told him about my experiences in London, how friends who'd come to it later on were evangelists for it, wouldn't miss a day on the bike now. Rain or shine.

'Aye, you canne whack it,' he said. 'The money saved, never late, the exercise. But the thing I love most is getting somewhere under my own steam, like it's some ancient thing. I can't explain it easily.'

'John Forester, the cycling writer, described it in his book *Effective Cycling* as something like the complete satisfaction you get from arriving because your mind has chosen the path and steered you over it,' I said. 'Your eyes have seen it; your muscles have felt it; your breathing, circulatory and digestive systems have all done their natural functions, and every part of your being knows you have travelled and arrived. That's hard to get from a bus ride.'

'Sunds about reet,' Sean said.

We emerged from the tunnel and Sean insisted on giving me a tour of the Tyne's north bank, through North Shields and on to Tynemouth.

'Where you staying taneet?' Sean asked.

'Dunno really.'

'One of the kids my wife teaches,' Sean said, 'their parents have a B&B in Whitley Bay. I can take you there if you like. And it's Friday. Friday neet in Whitley Bay. You wouldn't want to miss that.'

'What happens on Friday in Whitley Bay?'

'You don't know? Are you in for a treat.'

We pulled over in Tynemouth.

'See that building down there,' said Sean, pointing to a blue and white weatherboard house sitting at the mouth of the Tyne. 'That's the Life Brigade. Run by a lovely old guy called Bill Scott. Full of bits of old wrecked ships. You should check it out if you get the time.'

Tynemouth and Cullercoats were lovely, with wide sandy beaches and rows of handsome Victorian houses along the front looking out to sea. Sean said people who lived there worked in Newcastle, and I imagined what a spectacular arrangement that must be.

Sean took me to the B&B in Whitley Bay, knocked on the door, said his hellos, then handed me over, like I was the baton in some great British coastal relay, which, at times, felt not far from the truth.

I had a shower and headed out. There was a stream of bikers going up and down the front on Harleys, and joggers and cyclists. There was also an awful lot of police. On the doors of every bar, and it seemed that the only buildings that weren't bars were take-aways, stood a brace of bouncers with short hair and even shorter necks, talking into walkie-talkies. There was an edge in the air, an atmosphere of fevered anticipation.

By around 9 p.m., the joggers and cyclists had been replaced by men dressed as Bananaman and the Pink Panther, and girls in dresses so small and tight that you'd be forgiven for thinking they'd misordered their size from a catalogue and couldn't be arsed to send them back.

The advent of going out in fancy dress had occurred during my lifetime – ditto going to the cricket dressed as Elvis or in drag – and I can't for the life of me work out why Brits have embraced it so robustly. I can't imagine a group of Italians turning up to a trattoria dressed as St Trinian's schoolgirls. Or going to the opera in hula skirts. Or maybe they do.

I went into the Avalon, a bar whose walls, covered as they were with bits of old motorbike, suggested to me that here was a biker pub. It was packed. A cluster of men all wore matching T-shirts, printed with the same photograph of a man, above which was the legend: 'Barry's Getting Married!!!' I grabbed a pint and took it outside.

A group of girls dressed in pink latex nurses' outfits went by pushing a similarly attired young woman in a shopping trolley with

L-plates attached front and back. A group of lads outside a pub shouted 'Get your tits out!' and the girls dutifully obliged, so that at least a dozen pale breasts in various shapes and sizes lined up and wobbled in front of me.

The evening wore on. A group of men strolled by carrying pints of bright green goo. A scuffle broke out on the opposite pavement. A middle-aged woman sat on the kerb and put her head between her legs, releasing a cataract of watery vomit. A group of nuns wobbled past. Loud music blared out from the bars. It was easy to imagine David Attenborough's hushed, dulcet voiceover:

'And here we have Henus geordius *and* Staggus scotus *gathered at their watering holes, engaged in ritualistic courtship behaviour, exposing their bare backsides to each other, many wearing traditional tribal grass skirts or togas. At a certain point in the ritual, some of the tribe members will collapse exhausted to the ground, while others will engage in the serious business of rutting. At this point, tribal elders in blue uniforms will present them with ceremonial bracelets. At some stage of the evening, mating will occur, often done publicly so fellow tribe members can communicate their appreciation.'*

I went into a cavernous pub, where the crowd stood ten deep at the bar, upon which several women were dancing. On podiums there were more women dancing; muffin-tops cascading over their short skirts. The music was so loud it felt like my ears were bleeding.

A man next to me was dressed as Pinhead from *Hellraiser*, having to drink his pint through a straw. Next to him was a Ninja Turtle. The whole room was a heaving, sweaty mass, all ages present from teenagers to pensioners. I'm guessing with the heavy police presence that trouble must occur, but the atmosphere to me felt anything but malevolent. It was a life-affirming experience standing there, watching it all unfold in its unselfconscious glory. So life-affirming, in fact, that I could have almost saved myself the cost of a B&B.

'Friday night in Whitley Bay, eh?' said Bill Scott, the next morning. 'I had many a canny night out there when I were a young man, ye bugger.'

I was standing in Bill's lovely garden, overlooking the Tyne. The sun wasn't out, but I was wearing sunglasses. I felt terrible, but probably not as terrible as Bananaman, whom I'd earlier passed asleep on a seafront bench in Whitley Bay. One could only hope that he wasn't on the superhero roster that day.

Taking the advice of Sean, I'd pedalled back a few miles south to the Tynemouth Volunteer Life Brigade watch house. Even though I'd turned up unannounced, Bill had agreed to drop his deadheading and show me around.

I was finding it difficult to talk in any coherent manner, my tongue somehow having become too large for my mouth and coated with what felt the contents of a Hoover bag. But luckily Bill, five foot tall, if that, and 80 years old but looking at least 20 years younger, was a talker.

We went into the living room. His wife Cath ('only Catherine on Sundays') brought us biscuits and tea, served in a fine china teapot. Bill had a neat little grey goatee beard and was wearing a collar and tie. Cath, wearing a floral dress, was immaculately made up, with perfectly coiffured hair. They made a very handsome couple. That's one of the things I remembered about my own grandparents: how they were always smart. I'm hoping that one day I will wake up and some switch will be thrown and I will stop being a slob. But I doubt it. Today's elderly people will probably be the last of the snappy dressers.

Bill started telling me about how the Life Brigade was founded.

'See those rocks just above the waterline? Black Middens reef, that is. In 1864, the SS *Stanley* was carrying 12,000 dictionaries and thirty-six choirgirls from Aberdeen to London, on their way to sing at a Christmas concert. There was a terrible storm, and the *Stanley* came to the Tyne for shelter, along with the schooner *Friendship*. *Stanley* hit the reef. *Friendship* too. A lifeboat, *Constance*, got to them but couldn't get aboard. They just had oars, see. *Constance* was wrecked too. Two killed on the lifeboat, all hands lost on the schooner, and only two of the choirgirls survived on *Stanley*. It were a terrible, dark night. People stood on this headland said they could hear screaming all night. Ye bugger.'

After the tragedy, the first coastal rescue station in the country was set up at Tynemouth and 100 men volunteered for duty. 'Aye, had nee money then, and we still got nee money,' said Bill, who'd been watch keeper at the station for 28 years.

As Bill spoke I looked around the room. Everywhere was evidence of a life lived intimately connected to the sea: ships' bells; ships in bottles; oil paintings of ships struggling though mountainous waves; photos of various modern ships; painted plates with ships on. It wouldn't have tested the *Through the Keyhole* panel for long. There was also a framed photograph of the Queen greeting Bill and Catherine (I'm assuming she was Catherine when meeting the Queen).

'She asked what the cat's name were,' Bill said. 'So I told her "Rollo". "What an unusual name," she said. "Arise, Sir Rollo." She knighted the bloody cat! Ye bugger. She were lovely.'

The ground floor hall of the watch house was like the aftermath of the world's greatest multiple shipwreck: dozens of great carved figureheads hung from the walls, looking down on us – mostly doe-eyed women, but also giant fish and other sea creatures, painted in vivid colours; barrels hung from the rafters ('every one saved somebody's life'); there were breeches buoys for taking people off floundering boats; ships' clocks; wheels; bits of railing; lanterns; sepia photographs of wrecks; old life vests; and name boards, mostly wooden and ancient – HMS *Brave*, *Mystery*, *Amalie*, *Light of the Lantern*. Bill knew the story behind every one, how the boat had perished, how many hands had been lost. There were only two of us in the room, but hundreds of ghosts.

'See that one there,' said Bill, pointing to a pair of decorative figureheads and a name board adorned with various symbols. '*City of Bristol*. The two female figures are for the women they'd meet. The horn of plenty for the goods they would get. And the star was to guide 'em. She went down in 1870. They never did get any of that stuff.'

We walked up the narrow, wooden staircase to the second floor, then up some steep stepladders to the top-floor watch room, a small garret high over the Black Middens and the mouth of the Tyne, with wide views of the North Sea beyond. In the middle of the room was a searchlight. To our left, on top of the adjoining hill, was a grey concrete bunker-like building.

'That used to be the coastguard building. John Prescott got that closed down when he worked out we'd do it for nothing. And him a bloody seaman!'

Bill was standing next to a figurehead. It was from the *First of May*. She looked like a heroine from a Regency costume drama, her right hand clutched to her chest, as if she were about to faint. I asked if I could have a photograph of Bill with her. She came up to his shoulders. 'She's me girlfriend,' he said. 'Sometimes at night, I comes up here and gives her a little kiss. Don't tell Cath.' Then he rested his right arm on her head for the photo, which seemed a little ungallant.

'You only really had two choices round here: sea or pit. I went to sea when I were fifteen. Back then you couldn't hear yourself talk round here because of the noise from the riveting in the shipyards.

'On my first trip, we hit terrible storms in the Atlantic. People breaking their arms and legs. Four new boys there were, but I were the only one to keep going after that. I loved it.'

All the while Bill was talking, he was scanning the North Sea for ships. Old habits died hard.

'Once, we were picking up grapefruit in Florida. There were these black men carrying these strange yellow fruit. "What you lookin' at boy?" one of 'em said. Well, they gave me about twenty bananas and I ate all of 'em one after the other. Had to go to hospital to get pumped out. Nurses kept comin' in to laugh at the English boy who'd eaten twenty bananas. Ye bugger!

'When I came back here on leave, I were king of the castle. I used to go to fifty-bob tailors, jump the queue as seamen always had priority as their time ashore was short. I paid with beautiful big, white fivers. Publicans would tell me I had to write my name and address on the back of them buggers. I used to buy joints of meat for grannies in butcher's. I felt like the king.'

Bill was in full flow now, the memories of a lifetime coming thick and fast.

He'd worked on the ferries in the Bass Strait between Victoria and Tasmania – 'that were a rough bugger' – survived a mutiny off Queensland, and had a business shooting crocodiles in northern Australia. 'Skin for handbags, tails for meat, feet for Thai table legs.' His Dutch partner was a drinker. 'We had to pull the crocs onto the boat, spike 'em through the brain. Dangerous enough when you're sober, but he were always full of gin. Ye bugger.'

In Mount Isa he'd landed a job sweeping the floor of a rough boozer. 'Wouldn't let me down the copper mines, see. I was a seaman. Aussie seamen's union was communist troublemakers they reckoned.

I earned more sweeping all the money off the floor than I could have earned down the mines. Rough as guts the place was, but they were so rich they'd just chuck money away.' He started to chuckle.

'Met a bloke in Isa. Geordie lad he were. He'd headed straight to Newcastle, New South Wales, cos he thought he'd feel at home. But he didn't get on down the pit there, and they asked him if he could do anything else. He told them he used to ride horses in England, so they gave him a job as a cowboy in the rodeo. But here's the thing – he used to look after the pit ponies in England. Never ridden a horse in his life! And here he was, a bloody cowboy rodeo rider! Ye bugger.'

Bill stared out to sea. It was his magic portal, across which lay adventure and his youth. He carried on staring out to sea for another minute or so, his back to me, his left arm resting on the *First of May*'s head. Below him, a couple were pushing their bikes towards the water to dip their wheels in, a rite before setting off on the coast-to-coast ride, which can start or finish in Tynemouth.

'Couple of your mates doon there,' Bill said. 'I envy your freedom. Travel's a bugger when it's in your blood.'

I wondered if he had any regrets about coming back home.

'Aye, we like to moan about the weather and everything. And the big companies and pits are all gone now. It's buggered, finished round here. We had it lucky really. But at the end of the day there's nee place like England. It takes some whackin'. I'm proud to be an Englishman.'

We both stared out to sea. I felt an absurd tingle of pride at being an Englishman myself.

'See that boat out there at anchor,' Bill said. 'Russian, waiting for a berth. Bringing coal. We're sitting on millions of tons of the stuff and we're importing it.'

He stared at the Russian boat for a while. The two cyclists set off to traverse the country.

'That used to be a joke, that, "selling coals to Newcastle",' he said, shaking his head. 'Ye bugger.'

The industrial north-east finished as abruptly as it had started. One minute I was riding past old slag heaps and decrepit factories and through eviscerated former pit towns, the next I was in stunning open countryside. I felt a wave of calm.

The NCN1 took to the coast again, either following deserted roads or traffic-free tracks, ducking through the high sandbanks and grasslands, skirting the stunning expanse of Druridge Bay, whose beach stretched before me seemingly for ever, and on whose sand I could not see a soul. There was the perfect mix of sun and cloud, the seascape luminously lit, the kind of sky that in a Renaissance painting would have nymphs and deities dancing on it. At sea, a slick of black eider ducks disappeared to fish en masse and reappeared a minute later.

My mobile phone went. It was a friend from London.

'What the fuck is that noise?' she said.

'What noise?'

'Sounds like you're in the middle of a car park and all the alarms are going off.'

'That's the birds.'

'Oh.'

'I know.'

The track followed the banks of the River Coquet, sheathed in mist. In front of me, rising from the haze, a hill atop which were the silhouetted ruins of twelfth-century Warkworth Castle, another one straight from a fairy tale, where Shakespeare had set three scenes from *Henry IV, Part 2*, describing it as 'this worm-eaten hold of ragged stone'. Nikolaus Pevsner reckoned the approach into Warkworth 'one of the most exciting sequences of views one can have in England', and I reckon he wasn't far wrong.

The Northumberland coast is an Area of Outstanding Natural Beauty, and called the Castles and Coast route by the National Cycle Network, and here again was a place in my own backyard to which I'd never been. It was magical. Yet even in summer there seemed to be few people around to enjoy it.

I stopped at the village shop in Warkworth to buy some bananas, declaring to the woman behind the counter, apropos of nothing, that she lived in possibly the most stunning part of the entire country.

'We know,' she said. 'But don't tell anybody.'

I passed the red-roofed cluster of houses at Alnmouth, looking like Edwardian semis from a London commuter town had been stuck on a tongue of land sticking out into the sea. Then through

Boulmer, where small stone cottages had piles of lobster pots drying in their gardens and the strong onshore wind filled my nostrils and head with an overpowering smell of the sea and a nostalgia for my early family seaside holidays, when the sea always seemed to smell more like the sea than it does now.

The coast track crossed small wooden bridges and then turned into a muddy single track, which the Ridgeback grumbled about but I didn't, quite happy to slip and slide and sing at the top of my lungs.

I did a quick whiz around Craster, a beautiful village built of local black basalt whinstone with a natural harbour and a cluster of tearooms, pubs and restaurants all displaying chalkboard menus, where you could have anything you wanted as long as it involved the world-famous oak-smoked Craster kipper.

Feeling hungry – as ever – but still phobic about seafood and cycling, I eschewed Craster's famous delicacy and stopped instead at a burger van by the side of the road, where a man in a smart shirt and tie and a strong Scots accent went through his various combinations of kipper burgers. Upon hearing of my reluctance to combine seafood and cycling, he directed me towards an Auchtermuchty burger, consisting of haggis and bacon, a culinary tribute to his hometown. As I ate, the man told me that he'd invented the burger because nobody believed him that such a place really existed when he found himself stranded in Craster after a failed love affair with a local girl.

He played the bagpipes at local pubs and music festivals, and held a Burns Night every year on 25 January. I said I was looking forward to Scotland, which induced a kind of misty-eyed longing from him. As I cycled away, past the magnificent, moody ruins of Dunstanburgh Castle, I was full of haggis and bacon, and full too of the conviction, articulated by Graham Swift in his masterpiece *Waterland*, that man 'is the storytelling animal... He has to go on telling stories... As long as there's a story, it's all right.'

Chapter 9

*'Life is like riding a bicycle – in order to keep
your balance, you must keep moving.'*
Albert Einstein

'No whistling!' the skipper said to me. 'That's unlucky on a boat.
Brings storms.'

'Sorry.'

He'd shot me a look. Seamen take these kinds of things very
seriously. I wondered whether there'd been a lot of whistling at the
mouth of the Tyne over the years.

I'd been cycling through Seahouses when I'd seen a board
advertising cruises to the Farne Islands. I'd heard of the Farnes,
knew vaguely they were something big in the world of seabirds, but,
like so many islands off the coast of Britain that I'd vaguely heard
of, I'd have been hard pressed to put my finger on them on a map.
I looked at my map on the top of my bar bag, and put my finger on
the Farnes. There.

The boat was called the MV *Glad Tidings*, and would be sailing
in 10 minutes. I took the boat's name as a sign and bought a ticket.
The woman in the little booth told me I could leave my bike in a
shed full of smoked kippers and frozen fish on the quayside. I hoped
it would forgive me in time.

'Should I lock it?' I asked.

'Why?' the woman replied.

And that's how I came to be chugging across the milky stillness
of Inner Sound, heading for the Farne Islands. I'd been happy.
When I'm happy, I tend to whistle. Now I sat there on the deck of
the *Glad Tidings* – the *Glad Tidings*! – sulking like a scolded child.

Sitting next to me was an elderly couple, as excited as children
off to Disneyland, binoculars in hand.

'You got a hat?' the woman asked me.

What was she, my mother?

'No,' I said. 'It's not cold.' And it wasn't. It was a glorious June day.

'Oh, dear,' she said.

The boat passed close by skerries and sea stacks packed to bursting with shags and kittiwakes, guillemots and razorbills, the noise levels like pre-pubescent girls at a boy-band gig. Common seals lolloped on rocks just sticking out of the water and regarded us with mournful eyes as we glided by. Puffins flew past inches above the water, their bodies seemingly too big for their tiny wings, which they flapped frantically, the sand eels dangling from their beaks giving them the look of Edwardian gentlemen.

We looped around Longstone Island, from whose lighthouse on 7 September 1838, we were told over the boat's PA, William Darling and his 22-year-old daughter Grace rowed out in a ferocious storm to save passengers of the steamship *Forfarshire*, smashed to pieces on the rocks.

'They'd probably been whistling,' I said to the elderly man.

'Eh?' he said.

'Eider duck,' said his wife, pointing off the port beam.

The voice on the PA went on to tell us how, in an early example of celebrity obsession, Grace's heroism had catapulted her into the national spotlight. She'd been pursued for locks of her hair and had many offers of marriage, the lighthouse being plagued by unwanted visitors. It's a pity she lived when she did. Had she been born 150 years later, she could have done a double-page spread in the *News of the World* in her knickers and become a tabloid Darling. Instead she died, aged just 26, from tuberculosis.

We were put ashore on Inner Farne. While waiting in the queue to buy a ticket at the National Trust office, everybody else but me produced a hat and put it on.

'Have you got a hat?' asked the man in the ticket office.

What was it with these people?

'No.'

'Oh, dear.'

We proceeded along a boardwalk, through the sea campion and scurvy grass. Down on the floor, peeking out from behind plant stalks, I caught the occasional glimpse of a little red mouth, pumping furiously. I felt a little gentle tap on my shoulder and turned round. I looked at the elderly woman.

'It wasn't me,' she said, and pointed to her hat.

There was another tap.

'Now look…'

But instead of the old woman, I was confronted with a scene even Hitchcock could not have dreamed to choreograph. I was besieged by birds, dive-bombing, strafing me, dozens and dozens of them, pecking at my ears and thudding on the top of my head, like somebody playing an allegro on it with their fingers. And all the while came this unearthly squawking and screaming.

'Arctic terns,' said the elderly woman, smiling. She was smiling because her ears and head were tucked under a thick woolly hat.

'Jesus!' said I, whose ears and head were not.

'They've just had chicks,' said her husband from under his hat. 'They're just protecting their nests.'

I'd like to be able to say that I handled the assault with a calmness and serenity befitting a middle-aged former rugby player being pecked by small birds. But I did not. I ran down the boardwalk, arms flailing, like somebody having a seizure. I'm not quite sure where I thought I was running to, though, seeing as I was on a tiny island in the North Sea, but run I did.

Everywhere I looked on the ground, I could see a nest. And every time I dared look up, all I could see was squadron after squadron of terns, lining up for their raid. Some, frustrated no doubt by the big flock camped flapping and squawking on my head, contented themselves instead by fly-by shitting. I hadn't paid to have so much bodily fluid dumped on me since seeing the Clash back in the day.

Still, they say it's lucky having a bird shit on you. So, judging by the amount of guano I was covered with, and subtracting the whistling on the boat, I calculated I was due good fortune until I was 246.

I liberated my bike from the kippers and the frozen fish. If it had been able to talk, it might well have said: 'What the hell happened to you?' But as it's just steel and rubber, I was spared having to explain the welts and the blood and the rivulets of white shit streaking my face.

I carried on up the coast. Bamburgh Castle towered over me majestically on its basalt crag overlooking Budle Bay. The

Northumberland coast was like riding through your own private Arthurian legend.

Shortly after, I got my first view of Lindisfarne, or Holy Island, sitting a mile off the coast and connected to the mainland by a narrow causeway that is submerged twice a day at high tide.

Back in Walsingham, Bishop Lindsay had told me about a Franciscan monk, Brother Damien, who lived on the island, and said to be sure to say hello when I was passing. I was carrying a message from a messenger of God. Who was I not to deliver it?

At the start of the causeway, I checked out the times of the tides on the board. It looked as if I had plenty of leeway to make it across, but the unequivocal warnings on the sign about the strength and speed of the tide when it raced through the channel made me nervous. Unlike those who sped across the causeway in cars and buses, I would have to pedal into a strong headwind, and factor in the time it would take to push if I got a puncture halfway across. I looked at the tide table again. Was I reading it correctly? It could be a costly mistake if I wasn't.

I decided to go for it. After all, I was carrying a message from God (once removed) and was covered in enough bird shit to enjoy some luck. But as I pedalled out, passing the tall wooden escape tower for the stranded, and seeing as I wasn't sure whether I was technically on land or at sea, I refrained from whistling just in case.

The island, just over a mile square, was crawling with day trippers – so that's where everybody was – packing the village's old narrow streets, faces pressed against front windows like they were in a diorama, queuing out of the door for tea and cakes at Pilgrims Coffee House.

I visited the museum, where I found out how St Aidan of Iona established the first monastery here in 634AD, developing a reputation for artistry, exemplified by the Lindisfarne Gospels. And then I read about the Viking raiders, for whom art held considerably less appeal than slaying monks.

Then I went looking for Brother Damian. There were plenty of signs that read 'no camping on the island', so I would have to keep one eye on the time if I was to get across the causeway before it was submerged again. I visited Damien's house and then the church, but he wasn't at either. But I was looking for a man dressed as a monk, on a tiny island – how hard could that be?

I stopped to asked a man working in his garden if he knew where I might find my monk. But he spoke before I did.

'Come farrrr?' he asked, in a rolling accent that seemed part Dutch and part Northumbrian. He had sparkling blue eyes and the face of the sea, so craggy that next to him Samuel Beckett would look like a fresh-faced ingenue.

'London.'

'You can sell the south. Waste of space. England starts at Hadrian's Wall far as I'm concerned.'

'Lived here long?'

'I was a seaman. Sailing past one day, saw this place, thought I'd settle here. Ye bugger.'

How cool was that? No brochures, no planning. Just sailing past and decided to settle, like an ancient Polynesian mariner alighting on Bora Bora.

'Sounds romantic.'

'Nothing romantic about living here,' he said. 'People come to live here with romantic ideas, but when we're cut off in winter, no food, no power, they change their minds. They don't last long.'

He rolled a fag. Lit it. Took a long drag. Exhaled slowly.

'Aye, give me a knife and a rifle and I can survive here, nee bother.'

'I'm looking for Brother Damian.'

'The other one ran off with the hotel owner's wife, made the papers and everything.'

'He's a Franciscan… The other one?'

'Used to be the two here. Now it's just Damian. You could write a book about this place and what people get up to. It's living on an island what does it, see. Everybody knows everybody's business.'

'So, any idea where he might…'

'See that house? Coupla poofs live there. Got nothin' against poofs, mind. Nice fellas. Come up from London three times a year…'

'I can't stay long because of the tide…'

'I could tell you some stories…'

'So I'm in a bit of a hurry…'

'See that house over there?'

Thirty minutes later, and with the entire collected shenanigans of Holy Island's populace catalogued in my brain, I headed for a

Christian retreat centre where the man with the crumpled face had finally told me I might find Damian. He wasn't there.

'Have you eaten?' asked a softly spoken man with kind eyes whose name was Ian.

I said that I hadn't, but that I was keen to find Damian before the tide…

A woman entered the dining room carrying a huge saucepan of steaming spuds, followed shortly by a young man, barely out of his teens, carrying a platter of chicken, sizzling from the oven. Food and cyclists: it's the equivalent of a hypnotist swinging a watch on a chain in front of your eyes.

The food was dished out, some wine poured. I wolfishly tucked into the full plate before me. It was delicious. But it still all felt a bit odd. How often I had travelled in Africa, or Asia, and been invited by strangers to join them for dinner, with not a sense that what I was experiencing was anything other than kindness and hospitality for a traveller. But I had not expected this, not here, in my own country. And even though I had met with so much kindness already, it still felt aberrant. I could only think that my views about my fellow country-men were based on the media diet of stories focusing on the worst aspects of us, convincing me that we are a mean-spirited little island. It was taking time for these deeply held prejudices to be wormed out.

'I have to tell you that I'm not a Christian,' I said, but only, obviously, after I had cleared my plate. This clearly was a habit I still hadn't managed to shake when confronted with Christian charity.

'All are welcome here,' Ian said. And I felt flushed with shame.

Over cheesecake, Ian told me how he'd come to be working on Holy Island. He'd been a copper, then a prison chaplain, and afterwards worked as a missionary in Ghana and Jerusalem.

'In Jerusalem, we built the Abraham Tent in a refugee camp, where Jews, Muslims and Christians sat down and talked. When people told their stories and others listened, you could see the relationships transform before your eyes. We're all born with an innate need to tell our stories, the old campfire of yore. It's impossible to harbour suspicion and hatred for someone if you hear their stories.'

More wine was poured. I had a nice buzz going now.

Ian continued: 'Politicians see talk as a weakness, but sitting down with your perceived enemy is the strongest, smartest and ulti-mately only productive thing you can do.'

It was a joy to listen to Ian. Such sentiments are often uttered forth from the mouths of teenagers filled with utopian ideals, yet they rarely seem to survive into adult life. And yet here was a middle-aged man who'd worked as a policeman and in prisons and in the hate-filled cauldron of the Middle East, and his optimism for the human spirit was undimmed.

'In all my time in prison or working as a copper, I've never met a single person who I thought was evil. These were people who had done bad things, very evil things, but that doesn't make a person evil, just a person who'd done evil things. We're not much different from plants. If you feed us and water us and give us the right conditions for growth, we will grow strong and healthy.'

I imagined how that concept would play out in the offices of the *Sun* or the *Mail*.

'I went to a council estate in Newcastle once, people living in tiny, damp boxes. It was little different from prison. I was visiting the relatives of a murdered little girl, whose assailant had been locked up in the nick I was working in. Some friends of theirs inside had attacked who they'd thought was the killer and beaten him badly. But it was the wrong man and he later killed himself. Being with that family that day, on that grim estate, with their little girl murdered, it was easy to see how these things just perpetuate.'

I went back to the church. In the porch was a grey-haired man wearing sandals and a monk's cassock tied around the waist with a rope girdle. I'd found Brother Damian at last. But it had taken so long I couldn't remember why I was looking for him.

I went to speak.

'Sssssshhhhh,' Damian said, and pointed up to a semi-circle of mud and grass, stuck on the wall above the door. 'Wait.'

We stood in silence, the only sound the wind whistling and moaning though the trees. The faintest of chirruping started up and built into a crescendo as four or five little mouths appeared above the rim of the nest, groping blindly. A few seconds passed, then came a flash of black as a swallow flew into the porch and, amid a frenzied blur, dropped food delicately into each of the mouths, before flashing by us and out again. The chirruping became a diminuendo, the little puckering mouths receding from view, one by one, until all was quiet once more apart from the wind.

'The same swallows come back here from Africa each year,' said Damian, staring up at the nest, a look of reverie on his face. 'How do they do that? And how do the chicks know Mum is coming to the nest when she's still hundreds of yards away? It's a true miracle.'

I looked out from the porch, across the strait. The tide was starting to fill the Fenham Flats. I remembered why I'd been looking for Damian.

'I've brought a message for you, from Walsingham. Bishop Lindsay says "hello".'

'That's a lovely gift to bring.'

'They looked after me well. It was the least I could do.'

'Did you meet the Franciscan brothers there?'

'I didn't.'

'We're back in Walsingham now. Assisi and Canterbury too. So Holy Island fits well into that scene.'

I'd never met a monk before. I wanted to ask him about his life on the island, what brought him there. But time and tide, quite literally in this case, waited for no man.

'I've got to go,' I said, pointing to the straits and then at my watch.

'Do you have a tent?' Damian asked.

'I do.'

'Then you're welcome to camp in my garden. The last people to camp there were the Vikings.'

'That long ago?'

'No, no,' Damian laughed, a great loud guffaw that made his whole body shake. 'A group from a Viking society came here last year to mock up a battle by the priory. Come.'

We walked back to Damian's house. He took me into the back garden and showed me a place, next to a bed of red-hot pokers, where I could pitch my tent. The garden sloped away to the strait, which looked quite full now.

I noticed a cross on a tiny island in the middle of the water.

'Hobthrush,' Damian said. 'Aidan's successor, St Cuthbert, exiled himself on it before moving to the Farne Islands. Did you go to the Farnes?'

I pointed to the bird shit all over my shirt.

'Ah, yes,' chuckled Damian. Then: 'When you've put your tent up, come inside and we'll have a chat.'

When he'd gone and my tent was up, I sat there for a little while, looking out over the water, past Cuthbert's little island, and towards the mainland. From somewhere unseen at the foot of the garden came moaning noises, like a rusty gate, or cartoon ghost noises. The world seemed to stop. I felt a profound serenity wash over me. This was what Cuthbert must have seen every day. I could have sat there for ever.

When I entered the house, Damian was on the phone. He gestured for me to sit down. For the next 15 minutes, his soft, compassionate voice was the only thing filling the space. It ebbed and flowed like a piece of fine classical music.

'Her husband passed away recently,' he said, after putting down the phone. 'She's struggling.'

Damian made some tea and produced a plate of biscuits. The hypnotist's pendulum swung.

'What's that moaning noise I could hear out there?' I asked, shovelling a couple of custard creams into my mouth.

'Like ghosts?'

'Yes.'

'That's the seals. They're always there. A Brazilian staying here once went quite mad because he thought the island was haunted.' He chuckled again.

I asked what had led him to Holy Island. He told me he'd qualified as an accountant in 1964, aged 23. But his father, a deeply religious man, had encouraged him to take up God's work. By 24, he'd taken up his Franciscan vows and celibacy. After working all over the world, he'd come to Holy Island in 2003.

'When you've done your job and served all your brothers, what do you do with the old one?' he chuckled to himself. 'Put him on an island! No, no, it was a lovely gift.

'But I wasn't welcomed here with open arms. I wasn't a young vicar with a wife and children. I had to be tested. The islanders were under monks in the distant past and I believe that's why the villagers were resistant at first. They don't like being told what to do. I tried to bring a light touch. The problems here – fishing problems, tourists, an ageing population – all call for a certain pastoral care. One day, I was asked to go and bless a new lobster boat. They took me out on it. That's when I felt I'd been accepted.'

'And what happened with the other brother?' I asked. The gossip in me was dying to know.

'Ah! That was all a bit of a mess. Some islanders said live and let live. Some said "tut, tut". Nature took over!'

And how, I wondered, did this island parish differ from places he'd been before?

'These people have a quite unique relationship with nature,' he said, pouring the tea. 'They have to. Until fifty years ago there was no road. They only had ponies and traps. They navigated across the sands using sticks to find their way through the quicksand. No electricity. No mains water, just a spring. It's a relationship with nature that's largely been lost in the modern world. The people of Holy Island are still coming to terms with these changes, being catapulted into the twenty-first century. But living in a place that gets cut off every day from the world preserves some of those ancient feelings. Keeps the world at arm's length.

'We know we're going to get invaded, especially on sunny days. But there's a rising to the occasion, which the community does in a very united way. When the tide comes back in, there's a sigh of relief; an immense contrast of calm and peace and a "thank goodness they've gone". That's the tidal demand on their lives. An ebb and flow, a rhythm to their lives.'

The phone went. Damian apologised, and then picked it up. I imagined he never left a ringing phone unanswered. It sounded as if it might be the same woman again. I could hear faint sobbing down the line. Damian closed his eyes and nodded.

I gestured that I was going outside, and walked around the ruined priory and the graveyard, the gnarled and puckered sandstone radiant in the last rays of the sun, and then through the village, now deserted, like a scene from an apocalyptic movie where I'm the last man on earth. I walked out onto the headland, past the fishing cobles, many upturned and converted into sheds, and towards the magnificent Tudor castle, clinging like a limpet to the top of Beblowe Crag. The sun had disappeared below the horizon now, its great pink and orange valediction fanning across the sky, bathing Holy Island in a celestial light.

I found a spot on the shore and sat there, surrounded by delicate little pink and purple flowers, staring out to sea. Time seemed to have a different quality when you were cut off, unable to go anywhere, relieved of choice. I thought of the philosopher Blaise Pascal's observation that all man's troubles stemmed from his inability to sit quietly by himself in a room. There was no problem sitting quietly on Holy Island. It commanded it.

A colony of seals moaned from somewhere in the gloaming. Dark shadows of seabirds flitted past. Unseen, oystercatchers fussed noisily. Then the ensemble seemed to settle down for the night and it was just me and the wind. Damian had spoken of the island having its own 'tangible goodness'. I could feel it. If there was ever a place that could convince an atheist of his folly, Lindisfarne was surely it.

The next morning I was actually further away from God than usual, having woken up lying on the cold ground, my inflatable mattress limp and deflated under me. It had been going down gradually during the nights, but the leak was slow enough to see me through. Now it looked as if it had had it. And it wasn't only my mattress that was suffering wear and tear. It had rained heavily during the night and my feet were submerged. I would need to do some repairs.

Stiff as a board, I continued up the Northumberland coast, mostly on traffic-free cycle track. It made an incredible difference, not having to share my space with cars. My mind was free to wander, the bike free to wobble and meander along, unworried about the consequences, my ears not constantly tuning in to noises behind.

I'd become amazed how much I could tell about a vehicle approaching from behind: how big it was; how quickly it was travelling; how aggressively it was being driven, even; and, perhaps most amazingly, being able to extrapolate, from all that noise, how much room it was likely to give me while passing – and all deduced only from sound.

I lost count of the number of times I braced myself based on this information. And, sure enough, somebody would whoosh by me with inches to spare, busy chatting on a mobile or engaged in an animated conversation with their passenger. It was as if cycling reactivated some long-lost sixth sense.

But such worries were not mine that morning. The track followed the cliff-tops, the only obstacles I had to worry about being the sheep. There must be something about bicycles that reminds sheep of predators, because whereas they seem largely indifferent to cars, they freeze in panic when approached by bike and then, weighing up their options, flight or fight, stare transfixed for a few seconds. Then they piss themselves. Every time.

All the way up the coast I had lamented not having a bell. With so many promenades and tracks shared with walkers, it would have been good to give them a friendly little tinkle to let them know I was behind them. Who knows? Maybe it would work with sheep too.

There were a lot of sheep on the cliff-top that day. And a lot of incontinence. But then I met what appeared to be the hardest sheep in Britain, who stood his ground, blocking the track. I stopped. He stamped his feet, as if about to charge, then took a few angry steps towards me. We stared at each other. He took another step forwards. Stamped his feet again. Made a snorting noise. He was now only about 10 yards away. It was a tense moment. Then he pissed himself.

Around a headland and down a long hill and, whoooo, there were Saltires everywhere, and pubs called the Rob Roy, and newsagents with Irn Bru hoardings alongside shops selling kilts. When I stopped for directions to a bike shop (my back wheel had pinged again as I pedalled away from the sheep stand-off, so Mr Pissy had had the last laugh), the man asked me if I was Ken. I had arrived in Scotland, obviously. Except I hadn't. Berwick-upon-Tweed had changed hands from the Scots to the English 14 times between 1174 and 1482, and when the music last stopped, England was holding the parcel. Nobody, however, seemed to have told the townsfolk.

Norman in Wilson's bike shop reckoned I was carrying too much stuff. 'Last time I saw a bike so heavily loaded was with an East German welder touring Scotland on holiday. Arms as big as my thighs,' he said. 'Mind, she were a lovely wee lassie.'

Norman's workshop was full of bikes waiting to be repaired. I feared I might be joining the back of a very long queue.

'If tourers come in, we always try and get them on their way again as soon as possible,' Norman said. 'I'll fix your bike after we close tonight. Nay bother.'

I thought that his extraordinary kindness merited me making some other purchases. I remembered the bell. That should create a massive spike in his finances.

'Could you fit a bell on the bike as well?'

'We've only got those left at the moment,' he said, pointing to a wall at the other side of the shop.

'Whatever,' I said, not following his finger. 'A bell's a bell. See you tomorrow morning, and thanks again.'

'Nay bother. But you might want to think about getting rid of some stuff.'

'I will.'

I walked around the corner, and up a side street. I had never been to Berwick, but the view from the top of the cliffs as I'd approached the town, with its roofscape of bright red pantiles and its three bridges side by side spanning the Tweed and three eras – medieval (old road), Victorian (railway) and Art Deco (new road) – had suggested a place worth exploring. As I'd only covered about 20 miles that day, I'd not have stopped if my back wheel hadn't pinged. My bike was certainly playing its part in shaping my journey.

Unable to camp until I fixed my mattress, I knocked on the door of a stately Georgian townhouse flying a wooden B&B board. A man answered. They were full but, perhaps seeing a man with four bicycle panniers and no bicycle, he took pity on me and said I could sleep in the junk room at the top of the house.

'Is there discount for that?' I asked.

'There's no charge at all,' he said. 'I'm a cyclist too.'

Ian helped me carry my stuff up the two flights of stairs and into a small room at the top. The floor contained a lifetime of accumulation: climbing gear, boxes of books, old lamps, rolled-up rugs. Against one wall was a set of children's bunk beds. The frame was covered in Panini footballer stickers from the eighties, all curly perms, porn-star moustaches and tight shorts. The bottom bunk had a *Doctor Who* duvet on it, resplendent with Cybermen and Daleks. I wasn't sure whose room this was, but was working on the assumption they wouldn't be coming back any time soon. I felt like a family guest, which in turn felt very nice.

Ian asked if I'd eaten. 'Okay, I'll go down and prepare something. Twenty minutes?'

I laid out my stuff on the top bunk. Norman was right. I was still carrying far too much stuff around with me. Thus far, I had been lucky in that my wheel had buckled close to large towns with bike shops. But I was just about to enter Scotland and, after the populated central belt, would be heading into some of the most sparsely populated and remote parts of Europe, where a bike shop could be several days' pushing away.

I set aside, in a pile to send home, my smart shoes, one of my cycling tops, my sole remaining smart shirt, the aftershave, the moisturiser, and my big can of shaving gel. I could get by with soap and water. Then I slipped my mattress and tent out of the camping bag and took them downstairs.

'Going camping?' said Ian.

'Just need to fix these. Both are leaking.'

'Let's do it in the garden. There's lots of space out there.'

The garden was lovely, with wisteria-covered thick stone walls, a large vegetable patch and plenty of fruit trees and beds bursting with lupins and irises and roses of every shade. Through an open door into an outbuilding in the corner, I could see a potter's wheel. 'I'm a potter,' said Ian, 'and my surname is Kilne!' Oh, the joys of nominative determinism. I might change my name to Mike Bike.

Ian took my tent, draped it over a washing line and helped me run silicone over the seams.

I loved fixing things. But it hadn't always been that way. Not so long ago I'd happily throw things away and buy new at the first signs of wear. It's what we're encouraged to do nowadays, of course, almost the patriotic duty of citizens relying on an economy that runs on the endless acquisition and disposal of stuff.

But a few years ago, when my fridge stopped working, I had found myself in a large electrical store looking at new ones. All the new fridges offered the same basic function: to keep food and drink cold. Some had chrome doors, and others fancy gadgets like ice machines or fast-freeze compartments that I never knew I needed. But there I was, crippled by choice, when all I wanted was a fridge that worked.

I went home empty-handed and flicked through the Yellow Pages, looking for a fridge repairman. I eventually found a guy. He came around. He was quite old. He only did it to top up his pension, but there wasn't much of that type of work around any more. I made him tea as he removed the plastic covers inside the fridge and pulled and tweaked at the wires. As he worked, I found out about his family and how he'd come to Britain as a young man from Poland to escape the Nazis. He told me how he'd met his wife at a dance in Hammersmith, 'the most beautiful girl in the room. I could hardly breathe when I danced with her', about his kids and his grandchildren. The fridge was still going strong and I sometimes thought about the old man when I reached for the milk. We exchanged Christmas cards for a few years. I didn't get one last December. Perhaps he died.

I blew up the mattress, filled an old zinc tub in the garden with water from a hose, and dunked it. No bubbles. I had a feeling that the mattress was a goner. I propped it against a wall, pinned down by a wisteria branch. I'd see if it was still up in the morning.

In the kitchen, Ian's partner Diana was packing a trombone into its case. 'Got to fly,' she said. 'Rehearsals.' And she was gone. 'We both play,' said Ian. 'I'm the French horn.'

After lunch, Ian offered to take me on a tour of Berwick. We walked along the high street, with more boarded-up shops and closing-down sales and, of course, the Woolies gap. We climbed onto the city's thick Elizabethan walls, surrounded by ditches on three sides and the Tweed on the other, with immense bastions whose arrowhead shapes ensured that every part of Berwick could be covered by fire. There were sheer, unguarded drops from the ramparts, maybe 20 feet down to grass. 'They keep finding drunks at the bottom, but nobody seems to come to much harm.' There were no signs, though. I liked that.

From high, we could see the toy-like trains running across the bridge and look down over the rooftops of the elegant Georgian mansions which, Ian explained, are evidence of Berwick's wealthy heyday as a flourishing seaport between 1750 and 1820. It was a gorgeous little town, the quality of the light extraordinary, like seeing the world in sharp focus for the first time.

We walked past the finely proportioned army barracks, designed by Nicholas Hawksmoor in 1717, and came to a board, on which was a laminated print of a Lowry painting, depicting an alleyway and stone steps. I looked up. The scene was in front of me, almost unchanged.

'He used to come here on holiday to paint,' Ian said. 'He was enchanted by Berwick, loved the quality of the light. There's a Lowry trail now, with paintings standing next to the places he painted.'

Ian knew a lot about Berwick, and seemed to know everyone
we passed, and them him. I assumed he'd lived there all his life.

But no. After his doctorate in geology from Oxford he'd moved
to London and ended up working for BT. 'Then two years ago I
found myself approaching fifty, so we gave it all up and came here.
Didn't know the place at all really. But for a geologist, the coastline
is amazing.'

As we walked, he told me about the move up here. It had been
a hard two years in terms of the B&B, setting up and developing
the business, but things were getting better. He had plans to run
residential pottery courses and maybe also offer geology walks along
the fossil-rich local beaches.

'It's a pipe dream for now. But then, so was moving here.'

Next morning, Norman, good as his word, had mended my wheel.
He held the hub with his fingers and spun it. 'Good as new,' he
said, and he bent down to insert it into the drop-outs at the end of
the chainstay, nimbly threading the chain over the rear sprocket.
'Mind, it'll go again if you're carrying all that gear.'

'I've got rid of some,' I said.

'Dad, can I have one of those?' said a little girl's voice behind me.

I turned round and followed her five-year-old finger to my
handlebars. For there was a bright pink bell, upon which was
Winnie-the-Pooh in a leather flying hat and goggles, staring at a
purple butterfly with a big, stupid Pooh grin on his face.

'Nice bell,' she said.

'It's all we've got at the moment,' said Norman.

It was not quite the look of the rugged round-Britain cyclist.
But the look on Pooh's face seemed perfectly appropriate for what
I was doing.

I rode back to Ian's house, tinkling my new bell constantly, for
all the world like a five-year-old child. And there must be something deeply resonant about the sound of a bicycle bell, because
when people turned around upon hearing it, they always seemed
to be smiling.

Ian was waiting for me with his bike. For instead of pressing on
to proper Scotland, after listening to Ian talk with such passion
about the geology of the coast, I'd offered myself up as a guinea
pig to take a proto-tour.

'Nice bell,' he said.

We rode south, across the narrow medieval bridge, and climbed a steep track until we were riding along the cliff-top, as ever a treat to be riding without luggage again. The day was gloriously stormy and tempestuous, with curtains of rain draped down from a black pelmet out at sea. The water was angry, snarling.

I asked Ian if he was happy.

'If you'd asked me that a few years ago, I'd have said no. But now I'm pretty happy most of the time.'

'What's changed?'

'Well, apart from the room to breathe and the relationship I've got with this,' and he swept his arm towards the sea, 'I think the biggest thing is that now I have a connection to an end product. Whether it's making pots or running a B&B or playing for an audience, you're part of the whole process. Completing circles. I've never had that in a job before. It feels important.'

We rode across a meadow of wild thyme and early purple orchids, upon which danced white butterflies. A skylark fluttered into the air. Ian pointed out a pair of enormous gannets swooping low over the waves. In the distance, Holy Island was pinpricked by a shaft of soft light that had pierced the clouds.

'You?' he asked.

I said that since leaving London I'd become far less tetchy, had started to like other people a lot more. I wasn't exactly sure why, but I suspected being outdoors in nature all day and the exercise was a big part of it all. I told him I'd been having really vivid dreams recently where I lived in a tree house. They were always very happy dreams. The thought of one day having to live once more in a small concrete box in a big city without birdsong seemed impossible.

'It makes me wonder if I can ever do that again,' I said.

'I feel the same,' Ian said.

We propped our bikes against a fence.

'Should we lock them?' I asked.

'Why?' said Ian.

We walked down along a path, towards the beach, winding our way through clumps of viper's bugloss and yellow vetch and wild geraniums. Ian touched his ear. There was a delicate 'chat, chat, chat' coming from the gorse. 'Stonechat. Amazing song, eh?'

On the beach, Ian beckoned me to take a seat on a large black rock.

'Now a geology lesson,' he said.

With great passion and a big piece of driftwood, he drew a timeline in the sand, and explained to his classroom of one how the work of James Hutton had created a paradigm shift in the conception of geological history, freeing it from the straitjacket of religious orthodoxy. Working with the principle of a much greater depth of time had allowed Darwin's theory of evolution to come to fruition. Ian's blackboard was the cliff behind, with the geological strata clearly marked. Being a thickie in matters geological, I couldn't follow everything he said, but his animation, aliveness, held me rapt. I could imagine him being miserable in a big city.

We went to look for fossils. It wasn't hard to find dozens of crinoids, or St Cuthbert's beads as they also known. We went our separate ways looking for more.

'Mike! Mike! Over here. Quick.'

What had he found? An image of Jesus in the limestone? A body?

Ian pointed to a mass of chaotic squiggly lines on a rock.

'That,' he announced, 'is by far and away the best example of bioturbation I have ever seen.'

We stared at the rock for a while. Him in awe, me in ignorance, what with not having the foggiest idea what bioturbation was. Finally, Ian looked up at me and smiled.

'You must think I'm an idiot, getting so excited about a few lines.'

'No, no,' I said. 'Quite the opposite.'

Chapter 10

'Get a bicycle. You will not regret it, if you live.'
Mark Twain

There didn't seem to be too many quiet-road options heading north out of Berwick. In fact, every route ran due west except the A1. So I decided to take it. I mean, how bad could it be? The answer, of course, was very, very bad indeed. Ordinarily, the constant stream of lorries and coaches haring past inches away from me at motorway speeds would have been bad enough. But factor in the gale-force westerly crosswind that had me swerving like a drunk, the cold, needle-like rain that flew into me like a hail of bullets, and the long, slow drags up the hills, and it all added up to possibly the least fun you could have in a saddle. Although Tommy Simpson would probably have begged to differ.

I pulled over and dug out my iPod. I figured that my ears were of no practical use to me on that road. Every approaching vehicle sounded like it was going to mow me down, all amplified by the menacing hissing noise of tyres on wet tarmac. If I was going to die, I might as well go down listening to something soothing. I scrolled through and clicked on *Concierto de Aranjuez*, and soon I was cocooned within a safer, friendlier world, though the logistics of the situation saw me having to fiercely resist conducting with both hands during the rousing string sections, as is my custom.

A few miles up the highway to hell, a big blue sign with a white cross at the side of the road announced *Fàilte gu Alba*, which was handily translated for non-Gaelic speakers as Welcome to Scotland. After the mandatory self-timer shot of me by the sign, I took a moment. I had cycled to Scotland! From London! I wanted to share this with somebody. But as everybody else was speeding past at 80mph in the pouring rain, I had to be content with talking to my bike.

'We've cycled to Scotland!' I said, patting it on the handlebars. 'Me and you.'

Had it been a Herbie-type bike, it would have pinged its bell. But it wasn't, so I pinged it for it.

For the rest of the morning, I played a game called Beat the A1. The rules were quite simple. You took the first exit off the murderously busy road, spent half an hour or so climbing and descending the steep little country lanes of the Lammermuir Hills, before reappearing on the A1 about 100 yards further on from where you had left it. The A1 always won. It was a stupid game.

Past the high, jagged cliffs of St Abb's Head and before me was the wide expanse of the Firth of Forth. Rising from the haze in the Forth was Bass Rock, containing the largest single rock colony of northern gannets in the world, their presence, or rather their guano, from a distance giving the island the look of a cream-topped Christmas pudding.

In North Berwick, I stopped for lunch at a greasy spoon café. The menu was full of things I'd never heard of: link or square sausage, red, white or fruit pudding, Scotch or macaroni pies, tattie scones, bridies, morning rolls. It was a whole new culinary lexicon, a foreign country. I asked the man behind the counter what the difference was between the types of sausage, but he had to ask me to repeat myself because he didn't understand what I was saying, and I in turn had to ask him to repeat this request, because I didn't understand what he was saying either, apart from the word ken, which was ironic really, seeing as I didn't ken at all. This made me feel like some southern smartarse, and I could feel myself affecting a ridiculous Scottish accent, which would have done nothing to disabuse him of the idea that all Englishmen are smartarses.

I finally established, I think, that fruit pudding was very nice. But then I imagined I must have misheard him, because when he offered me a taster of that slab of suet peppered with raisins, it was not very nice at all. I eventually went for black pudding in a morning roll, which was unctuous and gooey and, quite simply, heaven in a bun, unlike any black pudding I had ever tasted before. So I ordered another, naturally.

Edinburgh only detained me long enough to buy a new Thermarest mattress to replace the one that I'd reluctantly had to concede was unrepairable back in Berwick-upon-Tweed. Edinburgh is one of my favourite cities, but I'd been there enough times in the past and, having read while I was stuffing my face with black pudding that Scotland contained two-thirds of the British coastline, I was keen to crack on.

The Forth Railway Bridge hove into view, from a distance looking like a great, humped sea monster, and from up close like the ultimate Meccano set. There are some man-made objects that people feel compelled to gape at open-jawed without really knowing why. I remembered how people would stop and gaze up as if bewitched as Concorde flew over London on its approach to Heathrow, people who maybe otherwise had no interest in planes, like there was some recognition, in the Platonic sense, of its perfect beauty. I've no idea what it is that great design triggers in us, but I know that it's timeless, universal. And I also know that the Forth Railway Bridge has its place, for me at least, in that great architectural pantheon, but I wouldn't know where to begin explaining why.

I bounced my way alarmingly across the Forth Road Bridge – a mate of mine reckons it's falling down and I reckon he might be right. As ever on the big bridges, the Samaritans had their phone number on little boards dotted along the railings and shrivelled bunches of flowers hung limply. About halfway across, a woman, wearing a ball gown and pearls, walked past me in the opposite direction. She looked like she'd been crying. I watched her, uncertain what to do, until eventually she cleared the bridge.

At the end of the bridge, I turned right and picked up the National Cycle Network's Route 76, a stunning track that hugged the north bank of the Firth of Forth, through dense woods and past waterfalls, the trail cutting underneath the railway line by way of narrow little tunnels. Edinburgh sparkled in the sunshine on the other side of the firth, Arthur's Seat looming over it.

I found a campsite right by the water's edge. It had a lot of signs up, but I didn't care. There were giant flags flying from tall poles – Germany, France, Scotland, Wales. No St George's cross, though.

I rode my bike past touring caravans, where some of the owners had assembled little white click-and-fit plastic fences around their pitches. I'm assuming that they must carry these things around with them, for the caravans were of the mobile variety and not those big metal boxes with toy wheels on the bottom to circumvent planning laws.

Within many of the 'walled' pitches were rotating washing lines stuck into the earth and tables set for dinner, standing upon rugs. One woman was using a Flymo to trim the grass of her territory. Man and nature in perfect harmony.

I pitched my little tent, inflated my new mattress, climbed in and just lay there for an hour, utterly spent from the day's efforts, skin tingling deliciously from the windburn, lips cracked, listening to the oystercatchers fussing around, the flags flapping and whip-cracking in the wind. I had come to love that magical time of half-sleep, emptying my mind of the day's events, listening to the world beyond the fabric. There was only one thing that could have made that situation even more perfect then, and it happened soon after. As the inside of my tent turned to grey and then to black, the pitter-patter of rain started drumming on the fabric as I slipped into the sleep of the just.

I rode along the mercifully flat East Neuk of Fife, neuk being the Scots word for corner. Golf courses came thick and fast now, the shoreline made up of golden sandy beaches. I pedalled through the handsome, formerly wealthy fishing villages of St Monans, Pitten-weem and Anstruther – names to be reckoned with, dripping with stoic Scottish dependability. Then on to gorgeous Crail, with its pretty little harbour. Behind the harbour clustered houses with Flemish crow-stepped gables, pantiled roofs and outer stairs, testi-mony to Crail's life in the seventeenth and eighteenth centuries, when it became the largest fishing market in Europe and its fisher-men would return from all over Scandinavia and northern Europe and copy the architectural styles they'd seen. Upon the tiered tower of the ancient tollbooth was a copper weather vane in the shape of a capon, or dried haddock, a reminder that these fish were partly what made this coastal area of otherwise poor Fife so wealthy that King James II had called it 'a fringe of gold on a beggar's mantle'.

'A delight; an old grey town of ancient houses and monastic ruins,' H.V. Morton had written about St Andrews in his 1929 book *In Search of Scotland*, 'full of men in plus fours and women with golf bags on their tweed shoulders; of undergraduates in splendid scarlet gowns; of happy meetings in cake shops.' And not much seemed to have changed since. As I rode down the main street, the town's twin communities – golfers and students – were out in force.

Every other shop seemed to be selling golf equipment, while every pavement café and cake shop was thronged with young, shiny people in scarlet gowns, engaged in happy meetings, their mortar boards lying on tables like so many black fruit bowls. The scarlet gowns had been introduced back in the Middle Ages so that students could be spotted easily when entering brothels. Divinity students were spared this tagging, presumably because they were above suspicion.

With the students sat parents and grandparents, brothers and sisters, all in their Sunday best. For it was late June and graduation day. The cars driving past containing gowned students and their families – Bentleys and Rolls-Royces, top-of-the-range Mercedes and BMWs – spoke of the demographic from which the university, founded in 1411 and known as the Oxford of Scotland, drew its students.

I pulled over and watched the scene for a while, parents beaming with pride, fussing over their little stars and taking photographs. The students, perhaps, were caught up in one of those strange moments when previously quite separate worlds collide. I thought about my own graduation. It might have been yesterday. I remembered feeling simultaneously, in the presence of my parents and my peers, like a boy and a man and all points in between, on the threshold of something – an ending, a beginning, a sense of loss – yet relishing the prospect of great adventures ahead. I could have watched that scene all day.

'Come far, buddy?' said an American voice from behind me.

'Gee, that's some road trip,' he said, after I'd told him.

He held out his hand and introduced himself as Frank Fotheringham Jnr the Third or some such, from Omaha, Nebraska, US of A. I love the way Americans do that: full name, city, state of origin and country straight up, opening gambit, no messing about. I couldn't imagine myself ever introducing myself as 'Mike Carter, London, Middlesex, England, Great Britain. How you doing?'

It's an intriguing insight into cultures: the information we deem to be important to impart first up to a stranger, and the information we seek. In England, the thing everyone generally wants to know, way before you get around to exchanging names, is what you do for a living. I'd never really thought about it much, until a friend of mine, English but living in France, explained to me that to most French people such a question would be considered rude. For what the English are really wanting to know, reckon the French, is how much money do you earn? Are you better than me? Worse? Once we've got that out of the way, we can decide whether we're interested in pursuing the conversation or not. For the French, this is evidence writ large of the hardwired English obsession with class; their avoidance of the question evidence of the spirit born of 1789.

Frank Fotheringham Jnr the Third had flown halfway around the world to play a round of golf. More specifically, he was going to play the famous Old Course links at the Royal and Ancient, an experience that can cost up to a mind-boggling £1,200 a round. Frank Jnr said the words 'Royal' and 'Ancient', in his Midwestern drawl, as if they were invocations to the gods. He had dressed up as Rupert the Bear for the occasion.

'My buddies back home are jealous as hell,' he said.

The R&A, as it's known to golfing cognoscenti worldwide, is, of course, considered the spiritual home of golf, where the rules of the game are determined and some of the greatest Open Championships have been held. But it is the Americans who seem to revere it most of all, almost as Muslims do Mecca, a place every golfer should visit at least once in his or her lifetime. 'St Andrews affects the American golfer much as Stratford-on-Avon affects the American college girl,' Morton noted.

I wished Frank Fotheringham Jnr the Third a pleasant round and rode off down towards the curve of the bay.

A little path ran alongside the wide, almost painfully green, joint fairways of the first and 18th holes, and then cut across them barely a short iron from the first tee. I tried to time my dash across the fairways between drives, but put on my cycle helmet for the first time since Norfolk just in case. Once on the other side, I settled by the famous little stone bridge that I'd seen countless times on TV, and which, over the years, had carried the golfing gods to triumph or disaster over the serpentine burn that runs across the course.

There I sat as a succession of well-fed golfing foursomes made their way up the fairway, most of them dressed in outfits of which

PG Wodehouse might approve. The accents were mostly American, the shots played mostly terrible, sending huge divots of the hallowed turf flying like small landmines being detonated, the ball dribbling a few yards towards its ultimate destination. They would stand on the famous bridge for a photograph, clutching each other tightly around the back, raising thumbs and shouting 'awesome' or 'St Andrews, man!' as the shutter clicked, before striding towards the final green, chattering loudly, detonating their landmines as they went. It was strangely comforting to watch such sacrilege.

I looked up to the large windows of the august members-only clubhouse. There, old white men with bulbous thread-veined noses protruding from granite, patrician faces stared grimly out at the carnage and the high-fiving, no doubt doing the maths. This made me warm to the American golfers even more.

The Tay Bridge was my favourite bridge of the trip so far. This had little to do with aesthetics, though. No, it was just that the bridge was all downhill, three miles of it, sucking me into Dundee like a black hole. Cyclists are easily impressed. Towards the North Sea, I could see dotted a collection of gargantuan oil rigs, brought into the shallow waters of the Tay for repair or decommissioning, looking like sci-fi monsters taking a crap. The air was full of heavy thudding from the rotors of Chinook helicopters buzzing around nearby RAF Leuchars.

At the end of the bridge, I saw a sign for NCN1. I had spent so much of this journey so far on it that it was always like seeing an old friend when I picked it up again. Another sign underneath informed me that I'd need photographic ID to take NCN1 through the docks. Photographic ID? I didn't have anything with my photograph on it. Come to think about it, I didn't have anything with my address on it either, and no easy access to such things, seeing as all my papers were hundreds of miles away. I'd been on the road for over a month and had nothing on me that could identify who I was apart from a name on a debit card. I hadn't got my passport or my driving licence. It was the first time I'd thought about the general anonymity of travelling this way: I must have appeared on thousands of CCTV cameras since I'd left home – with 4.2 million cameras, or one for every 14 people, Britons are after all the most watched people on earth – but with no registration number, nobody could know who I was, where I'd been or where I belonged. I was a vagrant, a nomad, a nobody. And do you know what? It felt bloody marvellous.

There can't be too many countries left where citizens are allowed to roam freely without photographic ID or papers of identification. For all those years when New Labour were intent on introducing ID cards, I'd felt strangely indifferent about the whole thing, unable to muster much enthusiasm one way or the other. But standing there, under the Tay Bridge, feeling the freedom of belonging nowhere, I understood why having to carry an ID card would completely destroy that.

'Got any ID?' the security guard asked at the kiosk.

'No,' I said. 'I haven't got anything.'

'Driving licence, library card, bus pass…?'

'Nothing.'

'Nay bother, like,' he said, waving me through. 'Just stay on the bike path.'

I'm not sure to this day what they've got concealed in Dundee docks that would merit such security, so stringently laid out yet so woefully executed. All I saw was an old lightship, scrapyards and several oil rigs rusting away. Maybe they really were sci-fi monsters taking a dump.

I came up behind a woman out walking her dog and tinkled my bell. I loved having a bell, and can't recommend them highly enough. The woman turned around and, as always happened, smiled and stepped out of the way. Dogs, however, were a different matter. This one, a Skye terrier, stood his ground. 'He'll nay git out ya way,' she said. 'You'll have te git out of his.' I tinkled my bell again. Dogs either don't respond to bells or think such things beneath them. The terrier just sat and stared at me with imperious disdain as I manoeuvred around him.

The esplanade became a track sandwiched between an MoD firing range on one side, with red flags flying and signs warning 'Do not touch anything. It may explode and kill you' – signs which even I had to concede were probably justified – and the front nine at Carnoustie, witness to some of the finest golf ever played and, on the day I passed through, some of the worst. Once again my helmet

went on, as robust expletives rang out, followed by cries of 'Fore!'
Balls whooshed around my ears and pinged off the walls.

At a roundabout, I looked at a road sign containing a good slice
of Scottish football's lower divisions: Arbroath, Brechin, Forfar,
Montrose. I'd had no clue where these places were when the official
results were read out at 4.45 on a Saturday afternoon, and I didn't
care. To me they were always an annoying hiatus that must be
endured before the interviews with players and managers from
'important' matches could be aired. But now I'd been there, could
put a place to the name, I doubted I would be as impatient in
future. It would, I was sure, be the same when looking at the
national weather forecast.

Thoughts about lower-league football in Scotland were almost
my last. For coming off that roundabout without paying attention,
I nearly went under the wheels of an articulated lorry, my closest
shave since leaving home. So now the fortunes of Brechin and Forfar
on the pitch will, for me, be inextricably and for ever more caught
up with the hissing of air brakes, the smell of burning rubber and a
volley of abuse that I couldn't understand but whose sentiments
were perfectly clear. My, Scottish lorry drivers are good at swearing.

The smell of burning was pretty strong in Arbroath too. But this
was an altogether more pleasant aroma: the smell of Arbroath smok-
ies – the haddock being smoked over woodchip fires for which the
town is famous. Local legend has it that a fish store caught fire one
night, consuming barrels of locally caught haddock packed in salt.
The result was thought to be just a lot of written-off fish, until
someone tasted the remains.

I rode along the walls of the lovely little harbour. Boats were
offloading their catch, others getting ready to head for sea. The
massive ruin of the red sandstone abbey rose from the town.

A battered blue enamel sign on the wall announced that it was
in Arbroath's abbey in 1320 that the Declaration of Independence
over England was signed after Robert the Bruce's victory at
Bannockburn. The sign had been provided by Springfield Gospel
Hall. 'Scotland,' it read, 'was once known as a Bible-loving nation
and had been richly blessed...' The past tense perhaps being the
point, because alongside it advertised a 'Sunset service, here at the

harbour, every Sunday. Bright singing. Testimonies. Gospel messages. Bring a friend.' I thought that a sunset service sounded just lovely, but alas it was a Tuesday.

Just south of Montrose, a wet and sticky sea mist came in, what they called in eastern Scotland a haar. The day was sliding into evening now, and with no idea where I was going to stay, I pressed on through Montrose, following the cycle route through the docks, with deep-water fishing boats and oil-rig supply vessels, and started looking for somewhere to pitch my tent. Since the Land Reform Act of 2003, wild camping has been legal in Scotland, the only conditions being that you behave responsibly and don't inconvenience others.

I was hugely looking forward to wild camping by the deserted lochs and in the desolate mountains further north. When I'd set off from London, this was one of my great fantasies – remote; showering under a mountain waterfall; no signs. I hadn't anticipated pitching my tent away from campsites this far south. But it was a good feeling to know that if the worst came to the worst, I could pitch almost anywhere and not be woken up and evicted in the middle of the night by an irate farmer, policeman or campsite owner telling me that hanging my underpants off my tent was illegal.

The road dipped under the graceful curve of the disused Kinnaber viaduct just north of Montrose – more of Dr Beeching's handiwork – and then ran along the rugged coastline south of St Cyrus. I disturbed a huge raptor feasting on something by the side of the road. I didn't get too good a look at it, but I convinced myself it was a golden eagle, although it was more likely a buzzard, which had become so common a sight to me that they had lost nearly all their wow factor. Which was a shame, because if you saw a buzzard sitting in your city garden you'd be telling the story for the rest of your life.

It was there that I was stopped in my tracks by an extraordinary sight. For in front of me was a modest farmhouse surrounded by fields, but instead of the fields being filled with wheat or maize, they had been sown with junk: as far as the eye could see, there were old wheelbarrows, rusting lawnmowers, lamp stands, bits of bicycles, electric fires, suits of armour, old coat stands. It was a crop of bric-a-brac. Dozens of trestle tables groaned under mountains of tea sets, porcelain figures and chandeliers. Decrepit caravans sat rusting. Old doors and windows propped each other up like structures built from playing cards. It was like a tornado had gone through a department store and dumped it in a field.

I propped the Ridgeback against a wall, next to a tangled heap of rusty and broken bikes. I felt bad about this, as if I was dropping a pedigree off at the dogs' home.

'Can I help you?' said a middle-aged woman with shoulder-length blond hair and a warm smile.

I explained that I had just been cycling past, had seen this extraordinary sight and wondered what was going on.

'Come in for a cuppa,' she said.

I followed her into the farmhouse, along a dark corridor stuffed with boxes of magazines and piles of clothes and knackered dolls and more suits of armour, and into the kitchen, where, around a big wooden table piled high with old pots and pans and crockery, sat a cast of adults, young and old, some holding babies, while various terriers and collies and cats chased each other or dozed in baskets and twitched their legs, dreaming of chases.

'This is Mike,' said the woman who'd brought me in. Her name was Heather. She introduced everybody. There was William, a son, who was visiting from university, Chay, an old man sitting in the corner, nursing a bottle of Scotch, and Christina, a striking Amazonian woman who rose to shake my hand and towered above me. 'I only came to buy a teapot,' she said. 'That was four years ago and I'm still here.'

'That's Fester,' Heather said, pointing to a young Jack Russell, who was chasing another Jack called Sam. Tess the elderly collie sat quietly and watched the chaos through rheumy eyes. 'And the bairn's Nairn.'

'Och, you smell bad,' said a young woman, holding up Nairn and sniffing his bottom. There were introductions made to the other half a dozen people in the kitchen, and explanations made as to where they fitted into the grand scheme of things – friends, daughters – but I was so overwhelmed with all of this that my brain was full.

Tea and biscuits were placed in front of me, and then everyone went back to their conversations. I just sat there for a while, tickling Tess under the chin and trying to work out if I'd been adopted.

'Are you staying the night?' asked Christina.

'I don't—'

'Great,' she said. 'You can sleep in one of the old caravans.'

And that was that. I thought about what she'd said about only popping in to buy a teapot, and wondered whether this was where my bike trip ended.

After about 30 minutes, a man entered the room.

'Hello, darling,' said Heather. 'This is Mike. Mike, Peter. Mike's our guest for the night.'

Peter, who was aged about 60, had a farmer's tan and a battered tweed cap on his head. He, too, had a warm smile.

'Lovely,' he said. I was waiting for him to ask me what I wanted, or what I was doing sitting in his kitchen, like you might if you came in from work and found a stranger in your house, but he didn't seem remotely curious.

'They been looking after you?' Peter said.

'Aye,' I said. 'Very well.'

'Dinner'll be about half an hour,' Heather said to Peter. 'Why don't you show Mike around?'

He led me into a large living room, where sofas of varying vintages and states of repair sat on the floor and leaned against the walls. We had to step over boxes of garden tools and carriage lamps and piles of old wedding dresses. There were rolls of razor wire and carpet, ceramic tiles, old shoes, a blacksmith's bellows. An old kayak was propped against one wall alongside half a dozen grandfather clocks and cartwheels. Peter pointed to the ceiling and the metal beams that ran across it. 'Got those from a North Sea oil rig,' he said.

Peter explained that he'd been a cattle farmer all his life, exporting beef to France, but had been ruined by BSE. 'Lost a third of a million pounds. Everything gone, overnight. I'd never had a bad debt in my life. We lived in a caravan for a while, then started buying things to do up this house. I bought too much and had to start selling it. That's how the business started.'

We walked out of the house and towards a huge barn, whose walls were built of old doors and house windows, like a jigsaw puzzle of a house painted by Picasso. Outside, a pheasant was having a fight with itself in a mirror. Inside, it was stuffed to the ceiling with old furniture.

'Too-easy finance has destroyed the second-hand market, encouraged debt, created a wasteful society. Look at this,' said Peter, pointing to an old oak table with graceful curved legs. 'Beautiful. This will still be here in a hundred years. Now look at this rubbish. This might not be here in five minutes' time.'

Peter explained how he'd been naïve about the value of things when he started, but had learned quickly. Had to. 'We even have people from Christie's come here regular now.

'People include us as part of their holidays. Looking for treasure, I suppose. Sometimes we've got more cars outside than Tesco's. It's weird who goes for what. People come and load up shipping containers and send it home. We send old furniture to Florida. The Milanese love fine china. The Norwegians buy the lawnmowers. Alaskans go for the old hot-water bottles. You see patterns emerging.'

We walked into another barn, this one full of shelf after shelf of hand-painted china, silver cutlery canteens and crystal vases. Boxes of old Ordnance Survey maps, 78rpm records and cellophane-wrapped birthday cards that were never sent littered the floor. Choral music played from unseen speakers. It all felt very intimate, somehow, being so close to the personal belongings of so many others. 'People don't tend to use their good stuff, so when they die it's often in boxes as new,' Peter observed.

He showed me a box of assorted royal memorabilia, commemorative mugs of the Queen Mum, and Charles and Di's and Fergie and Andrew's weddings. 'Scotland's not the place to sell that kind of stuff,' he said. 'Now, let's get you to your caravan before dinner goes cold.'

We walked over to one of the old caravans. Peter opened the door and brushed away the cobwebs. 'There's a bed somewhere at the other end if you can find it. See you inside in five minutes.'

I climbed over boxes of *Military Modelling* magazines from the seventies and a pile of old eight-track car stereos. Under a mountain of old ball gowns I found the bed. Next to it was a box of old railway magazines. I lay down and flicked through a copy of *Modern Railways* from 1977. That was the year when I'd started trainspotting with an obsession bordering on a pathology. At the time, I believed that I simply loved trains. But as an adult, I'd started looking at it differently: that collecting numbers was my way of regaining order, control, among the chaos. It wasn't a massive leap to see some parallels in that caravan.

In the kitchen, a vast platter of steaming lamb was put on the table. Chay had worked his way through half of the bottle. Nairn was asleep in the corner. Tess didn't look as if she'd moved. The Jack Russells were still chasing around. There were two or three new people there. I didn't catch their names. Nobody asked me what I was doing there. Nobody seemed to care. People traded their stories of the day. It was all so *Darling Buds of May* and all so lovely that I could understand why Christina had never left.

'Fancy coming to tonight's auction?' Peter asked me.

'If we've got a guest, maybe you could take the night off,' said Heather, rolling her eyes in what seemed like exasperation. But Peter didn't appear to be listening. 'Come on, we're late.'

I wouldn't say Peter drove the 10 miles to Inverbervie quickly, but by the time I'd done up my seatbelt it was time to take it off again. The combined effect of his driving and the fact that I'd got used to travelling the roads at a sedate 10mph had made my head spin, the world flashing by in hyperspeed like I was in some video-game Grand Prix.

As we walked into the village hall, the people all turned to clock us and seemed to crumple at the sight of Peter, as if Usain Bolt had turned up for the parents' race at sports day.

'Anything you fancy, just let me know and I'll get it for you,' Peter said.

'I'm on a bicycle.'

'Do you need a pump? There's one there.'

The sale started. Peter's number was 482. First lot: Austin Maestro car manuals. A few bids, then 'sold to 482'. Binoculars: to 482. *Star Trek* paperbacks: 482. Work boots, used, size 10. 'Surely somebody will give me a pound? 50p? 482.' A few people drifted out of the hall. Soon, an old electric meter, 20 boxes of screws, Airfix kits and Meccano sets and an old mirror adorned by Roman eagles had been assigned to 482. Four hours and £1,300 later we were driving back towards the house, considerably slower this time, an appetite sated, a contented silence pervading the car.

I wanted to ask Peter about his collecting. I ran the question around in my head, but any way I phrased it sounded rude, impertinent, to a man who'd been so generous to a stranger. What business was it of mine anyway? But before I knew it, the words were tumbling out of my mouth.

'Do you think you might have become just a little bit...' I paused.

'What?'

'Well, obsessed,' I replied.

There was a silence. Peter smiled slightly, the smile of a man who must have been asked the same question a million times.

Finally, he spoke. 'People have become very wasteful these days, throwing things away that are still useful. We live in a culture where things and people are disposed of just like that. I don't think it's right. Would you call that "obsessed"?'

I felt bad for bringing it up, like I knew I would.

No, I said, I wouldn't.

Chapter 11

'Melancholy is incompatible with bicycling.'
James E. Starrs

The landscapes were definitely getting wilder now, the hinterland to my left more unkempt, the coastline on my right craggier. The weather was getting into the spirit, too: a sharp easterly raced across the sea, having me rummaging for extra layers, and gloomy clouds hung low over the water, turning the day into perennial dusk. I passed my first field of Highland cattle, and stopped to take a picture. Like all the cows I'd encountered, there followed a familiar pattern: one or two of the animals would look up from their grazing at the stranger in their midst. Then one or two more, until the whole herd was staring; even the ones dry-humping each other would dismount and stop and stare.

Then, slowly, in ones and twos, the animals would walk towards me, until they were all against the fence, inches from me, mouths chewing, as if engaged in a mass bovine greeting. The Sancho Panza in me always concluded that the cows were expecting food, but my Don Quixote knew that cows were sociable types, wanting to chew the fat, have a nose. I always ended up talking to them: how you doing, Mrs Cow? What's the grass like in this part of the country? It's impossible to ever be lonely on a long bike ride through cattle country. All you need to do is pull over by a field of cows and soon you have all the company you could ever want.

I rounded a headland, and there in front of me was the brooding thirteenth-century Dunnottar Castle, sitting on a mesa surrounded by churning, boiling seas and soaring 160-foot cliffs on all sides. So impenetrable was its position that a small garrison of men had held out against Cromwell's army for more than eight months to save the Scottish crown jewels that had been stored there for safekeeping. Looking at Dunnottar from the cliff-top, it was hard to imagine where you'd even start trying to storm it. I made myself a promise that if I ever won the Euromillions, and decided to buy myself a globe-destroying ray gun and a fluffy white cat, I would base myself at Dunnottar. It was that kind of place. It also replaced Bamburgh at number one in my Top 10 of spectacular British castles.

In a small village, with fishing nets strung between poles to dry, I popped into a post office to buy a flapjack. I didn't know what was more incongruent: the fact that I'd found a village post office in twenty-first-century Britain still functioning; or the fact that Michael Jackson's 'Billie Jean' was playing loudly from the radio that belonged to the little old lady behind the counter.

'Like this?' I asked her, pointing to the radio as I handed over my money.

'Och, no, it's awful,' she said, pulling a face like she'd sucked on something sharp.

'Why don't you change the station?'

'It's on every one.'

I crested the hill above Nigg Bay, and below me was the urban sprawl of Aberdeen, the low cloud ceiling and grey light combining with the granite buildings from which the place earns its austere moniker, to make it one of the most depressing-looking cities I'd ever seen. And that's from someone who comes from Birmingham. I'm sure Aberdeen is a very different place in the sunshine, but as the cycle route dropped me down among the sprawling industrial boat-yards, full of oil-rig supply vessels, and passed the fish-processing units, then across the River Dee on Victoria Bridge and into the bus dodgems on Union Street, all I wanted to do was get out the other side, preferably in one piece. The cities I'd passed through on the trip were always a shock after the soporific peace of the countryside, and I always felt like an Amish child visiting the big smoke for the first time, eyes wide in horror at the pace and intensity of life, the noise, the lack of space.

But soon I was lost. I popped into a newsagent's to ask the way. The man launched into a set of directions, which would have been complicated under normal circumstances, but in Aberdonian, which sounded like Billy Connolly doing a poor impression of the Swedish chef from *The Muppets*, had been doubly unfathomable. I caught the word 'reet' a few times, and 'street on' and 'atween', which I could hazard a guess at, and 'aneth', 'bide' and 'braw', which I could not. I just stood there trying to nod sagely at the appropriate moments. 'Ken?' he said at the end.

'Thriller' was playing on the radio. What was it about this part of Scotland and the King of Pop? The man behind the counter was young, maybe early twenties.

'Affa, eh?' he said, thumbing in the rough direction of the radio.

'Affa?'

'Terrible, ya ken.'

Now, I wouldn't describe myself as Michael Jackson's greatest fan. And I think one must make up one's own mind about Bubbles the chimp and the pyjama parties and the melted nose. But I remember first watching the 'Thriller' video in 1984 in awe as MJ and his zombie pals jerked around the gravestones. It had been a seminal moment in music history, the precursor to the music video age. And on top of all that, it still remained a classic pop song.

'How can you say it's terrible?' I said. 'To be honest, I think it's great.'

The man shook his head. And, happy that I'd defended the reputation of one of our more maligned icons, I flounced out.

The easterlies picked up in intensity as I headed north out of Aberdeen, and soon I was riding in italics again. But I'd seen the map; I knew what was coming. And after Rattray Head, as the great slab of Aberdeenshire ended suddenly at the mouth of the Moray Firth, I pointed the bike due west. I was flying, 20mph up the gentle, rolling hills, 45mph down them. I was singing at the top of my lungs. It seemed like for ever since I'd had a tailwind, especially one of this strength. I was Lance. I was Superman. But not for long.

For just past Fraserburgh, the landscape changed abruptly and dramatically, from rolling hills to cliffs. It was as if a giant had taken the coastline and smacked it from both ends with a pair of house bricks. No wind was going to get me up these. For the first time since Yorkshire, I was off the bike and pushing.

I rolled down the near-vertical dead-end lane into the tiny village of Pennan, which consisted of a row of 30-odd whitewashed fishermen's cottages nestling under the high sandstone cliffs that separated it from the outside world. It felt like a secret place, forgotten. It was simply gorgeous. On the narrow pebbly beach sat brightly painted little fishing cobles. In its centre was a tiny harbour and an old-fashioned red phone box.

I'd never been to Pennan, but I was having the strangest sense of déjà vu. It all looked so, so familiar.

A woman walked past. She pointed to the bike and asked where I'd cycled from. Her name was Sue and she ran the village's only B&B.

I was gobsmacked that there weren't more places to cater for tourists. I thought they'd be fighting them off.

'Holidaymakers don't tend to come. They think it's always misty and freezing here,' she said. 'They pass us by and go straight to the West Coast. But when they do come they're always amazed because the climate here's lovely.

'Of course, we get a few people come here because of the film.'

'The film?'

'*Local Hero*. It was shot here.'

That was it! No wonder the place looked familiar. *Local Hero* was one of my favourite movies, one I must have seen at least a dozen times. For some reason, I'd always assumed that 'Ferness', the village in the film, was on the West Coast somewhere. But now that Sue had said it, I could see it all: there was the pub where the locals had plotted against the oil developers; there was the little road along which the mystery man on the moped had torn up and down going who knew where; there was the little quayside where the fishermen landed their catch; and there, on the pavement opposite me, was the phone box. The phone box from where MacIntyre had called back to Felix Happer in Houston, and from where Mac had seen the Northern Lights and had his epiphany about the oil companies desecrating this sacred spot. It all seemed a rather neat plot point that a real village playing a fictional town under threat of being ruined by development had also been largely spared.

'As far as I'm aware,' Sue said. 'That's the only listed phone box in Britain.'

She took my picture standing in it, one of my most treasured photographs from my trip. Serendipity had brought me to Pennan. Serendipity had introduced me to Pennan's only B&B owner. It seemed that the universe had plans for me to spend the night here, have a drink in the pub, maybe sit on the beach and watch shooting stars. Oh, how mysterious are the ways of the cosmos.

'Can I book a room for tonight?' I asked Sue.

'We're full,' Sue said.

Serendipity my arse.

'They're not keen on people camping here either, seeing as we're such a tiny village. But people camp on the beach in Gardenstown next door.'

I rode along the sharply corrugated coastline, up and down, with incredible views out over the North Sea. Then I dropped down a steep road, along a series of white-knuckle hairpins that took me from a chimney to the same house's front door in just a few metres. Gardenstown was bigger than Pennan, but just as dramatic, hemmed in by big bluffs, with raptors gliding on the thermals. I rode along the narrow main street, flanked by whitewashed cottages. If this place were in Cornwall or Devon, it would be rammed with bijou hotels and B&Bs, craft shops and coffee shops. But here there was next to nothing, and hardly a soul abroad.

A couple on the main street asked me 'the question' and we exchanged pleasantries. Clare and Steve were renting a cottage in Gardenstown for the week, and lived in Edinburgh. I said how amazed I was that these places along the coast weren't mobbed and got the same response as I had from people on the Northumberland coast: 'We know. But don't tell anybody.'

I said goodbye and rode around another switchback, heading for the beach and a place to pitch my tent. By the time I'd rounded the corner, Clare had taken a narrow stone staircase and was standing in front of me.

'Steve and I were just talking. If you've no plans for tonight, we'd love to have you round for dinner. We're having a barbecue. We'd like to hear some of your stories.'

'That would be great,' I said.

I pushed my bike across the beach and found a glorious spot on a high ledge looking out over the water. I noticed Steve making his way towards me.

'We've just been chatting and, well, we've got a spare room and it seems such a waste. Why don't you come and stay with us tonight?'

Serendipity, I apologise for being so rude.

So, soon after, I was doing my laundry (the second-most exciting thing for touring cyclists), and soon after that drinking wine and eating venison burgers (the most exciting) on the terrace under a million stars.

Clare and Steve were terrific company, funny and sharp, and I laughed so hard at their stories that red wine came out of my nose.

I asked them about north-east Scotland's obsession with Michael Jackson.

'He died,' said Clare.

'What?'

'Terrible, eh?' said Steve.

And I thought back to the newsagent's, and telling the man behind the counter that, far from being terrible, it was great. This I relayed to my hosts, and it was their turn to have red wine coming out of their noses.

The night wore on into the small hours. I finally went up to my room, exhausted from laughter, and lay on my big comfy bed, looking out of the huge picture window onto the sea, silvery with the moon. As I scanned the heavens for shooting stars, I felt like the luckiest man alive.

There was sunshine and tailwinds the next morning. Could life get any better for a cyclist? Well, yes, actually, it could, because after passing through the elegant towns of Macduff (it really exists!) and Banff, and the picturesque little fishing ports of Whitehills and Portsoy, the National Cycle Network's Route 1 delivered up one of the finest sections of largely traffic-free riding I'd experienced since leaving London. And to put the icing on what was already an exceptionally nice cake, the section in question was on the track bed of the former Aberdeen–Inverness railway line in all its flat-as-a-pancake glory.

It started in Cullen, where the disused viaduct took me high over the rooftops of the town, and continued for mile after mile, past distilleries and ruined castles, through deep cuttings and pine woods, and alongside the Moray Firth, sparkling in the sunshine, a blue of such deep intensity that it inspired H.V. Morton to call it

> … a blue so blue, and yet so soft, that to look at it is to think of the islands of the Hesperides or the land of the Lotus Eaters. It is a colour not of this world: it is a paint they use only in heaven.

Beyond the firth rose the distant hills of Cromarty and Dornoch shimmering in the heat haze. I would be there soon enough. A couple of crows loudly and bravely harassed a buzzard. I scanned the water in vain for a glimpse of the famous Moray dolphins. It was a view, Morton had said, that could almost break the heart, and at that moment I knew exactly what he meant.

At Garmouth, the track went across a glorious metal truss bridge that was more River Kwai than Spey, and shortly afterwards I was pedalling alongside the runway at RAF Lossiemouth, fighter jets spewing fire and screaming into the skies. It was like a low-rent version of the scene in *Top Gun*, with an overweight middle-aged man in Lycra shorts playing the Tom Cruise role, and the Ridge-back playing the Kawasaki Ninja 900. And to increase the similitude, I sang 'Take My Breath Away' as I pedalled frantically after the jets until I had to stop because I couldn't breathe any longer.

The sky grew purple, then black. A sign heralded the village of Findhorn. Findhorn? It rang a bell, but I couldn't quite place the name.

The heavens opened in the manner that would have animals lining up in pairs. I scurried for cover, finding myself sheltering, like a drowned rat, in the doorway of a large house. I took off my shoes, wrung out my socks and waited for the storm to pass.

The door opened and a woman with spectacles and a kindly smile asked if I'd like to go inside, where tea and biscuits would be served. That was very welcome, if unexpected, but not quite as unexpected as being shown into a large living room where around 20 men and women sat on sofas clutching notebooks.

'Are you here for the flower remedy class?' asked one.

I was standing there, barefoot, dripping wet, in Lycra. There were any number of fantastically witty responses to the question that any fantastically witty person would have reeled off.

'No,' I said.

The woman returned with the tea and biscuits. She explained how the Findhorn Flower Centre used flowers grown in their own gardens to create homeopathic medicine. The people in the room were on a residential course.

Flowers. Homeopathy. Findhorn. It came back to me where I remembered the name from. Findhorn was the famous hippy community founded in the 1960s. All free love, drugs and shitting on cabbages. So this is where it was. I looked again at the people on the sofas. There were no kaftans in sight, no flowers in their hair, nobody barefoot, apart from me. In fact, everybody looked disappointingly normal and middle class. Like civil servants or teachers or, well, like me. Even hippies, it seemed, had been gentrified.

'Findhorn,' I said. 'The famous...'

I wanted to say hippies, but the word sounded rude sloshing around in my head.

'...alternative lifestyle people.'

'I think you might be confusing us with the Findhorn Foundation,' she said. 'Quite separate. They're next door.'

After eating the flower people out of biscuits, I saw that the rain had stopped, so I left and popped into the Findhorn Foundation. There was a campsite, with a few teepees on it, and caravans with grass roofs and a shop that accepted the eko, Findhorn's own currency. On the shop's noticeboard were signs for upcoming courses: 'Thrival Living Skills for the Upcoming Times' and 'The Bright Side of Cataclysm – the Adventure of the Universe Depends on Our Ability to Listen'. On a small patch of grass in front of the shop, a man stood on one leg and played the flute. Two young women with American accents, one clutching a copy of *The Nine Faces of Christ*, were discussing their chakras.

'Oh, ya.'

'I totally, like, feel that.'

'Ya, you should go with that feeling.'

This was more like it. The piss-taking stories I could pick up here could keep me going for years. It wasn't that I disliked hippies or anything. It's just that their earnestness generally annoyed the big-city-dwelling cynic in me.

I met Carin, one of the Foundation's administrators, who offered to give me a tour. Carin was originally from Australia and moved to Findhorn after she developed health problems, problems that largely disappeared after the move.

As we walked, Carin explained how the community had started in 1962, when Peter and Eileen Caddy and Dorothy Maclean, broke and homeless, settled in a small caravan in the dunes that surround Findhorn Bay.

'Dorothy found she was able to intuitively contact the spirit of plants, called devas,' said Carin.

'Did she?' said I.

'These devas gave Dorothy instructions on how to make the most of the poor, sandy soil.'

'The plant spirits gave her instructions, huh?'

'And following these principles, their garden produced spectacular results, including forty-pound cabbages, and became famous for demonstrating what can be achieved by cooperating with nature instead of imposing on it.'

'Right.'

Carin showed me the Foundation's Living Machine, a reed-bed system for processing sewage, and then we moved on to the Universal Hall, a 300-seat concert venue with a sedum roof that's hosted the National Theatre of Scotland and the BBC Symphony Orchestra, among others.

The Foundation was now a charitable trust, Carin said, and in the 1980s the eco-village was built. They get 4,000 visitors a year from 70 countries, who come to take part in Experience Weeks, where they're put to work in the gardens or in the kitchens in exchange for meals and accommodation. 'It's a chance for them to experience the principles on which the community is based: inner listening, connection with life, and inspired action.'

Visitor numbers, Carin said, were rising each year. I asked why she thought this was the case. She paused.

'It's hard to explain without sounding painfully right-on, but I think people are increasingly rejecting the modern orthodoxy of materialism. All that wealth seems to have come at the cost of communities, and if there's one thing we know here it's that community is vital for humans to thrive. I think the collapse of the banks confirmed to many that the way we've been living these past thirty years is neither sustainable not conducive to real happiness.

'We've just been quietly getting on with our lives here, eco-living, recycling, bioplanting, living sustainably with nature. Even just a few years ago, these things were viewed by the mainstream as, well, a bit oddball. But now they're being seen as conventional wisdom. We've got guys bidding for water-treatment plants in Shanghai, and other projects. The funniest thing is RAF Kinloss next door. The Home Office used to have a file on Findhorn, in which we were dismissed as "harmless eccentrics". And now the RAF base is asking for our advice on building wind turbines, a biomass system and a Living Machine.'

'Looks like your time has come,' I said.

'Maybe. But we're not holding our breath.'

We followed a sign that read 'Field of Dreams'. Carin explained how up to 700 residents lived full-time on site now – herbalists, healers, potters, teachers, doctors and builders among them – bartering their skills for food or services. They lived in a variety of abodes, from caravans to chalets with 'living roofs' of grass and wild flowers to houses built from recycled whisky vats. 'Like that one,' she said, pointing to a round wooden structure with windows cut into it, like something from a fairy tale. Behind the house were the Foundation's four large wind turbines that provide much of its energy needs. 'Would you like to have a look inside? We'll see if Craig will show us around. He's a good guy.'

'Come in,' Craig said, with an antipodean twang.

Craig was 67, but with the youthful eyes and bouncing energy of an excitable child. The inside of his wooden whisky vat home was extraordinary. There's something magical to me about a building with no corners. I thought about ancient structures, the Iron Age and Saxon roundhouses, the rural houses of sub-Saharan Africa, the yurts of Mongolia, the teepees of the Native Americans: all round. I wondered why in the west we've become fixated on boxes.

Craig had been at Findhorn 41 years, had built his own house with no previous experience. Rooms off the main chamber were made up of smaller whisky vats. 'Whisky used to be blended in these, and now people are. We got married right there,' he said, pointing to the floor, 'and had our first child right there too.'

We walked out into the garden. It was like The Lost World, a wild profusion of garlic, enormous poppies, feral potatoes, cherries and currants of every hue. Chickens clucked around. 'I'd say 50 per cent of all this is self-sown,' Craig said. 'This is all built on sand dunes. Whatever the spirit of nature you've got, you work with it, not impose on it. Permaculture isn't just gardening. It's an attitude to life based on observation.'

He bent over, ripped up what looked like a weed with bright yellow flowers and thrust it in my hand.

'Wild brassica. Try it, it's good.'

And it was.

He gave me a cup of rainwater from a barrel, which was crisp and delicious. Craig explained how he mixed nine parts water with one part urine to feed his plants.

'More brassica?' he said.

'No, I'm good, thanks.'

Craig got much of his meat from roadkill, but he had a treat coming up, he said, pointing to a wild pheasant clucking noisily and pompously at the edge of the garden. 'Ate all my beetroot,' Craig said, and then smiled. 'Beetroot-infused pheasant. Hmmmm.'

As we walked away, Carin suggested that I stay the night. I'd been thinking the same thing. I went off and pitched my tent, grabbed a quick shower and met Carin in the Community Centre for dinner, where we stood in a big circle with our fellow diners to bless our food and then all had a hug. There was a lot of hugging at Findhorn, and a lot of laughter.

At our table were Nick and Katie, two twenty-somethings from south London visiting Findhorn for a week. They were setting up a Transition Town in their area, a grass-roots movement to foster communities in cities based around allotments and pooling resources.

'We didn't know our neighbours, and now we do,' said Katie.

'We're part of the most useless generation that has ever existed,' said Nick. 'All those skills – knitting, cooking, darning, building, mending things – all lost. We want to learn them.'

I told him about my fridge.

'That's it,' he said.

After dinner, I looked at the programme of events.

'I want to go to Sacred Dance and then to Taizé singing,' I said to Carin.

'You just want to take the piss,' she said.

And she was right, of course. But as I danced around with the group laughing and pretending to be skylarks and, after, as I sat in the Gaudiesque little stone cottage of the nature sanctuary surrounded by people with flowers in their hair, with the most exquisite singing filling the air, I was too busy enjoying myself to remember that I should have been taking the piss. At the end, we all stood and put our arms around each other. 'We are a circle within a circle that never ends,' we sang, swaying gently like so many drunk girls at the end of a hen night. When the RAF adopts this, too, I thought, we will indeed have travelled far.

Later that night, as I lay happily on my back in my tent, a big grin on my face, it occurred to me that two quite significant things had happened to me on the trip so far. One: I had developed thighs that made sleeping on my side so painful as to be almost impossible. And two: I had, along the way, somehow become a hippy.

I stopped off at Culloden, one of the most atmospheric battle sites I'd ever been to, sitting there all lonely, surrounded by mournful pine forest and scowling hills. The son et lumière provided by nature doubtless helped to evoke the right spirit, with the sky full of black malevolence and thunder. I went into the visitor centre and then into a small room whose four walls were screens onto which were projected re-enacted battle scenes of such graphic violence that I actually found myself surrendering. The Jacobites lost, by the way, just in case you don't know how it all worked out. Hope I haven't ruined it for you.

The long eight-mile freewheel down into Inverness became a terrifying ordeal after the clouds tore open and dumped their contents, turning the road into a river. My brakes were not at their best in such conditions and, seeing as any potholes were under several inches of water, I think I managed to find most of them. I was getting used to such drownings, and had developed a genuine indifference to them. The gods had clearly cottoned on to this, though, because they then decided to unleash a murderous salvo of hailstorms.

By the time I got into Inverness, the lightning had joined the party, spitting fury and prompting young girls and middle-aged cyclists to shriek with fear.

Over the vertiginous span of the magnificent Kessock Bridge, where the Beauly Firth met the Moray Firth, and onto the Black Isle. As soon as my wheels touched the isle, the heavens abruptly turned off the taps and the sun broke through with intensity, turning the tarmac into a fizzing and sizzling hotplate. You've got to love the British weather.

A long, sharp climb out of Fortrose, and then a lovely long descent the other side, with spectacular views across the Cromarty Firth, dotted that day with oil rigs and cruise ships. The firth, one of the most sheltered deep-water bays in the world, is noted for its role in protecting destroyers in both world wars and, in my flat at least, as being one of the last words I hear before I go to sleep.

You see, it's not only nuclear power stations and lower league Scottish football clubs that I've been ticking off on this journey, but also points where the Shipping Forecast met land. How many times I'd lain tucked up in my warm, cosy bed on a foul winter's night, in that glorious half-sleep, hearing the names called out, followed by forecasts of severe gales and squally showers in wild, barren places called Malin and Fair Isle. I'd imagine bearded old sea dogs in sou'westers and oilskins gathered rapt and wide-eyed around crackling boat radios, saying: 'Best we call it a night, wee Hamish, there's a fearful storm bruin.'

But somehow, it was always Cromarty that I'd wait for most eagerly, and I've no idea why. I always look out for St Mirren's results as well. And I've no idea about that either. I don't even know where it is.

The Cromarty–Nigg car ferry is the last surviving ferry across the firth and what used to be the main route north for kings. Hence its name: King's Ferry. The traffic was backed up on the quayside, and as the Cromarty Rose bounced and bucked towards us, I could see why. It is the smallest car ferry in Britain, with one ramp for on and off, room for two cars only, and on its deck a little turntable for swivelling them around at the other end. As the round trip took 30 minutes including loading, I estimated some of the cars waiting would be there for four hours. But people seemed happy to sit in the sunshine, eyes closed, fingers thrumming to the tunes from their radios.

The crewman called me on first. That's another great thing about bicycles and ferries. How very civilised. We set sail. There was no safety announcement about what to do in the event of the boat starting to sink. I liked that. I mean, you're on a boat. It starts to sink. You know it's sinking because there's a loud alarm going off and water up to your knees. What do you think you'd do? Play another round of deck quoits, perhaps, or do a routine from *South Pacific*? I'm guessing you'd jump into the lifeboat.

We chugged out into the middle of the channel, past the North and South Sutors, the giant stacks that stand sentinel over the firth's entrance. Beyond the firth, the monster hills of the Highlands proper loomed.

I got a text message. It was from a woman called Kendal. She'd read about my trip in the *Observer* and had contacted me via the newspaper. Her dad, Jack Allen, was also riding around the coast of Britain, but clockwise. He'd set off from Liverpool and was just two days away from John O'Groats. I was really looking forward to meeting up with Jack, exchanging yarns, comparing experiences of riding the coast road. It seemed fortuitous that we would cross paths at John O'Groats, such an important place in British long-distance, self-powered journeying.

I texted Kendal, said I'd try and make it to meet Jack. By my reckoning, I had about 100 miles still to go but already the shadows on the road were growing longer. A good day's riding tomorrow should see me make it to the north-east tip of Britain but, looking up at the hills in the distance, it would be a hard day in the saddle.

I sidled up to the first mate, having a cigarette in the bow.

'Yet another point on the Shipping Forecast I've been to,' I said.

'The what?'

'Shipping Forecast. Cromarty. You know.'

'No.'

'On the radio.'

'I don't listen to the radio.'

'Oh.'

Those winter London nights would never be quite the same again.

I joined the main A9. I'd had a look at the map and it seemed that there was no option if I was to carry on following the coast. The sheer scale of the mountains inland and the barren interior meant that there wasn't much scope or call for minor roads. Unfortunately, this also meant that everything heading north was on the A9, and it was hideously busy, the worst kind of road for cyclists – great scenery, but with one lane each way of heavy traffic, squeezing past, I was far too terrified to survey it.

This was also the first time my journey had converged with the main route taken by those doing the Land's End to John O'Groats ride (Lejog or Jogle for acronym lovers) and I wondered how long it would be before I saw one.

Twenty seconds later, two young men in Lycra and charity shirts swooshed past me. 'Keep going,' they said. 'Nearly there.'

'No. I'm not doing the…' but they were gone before I could finish my sentence.

Coming in the opposite direction was a couple on a tandem, with purple balloons tied to their machine. 'Keep going,' they both said.

It was early July now, the peak season for Jogles and Lejogs. In most lay-bys was a support van tending to end-to-enders, decorated with sponsors' and charities' names, riders lying prostrate on the ground having their legs massaged. At regular intervals, in both directions, I saw walkers lugging huge backpacks, groups of walkers dressed as the Village People, groups of men on vintage motorcycles, men and women on Harleys, solo cyclists in skinsuits and aero helmets tucked low on tri-bars, cyclists in great packs, a Model T Ford festooned with Lejog stickers, recumbents, and a man in a pink tutu. It was quite the party, like some weird pilgrimage crossed with a Pride parade.

'Keep going,' they all shouted.

I gave up trying to explain and in the end just opted for 'Great. Thanks,' and returning the thumbs up. But I felt like a terrible fraud.

The fraud feeling was accompanied by something else. I had become used to being the novelty act, the laden loner pedalling through the landscape, the recipient of smiles and waves and friendly questions. In my shallow way, I quite liked that. And now I was just part of the crowd, unremarkable compared to the people doing it faster, madder, better. It felt a bit like I was mediocre me again, back in the rat race, surrounded by people with whom I always felt I should be competing. I didn't like the feeling at all.

At Dornoch Bridge, I passed a sign saying 'John O'Groats 85 miles'. Even though the north-east tip of the British mainland was only about a third of the way of my journey, I still felt a small lump in my throat. It would be the first major milestone, the northern edge of the island. From there I would have to head west and then, not long afterwards, south. There were still many, many miles to go but, as any schoolboy knows, it's all downhill from Scotland.

I camped for the night in Brora, in a field full of rabbits, and set off early the next day to cover the 65 miles to John O'Groats.

After Helmsdale, the scenery became more dramatic, with ravines and steep cliffs and summits hidden by cloud as the road followed a long, relentless climb to a high plateau, with spectacular views over the wild North Sea from the Ord of Caithness. Even the engineers who'd built the railway line from Inverness to Wick gave up on the impossibilities of taming the coast here and took their track inland seeking valley floors.

At Berridale, the road plunged down into a deep ravine, then steeply up onto bleak moorland, freezing cold and shrouded in a thick, milky fog, from which trucks would burst and cyclists would emerge wraith-like. 'Keep going...'

I was having a bad-energy day, a familiar experience for any cyclist. I'd eaten enough, I'd slept well, I could not have had more inspiring scenery to pedal through. Yet my legs were dead weights, my heart heavy. It was just one of those days when you have to remind yourself to turn the pedals, count the strokes if necessary. It was the first day since leaving London that cycling had felt like a chore.

At a croft by the side of the road on a cliff-top I pulled over and asked the farmer if I could fill my water bottles.

'If you were on a motorbike, I'd tell you to fuck off,' he said, apropos of nothing.

At that moment a group of motorcyclists roared past.

'Fuckers!' the farmer screamed at them, shaking his fist. 'Would ya look at them bastards.'

He loved cyclists, he said, would always allow them to sleep in his field for free. But motorcyclists? Never.

'Why?' I asked.

'Why?'

Another biker came past. 'Fucker!' the farmer yelled after him. 'That's why,' he said pointing after the biker. But that was the closest I got to an explanation.

I rode through Wick and then across exposed wild and barren moorland, where purple heather and delicate little yellow flowers danced in the sharp onshore wind. The road undulated up and down and I had to count my pedal strokes just to get up the climbs. Finally, at the top of a rise, I looked down over the coastal plain where mainland Britain abruptly ended: a scattering of whitewashed cottages in a flat, dreary landscape clinging to the edge of the Pent-land Firth, with the Orkney Islands and the waters of Fair Isle (another one chalked off the Shipping Forecast) beyond. It really felt like the very edge of the world.

I stood there surveying that scene trying to work out why I felt so low. It didn't make much sense. I'd just ridden 1,600 miles from my front door in London to the very top of the island. Soon I would be turning west, then south and, eventually, east again to ride back to my front door. Perhaps it was because John O'Groats had been the first target, and now there it was. It was a staging post, sure, but it was also an ending and, as I was beginning to understand, I have always found endings painful and difficult. Maybe I was just still feeling the effects of the storm in Inverness when I'd been soaked to the bone for a few hours. More likely it was just down to the fact that with life, as with the road, there were ups and there were downs, and there wasn't much to be done but keep on pedalling.

I rolled down the final hill. Perhaps when you're feeling a bit under the weather, John O'Groats is not the best place for you. You might be forgiven for thinking that Groats was the Norse word for shithole, seeing as the place consisted only of a few unappealing-looking guesthouses, a coffee shop, a closed-down pub and loads of cyclists wandering around wearing a simultaneous look of euphoria and disappointment. But in fact the place got its name from a Dutchman, Jan de Groot, who'd established a ferry link with Orkney in 1496.

There was the famous signpost, of course, next to which you could have your picture taken for £9.50 by a man whose spectacular grumpiness suggested that in snapping giddy end-to-enders who'd dreamed for months of seeing that sign, he'd not quite found his ideal vocation.

I thought I'd beat the system and save myself some money by waiting until he closed and then getting someone to snap me with my camera. But, wise to such tricks, at 5.30 p.m. he just took down the sign and locked it away in a shed.

I pitched my tent on a campsite overlooking the Pentland Firth. It was full of bicycles: singles, tandems, recumbents. It was easy to spot the people who'd just finished. They were drinking cans of beer and grilling great slabs of meat on barbecues, laughing expansively, swapping tales of the trip. Those setting off next day busied themselves with their bikes, and sat around outside their tents pensively.

I walked up the road in search of some food. I found a pub full of spectacularly pissed motorcyclists. I ordered bangers and mash and took it outside to the beer garden. A biker with a grey goatee beard introduced himself as Jesus. He seemed like a nice man, as you might expect, but soon after saying hello he fell off his chair and never got up again. His girlfriend, who never told me her name, explained how they'd been up solid for three days and nights at a heavy metal music festival being held in a nearby barn.

'We're fucked,' she said.

'Nice shirt,' a young man said to me. He was dressed as a Playboy bunny, his testicles bulging through his white Y-fronts underneath his black leotard. He was with a group of friends from Thurso who'd come to John O'Groats for a stag weekend. They were all dressed as Playboy bunnies.

'Where'd you get it?'

'Not sure.'

We both sat there for a few minutes, saying nothing. Jesus was now snoring on the floor.

'Nice shirt,' the young man said again, and reeled back off to join his friends.

I headed back to the campsite. The weather was now what they call in these parts dreich, a drizzle of low cloud reducing visibility to a few yards, and the temperature had dropped significantly. I climbed into my tent, the outside soaked, and lay there awake for an hour, maybe more, in the perpetual twilight of a northern Scottish summer's night. In the distance I could hear what sounded like a man screaming in pain accompanied by electric guitars. I hoped Jesus had risen to enjoy it. From somewhere closer came the elegiac moan of a foghorn.

'Mike?' a voice called. 'Is that you?'

I was packing away my tent. I turned around to see a beaming, mischievous grin emerging from under a peaked cycling cap.

'Jack,' he said, holding out his hand. 'Jack Allen. I believe my daughter's been in touch with you.'

We went for breakfast at the coffee shop and ordered bacon butties. I asked Jack what had inspired him to ride around the British coast.

'Mostly to do with my daughter, Kendal,' he said. 'She worries about me when I'm abroad, you see. So instead of going off cycling for six months in South America or Alaska, like I do most years, this time I said I'd bike round Britain, so she can keep an eye on me.'

Lest anybody should think that Kendal sounds like the over-protective kind, I should explain that Jack was 74 years old.

A former plumber from Stoke-on-Trent, he told me how his taste for adventure had started after his divorce 25 years earlier. Since retirement, there'd been no stopping him. He fired off anec-dotes from his road trips: the bears in Alaska around his tent; the fantastic scenery in New Zealand's South Island; the scrapes he'd got into in Mexico. And after every story, he'd remove his cap and scratch his head as if in wonder at the world and everything it had to offer.

'If I'm in London, on a bus or the Tube, I can get so lonely in a crowd: all them people and nobody will talk to you. But in the wilderness I can be totally happy. I do like people, but if you can learn to be on your own – now that's the real secret to happiness.'

I asked him how his trip had been so far since he set off from Liverpool.

'What a country we've got, eh? Especially Scotland. My God! You're in for a treat on the West Coast. How about the ride up from London? What's that like?'

I told him about some of the highlights, where he could find good bike shops, decent campsites. I also told him that the hills hadn't been too bad. He reciprocated in kind. And even though I knew that the road I would take around the rest of the High-lands went through some of Britain's most mountainous terrain, he dismissed it as being 'just a bit lumpy'. This followed the unwritten rule of cycle touring: you must always understate the severity of hills.

We finished two bacon sandwiches each and walked outside. We lifted up each other's bikes. This is another unwritten rule, checking out the weight, like a bizarre courtship ritual or two dogs sniffing each other. If anything, Jack's load was heavier than mine and, coupled with the fact that his knees were 28 years older, I felt reassured by that.

I wanted to spend more time with Jack and suggested we ride together to Duncansby Head, about a mile and a half away, the true top right-hand corner of mainland Britain.

I was soon puffing up a steep hill in my grovel gear. Jack was pedalling effortlessly. 'I've got three gears I'm not using if you'd like to borrow one,' he said, winking. 'And you, such a young 'un.'

Jack gave me a friendly lecture about not wearing my helmet. I tried to explain the freedom thing, but he didn't look convinced.

As we rode, I asked him about his seemingly unquenchable passion for the road. 'I love me little tent, cost me twenty pounds, and my blow-up mattress, more than I love me own bed. They're like friends,' he said. 'The real excitement for me is not knowing each day where I'm going to end up. This is all a total pleasure for me, makes me so happy to be alive.' I felt so in awe of this man, at his infectious enthusiasm for everything life had to offer – 'people are great; so friendly', 'beans, rice pudding and custard. A feast for three quid!', 'it came down in buckets the other day. I love cycling in the rain!' – that I just grinned at him like a star-struck fan.

But my admiration for Jack had a selfish element. I'd read a few years earlier about research that had concluded that, in terms of happiness, life tends to follow a U-shape. We start off full of youthful brio and optimism and gradually, as we progress through the first half of life, lose much of that until, roughly in our mid-forties, we are at the bottom of the U. Given a prevailing wind, enough money to live on and decent physical health, people in the second half of life reported getting happier and happier again.

It was a report that I'd found myself thinking back to frequently. Certainly, for myself and many of my friends, mostly in our mid-forties, a sense of ennui and lassitude seemed to have been gradually creeping up on us during this past decade. It wasn't just connected to the physical implications of ageing, but the jadedness that accompanied it. More terrifying was the thought that maybe this was it: life not as a U-shape but a line running down from left to right. That's more or less how I'd felt about life before setting off from London.

And yet here was Jack, as sprightly as a teenager, eyes, like 67-year-old Craig's back in Findhorn, or 80-year-old Bill Scott's in

Tynemouth, burning with the light of a child, engaged with the world. What was that? Luck? Genetics? Whatever it was, he gave me hope for the future, did Jack.

We propped our bikes against the fence by the lighthouse at Duncansby Head and walked, joking and pushing each other like a couple of schoolboys, across fields of wild thyme, purple butterwort and pink thrift, and along the top of the pastry-cutter cliffs. We reached the end of the path and looked out to the extraordinary rock formations and giant sea stacks, shaped like witches' hats, thousands of seabirds encircling them.

'Wow,' I said.

'Makes you glad to be alive, eh?' said Jack.

After a couple of hours, it was time to part.

'We're like ships passing in the night,' I said.

'Yes, hardships,' said Jack, laughing.

At the junction, where one road went due south and the other due west, we hugged.

'See you in the West Country in a couple of months,' I said.

'The way you cycle, I'll probably have finished by the time you get to Liverpool,' he said, and winked for one last time, his whole face creasing.

'Cheeky bugger.'

'Safe cycling, Mike. Be good.'

And with that, I watched him pedal off, that lovely man, heading into the unknown and adventures anew. I stood there watching him, getting smaller and smaller, until he disappeared over the brow of a hill. And standing there, on my own once more, thinking about the thousands of miles of road ahead, I felt, for the first time on that trip, quite lonely.

Chapter 12

'I never want to abandon my bike. I see my grandfather, now in his seventies and riding around everywhere. To me that is beautiful. And the bike must always remain a part of my life.'

Stephen Roche, Irish winner of the 1987 Tour de France
and Giro d'Italia

The dark mood had passed next day as I flew along the roof of Britain with a brisk easterly tailwind, past the Castle of Mey and the dome of Dounreay nuclear power station, and then into Sutherland, where the land passed from flat to seriously buckled once more, all magnificently bleak moorland with barely a house or car to be seen.

The road ran right next to the sea, the coastline staggering in its wild beauty, with fabulous rock arches and golden sand beaches in sheltered bays with not a soul on them.

In Bettyhill, high above Torrisdale Bay, with a wide deserted beach pounded by breakers that was so beautiful it defied belief, I went into a pub for some food. It was 11 a.m., and the only other two occupants of the room were an old man swaying on a stool at the bar, spectacularly drunk and talking to himself, about what I had no idea, and a middle-aged woman sitting at one of the tables, eating egg and chips.

I picked up a menu. There was chips, egg and chips, and double egg and chips. I ordered double egg and chips, and extra chips, naturally.

'Hello,' I said to the woman.

'Hello,' she said back, in a strong Midlands accent.

'Long way from home?'

'As far as possible.'

'Oh?'

She was straight into it. 'Gave him a second chance. But it was a mistake.'

'Sorry.'

'Had to get away.'

'Right.'

'It was hard giving away all my furniture, everything, but it's so expensive to store and I didn't need it. People here have been very kind. Given me all kinds of stuff.'

My food arrived. I tucked in. The woman carried on talking in staccato bursts. 'He' was alluded to a few times, but she always held back from going into details, as if the hard-won physical distance, the hundreds of miles and the mountains that separated her from 'him', might be breached if she brought 'him' into the room.

She'd travelled in the US – 'Walked everywhere. People thought I was mad' – and she'd recently done a TEFL course, in Edinburgh. She was thinking of going to Africa to teach, or the Far East, for a fresh start.

'I like to keep moving,' she said. 'I always feel alive when I'm moving, you know.' There was something in her narrative that seemed very familiar.

'You've certainly got as far away as you can in this country,' I said.

'I'd go to the moon if I could.'

I left the pub and followed the single-track road, up and down the Sutherland hills, glimpsing, occasionally, in the far distance, the silver track threading its serpentine way between the peaks and across the carpet of green and purple, the scudding clouds dragging ever-changing shapes across the ground. And, still, there was barely a sign that humans ever came here: no buildings, no power lines, no vapour trails. There was just silence. Immense silence.

The road emerged high above the magnificent Kyle of Tongue and I freewheeled down the steep slope. After crossing the causeway I turned right, following a narrow road alongside the inlet to the tiny village of Talmine; there, at the bottom of a near-vertical track and right on the beach, I found a deserted little campsite, where a sign said £7 a night. I went over to a woman who was chopping down nettles with a scythe, and gave her a tenner. She gave me back £8. I pointed to the sign.

There was a beat. The woman looked at me. This was something I'd noticed about people in the Highlands. There were often pauses in conversation, as if the peace and pace of life had slowed everything down.

'Och, don't worry about the sign,' she said.

After pitching my tent, I rode back up the steep hill, into Talmine, and went into the only pub for a pint and something to eat. At the bar, a group of locals were singing Rod Stewart numbers. Badly.

As I stood at the bar, I was bombarded with questions. Where are ye from? What are ye doing? Will ye have another? Och, go on. Drinking alone is not an option in rural Scotland. Every pub feels like your fantasy local. Like the Queen Vic but without the aggro.

A man with a Yorkshire accent introduced himself as Tony. He looked and sounded like Brian Glover. 'And this is my wife, Karen,' he said, pointing to the woman next to him.

Tony asked what I was doing in Talmine. I told him about the ride.

'For charity?' he asked.

'Just for the hell of it.'

'Fantastic. When I were a boy in Leeds, I used to dream about Scotland, read all about it. Came here when I were 20 for the first time. Cycled round it. Now we're coming here to live.'

Tony, now 40, explained how he and Karen were building a house in Talmine. 'Have you ever seen anywhere so beautiful?' he said.

Tony said he hated cities, but especially London. 'How do you live there? Nobody talks to each other. It's not human. Pint?'

A woman breezed past, balancing four plates of food.

'This man's cycling round the British coast,' Tony said to her.

'Och, you'll be needin' a good breakfast tomorrow, then,' she said. 'Come on up. It'll be on us.'

The singing started up again. 'Flower of Scotland' this time. I was stuck in a round with four or five of the men now. Everybody looked like they were there for the duration. I doubted that there was such a thing as a closing time in such a remote place to save me. It was going to get messy, but after the sixth pint, I ceased caring.

'Have ye met the midges yet?' asked one man.

I said that I hadn't.

'Wee bastards,' said another.

'Awful fierce on the West Coast.'

'Aye, kill one and a million come te tha funeral.'

'People ha threw themselves offa cliffs to escape.'

'Ye need to git yourself some of that cream.'

'That shite dinna work.'

'Pint?'

'They reckon the SAS use it. Fuck knows what's in it if it'll keep those wee bastards away.'

'Aye, fella serves it in the shop just over by.'

'Yous're all talkin' shite. Nothing works on the fuckers.'

'And the cleggies?' asked one.

'Cleggies?'

'Aye. Flies. Big biting bastards. You'll be meeting them soon enough.'

'Pint?' the landlord asked, on the house.

'Aye,' I said. It was all I could say by now.

'Will you be going up to Cape Wrath?' the landlord asked.

'Aye,' I said.

'Well tell the ferryman he's a useless, lazy bastard from us.'

'Aye. Useless,' came the chorus, then laughing.

'Lovely man all the same,' said one.

'Aye,' came the chorus.

'He keeps his change in a tin fulla sea water so the coins are rotten,' one said. 'When he goes to offer it to passengers, they always say "Dinnie botha. You can keep it."'

More laughter.

'Aye. He's a character alreet.'

The stories started coming thick and fast: about the late, legendary Christy, 'the George Best of Talmine', who came back into the pub ashen-faced one night after meeting a talking horse, followed by the two men who'd been hiding behind the wall ('It even knew my name,' he'd said); about the youth who'd been caught in flagrante with a cow; the local scandals kept coming.

I looked at my watch. It was 2 a.m.

'Will you have a wee dram?' the landlord asked. 'Nightcap. On me. Whatever you want.' I looked up at the wall of Scotch. I knew it was a terrible idea.

'Aye,' I said.

Shortly afterwards, somebody started singing 'Maggie May'. I'm pretty sure it was me.

*

With its low, white inner, my tiny tent could sometimes feel like the inside of a coffin. And some mornings more than others. This was one of those mornings. Lying there, head thumping, I wasn't sure where I was, or even whether I was alive or dead. I could hear waves breaking, and the relentless splatter of rain on the outside of the tent, so if I was dead, I was at least in a place that was wet and not hot. That was a good start.

As hangover cures go, a bike ride across bleak moorlands and up and down mountains in the pouring rain, with howling wind making Hammer Horror sound-effect noises, is not the best. The only hazards I had to worry about were the sheep all over the road and the improbably huge cleggies, whose name I now knew, and who seemed to find gnawing away at the flesh of a hungover man lumbering up hills, unable to outrun them nor dare to remove his hands from the bars to swat them, too good to resist.

But by the time I'd cycled the 10 miles to Loch Eriboll, with the peak of Foinavan towering above it, a strip of cloud snagged on its summit, I was at least beginning to feel human again. But then again, the scenery in this part of Scotland, one of the least populated areas of Europe, could not fail to be restorative.

Eriboll, a deep-sea loch running 10 miles inland, hunkering under a ceiling of low cloud, lay before me like a pool of mercury. In the seventeenth century, the Brahan Seer, a sort of Scottish Nostradamus, had prophesied that Loch Eriboll would be a place where a conflict would one day end. In 1945, German U-boats had come into the loch to surrender at the end of the Second World War. It's not recorded whether Mr Seer had managed to get himself down to Ladbrokes.

Servicemen based here during the war to protect the convoys passing through the Pentland Firth had nicknamed it Loch 'Orrible. And as I followed the road around its shores on that cold, wet, blustery July day, passing ancient derelict crofts abandoned during the Highland clearances, peat cuttings piled up like Jenga stacks, I shuddered to imagine what those servicemen must have endured in the thick of a harsh Scottish winter.

In Durness, a sign pointed off to the John Lennon Memorial Garden, which I followed. I found myself in a beautiful little patch of wild flowers and driftwood backed by brooding hills. A weather-battered sign informed me that Lennon, whose aunt had married a local man, had spent happy childhood holidays in Durness. In the song 'In My Life' from the *Rubber Soul* album, Lennon reflected on places and people that he loved: one of the places was Durness, and some of the people the family and friends he had there. Next to the sign were three simple stones, carved with some of the lyrics.

John had also been a bit of a bike nut, and I remembered reading about him talking about getting his first bicycle. 'I lived for that bike,' he'd said. 'Most kids left their bike in the backyard at night. Not me. I insisted on taking mine indoors and the first night I even kept it in my bed.'

It had been a relief to read that, to realise that I had not been the only child to take his beloved first bike to bed with him.

But the sad truth is, I still do. At home, the Ridgeback, the steel workhorse, lives in the shed, but it has a love rival: for I also have a Colnago C50, a black carbon-fibre Italian dream thoroughbred racing bike. It lives in my bedroom between rides, though the fact that I don't sleep with my arms draped around it should be seen as progress of a kind. To me, it is as exquisite as anything by Rodin or Michelangelo, and I can find myself staring at it for ages, transfixed by its beauty and its graceful lines. I run my hands gently along the tubes, shaped in cross section like a clover leaf, or more accurately, the company's Ace of Clubs logo, all lovingly hand-crafted at Colnago's factory in Cambiago, just outside Milan. And I realise that these are things probably best kept to oneself on a first date.

It cost the same as a small family car, would probably snap in two if it was asked to carry half the weight the Ridgeback does, and any half-decent racing cyclist would beat me on it if he or she were riding a butcher's bike. But that's not really the point of owning a beautiful bicycle. For not only does having one somehow connect you to the passion of the artisans who produced it, and to the heroic exploits of the supermen who've powered those machines to racing glory over the years, the Colnago is the only truly great work of art that I'm ever likely to be able to afford. And I get to ride it. Try riding the statue of David and you'd have some explaining to do.

*

I stocked up on supplies at the local shop in Durness. In my fuddled state leaving Talmine that morning, I'd forgotten to get some of the midge cream that the guys in the pub had recommended. I asked the woman behind the counter about it.

'Aye, we've got some just there.'

I followed her finger. She was pointing at a display of a moisturiser called Skin So Soft, by Avon.

'Does it work?'

'Only if you put so much on that the wee beasties slip off ye,' she said. 'But even if it disney, at least you'll be looking a lot younger.'

I grabbed a bottle, and then some bread and cheese for my dinner that night. Where I was going there would be no restaurants. Or pubs. My liver was happy about that.

I pedalled two miles out of Durness and hid out of the rain in a little bus-stop-like shelter with around half a dozen others. After about 20 minutes, a tiny boat with a small half cabin came into view.

The ferryman tied off and came up the steep stone jetty. I had my message to deliver from the locals in Talmine. But I bottled it, unsure as to how wise it would be to call a complete stranger a 'lazy, useless bastard' apropos of nothing in front of a bunch of people. Especially as without him I wouldn't be able to get across the Kyle of Durness and onto the track that leads to Cape Wrath – the only way to get to the north-western-most tip of the British mainland. Besides, I had a sneaking suspicion that by delivering my message, I would become part of the rich barroom story collection that would in future run from talking horses to cow-shagging youths to the cyclist that got his bike thrown overboard from the Durness ferry.

The rest of the passengers clambered into the tiny boat. The ferryman took my panniers and tent bag and carried them down the slipway. I followed, with my bike, slipping and sliding on the algae. The passengers were wedged in like sardines, the boat literally packed to the gunwales. But the ferryman insisted there was room, and I climbed on and squeezed my ample arse between a nice elderly Japanese couple, who smiled at me politely and nodded their heads several times. Once I was seated, the ferryman handed me the bike, which, lacking anywhere else to put it, I had to wear around my neck, the nice Japanese couple taking a wheel each in their laps. They were too polite to say anything and just nodded. My bags were loaded and distributed among the rest of the passengers, who all of a sudden looked like Dunkirk evacuees.

And thus we cast off into the choppy Kyle of Durness to tango between its shifting sand bars, me with my bicycle necklace, the Japanese couple pinned under its wheels, the other passengers buried under all my luggage as the ferryman collected the fares and was told to keep the change, seeing as the coins he was offering in return looked as if they'd been marinating in sewage. 'Plenty of Guinness for me tonight,' he said, as the little boat rolled and pitched alarmingly across the kyle. 'Glug, glug, glug.' And he held an imaginary glass to his lips and cocked his wrist.

Once across, we all disembarked and the other passengers piled into the waiting minibus that would carry them the 11 miles to the lighthouse at Cape Wrath. The Ministry of Defence has owned the entire 207-square kilometre cape since the early twentieth century and uses it as a bombing range. Nobody lives there full-time. When there's no bombing, they allow the minibus to run – unless you bring a bike, it's the only way to get to Cape Wrath.

I put the luggage back on my bike and set off towards the end of the world, climbing a steep, slippery slope onto the moorland with wide views over lonely, lovely Balnakeil Bay.

The single-track road had obviously taken more than a few direct hits over the years and seen a few battle tanks rumble along it, for it was truly terrible, rutted and pockmarked, the bike taking some sickening cracks, my arms and shoulders feeling like I was drilling the surface, not riding on it. I'd managed not to buckle a wheel since Berwick-upon-Tweed, and was suddenly struck with the likelihood, or otherwise, of finding a bicycle repair shop in this sparsely populated part of the world.

But despite the comedy road, I was excited about riding towards Cape Wrath. Is there a more evocative name in Britain? I'd been slightly disappointed to learn from a fellow ferry passenger that the name refers not to the fury of the seas that pound the cliffs, but is from the Norse word *hvarf*, meaning turning place, the point where Viking warships used to turn east for home or south to the Hebrides. But still, it was a place I'd long looked at on maps of Britain and wondered what such a remote, wild place might look like.

And there I was, cycling alone though its majestic bleakness, that desolate wasteland, only a few living sheep and countless bleached bones, the landscape treeless, pockmarked with little oily burns that sparkled like mirrors. Beyond the land, just infinite sea and sky. The Parbh, as the land is known, was once home to vast numbers of wolves, and it wouldn't have surprised me in the least to hear a distant howl.

I've been lucky enough to have travelled to some of the remotest places on earth – the great Arabian Empty Quarter, the Alaskan wilderness, Siberia. All those places have an ineluctable sense of their own isolation; it defines them. You travel in those empty places and feel like the first human ever to set foot there, or the first visitor after a terrible catastrophe. Cape Wrath felt like that to me.

The last minibus bringing people back from the cape passed me, and then I was alone. I had the thought that if I fell off my bike and broke a leg, or started bleeding heavily, I would probably die: nobody would know; nobody was expecting me; there was no phone signal. The thought, far from making me frightened, just made me smile, for it felt like I was truly living.

The wind picked up. After about an hour, I climbed a final hill, turned a final bend, and there it was: 3,000 miles east of America and south of nowhere, the famous lighthouse, built in 1828 by Robert Stevenson, grandfather of Robert Louis, sitting atop some of the highest cliffs in Britain, where two seas collide. It was one of the most spectacular places I had ever seen. The light was automated in 1998, operated remotely, like all lighthouses in Britain now, by computer from Edinburgh. So who was the man coming out to greet me, followed by six barking spaniels? It would appear that somebody did live on the cape. I felt a pang of disappointment that I was not alone.

'Hello,' the man said. 'Don't mind them. They won't bite.'

His name was John, and he'd been living at the cape for two years full-time, and eight years part-time before that, renovating the lighthouse's outbuildings and turning them into a little café for the minibus visitors. It had opened for the first time earlier that year.

'Go and put your tent up and come over by for a wee cuppa tea,' he said.

I pushed my bike into a field. The wind was very strong now, blowing in staccato bursts, so walking had to be done in timed intervals. Alongside one edge of the field was a thick wall standing 15 feet high, made from stones each the size of a coffin. In places the wall had been flattened, by shelling or the wind I knew not, but I suspected the latter. And as tempting as it was to tuck into its lee, I measured about 20 feet from its base and pitched there.

I met John in the little café, The Ozone. 'In winter, you can smell the ozone up here,' he said. 'It comes from the Arctic. Hence the name.' The café was basic, a few plastic tables and a serving hatch, beyond which were shelves of crisps and chocolate bars, soft drinks and a couple of urns for tea and coffee.

'We've no mains water or toilets, and the power comes from a small generator,' said John. 'So we're limited as to what we can offer.'

John poured the tea and dropped a couple of Kit Kats on the table. The six spaniels sat around John in a semi-circle.

John told me how he and his wife Katherine had bought the building 10 years ago for £25 on a 25-year lease. They'd been living in Glasgow at the time, where he'd manufactured window blinds, but he'd long had a dream of doing up a building at risk, preferably one that was remote. So when the lighthouse at Cape Wrath came up, it was too good to pass up.

'The windows and doors and roofs were off. It was pretty derelict. We lived in Durness and travelled up daily to do the work. It's taken us 10 years to get it like this.'

He told me about the storms, about the 140mph winds that regularly rip the roof off, demolish the walls and send the dogs pitchpoling like tumbleweed.

I asked where Katherine was. John told me she was in Durness, where she worked. She spent three days a week at the lighthouse.

Did the isolation ever bother him? He looked at me as if I were simple.

'I sit here and watch the fin whales and dolphins cruise past. The deer come here at night to graze. I breathe what almost feels like pure oxygen. People come here on the minibus and walk around with their mobile phones held high, trying to get a signal. When they get back to the ferry within range, all their phones start bleeping and it's as if they breathe a collective sigh of relief. No, I wouldn't go back down the road again for anything.'

I went for a walk and sat at the edge of the world watching the kittiwakes and the fulmars and the razorbills. To the east I could see the Clo Mor Cliffs, great sandstone bluffs which, at 900 feet, are the very highest in Britain. From below me, in a cove, came the fearful crash of water colliding with rock, the spume carried on the wind to where I sat. 'On this dread Cape, so fatal to mariners...' Sir Walter Scott wrote in 1814. 'There the foam of the sea plays at longbowls with a huge collection of large stones, some of them a ton in weight, but which these fearful billows chuck up and down as a child tosses a ball.'

I climbed the steep hill behind the lighthouse and looked out on the vastness, 270 degrees of sea. It was like sitting in the gods at the theatre. It was late now, maybe 10 p.m., in the perpetual twilight of a northern Scottish summer night. The lighthouse light flickered into life, its beam sweeping across the ocean and then the hill, catching me in it.

The wind was violently strong, threatening to knock me over, the sea below me a maelstrom of whitecaps and churning water. A freighter battled north, its bow disappearing in the swells before popping up again. Ball cotton was flying around, creating a blizzard. A herd of red deer appeared in silhouette on the ridgeline. I don't think there had been a moment in my life when I had ever felt more at peace; yet the raw elemental intensity of the place was making me emotional to the point of tears.

Eventually, reluctantly, I staggered back to my tent and climbed inside. It was getting battered and I found myself clutching the ground with my fingers. In the morning, there'd be torn canvas and several of the guy lines would be ripped to shreds. But I just lay there, smiling, not wanting the night to end.

Chapter 13

*'I love the bicycle. I always have. I can think of no
sincere, decent human being, male or female, young
or old, saintly or sinful, who can resist the bicycle.'*
William Saroyan

The Sabbatarians were predicting the apocalypse. Dark forces were
going to descend on the Outer Hebrides. The archipelago had hitherto been spared the attentions and excesses of mainland evildoers,
but the start of Sunday ferries from Ullapool across the Minch to
Stornoway in a few days' time was, according to a man interviewed
in the local paper, going to unleash hell.

It was difficult to imagine, cycling across the barren, marshy
interior of northern Lewis, what kind of criminal mastermind would
be targeting the islands. International peat traffickers, perhaps?

The previous day, I'd cycled the 70 miles south from Cape
Wrath. The ride, through more gloriously bleak wilderness and then
through the rock-strew glens, dark, brooding lochs and the glow-
ering mist-covered peaks of the Assynt Mountains, had only intensified my spirits, soaring after the time spent with lovely John and
his spaniels at the cape.

The roads were quiet, buzzards as common as sparrows, the
dreich weather was keeping the cleggies off and all was right with
the world. The only problem I had was at the passing places on
the single-track roads, when I'd swing over to allow the car behind
to pass, then swing out after it had gone by, only to discover that
most vehicles in these parts were towing things – trailers full of
sheep peering out, mostly – into which I'd nearly collide, swerving
violently back to avoid them. The sheep tended to look uncon-
cerned with my ordeal. I guessed they had other more pressing
worries, like what awaited them at the other end of their journey.

I was heading south now for the first time on the trip and
although there were many miles left to cycle – the small matter of

the rest of Scotland, northern England, Wales, then south-west and southern England – the thought of hitting areas with lots of people in them didn't exactly fill me with joy. I felt like I could have quite happily cycled through that wilderness for the rest of my life.

Thus, when I got to the top of the last climb and looked down on Ullapool, nestling as pretty as a postcard at the head of Loch Broom, with the Isle of Lewis ferry sitting at the quayside, I knew straight away that I should go to the Outer Hebrides, another place I'd had no reason to visit before, but had long wanted to see. This was in part because it was the place adults of my youth used to use metaphorically as the edge of the world, as in 'blimey, it's like being in the Outer Hebrides' when they were in fact in the Lickey Hills just outside Birmingham. Much in the same way they'd talk about being sent to Coventry. This kind of thing was very confusing for children. The first time I went to Coventry, I was amazed that people were talking to each other.

This was one of the greatest thrills of my journey: the freedom to make snap decisions about where I'd be waking up tomorrow; the constantly shifting shape of the adventure. The only routine I seemed to have in my life was the turning of the pedals. That suited me just fine.

But before I could freewheel down the long hill, I had to take a moment to listen to my little shoulder-mounted twin sophists, the angel and the devil, engaged as they were in a heated debate about what did and did not constitute a ride around the British coastline.

'To adhere to the purity of the journey, you've got to stick to the mainland,' the one who, in a cartoon, would be wearing angel wings was saying.

'Screw that,' said the one with red horns. 'Hark at her! Purity of the journey! Who are you, the Dalai Lama? Anyway, who's counting? Norris McWhirter (younger readers may have to ask their parents)? This is Mike's trip. He's allowed to make it up as he goes along.'

I weighed it up. I had set off to cover every inch of the mainland coastline, but I'd blown that as early as day one in Essex with my reluctance to ride down every out-and-back. The horny fella was right in that nobody cared apart from me.

I thought about what lay ahead. There'd be many islands off the West Coast of Scotland that I could use as stepping stones, then, later, Anglesey and the Isle of Wight, and little islands such as Walney off Barrow-in-Furness and Portland in Dorset. I didn't really want to miss out any of them. Or, at least, I wanted to have the freedom to choose.

The devil was on the money this time. With me, I'm afraid to say, he usually tends to get his way.

And thus it was, after a brief stop in Stornoway to buy some sealant and a needle and thread to repair my Cape Wrath-ravaged tent, that I'd found myself riding across Lewis. If I'd had any slight regrets about the deviation from the original plan, the empty roads and vast skies kept them subdued.

I soon ran into a little local difficulty. My road atlas, gifted to me by that kind shopkeeper back in London's East End, had place names only in their Anglicised form. Now, the Outer Hebrides is a very strong Gaelic-speaking area, over 50 per cent of the population in the 2001 census spoke the language, so many of the road signs are in Gaelic. Navigating in a foreign country whose language you know nothing of is not so difficult when you're looking for Milan, where the simple addition of the letter O on a road sign would foil not even the most dim-witted. But when you're looking for, say, the Butt of Lewis, and the sign offers up Rubha Robhanais in one direction and Gearraidh na h-Aibhne in the other, would you know which way to go? Me neither.

Of course, things are further complicated by the fact that Gearraidh na h-Aibhne, in all likelihood, if it isn't indeed the Butt of Lewis, is pronounced Milton Keynes or somesuch, just as Steòrnabhagh is pronounced Stornoway and the Outer Hebrides becomes Na h-Eileanan a-Muigh.

In the end, I smartly deduced that 'na' probably meant 'of' and therefore Gearraidh na h-Aibhne was probably correct. It wasn't. Thus I never did get to the Butt of Lewis, but I did get to learn from a cyclist I met on the road that Gearraidh na h-Aibhne was pronounced Garynahine, and that he lived there, and that his name was Norman.

'And how do you spell that?' I asked.

'N-O-R-M-A-N,' he said.

We rode together down the rolling west coast of Eilean Leòdhais, or Lewis, through isolated crofting villages, and across treeless moors of blanket peat dotted with small grey lochs, the spine of huge mountains that divides Lewis and Harris – not separate islands at all but two halves of the same landmass, the third largest island in the British Isles after Ireland and Great Britain – rearing up in the distance. How could a landscape so spectacular and empty be in Britain, one of the most populous countries in Europe? I was pretty sure that if I asked Norman, I'd get the stock answer I'd got from all the other spectacular but empty places I'd cycled through: 'I know, but don't tell anybody.'

Occasionally, we'd pass a graveyard in the middle of nowhere, surrounded by a low stone wall, with tall and slender columns for graves, like chess-piece bishops.

I said goodbye to Norman, and followed a sign for the Callanish Standing Stones, thankfully in Gaelic and English, although Calanais wasn't a stretch, and cycled up a steep track to a little plateau upon which stood the 47 slabs of gneiss that make up the 4,000-year-old prehistoric site. It ranks in importance with Stonehenge but, in my mind, knocks spots off it, the stones standing sentinel over a steel-grey loch, with mountains behind it, as opposed to the A303. And there were none of the entry fees nor fences keeping you at a distance nor fast-food joints that have commercialised the Wiltshire site to such an extent that it surely cannot be long before actors playing druids will be posing for photos.

The Callanish stones are set out in a Celtic wheelcross, with a burial cairn at the centre. The central pillar casts its shadow along the entrance passage into the grave only at sunset on the days of the equinox. Yet nobody really knows for sure what Callanish was built for. And that, I thought, as I wandered alone among the stones, all primal and inexplicable, running my hands over them and not in the least bit tempted to graffiti or damage them, was as I hoped it would remain, for some things should remain a mystery.

I followed a dead-end road for 20 miles, the climbs brutal, trying to ignore the voice in my head that was screaming 'What's the point, when you've got to come all the way back?' A huge red stag, with the biggest set of antlers I've ever seen, stood on a rocky outcrop near the side of the road and watched me ride past. The voice was quiet after that.

At the end of the road, I found an empty field full of yellow
wildflowers, right next to the vast expanse of Uig Sands, that advertised itself as a campsite but, with its lack of any facilities whatsoever,
should probably more accurately call itself a field. I walked across
towards the sands, hundreds of rabbits ghosting through the long
grass all around me, only their ears and white tails betraying their
movements, like I was being stalked in a horror movie that, thinking
about it, wouldn't be particularly scary. I pitched my tent and cycled
off to find someone to pay, eventually seeing an honesty box next
to a croft with a handwritten 'Camping £2' on it in red felt tip. I
was about to drop my money in it when I heard a voice.

'Hello, there!' it said, in that beautiful, soft Hebridean lilt, two
parts Scandinavian, one part Scottish.

I looked up to see an elderly man in a plaid shirt coming from
around the back of the croft and walking towards me. In a weird
optical illusion, when he was quite far away he looked tiny, but he
didn't get any bigger when he was standing next to me. In fact, he
was barely taller than my handlebars.

He introduced himself as Donald.

Behind him, through the window of his living room, I could
see a balloon on the ceiling with 100 written on it. I looked at
Donald. Then looked at the balloon again. I wanted to ask. But it
seemed beyond rude to accuse a man of being 100 years old if he
was nothing of the sort, even if he'd have had to stand on a box to
punch my lights out.

'How long have you lived here?' I asked.

There was a big pause, long enough to invite the thought that
maybe he hadn't heard me, then I remembered the pace of things
up here.

'All my leaf,' he said, eventually.

'And, er, how long would that be?'

Long pause.

'Seventy-two years noo.'

'So whose is that?' I asked pointing to the balloon.

Long pause. A corncrake amply filled the silence.

'Have ye time for a wee coffee?'

We sat in the kitchen. Donald made the drinks and plonked a
big plate of chocolate fingers in front of me. The polite guest in me

wanted to nibble away at one or two. The cyclist in me scoffed around a dozen in quick time.

'All that cycling meeks ya affa hungry, I'd say,' said Donald.

We sat there for a while in silence. I wasn't sure what, if anything, we were waiting for. The clock on the wall ticked loudly. The corncrake was still making its racket outside.

'How about those rabbits?' I said.

'Aye, tis like a plague this year.'

Another long silence.

'Can they climb?' asked Donald. 'Only I wouldne want them getting into my garden.'

'I don't know.'

'Oh.'

The clock ticked. The corncrake craked.

'Are ye done?' Donald said, pointing to the now empty plate.

'Aye.'

'Then come with me.'

We walked through a door into the next room. Sitting there in an armchair was Catherine, Donald's mother, the new centurion, eyes aflame.

'Mudda, this is Mike,' said Donald.

I'd never met anybody who was a hundred before.

'I feel like curtseying,' I said.

'Och, get awee,' Catherine said.

I noticed the telegram from the Queen, hanging from the wall.

I asked Catherine about her life. She'd never been off the island. She'd had five children, all of whom except Donald had moved away.

It was incredible to sit there looking at that remarkable woman and think about all the things that had happened in her lifetime: two world wars, the coming of electric light, the Russian Revolution, votes for women, the Internet, the sinking of the Titanic, nuclear bombs, men on the moon, the Great Depression, *Celebrity Love Island*.

'You must have seen many amazing changes in your time,' I said.

There was a pause, longer than usual. There was, after all, a lot to remember.

'Aye,' she replied, eventually. 'After the road opened, we didne have to take a boot to the doctor's.'

Another pause.

'And when the shop opened, we didne have to grow all our own fud.'

And it struck me then that change in the remotest part of one of Britain's most remote islands probably has a tempo all of its own.

The wind was ferocious the next day, a howling and a hollering. But it was coming from the north-east and I was heading south-west, so I couldn't have been happier. I went up the three-mile 10% climb to the pass between the peaks of Sgaoth Aird and An Cliseam, the archipelago's highest at 2,621 feet, as if it didn't exist. Even the cleggies couldn't catch me. Most of the little schools and municipal buildings I occasionally passed had small wind turbines attached to them, rotating so furiously that a few more and surely the entire island would take off and head out into the Atlantic.

I went to the public toilets at the bus station at Tarbert in North Harris. Inside the only toilet cubicle was also a shower. I'd not had a shower for three days, which is scuzzy, I know, but also wonderfully liberating. I stripped off, inserted my 50p and had a good lather. Right outside the window, somebody started playing the bagpipes.

The shower lasted five minutes, and so lovely was the combination of hot water, suds and the plaintive pipes that I put another 50p in the slot and went all over again. I emerged feeling reborn, glowing and happy, unlike the queue of people waiting to use the toilet with their legs crossed and the bus driver looking at me and tapping his watch.

I cycled across the narrow isthmus at Tarbert (Tarbert means isthmus in Gaelic, which explains why there are six towns of that name in Scotland) and into South Harris. As I hit the west coast of the island, the bleak, granite-strewn lunar landscape gave way to emerald machair grasslands, golden sands and turquoise waters, which gave it all the look of a golf course designed by the most benevolent of gods.

I rode for a while accompanied by a small, white owl, hunting in the daylight, that flew alongside me for fully 30 seconds or more before peeling off. Then, around the next corner, there was the golden expanse of Luskintyre Beach, sheltered and empty. I pulled on the brakes and stopped, just gazing in wonder, drinking it all in, unable to fully believe what I was seeing. The channel was drained and the flats were alive with squawking dunlin, redshank and lapwing. In the distance, the deep water of the sound was so blue it hurt my eyes, and beyond were the variegated gneiss hills of Taransay, their peaks flecked by quartzite and marble that sparkled in the sun so that they looked as if they were wearing tiaras. It was difficult to believe that anywhere so perfect could exist. This must be the Scotland that forms the dreamscapes of expats and exiles, sleeping fitfully in a tropical heat. I doubt there is a more beautiful spot on the planet, and I had it all to myself.

In Leverburgh, while waiting for the ferry to Berneray, I stepped onto the Butty Bus and ordered a black pudding and bacon roll. I liked to think that I had become a bit of a connoisseur in the arts of all things pig since I'd hit Scotland, and my hopes weren't exactly high for this offering from a van in a car park. Oh. My. Goodness. The black pudding, unctuous and gooey, dissolved on my tongue. The bacon, gammon thick, salted to perfection and rich with flavour, did the same. I almost cried. It was, without a shadow of a doubt, the most fantastic thing I'd ever eaten. But it also made me feel a little sad because, like flying in economy after you've experienced an upgrade, eating bacon and black pudding would never be the same again. I swore that if I ever got seriously rich, not only would I buy Dunnottar Castle, a ray gun and a white cat. I'd also chopper in my breakfast every day from that car park in Leverburgh.

Obviously, I ordered another.

'Good, huh?' said the man behind the counter.

'Hmmmmmssssssssyeeessshhh,' I said. My mouth was full, but there was no way I was going to let manners get in the way.

'The black pudding is from Stornoway, the best in the world. And the bacon is from North Uist. Bacon disne come any better than the stuff they produce there.'

I was trying to place the guy's accent. The odd word carried a Hebridean inflection, but I was guessing the Midlands somewhere.

'From Macclesfield,' he said. He used to be a long-distance lorry driver, taking boilers to Poole. He talked about his former life, the traffic jams, the constant sense of swimming against the tide, always being behind schedule. He shook his head as he was talking.

An old guy came onto the bus and the two of them chatted for a while as bacon sizzled on the grill. They talked about an upcoming cattle market, about the salmon expected off the Berneray boat, and about the first Sunday ferry.

'They're makin an affa fuss,' said the old man. 'Things change.'

'Been here three years now,' the man said to me after the old guy had wandered off.

'Ever miss England?' I asked.

The man looked out of the window towards the mountains and inhaled deeply.

'I'm going nowhere,' he said.

On through North Uist and across a five-mile causeway to Benbecula. I was still being blown south at turbo speed by the savage north-easterlies. Those lower Hebridean islands were gloriously flat, glorious from a cycling point of view that is, and largely inundated with water, criss-crossed as they are by a maze of lochs and vast mudflats, over which the road flies low on bridges and single-lane causeways like a join-the-dots puzzle.

On the mudflats stood stooped figures in silhouette digging for cockles, and as I passed by isolated crofts there would be a sharp aroma of burning peat. Almost all the outer isles use this free fuel, cut in spring and stacked to dry outside the houses until ready. The few trees around were stunted and bent in perpetuity.

South Uist looked much the same as North Uist, but the presence of a large roadside shrine to the Virgin Mary just over the causeway, and thereafter shrines every few miles, announced that I was leaving the predominantly Presbyterian northern isles, and entering the largely Roman Catholic southern isles.

I finally reached the tiny island of Barra, population 1,078, right at the southern end of the Outer Hebrides chain. Off the ferry, I headed north, looking for a place to wild camp, and came across an immense stretch of cockleshell strand that looked beyond perfect. Just as I was unloading my bike, a low droning noise in the distance grew louder and louder until a plane flew so low over my head that I was convinced it was about to crash. The plane proceeded to land smartly on the beach a few hundred yards from me. It was only then that I noticed the little control tower on the far side of the sands. I recalled seeing on TV a place in Scotland where the airport was on the beach, the only such airport in the world. Unfortunately, I hadn't recalled that it was in Barra.

I thought about the Darwin Awards, that collection of death by stupidity that celebrates the deceased's removal from the gene pool. 'Man killed by aeroplane after camping on runway' would have made a worthy addition.

So I headed south, around the island's 12-mile perimeter road, to the capital Castlebay, the first sight of which, as I approached it from the top of a steep hill, will stay long in my memory, with the fifteenth-century Kisimul Castle on a rock in the middle of the bay. The planning meeting to decide on a name for the town must have been a very short one.

I stopped off at the little supermarket and bought some food and a bottle of wine for the evening. In front of me in the queue, two elderly women were discussing the first Sunday ferry, due to depart from Ullapool for Stornoway the day after.

'I hear that the boot's broken doon,' said the one. 'They're having ta send a replacement up from Arran.'

'Aye,' said her friend. 'The Lord surely works in mysterious ways.'

I asked the woman behind the till if she knew a good spot to wild camp.

'People camp doon by the harbour there,' she said. 'Naybody'll mind. Tis a canny spot.'

And indeed it was. There were three or four tents already pitched on the patch of rough grass at the bottom of the cliffs, but I didn't mind sharing, seeing as how beautiful the view was.

I poured some wine into my plastic beaker and lay there as the sun disappeared behind me, setting the sea on fire, Kisimul Castle in dramatic silhouette right in front of me, the Caledonian MacBrayne ferry slipping quietly past it on its five-hour voyage across the Sea of the Hebrides to Oban. The wind had died down now, and all was still and perfect. I'd even seen that the forecast for tomorrow was for south-westerlies, meaning a tailwind back up the island chain to Lochmaddy where I'd catch the ferry to Skye. Could I have been any more blessed? I felt that the gods were smiling down on me and thanked them for their benevolence. The gods were actually scowling back down at me and saying: 'Right, let's screw this smug bastard over.'

'Great place to camp,' said a man, of late middle age, out walking with a woman I took to be his wife and a collie.

'Yes, isn't it,' I replied. 'What a view.'

'How would you like it if I camped in your garden?' he said. I had apparently missed the ironic tenor in his opening remark.

I looked at his wife. She was quite a bit younger than him. She was rolling her eyes at the man as if she'd seen this kind of thing all too often.

'Is this your garden?' I asked. I wasn't being sarcastic.

'Don't be sarcastic.'

'Come on, dear,' the wife said.

'You have all this wilderness, and yet you camp here!' His accent was definitely Scottish, but was much harsher than the islands. I was guessing Glasgow, definitely mainland somewhere.

I felt woefully ill-equipped for confrontation after all that time on the road. I wanted to tell him to fuck off, tell him to mind his own business. That would have come more easily for me in London, but I'd somehow lost the aptitude or appetite for conflict. Curious. Besides, he struck me as the type for whom everything is his business.

'I asked in the shop,' I said. 'About where I should camp.'

'They know nothing.'

'There were others already here when I arrived.'

'They are twelve-year-old boys!' he said, his face growing puce with rage.

I wasn't exactly sure what that meant. Did he think I was a kiddie-fiddler?

'What's that got to do with it?'

'They're twelve!' he said, again, as if that cleared that up.

He walked off. A few seconds later he was back for more. His wife had carried on walking.

'People like you are ruining it for everyone,' he said.

'I thought you were allowed to camp anywhere in Scotland,' I said. 'The 2003 Land Reform Act and all that, so long as you were sensible about it.'

'Well, the law is wrong.' And he stomped off, never to return.

I sat there for a while, my mood utterly changed, feeling terribly deviant and a little ashamed. The flaps of one of my neighbours' tents opened and out emerged a young man. He looked as if he was in his twenties.

'Hi,' he said. 'How's it going?'

'You're not twelve,' I said. I was talking to myself really, but the words drifted across to him.

'No,' he said, and walked off towards the pub.

I ate my dinner, finished off the bottle of wine, rather too quickly and angrily, and then crawled into my tent. It had been a weird evening, but it was just about to get even weirder.

Around midnight, in a fitful half-sleep, I became aware of footsteps on the cliff high above my tent. There was a crash as what sounded like glass smashed close to the tent, then another followed by a thump into the fabric. I crawled out just in time to see a shadowy figure running away. I looked down at my tent. There was a three-inch gash in the side wall and, next to it, the jagged base of a broken bottle. From somewhere high above me, trailing off into the night, I could hear laughter.

Chapter 14

'What's with these recumbent bicycles?
Listen, buddy, if you wanna take a nap, lie down.
If you wanna ride a bike, buy a f**king bicycle.'

George Carlin, comedian

If it hadn't been happening to me, it would have been one of the funniest things I'd ever seen. A grown man in Lycra shorts trying, simultaneously and with growing panic, to pack away a tent, apply a liberal coating of moisturiser and slap himself violently and repeatedly like a man on fire trying to put himself out.

The day had started just dandy. I'd taken the crack-of-dawn ferry from Lochmaddy in North Uist across The Little Minch to Uig in northern Skye, then ridden south across the island in glorious sunshine, grateful to have left the ferocious winds and horizontal rain of the Outer Hebrides behind.

The road through Skye had taken in some pretty big climbs and was busy with holiday traffic. But riding along the banks of Loch Snizort past fields of wild foxgloves, then through the lovely little capital of Portree with its pastel quayside houses, and afterwards pedalling in the shadow of the brooding black gabbro mass of The Cuillin, their saw-tooth peaks topped with puffballs of cloud, all was well with the world. My spirits were soaring, and the bicycle seemed to be magically powering itself, the chain running so smoothly that I sometimes had to check there was a chain. Even the altercation with Mr Angry on Barra was becoming a distant memory.

What with the ferry journey and a long, leisurely lunch in Portree, I'd probably only covered 40 miles that day, but by the time I got to Broadford, in southern Skye, I was ready to set up camp for the evening.

Mr Angry might have been just a whisper now, but he was audible enough for me to choose my site carefully, far from any houses and cliffs from which missiles could be launched.

I rode down a track across the grasslands lining Broadford Bay, and at the end found a little isolated graveyard and, beyond, close to the water's edge, a small patch of tufted grass as soft and bouncy as a double-sprung mattress. It was a late July evening, I was in the Highlands of Scotland, on the West Coast, and the gentle breeze had died completely. I was right by the water, I was surrounded by lovely, thick bracken and wearing just shorts and a T-shirt. What could possibly go wrong?

That question is aimed at people who have experience of the Scottish outdoors, who doubtless, as they're reading this, are shaking their heads just as Custer's men must have done when their general said something along the lines of 'Hey guys, chill. It's just a few Indians'.

For those of you unfamiliar with the scenario I found myself in, let what follows be a salutary lesson; I suffered so that you don't have to.

I unclipped my luggage and dropped it over a fence, then clambered over it myself. I'd just pitched my tent and started to unpack my other bags when I felt the smallest little ping on my arm, like a fine drop of rain. I looked up. The sky was cloudless. Curious. I felt another ping. I looked down at my arm. Nothing. What I didn't know at that stage was that I'd been scouted, like a raver looking for an empty squat, but instead of party-goers being alerted about the venue by text or email, on that still Scottish evening, pheromones were drifting towards the dense clumps of bracken with one clear message: 'Party time!'

The next time I looked up, I was encircled by a black cloud. Within seconds they were upon me, completely enveloping all my exposed flesh, going up my nose, down my throat and in my ears; my arms and legs were just a seething black mess of *Culicoides impunctatus*, Latin for blood-sucking little biting bastards, which in English we pronounce midges.

I had rather foolishly dismissed all tales of midge attacks I'd been told about, the people who'd jumped off cliffs to escape them or been committed to lunatic asylums, as rather hyperbolic and hysterical. After all, I'd encountered great swarms of giant mosquitoes in the tropics, locusts in Africa, and even, when I was a lad, had run into a wasps' nest, the legacy of which still has me fleeing like a great big girl when one of the stripy things comes close.

But nothing could have prepared me for the savagery of my first full-blown midge assault. They reckon that the Skye variety are the Special Forces of the midge world, and that up to half a million of them can join in an attack. But I reckon this must be an underestimate – they must get their numbers from the same source as the government does for protest marches. They were up my shorts now, gnawing and biting, crawling over the old crown jewels. If anything, the cloud was getting thicker. When would they be sated? Would they not stop until I was just a stack of bleached bones?

I was leaping and jumping and waving my arms around. At least I now knew how the Highland Fling had been invented.

The logical thing would have been to pedal away, mindful that midges can't fly at more than 4mph. But I had a slight problem in that my tent was up and all my worldly possessions were strewn about on the ground. I dived into my tent, but it was full of them. I remembered the Avon Skin So Soft, and ferreted around in my bag until I found it, proceeding to smear myself in great globs of the stuff. If anything, this only seemed to make me more attractive to the ladies (it's only the female midge that attacks. The blokes probably stay at home with their mates and a beer), so I went back into my bags and found my midge-net hat. Like the cream, this device is best used as a prophylactic, and is not so useful when it contains not only your head, but thousands of midges, that now seemed to be burrowing into my eyeballs. Think Room 101. If there'd been a cliff handy, I'd have jumped off it, no doubt about it.

I stuffed everything into my bags, threw them over the fence, then pulled out the tent pegs and poles and threw the tent over too. I then threw myself over, landing heavily on my left ankle, sending a shooting pain up my leg.

I mounted up, clutching the bars with my left hand, the right one clutching the tent, which I was now wearing around my shoulders like a poncho. And with that I was gone, heart pounding, broken, having to pedal with my right leg only. I knew that one day I would see the funny side of it. Say a Tuesday, in 2023.

I rode like that, south on the A87, not daring to stop. Only when I was over the Skye bridge at Kyleakin and onto the mainland did I pull over to pack away my gear properly and examine the damage. My traumatised brain was telling me that Skye midges would respect natural borders.

There were red angry welts and hives covering every inch of skin on my arms and legs, and, judging from the amount of itching occurring, all over my face too. I looked like I'd been blowtorched, my privates feeling like they'd been marinated in Deep Heat.

I rode around Kyle of Lochalsh trying to find a B&B. They were all full. I felt like crying. Finally, on the suggestion of a man in a petrol station, I rode a little out of town and knocked on the door of a house with no obvious outward signs that it offered lodgings.

An elderly woman half opened the door.

'Do you have a room?' I asked, whining pitifully, standing there scratching like a junkie going cold turkey, legs and arms bleeding.

'What's wrung with ye?' she asked.

'Midges.'

'Aye, hurd sid they prefer fat people all reet,' she said.

'Shove your room,' I would have said, had I had a shred of self-respect, and was in a buyer's market.

'Is that right?' was what I said, seeing as I didn't and wasn't.

She hesitated for a moment. Then said she'd had a cancellation, that the room would be £25, and that she'd like the money up front. I do believe that had she said the price was £250 I still would have taken it.

I climbed the narrow staircase, all distracted, confused and fat.

'I feel like I've been in a war,' I said over my shoulder.

'A war, ye say?'

My elbow caught a vase full of dried flowers, which toppled into a set of small porcelain dogs, the whole lot cascading down the stairs, landing in a broken heap at the woman's feet at the bottom.

'I'm so sorry,' I said raising my arms to emphasise just how sorry I was, catching a framed portrait of a young man in military uniform on the wall, which bounced down the steps and joined the heap but which, mercifully, didn't smash.

'That's my grandson,' the woman said, looking down at the portrait at her feet. 'He's in Afghanistan.'

My ankle was still tender the next morning, but luckily sitting on a hard, narrow saddle with testicles that had been scratched raw overnight took my mind off it. On the ferry from Armadale to Mallaig, I sat among my fellow passengers pawing at my bites, twitching and scraping away at my arms, legs and scalp. When, after five minutes, I looked up, I found that I had a whole seating section to myself.

Things got better in Mallaig when, cycling past the train station, the summer-only Jacobite steam service to Fort William was pulling out (It was hauled by 62005 *Lord of the Isles*, a K1 2-6-0 Peppercorn locomotive, if you're interested).

The track ran right next to the road for the first mile or so, and I raced the train, that hissing, living beast, wheels clanging, pistons pumping, all steam and fury, just feet from my bicycle. It was magnificent. I was waving at the families in the front carriage. They were waving back. I felt like I'd been dropped into *The Railway Children*. Whoooooooo went the whistle. Ping went my back wheel.

The Jacobite disappeared into the distance and I looked down at my wheel – three broken spokes and a buckle so bad that it was unrideable. Midges may like fat people, but Ridgebacks clearly don't.

I unclipped the brake cable from the calliper and pushed the bike back the few miles to Mallaig. Now, Mallaig is a beautiful, unspoilt little peach of a fishing port and no mistake, and no rational person could possibly find fault with it. But take a rational person and factor in a sore ankle, burning testicles and a knackered back wheel. Then add the fact that Mallaig has no bike shop, and rationality goes somewhat out of the window. I'd have to go to the nearest bicycle shop, in Fort William 40 miles away, which would mean putting my bike on a train, and the day's last one had just departed.

I pitched my tent on a little piece of dog-shit-covered grass in the car park next to the railway station for the early morning train, overlooking the Sound of Sleat.

I felt resentful towards Mallaig for its lack of bike shops. But I knew that wasn't the real source my resentment. That came from the fact that the freedom to go wherever I wanted whenever I wanted had become such a part of my life that to lose it, even for a day, felt like a terrible punishment, an imprisonment almost.

I sat on the sea wall and looked out across the sound. The light was soft, magical, the setting sun turning scarlet the islands of Eigg and Rum, the billowing clouds of oranges and lemons above them making it appear as if they were on fire. From somewhere, a seal moaned its ghostly recital.

*

With the wheel fixed, I headed south from Fort William on the busy A82 under an angry-looking sky, neon signs flashing warnings of severe rain and flooding on their way.

'Come far?' said a voice as I waited for the ferry across Loch Linnhe at the Corran Narrows.

I turned around to see a man sitting on a recumbent bicycle. He introduced himself as Aidan and told me that he lived in Strontian, about 15 miles up the road on the other side of the loch. His bike had what looked like home-made steel baskets straddling the back wheel. They were full of shopping.

'I've just been to Fort William for my shopping,' said Aidan, 55, but looking barely over 40. I worked out that was a 50-mile round trip. 'And also to get this fixed.' He held up a bandaged hand.

'What happened?'

'Chopped off my finger with a chainsaw,' he said, as if he was talking about getting a splinter. I was going to tell him about my near-death experience with the midges, but thought better of it.

The rain started to fall, but thankfully not quite as apocalyptically as the neon signs had predicted. We cycled together along the deserted road through Glen Tarbert (there's another one!), through the district of Ardgour and into Sunart, the entire peninsula – also comprising Morven, Moidart and Ardnamurchan – sounding more Middle Earth than middle Scotland. It looked like it, too: the road snaking through wild, remote wooded glens topped by rocky peaks, no sign of human life. Scotland had daily filled me with awe at its beauty, but this was surely one of its most magical corners.

I was lovely to be riding with somebody and Aidan was fine company, although it did feel slightly odd to be talking to somebody who was lying down. It felt like I had a sidecar.

'I rode normal bikes for years,' he said. 'But after trying a recumbent a few years ago, I was converted. Can't understand why everybody doesn't have one. They're much quicker and more comfortable.'

To prove his point, at the next hill, bearing a 15% gradient sign, he flew up without breaking sweat, leaving me puffing and panting in his wake.

Aidan told me a little history of the area. How it has been known since time immemorial as The Rough Bounds, and how it was the heartland of the Lord of the Isles, until relatively recently accessed only by sea and guarded at every headland by a fortress.

The town of Strontian, he told me, was the place where the chemical element strontium had been first found in the lead mines that opened in 1722, and thus the name. Who needed a guidebook when you've got a talking guide in a sidecar?

I asked him about camping in Strontian.

'You're very welcome to sleep at my house tonight. I like to help out fellow cyclists,' he said. I paused. I'd been on the road three months, and housed and watered by strangers on a regular basis, a level of kindness I never imagined existed in Britain. But old habits died hard, and the words 'serial killer' always flashed through my brain before I could catch myself.

'That would be great,' I said.

The glen opened up and we were looking down on Strontian on the banks of Loch Sunart, hemmed in by sharp hills, like another hidden kingdom. We pulled up outside a house.

'I stay here,' said Aidan. I loved the way Scots said that; so much more poetic than 'I live here'.

Aidan's house clung to the steep hillside high above the loch, surrounded by pine and spruce forest. He showed me around. The interior walls were lined in the oak and larch panelling he'd made, and gave it the look of a giant sauna. Aidan had made most of the furniture, too, and it was beautiful. 'I only use fallen wood I find,' he said.

We walked into the garden. Three very old-looking hens sat on a bench. On the floor was a runny mess of soft eggs.

'They're too old for eggs now, but I couldn't kill them. Not after all the food they've given us.'

I asked who 'us' was. Aidan lived there with his son, Barney. 'His mother died when he was only one.'

He'd been a single parent for many years, but had recently married again. His wife was away in London for a few days.

We went into his workshop. The walls were lined with exquisite guitars.

'You make these?'

'Yes. I have to buy the spruce for the bodies, but the rosettes are made from my sycamores in the garden. I manage to sell a few to passing trade.'

Aidan talked about working with wood, about his passion for the material. Down at the loch, he said, he had a sailboat he was restoring.

'She's called the *Twinklamee*. Built in Orkney in 1959. She's made from larch and oak with a pine deck.' He pronounced the names of the woods as if he were talking about precious stones. 'When's she ready, I'm going to take her out to the Western Isles.'

Aidan went off to dig up some potatoes and courgettes for dinner, which he cooked up on his Rayburn, hissing and fizzing under my wet socks. Aidan had insisted.

'That's what it's for,' he'd said.

He served the vegetables with home-made bread and a pizza carried back from Fort William. For dessert we had wild raspberries. I remembered back to Findhorn, and the comment about us being the most useless generation in history, having lost all the practical skills and knowledge our forefathers had accumulated. Then I looked at Aidan, and thought: not quite.

We sat there eating quietly as the light faded and the midges danced outside and pinged against the pane. Along the far side of the loch I could see the little lights burning from houses far from anywhere. On the radio, there was a recital of Shelley's works: 'Ozymandias', 'Ode to the West Wind', 'To a Skylark'.

Barney popped his head around the door to say hello and quickly disappeared again.

'He's about to go off to university, to study computer game design,' Aidan said. 'Imagine that! You can have a career designing computer games.'

Aidan had said the climb away from Strontian, up and over the mountains of Morven, was 'nothing to worry about too much'. He may well have said this to adhere to the cyclists' sacred code of understating the severity of upcoming hills, but it was perhaps more accurately a reflection of his own fitness – he'd casually mentioned over dinner how he'd sometimes ride a long loop down to Iona and back in a day, a distance of over 200 miles, just for the hell of it. Some people are just magnificent specimens – hardy, talented, kind, gentle, modest, curious, stoical, smart, physically strong – and I never cease to be in awe when I meet them.

Anyway, the 'nothing to worry about' hill was a monster, as I suspected it would be: 40 minutes of solid climbing, the gradient at a steady 10%, talking me from sea level to nearly 1,000ft in around four miles. The cloud was low, the drizzle steady, my sweat, mixing with the Avon Skin So Soft, the application of which had now become a morning ritual, stinging my eyes. At the side of the single-track road foamed down great cataracts, and from these I filled my bottles, greedily swallowing great peaty mouthfuls, the liquid as dark as stout.

The summit was in the clouds, the wind fierce and billowing, scattering the white in eddies to reveal, momentarily, desolate glens of moorland and scrub and, in the distance, the Isle of Mull, before all became white and silent once more.

I freewheeled down the other side, for six maybe seven miles, a stunning green valley of remote farmhouses and spruce forests. My speedometer hovered around the 45mph mark. Occasionally I'd meet a tractor coming the other way up the steep single track. I'd pull on my brakes but fail to stop, and all I could do was breathe in and pray as I shot through the narrow gap.

I caught the little ferry in Lochaline for the 15-minute trip across the Sound of Mull, and 20 minutes later, in the village of Salen, I was having a coffee with Nick Hand.

Nick, like Jack Allen's daughter, had contacted me when he'd read about my trip. Nick, who told me he was 52, was also cycling round the British coastline, clockwise like Jack, and had departed from his home in Bristol. We'd been in regular text contact, keeping tabs on one another. Our orbits had crossed in Mull.

We went through the ritual of lifting up each other's bikes, feeling the weight. I was happy to discover that Nick's bike was, if anything, heavier than mine. This could be explained by the incredible amount of electronic equipment he was carrying – cameras, lenses, laptop, voice-recording gear – for Nick was travelling the coast interviewing artisans and artists who lived by the water's edge for his blog, Slowcoast.

He'd done a lot of research before setting off, arranging interviews, putting a schedule together. He'd met some incredible people and a part of me was envious; the part that always feels as if I'm missing out.

Nick knew more or less to the day when he'd be back in Bristol; I only knew I'd be back in London any time between then and Christmas. Nick knew where he was going to be stopping most nights. Every night he edited his footage and audio tapes and wrote his blog; I just slumped with a glass of wine and stared into space. He'd been planning for a year, testing saddles and gear ratios and equipment; I'd just grabbed my bike and set off. Nick had been seen off by a big crowd of friends with banners and would be welcomed home by a similar scene; I'd just left quietly and would slip back into London. Nick couldn't have been a gentler, lovelier, kinder man, but it was hard for me not to feel just a little inadequate next to him. It felt absurd to make comparisons, but whether it's against a fellow round-Britain cyclist or the people living next door or the shiny family on the toothpaste commercial, it seems to be something I'm prone to do.

At times like that, I always have to remind myself of a quote given to me by a friend when I was young and troubled after my mum had died. It was a quote that had stayed with me down the years. 'One has to just be oneself. That's my basic message,' the Bhagwan Shree Rajneesh had written. 'The moment you accept yourself as you are, all burdens, all mountainous burdens, simply disappear. Then life is a sheer joy, a festival of lights.'

I asked Nick how his trip had been so far. He'd been terrified when he'd set off, from Bristol to Cardiff in the rain, afraid he was going to get crushed by the trucks and cars. He'd also been daunted by the scale of the thing he'd taken on.

'But after a few days, it hit me just how happy I was feeling. I had a stupid smile on my face the whole time.'

We ordered another coffee.

I asked Nick what had inspired him to do the trip.

'Well, I've always wanted to do it and thought I'd better get on with it before I was too old.'

I told him about Jack.

'Ah, there's hope for us all!'

We both took a sip of coffee.

'I'm not exactly sure why I wanted to do it, though. I think it was something to do with… wanting to "feel" the place, to know it, to get a sense of the place I was born. That make any sense?'

I said that it did to me.

'We live on such a beautiful island,' I said.

'Don't we.'

We sat there for three hours, exchanging stories of the road. Then it was time to head off in opposite directions. Nick gave me the address of some friends in Cardigan on the Welsh coast.

'Be sure to contact them. They're lovely and will look after you well.'

He asked me how the hills were ahead of him.

'Oh, not bad,' I lied.

I asked the same question.

'Nothing much to worry about,' he lied.

And with that we headed off in opposite directions.

I could imagine the meeting, as the ad agency creatives pitched their ideas to the Scottish Tourist Board.

'Okay. So there's a guy cycling on his own, through an empty but jaw-droppingly gorgeous landscape, with high mountains and heather-coated moorland on one side of him and a crystalline loch on the other. Say, Loch Na Keal in Mull, cos that's beautiful.'

'Like it. Like it.'

'And let's say he stops and pitches his tent by the loch, miles from anywhere, no people around, a few red deer maybe, cos there are a lot of them on Mull. And after drinking a couple of beers he goes for a swim as the sky catches fire from the setting sun, like one of them Italian paintings.'

'Saluting that. Great stuff.'

'And here's the killer. Just then, a lone bagpiper appears on top of a nearby hill, in silhouette, behind him the towering peak of Ben More. Slowly, the notes of "Scotland the Brave" drift through the still, languid air.'

'Now you're taking the piss.'

But I was in that commercial on the banks of Loch Na Keal. And sadly, apart from the piper – and God knows where he came from – it's unlikely anybody will ever believe me.

In the morning I bathed in the loch, sadly unaccompanied by the pipes this time, then cycled along its south side under high cliffs and past sheltered, sandy bays.

A cyclist pulled alongside me.

'All right?'

'Yeah.'

We rode together for 10 minutes in silence.

'Where you from?' I asked eventually.

'Pembrokeshire.'

More silence.

'On holiday?'

'Not really.'

A mile or two more. We'd cut inland now, moving across the rugged mountainous interior.

'Thing is,' he said, finally. 'I just did a triathlon, see. But my time was shit. So I thought I'd beat myself up over some Scottish mountains.'

'Right.'

'Bye then.' And with that he was off, powering up the steep slope in purgatory. I hoped his next triathlon was a more satisfying experience.

I cycled along the Ross of Mull, the scenery growing softer. To my right, across the loch on the Ardmeanach headland, I could see great cascades of water tumbling down the mountains. Ahead was Staffa, the island whose vast fluted basalt columns resembling organ pipes inspired Mendelssohn to write the Hebrides Overture. An eagle flew low and to my left, disappearing into a thicket of pines.

At the end of Mull, at Fionnphort, I hopped onto the little ferry, the flat-bottomed vessel rolling violently, slapping the swells, as it crossed the Sound of Iona. I looked down onto the car deck, at my bike straining at the appalling knots I'd tied in the holding rope. Any minute I expected to see her fly across the deck. But somehow everything held.

On tiny Iona, I found the campsite, pitched my tent and went off in search of the thing I'd been longing to visit for 15 years. As I rode, Iona looked stunning, with cockleshell white sand and vivid green slopes flecked with rust-red granite and carpeted with wild flowers.

Over 1,400 years earlier, St Columba had been exiled from his native Ireland, and crossed the sea to convert the heathen Picts to Celtic Christianity. He'd founded his church on Iona, making the island Britain's true cradle of Christianity and a place of pilgrimage ever since. But this wasn't why I'd wanted to come.

I rode up a short hill towards the abbey, leant my bike against a wall, and walked around Iona's sacred burial ground, Reilig Odhráin, said to contain the remains of 60 kings of Norway, Ireland, France and Scotland, including Macbeth and Duncan. I scanned the inscriptions: 'Here lies all that could die of Bruce Kenrick'; 'Penry Jones. A man of parts'. And then there was a rough-hewn, weathered slab inlaid with, in golden script, a quote from Alexander Pope: 'An honest man's the noblest work of God.' The name across the top read: 'John Smith'.

That was why I'd come. I stood there in the rain, quite alone, remembering May 1994 and the scenes I'd watched on television from that little graveyard as they buried the Labour party leader, dead from a heart attack aged just 55, a few hours after saying: 'The opportunity to serve our country – that's all we ask.' It felt like history had taken a wrong turn. I recalled how, even back then, before all that followed and all that has subsequently become, the loss, laden with presentiment, had felt cataclysmic, without knowing why. It is, of course, a mug's game to imagine what might have been; to believe that one individual might have taken the country in a completely different direction. But standing there that day, in the rain, with everything that was going on in Britain, and the prospect of what was to come, the need to believe in something felt important.

About halfway back across Mull I stopped at a little remote general store on the banks of Loch Scridain. I grabbed a flapjack and a coffee and sat on a wooden bench outside, lost in a reverie, gazing over the water to the towering giant of Ben More beyond.

A cyclist pulled up. He was blond and blue-eyed and, I guessed, in his fifties. He didn't have any luggage on his bike, but was wearing an enormous backpack. In a heavy Dutch accent, he asked if he could join me. Of course, I said. For if there was one thing I'd had confirmed to me on this trip, it was that cyclists were my kind of people. I imagined we'd pass a pleasant period swapping tales of the road and smugly congratulating ourselves on our good fortune in being alive.

'Where have you cycled from?' he asked.

'London,' I said, and waited for the 'wow!'

'Zat is not far,' he said, dismissively. That threw me. I immediately felt a little foolish for feeling self-important. I decided we'd got off to a bad start, perhaps confused by cultural considerations.

'I've just been down to Iona,' I said, breezily.

'Why?'

Why? What sort of question was that for a touring cyclist to ask? What, when, where were our staples. Why never came into it. Somehow, I didn't think explaining that I'd wanted to visit John Smith's grave was going to satisfy my Dutch friend.

'Because it's… erm… beautiful.'

'Pah! Fiona is not beautiful. The scenery is boring.'

I sat there, staring no longer up at Ben More but down into my Nescafé.

He pointed at my water bottles.

'Why have you got three? That's stoopid.'

It was like I'd stumbled into Monty Python's Argument Sketch.

'Well, some of the places I've been, it's a long way from…'

'And look at all the stuff you have. Stooopid! I just have a backpack.'

'I have all my camping gear…' I said.

'I just have a tarp. That's all you need.'

'And a laptop…'

'A laptop? Ha! Stooooopid!'

'I'm writing about my trip.'

'Then why don't you just go by car? That would be more sensible.'

'By car?'

'Cycling should be simples. You do it wrong.'

We sat there in silence for a while. I felt quite annoyed now, not to mention a little stoooopid. I wondered how people like the Dutch guy made it through life, demanding that the world fitted their prescriptions. It might explain why he was cycling alone. Then again, what was my excuse?

'Nice to meet you,' I said. 'I'm off now.'

'I vill come too,' he said.

So we set off, Sancho Panza and I. The road started to climb steeply through Glen More, waterfalls cascading down on either side, a thick, bubbling ceiling of cloud giving it the feeling of moving across the floor of a giant, smoke-filled room. An eagle flashed past.

'Why you not vear your helmet?' Sancho said.

'I don't want to.'

'That is stoopid.'

I was at breaking point. Here I was in the midst of such staggering natural beauty, and yet I was filled with such festering resentment that I couldn't enjoy it.

'Can't you go faster?' Sancho said. 'This is very slow.'

'Why would I want to?'

'Because cycling is better fast.'

I thought for a minute, trying to assemble the words that would explain my world view to this man: that the goal is nothing and movement everything; that we all have a different take on things and that that's just dandy. But in the end, the words that came lacked a certain sophistication.

'Why don't you just fuck off.'

He looked at me with the eyes of a wounded child and then silently pulled away up the slope. I felt terrible.

The Dutch guy was on the same ferry as me from Craignure to Oban back on the mainland. But he spent the crossing either studiously ignoring me or shooting me daggers, and who could blame him?

I disembarked in the rain and cycled south through Argyll and Bute into a sharp headwind along the fast and dangerous A816. I can't explain it in rational terms, but there's something about wet roads that makes motorists drive like utter tools. I've noticed it on my daily commute in London. A bit of water, and everybody's jumpy and twitchy and throwing caution to the wind. On the A816 they swept past inches from me, or drove right on my back wheel, revving impatiently until they could get past. Yet when it's dry, I find most motorists to be calm and courteous. Weird.

By the time I got to the little town of Lochgilphead, I was as grey and angry as Loch Gilp, seething and boiling as it was with whitecaps. I wanted to grab a quiet coffee and some lunch and calm down a bit, but every café was rammed with people sheltering from the wind and the rain, great queues at the counter, the windows all steamed up. This all only served to make me feel even more fractious.

At a table outside one café, under an awning, sat a man, hair the colour of straw, blue-eyed, early fifties. Next to him was a heavily loaded touring bike. He beckoned for me to join him. I didn't exactly feel I'd be the best company, and after my Dutch friend I was reluctant to be subjected to ridicule again so soon. But the man insisted, so I sat down.

'Come far?' he asked, with a gentle Scandinavian accent.

'Only London,' I said.

'That's very far.'

'And you?'

'Sweden.'

'Wow!'

He introduced himself as Anders. He told me he had recently lost his job as a managing director in a town in the far north of Sweden and was going through a divorce. He rolled up his sleeve and showed me a wristband a friend had given to him inscribed 'carpe diem'.

'It's such an cliché,' he said. 'But it's very true. There I was, jobless, middle-aged, getting divorced. One day, I said to myself: "Anders, you're fifty-two and you've never seen a whale." I don't know why a whale seemed so important, but I knew I had to hit the road.'

'Seen one yet?'

'Still looking. But I'm getting closer, I can feel it.'

We ordered a couple of coffees. Anders told me about his ride down through Sweden, across Denmark and then the ferry to Harwich. He'd ridden across England and through Wales and Ireland before arriving in Scotland.

'I've been playing golf as I've gone along. All the famous links courses in Britain I've always dreamed about. I played at Portrush, and Troon, now I'm off to St Andrews. I prefer to be in pure nature playing golf. Where the land and the sea combine. There's nowhere else in the world that can compare to the UK for this.'

After Britain, he planned to cycle across the US and then, if the money held out, around Australia, playing golf as he went. It seemed like such a mad adventure. I wondered what my Dutch friend on Mull would have made of it.

I asked him how easy it was to borrow clubs at these prestigious courses.

'I have my own.'

'Your own?'

'Sure. Look,' he said pointing at his bike.

I hadn't noticed, but as well as all the usual touring luggage and camping gear, strapped to the top tube were six golf irons and a putter. Attached by bungee cord to the rear panniers were a folded-up golf bag and a pair of spikes.

'That's insane,' I said.

'I know, I know,' he replied, laughing.

By the time Anders and I had gone our separate ways, my mood had been transformed. For there is nothing like time spent in the company of a Quixotic lunatic to make you feel that every-thing will work out just fine. As I headed south on the A83 in the rain, along the banks of Loch Fyne, I was once more singing at the top of my lungs.

By the time I got to the little lochside village of Tarbert, not only was I happy to be completing a line of three in my game of Tarbert bingo, but I was very much relishing finding a B&B to treat myself to a hot bath and a chance to dry off my gear. Alas, every room was taken.

I popped into the Co-op to buy some food for the evening and asked the woman if she knew anywhere good to camp nearby.

'Aye,' she said. 'Some people camp up at the castle.'

I rode up the steep little path and then pushed my bike across the grass, watched by chocolate-coloured horned sheep with little plastic indigo ties in their ears that gave them the look of Barbary pirates. In the shadow of Tarbert Castle, renovated by Robert the Bruce in 1325, but now just a ruin, I found a little grassy amphithe-atre in the rocks and pitched my tent in the centre of it. I then took my bread, cheese and wine and sat on a rocky outcrop, looking down from high on Tarbert below me, with its bright-coloured houses and boats at anchor, and out at the vastness of Loch Fyne beyond. The wind had dropped now and the world had a sublime stillness to it. I looked back at my tent in its little hollow and then at the magnificent view and the ruined castle, and I was struggling to think of a better spot I'd slept in all trip.

At around 11 p.m. I was just about to turn off my headtorch and go to sleep when I heard the faint sound of young male voices nearby. The voices got louder and louder until it sounded like they were just the other side of my bowl. Whoever they were, their conversation, liberally peppered with profanities and whooping, suggested to me that I was not in the presence of the Tarbert Temperance Society.

I held my breath, feeling suddenly quite vulnerable. In retrospect, on that dark night it would have been more sensible to keep breathing but turn off my headtorch.

'Hey, there's onla sum prick campin' up 'ere.'

Too late.

'Let's mash 'im.'

Suddenly, all I could hear was thumping footsteps running towards where I lay, and then the tent was taking great kicks and slaps from unseen hands and feet. A firework exploded. I remembered seeing Ross Kemp's TV series on the world's toughest gangs. I could recall the townships of South Africa and the favelas of Rio. But I couldn't recall an episode set on the Kintyre peninsula.

I struggled out of my sleeping bag, heart pounding, and unzipped the inner flap. In the little porch, all I could see in the beam of my torch was a thick cloud of black midges. I had a terrible flashback, and rapidly zipped up the flap again. Outside, the hooting and hollering was becoming frenzied.

I quickly convinced myself that it wouldn't be too long before my drunken young friends would tire of slapping and kicking and decide that what the evening really needed was a bonfire. And so this was the choice I presented to myself: burning to death in my tent or getting attacked by Scottish midges. I pondered the pros and cons. It was a tough call.

I quickly topped up the Skin So Soft, unzipped the flap and crawled out. Hell was unleashed. I was only wearing my underpants and the midges soon enveloped me. I ran out into the night, screaming obscenities and trying to sound like a wild man. But all I could hear was young male voices drifting off into the distance and laughing.

I climbed back into my tent. The gang may have left, but the midges decided to stay the night. I lay back and accepted my fate. I started to scratch and, I think, cry. The feast in full swing and showing no signs of abating, the thought occurred to me that it might actually be better if I immolated myself.

About an hour later, I heard voices approaching again. This time I was out of the tent in a flash, waiting for them. I picked out their faces in the beam of my torch as they came over the lip of the bowl. There were six of them, all only about 15 or 16 years old. There was a stand-off for a few seconds, them up on the ridge, me below them. I recalled the advice from *Danny Dyer's Deadliest Men*: take out the main man first then the rest would capitulate. To this end, I was trying to work out which one was the leader. The youths, no doubt, were trying to work out how best to take out a near-naked middle-aged man scratching himself to death.

The silence was eventually broken.

'Sorry, mister,' said one of the kids, looking angelic now. 'But we've lost a wallet from before. Can we borrow ya torch?'

And so the evening finished in a surreal fashion, with me in my underpants helping my tormentors to find their wallet.

'Why did you attack my tent?' I asked one of them.

'We thart ye wa frum a rival gang, come to tick our territory,' he said.

'Really?'

'No, not really,' he said. 'We're just bolloxed.'

Chapter 15

'If the constellations had been named in the twentieth century, I suppose we would see bicycles.'

Carl Sagan, author and astronomer

I huddled in the shelter from the rain with three other foot passengers for the early morning ferry to Arran, whose mountainous form rose vertically from the sea a few miles away across Kilbrannan Sound. Arran was to be the last of my stepping-stone islands in Scotland, and it was from there that I would catch my final CalMac ferry back to Ardrossan, just south-west of Glasgow on the mainland.

I'd spent the past month taking those ferries, hopping on and off them like one might a bus. If it's true, as I believe it is, that the most exhilarating way to approach a new land is from the sea, watching it gradually rise from the water, the anticipation building slowly, then I had been spoiled in Scotland.

One of the first things I saw upon disembarking in Lochranza was the Isle of Arran Distillery. It felt wrong to have almost circumnavigated Scotland and not paid my respects, so I took the tour.

Robin, my guide, was originally from Newcastle and had moved to Arran seven years earlier. His accent was a soft, heavenly blend, no pun intended, of Geordie and Scots. He'd always been passionate about whisky, and when he saw the job at the distillery advertised he'd felt like the gods were smiling down on him.

'My dad always said to me that drinking whisky was an adventure, because you just don't know what the next one's going to be. We always used to go off and work along the bars together. But we could never remember where we left off! When I came here, I thought I knew a lot about whisky, but I realised I knew nothing.'

As we walked around the copper stills, Robin explained the distilling process, the washing and the mashing and the role the different cask woods played in the final flavour. 'The raw spirit evaporates through the wood. This is called the angels' share. There must be some very happy angels up there!' He spoke in whispered reverence as if trying to explain the miracle of life itself.

He spoke of the resurgence in national pride and identity since the formation of the Scottish parliament. 'We've had a string of ministers through here in the past few years. We never saw them before.' He talked about the number of independent distilleries that have reopened recently that had been shut for years, and the growing number of small companies selling local produce.

'This is a vibrant place. We use each other's products on the island and sell each other's products. It makes sense to work together as a community. I can't help but think that other people could learn from what we're doing here.'

In the tasting room, Robin lined up a few bottles on the counter.

'Try this one, Mike. It's a ten-year-old, matured in bourbon and sherry casks. If you add just a wee drop of water it brings the flavours out, you can see the oils mixing together.'

I don't think I had ever drunk whisky at 10 in the morning before, and I was alarmed to discover that I quite liked it.

'Now this one is 50 per cent ABV,' Robin said, pouring me another glass. 'Lovely bouquet. Matured in a bourbon cask for eight years, then a pomerol cask for eight months.'

'Delicious.'

'Let it sit on your tongue for a while. Get some air through. The flavours should explode in your mouth.'

'Oh, they do.'

'And this is our Robert Burns, only five years old, hence its pale colour.'

'To Robert Burns,' I said, raising my glass.

'Fancy a liqueur?' said Robin.

'Why not?'

'This is Arran Gold, voted best liqueur in the world two years ago.'

'To Arran Gold,' I said.

I had originally planned to cycle the 14 miles down the east side of Arran to catch the ferry to the mainland from Brodick. By the time I emerged from the distillery, I had convinced myself that it would be a much better idea to go the long way around instead, a distance of over 40 miles.

I've read that back in the day cyclists in the Tour de France would have water bottles full of wine waiting for them at the bottom of climbs to give them a boost, and I could certainly feel how that would work as I powered along feeling superhuman. My decision to circumnavigate the island was entirely vindicated, for a while at least. Skirting around the mountainous interior, topped by Goat Fell at 2,800ft, the west coast of Arran was flat, with quiet, if appallingly potholed, roads and stunning views across the sound to the Mull of Kintyre, the famous song (or at least the first two lines, which were all I could remember) lodging in my brain and belting out of my gob on a endless loop.

Unhelpfully, the whisky wore off just in time for the hills of south Arran, a never-ending series of 20% climbs and drops. I considered retrieving the bottle of Arran whisky that I'd purchased at the distillery from my panniers. But on reflection, with the monster hills of Wales and the West Country ahead of me, I thought it could be a slippery slope that might lead to pills, blood transfusions and me sprawled on the floor of a remote Exmoor climb, telling some curious cows to 'put me back on my bike'.

As I rounded the southern tip of Arran I caught my first sight of Ailsa Craig, the magnificent 1,114-foot-high muffin-shaped volcanic lump that juts out of the Firth of Clyde and is known as Paddy's Milestone because it lies halfway between Glasgow and Belfast.

From the top of a hill, I could see a campsite right on the beach. Just offshore was the long, thin strip of Pladda Island, at whose head was a lighthouse rising like a periscope from a submarine. I decided to call it a day.

Now, I'm no paedophobe, but I would be quite relieved when the children went back to school. This was partly down the scarcity of B&Bs and campsite pitches during the holidays. But mostly it was because I was getting fed up with feeling like the Man Who Has Come to Do Terrible Things to Your Kiddies.

Imagine the scene. There you are, enjoying the carefree nature of a family camping holiday, kids running around, free, innocent, climbing trees, frolicking, playing with all the other children on the family-friendly site. Suddenly, a middle-aged man arrives. He's wearing Lycra. He's holidaying alone. Alone! On a bicycle. And hey presto! In the time it takes to pitch my little one-man tent, the

kiddywinkies have been ushered inside quicker than if the Child
Catcher had been spotted on the edge of town.

That had been one of the many joys of wild camping in Scotland: no need to explain yourself. But sometimes the lure of a hot
shower was too much to resist.

After I'd pitched my tent, a little boy approached me.

'That's a nice wee tent, mister,' he said.

'Thanks.'

'Can I have a look inside?'

'I'd rather you didn't…'

But before the words were out, the boy had disappeared into
the tent. Oh, Jesus. I could imagine the flaming torches.

'It's cool,' I could hear from inside.

A man was walking quickly in my direction. Explanations would
be sought. Needed. It's sad, but understandable.

'All right, mate?' he asked in a Glaswegian accent. I thought I
caught him suspiciously looking at my Winnie-the-Pooh bell.

'Good thanks.'

'On holiday?'

'That's right.'

'Lotta gear.'

'I'm on a long trip.'

'Where've you cycled from?'

'London.'

'All that way!'

'Well, actually I'm cycling around the whole coastline.'

At this stage, there always seemed to be a release of tension, as
if people can cope once a plausible narrative has been provided. I've
found that people are generally suspicious of loners. But if we can
justify our aloneness, dress it up as being an unfortunate but necessary consequence of some project, then it's acceptable.

But I knew what would be coming next.

'For charity?'

By now, I'd had a lot of practice answering this question and
had worked through various options. I'd tried lying and saying yes.
This answer seemed to be the one people wanted to hear and had
given me kudos. A double win.

But I'd had to drop it after a man had insisted I take a tenner,
and I'd insisted I couldn't, and he'd stuffed the note into my pocket

with a wink and said 'Good on ya.' For the record, I put it into the collection tin at a donkey sanctuary. Honest.

After that, I'd tried telling people that I was doing it just for the hell of it, but that only seemed to confuse them further. So in the end, I told them it was the result of a drunken bet or the fulfilment of a lifelong dream, and everybody could breathe easier and the kids could be released.

'Come on, son,' the man said. 'Out of the tent. Let's leave the man in peace.'

Word soon got around the campsite that I wasn't a sexual predator, and I even got invited by one nice couple with two kids to have dinner with them. It was lovely, sitting there with them under the stars, me contributing my wedge of Arran cheese with mustard and bottle of finest malt. We ended the evening swapping email addresses. The woman sent me a message a few days later. 'I'm a bored housewife,' she wrote, 'who's very broad-minded and not easily shocked. Fancy some email fun?'

I was tempted to write back, but in the end decided that I probably was easily shocked. But I was consoled at least by the thought that things are rarely as they seem and that few, if any, of us can truly or fully explain what we're doing and why.

It was a hefty culture shock to be back on the mainland and away from the remote Highlands and islands. In the port town of Ardrossan, many of the pubs had bars on the windows, the industrial estates had 'To Let' signs on their closed-down units and the terraced streets had boarded-up houses. I saw my first Iceland supermarket for weeks, and corner shops with starburst signs in the windows offering six cans of strong lager for a fiver. On the pavements litter swirled and eddied in the chill wind, there was graffiti on the walls and shattered windows in the bus shelters. There was a feeling of aggression in the air, of confrontation, an acceleration of everything, though it was more of an indefinable feeling than anything tangible. Taking NCN7 out of the town, across scrubby wasteland, I passed the charred remains of two burned-out cars and an eviscerated scooter. In the background was the ambient hiss from the dual carriageway nearby.

I doubted that Ardrossan was particularly or uniquely bleak compared with other mainland towns of a similar size, but the crossing from Arran to there felt like one spanning two completely separate worlds. As I rode south, I looked across to Arran, disappearing in the haze.

I pedalled along the Ayrshire coast into a strong south-westerly headwind. I wondered whether I would have this all the way to Land's End now. Passing the golf course at Troon I thought of Anders and wondered where he was, and whether he'd managed to see his whale yet.

Just south of Dunure, I stopped by the side of the road to read an inscribed stone block. 'The Electric Brae' it said at the top. This was the famous stretch of road where an optical illusion created by the lay of the land made it appear as if a car was rolling uphill when it was in fact going down. This is of course an illusion that cannot work on a bicycle. It might look as if you are going downhill, but your legs are sadly never fooled. Only a tailwind and whisky can do that.

I pressed on down the A77 right alongside the Firth of Clyde, riding past Ailsa Craig just off the town of Girvan. The island had always been present somewhere in my field of vision these past few days, like the moon moving around the sky on a cloudless night, and had acted as a pivot point as I'd moved around the long concave sweep of the South Ayrshire coast.

The NCN7 went inland, following the quiet lanes that climbed up through the forests and hills of Dumfries and Galloway. It was tempting to take it, especially as the coastal A77 was horrendously busy and dangerous, a two-lane highway that took all the traffic from the ferries at Stranraer to Glasgow. But taking NCN7 would mean cutting right across the headland and missing out a big chunk of the coast. I'd made a promise to myself that there would be no more cutting corners until I got home. There was nothing for it but to duck my head into the wind and pray every time a truck or coach squeezed past me with inches to spare, cursing as I went.

A 30-strong herd of brown bullocks ran alongside me in a field for about half a mile. That cheered me up.

I did a quick loop of the claw hammerhead that I'd always assumed was called the Stranraer Peninsula, but is in fact called The Rhinns of Galloway, which is far more poetic. I rode through great forests of tropical-looking trees, rhododendrons and azaleas that flourish in the mild climate of The Rhinns. And when I came to a clearing found myself looking at a landmass just across the water. I racked my brains to imagine what it could be. Not the Mull of Kintyre, surely. Nor the Isle of Man. I was pretty sure I was looking west, so it couldn't be part of the coast of mainland Britain. Then the penny dropped. I must be looking across the North Channel to Northern Ireland. I knew that the two islands came fairly close together, but had no idea that it was quite that near. It looked like I could swim across. It was another example of how my mental map of Britain would never look quite the same again.

The fishing village of Portpatrick was rammed with families enjoying that by now lovely sunny Sunday in early August. I rode past a pub, where a white-jumpsuited Elvis impersonator (the Vegas years) stood in the beer garden out front singing 'Love Me Tender'.

At the end of the old stone quay, a vicar in a brilliant white cassock was conducting a service, surrounded by a small knot of worshippers. Tied alongside was the Portpatrick lifeboat, on whose deck stood the crew, heads bowed solemnly. The vicar sprinkled his sermon with watery metaphors – 'God gives us our anchor', 'Imagine I was sinking in the sand and God saved me' – and the following rendition of 'For Those in Peril on the Sea' had the hairs on the back of my neck standing up, the profound silence that followed broken only by 'Jailhouse Rock' drifting across the harbour.

I skirted around Luce Bay and headed south-east, every village flying a sign at its end saying 'Haste Ye Back', which I thought was rather lovely. It had been an 80-mile day and I was feeling tired. My bike was feeling tired too, a state of affairs it communicated to me on arrival in Port William with the sound of a sickening crack coming from the rear wheel.

I dismounted and had a look. There was a big split in the rim. I might have been shedding stuff left, right and centre, but obviously not enough. And a broken spoke is one thing. Finding a rim for a touring bike in the middle of nowhere quite another. I felt like somebody had punched me in the stomach.

I pitched my tent by the water and went into the local shop – the shops in rural Scotland are delightful, like mini department stores selling a little bit of just about everything: food, chandlery, electric fences, rubber work boots, engine oil, camping gear. But sadly, generally no bicycle section.

I asked the woman behind the counter where the nearest bike shop was. She didn't know. Neither did the half a dozen people in the shop she asked. The third person she phoned seemed to think there was a bike shop in Newton Stewart, some 15 miles north.

'You'll need to be taking the bus if your bike's broken.'

'When's the next one?'

There was a further period of consultation, and a general looking at watches and shaking of heads.

'Tomorrow morning at 6.45.'

The rain was pouring down as I waited at the bus stop the next morning clutching my broken wheel. I could feel that familiar claustrophobia rising again at not being independent.

The bus eventually arrived, a small eight-seater minibus driven by an elderly man in a flat cap. We pulled off, bumping and meandering along the hedgerowed lanes, heading to all points of the compass, pulling into every little hamlet. The minibus had no shock absorbers, so my spine had to do the job.

We arrived in Newton Stewart 90 minutes later. With nearly an hour to kill before the bike shop opened, I wandered up and down the little high street in the rain, peering through the windows of the small independent shops, the butcher's and the fishmonger's, the bakery and the greengrocer's. I walked along the banks of the River Cree and came to a giant Sainsbury's with large orange banners announcing its grand opening in two weeks' time.

I remembered when my Sainsbury's Local opened a few years ago. The local shopkeepers, whom I'd got to know well over the years, said it would be the ruin of them and I pledged to them that I would never shop there. I'd kept that pledge for about a fortnight, before I was tempted by the better choice and lower prices. But I was ashamed of myself enough to take the back roads to the supermarket so that I wouldn't have to walk past the little shops clutching my orange carrier bags. I don't have to take the long detour any more, because many of the little shops have closed. The prices in the supermarket don't seem quite as low any more, and the staff there, nice as they seem, change frequently and are generally too busy to stop and chat. It's progress, of course, and my part in the demise of the local shops means I can't complain. But I do miss the sense of community that's now gone.

As soon as I walked into the bike shop, I knew I was stuffed. For it wasn't a specialist bike shop, but a store selling mainly children's toys. The bikes that were there were generally pink and possessing three wheels. The man was very nice, though.

He knew there was definitely a big bike shop in Dumfries, 50 miles away. But he also thought there might be one in Castle Douglas, on the same route at about halfway.

So, I had a plan. Get off in Castle Douglas, check out the bike shop. If I had no luck, I could hop on the next bus to Dumfries. Sorted.

I walked back up to the town square where the buses departed from. It was still raining. I looked at the timetable.

There was a whole cast of operators: Houston's Minicoaches; Andersons of Langholm; MacEwan's Coaches; King of Kirkcowan. There were asterisks and little dagger symbols everywhere. Some buses ran on Saturdays only, or the first Wednesday of the month, or only on market days. Some took different routes on schooldays to the ones they took at weekends or school holidays. Was it still school holidays? What day of the week was it? Monday. When was market day? My head swam. I'm convinced that Operation Desert Storm had fewer logistical problems than getting a bus out of Newton Stewart.

I asked a little old lady sitting in the shelter.

'Och, it's confusing, isn't it? Sometimes they dinne turn up at all.'

A bus pulled up. I asked the driver whether he went to Dumfries. He did. Via Castle Douglas? Only on Thursdays. I needed the bus just behind, he said. I didn't. That only went as far as New Galloway on Mondays. Market day, see. The one after that went past Castle Douglas, but on Mondays operated as the express to Dumfries and didn't stop. None of the timetables seemed to be coordinated, or the services connecting. I was in some *On The Buses*-meets-Kafka nightmare.

I watched all these buses pull away, my wheel dangling broken in my hand, and thought seriously for the first time about just packing it all in. But then I thought about the obstacles that my adventurer heroes had overcome in order to prevail – the frostbite, the loss of limbs, attacks by loin-clothed tribesmen, the insanity – and I imagined trying to explain how the Dumfries and Galloway bus timetable had tipped me over the edge. I figured that that the Explorers' Club wouldn't be booking me for a lecture any time soon.

Eventually I found a bus. It was one o'clock by the time it had visited every village on its way to Castle Douglas and had sat in the heavy, slow-moving traffic that filled the A75 every time we joined it. That journey gave me plenty of time to think about the madness of bus deregulation and all those bits of weed-covered and crumbling railway infrastructure that I glimpsed from my window from time to time. No wonder most people nowadays just hop in their cars. Who can blame them? It would have taken me three hours to cycle. Public transport had taken over six.

I got off in Castle Douglas. As the bus pulled away, I looked at the timetable. The next bus to Dumfries was in two hours. There was an asterisk. I looked at the legend at the bottom. It said: 'Mondays excepted.'

There was a bike shop. Hallelujah! And the man there told me he'd been fully booked, but just that morning a customer had called to cancel a wheel-building and so he could slot me in right now. Hallelujah and blessed are the wheel-makers. I do believe I said out loud that I loved him.

Proudly clutching my pristine new wheel, I arrived back in Port William at 8 p.m., some 13 hours after setting off. As I passed the little shop, the woman poked her head around the door.

'Och, we were getting worried about you,' she said.

For the next couple of days I rode along the Dumfries and Galloway coastline as it became the Solway Firth, indented with sandy coves and estuaries. NCN7 took me through some off-road sections of thick fairy-tale forest and also along some not-so-glorious sections of country back lanes that were a foot deep in water.

For the first time in nearly two months I could see England, the hills of the Lake District rising in the distance, shimmering across the firth like some mystical Avalon. I felt a tad emotional, like an emigrant staring from the prow of a ship returning to the mother-land after an adventure in the New World. Which was ridiculous, of course, but idealised and sentimental notions of home burn brightly. And somehow, when you've travelled every yard under your own steam, the sense of journey is magnified a thousand-fold.

I stopped off in Gretna Green. I followed the signs for the Blacksmith's Shop, riding up the driveway to the Gretna Hall Hotel and behind it into a courtyard. I was just in time to see a couple emerge through the archway to be showered with confetti by the two guests. I looked around the big car park and saw numerous other wedding parties clustered here and there. There was a white carriage drawn by a pair of white horses, a piper in full regalia, a pink stretched limousine, two poodles in waistcoats, people in Edwardian fancy dress. It looked like a wedding fair organised by footballers' wives.

A man in a light grey suit and a dog collar emerged from the Blacksmith's Shop.

'Hello,' I said.

'Are you getting married?' he asked.

'No. Just curious.'

'Do you want to have a look inside? I've got fifteen minutes before the next one.'

His name was Dom Frith and he'd been the Methodist minister at the Blacksmith's Shop marriage hall for eight years since retiring from his ministry in Carlisle.

'It gives me something to do and I really enjoy it. I'm seventy,' he said. 'You can't believe it, can you?'

'No,' I said. And I couldn't.

Don took me into the marriage hall. At the front was an old stagecoach, and in front of that an anvil on a wooden stump. Written on it in white lettering was 'The Old Anvil of the Marriages'.

'That is the old anvil of the marriages,' said Don, unnecessarily, and he picked up a ball-peen hammer from the floor and struck the metal block, sending a pinging noise ricocheting off the stone walls.

'That's how we confirm the marriage,' he said. 'Because back in the day, the unions were "forged" over an anvil by the blacksmith.'

Don explained how Gretna became a magnet for eloping couples whose motives could not stand the test of a formal betrothal with the parental consent required in England under the 1754 Hardwicke Marriage Act. Even today, couples come to Gretna because Scotland is the only place where parental consent is not required after the age of 16.

I asked Don what he thought about people getting married in fancy dress or having poodles as maids of honour. I was quite sure he'd deliver a sermon about the sanctity of marriage and the world going to hell in a handcart, but he just chuckled.

'I think it's all rather jolly,' he said. 'I've conducted a wedding where everybody was dressed as Elvis. I think it was the anniversary of his birth. I have people stopping off on motorbikes while riding to Land's End who marry in biker gear. There are people who dress up like fairy-tale characters. I've done a wedding in Welsh, with an interpreter, naturally. Just recently, a couple who'd been together for thirty-three years stopped off on their way to the Highlands on holiday and wanted to get married. Jeans and T-shirts. Lovely. I had the feeling that something very good was being celebrated.'

'You married, Mike?'

'Divorced.'

'Ah, so you have experience. We get a lot of people divorced from each other who come back years later to get remarried. I'm really encouraged by those people.'

'Are you married?' I asked Don. His sparkling eyes dimmed for a moment.

'She died a few months ago. This helps me to get out of the house. When I come here, I have to switch my mode from sadness to happiness. It's very, very helpful.'

'I'm sorry.'

He shrugged his shoulders and gave a forced smile.

'Well, when you marry again, you should come and see me.'

Marry again? I laughed at the suggestion. I hated that latterly acquired cynicism in myself, but what can you do?

'Maybe next time,' I said.

Don had to go. His next couple were walking towards us across the car park, attended by the two poodles.

'I'm happy I've seen the world-famous anvil,' I said to Don.

'Oh, this isn't it,' he said.

'It isn't?'

'The original one is up the road. There's a whole marriage business in Gretna these days.'

So I went off to the Original Old Blacksmith Shop Centre. I imagined I would have to follow that with a visit to the Truly

Original Old Blacksmith Shop Centre, but the woman at the desk assured me that I had found the oldest and most famous wedding venue in Gretna.

I watched a few newlyweds emerge from their nuptials, and surprised myself by feeling quite moved by it all, clapping along with the other tourists gathered around. That seemed like progress of a sort.

Just down the road was a hotel and I popped my bike against the wall and went in for a late breakfast. Sitting at the next table was a couple.

'Cycled far?' asked the man.

'Going round the British coastline.'

'For charity?' said the woman.

'No.'

'Oh,' said the man.

The waiter came over. I ordered a couple of boiled eggs.

'Just married?' I asked.

'This morning,' said the woman.

They came from the South Coast, had decided on a Gretna marriage to avoid all the fuss.

'We're not religious people,' said the man, whose name was Pete.

'We've been together six years,' said the woman, whose name was Karen. 'A lot of people didn't think we'd make it, because of the age gap. He's forty and I'm twenty-seven.'

'We wanted to do it our way,' said Pete.

'Bit selfish, but it's our day,' said Karen.

'I assumed they had a couple of official witnesses, but it was just two tourists in shorts and T-shirts with their kids. They were lovely.'

'Ceremony was short and sweet. He's a typical bloke, so I organised it all.'

'I'm happy to go with the flow. Just went there, they pulled out these witnesses. Job done. Bloody great.'

'When we came out, there were hundreds of strangers just clapping and taking photos. You feel like a movie star.'

'We don't enjoy the limelight very much.'

'Only a little bit.'

They were in full flow now, talking in short bursts, finishing each other's sentences.

'You read in the papers that sometimes the debt of getting wed lasts longer than the marriage...'

'...depressing...'

'...we don't need a kettle or a toaster...'

'...to be in debt and the marriage failing would be...'

'...depressing...'

'...wouldn't be great, would it?'

'My sister's done it twice before,' Pete said. 'I've held back. This is my first and last...'

'...you've bided your time.'

'I'm a bit older, seen a bit of life, done what I've wanted to do...'

'... a lot of people thought I'd regret coming up here, but I don't...'

'I'm proud of her. My family are proud of her too. I couldn't wish for anyone else...'

'...soppy git...'

And they hugged each other and shortly after said farewell and went off to start their married adventure together. And I sat there, at my table for one, hacking at the top of a boiled egg, with a big smile on my face.

I left the hotel and headed for the border, but got lost in the back streets of Gretna looking for the little road that runs south parallel to the M6. I felt hugely sad to be leaving Scotland.

I asked a man out walking his dog for directions. He scratched his head and thought for a while.

Eventually, he said: 'You go down to the roundabout... have ye eaten?'

'Erm, yes.'

'Well, there's a great chippy there if you're hungry.'

'Thanks.'

'Then you turn reet, past the "Welcome ta England" sign... have you got your camera? You wouldne want to miss that.'

'I have, yes.'

'Well, after that you follow the road... have you been to Carlisle afore? There's a bonny castle and a cathedral...'

'I'm not going to Carlisle.'

'Pity. There's a great B&B by the station…'

'I'm sticking to the coast.'

'Ah, you'll be going through Bowness-on-Solway, just over by. Great birdlife there. Do you like birds?'

'I do.'

'Och, fabulous they are this time of year.'

And as I eventually got away, and cycled past for the final time a sign saying 'Haste Ye Back' and, shortly afterwards, past a big sign bearing the Cross of St George, I realised that summed up in that final conversation is what I would remember most about my time in Scotland.

Chapter 16

'When the spirits are low. When the day appears dark.
When work becomes monotonous. When hope hardly
seems worth having. Just mount a bicycle and go out
for a spin down the road, without thought on
anything but the ride you are taking.'

Arthur Conan Doyle

The lambs were getting huge. They'd been an ever-present sight on my journey. From my saddle, peering over the hedgerows, or trying to marshal them out of the roads, I'd watched them grow, through May and June and now into August, from cute little bundles suckling gently to becoming bigger than their mother, ambushing her in twos and threes and feeding with such violent head-butting, little tails wagging like pumps, that they often lifted her clean off the ground. Sometimes I found myself shouting at them to treat their mothers with a little more respect. And that admission alone perhaps gives an indication of what over three months spent by yourself on a bicycle can do to a man.

The day would come soon enough when the lambs would disappear altogether, and with it a sense of time passing and a summer fast receding.

I use the term summer in its loosest sense, of course. For ever since I'd stupidly taken advantage of a Boots two-for-the-price-of-one sun cream offer two months previously, the bottles had remained full and unused in my panniers. And yet, as I pedalled along in the rain and the cold and the south-westerly gales, I kept thinking that that day, that week, that month, must be an aberration, and that the predicted 'barbecue summer' must be just around the corner.

Then I'd look at the calendar and see that August was already well under way, and I'd plan my murderous revenge on the Met

Office and their band of smiley autocutie propagandists, while remembering the John Cleese character's line in the movie *Clockwise*: 'It's not the despair, I can take the despair. It's the hope I can't stand.'

I rode alongside the mudflats and shifting sands of the Solway Firth, the Campfield Marsh nature reserve teeming with wading birds, as my Gretna friend had said it would be, the hills of Galloway engulfed by swirling mist beyond. The wild weather seemed to suit this English outpost perfectly. It felt elemental and abandoned, a frontier. The NCN signs announced that this was called the Reivers Cycle Route, named after the thieves and bandits who used to rule the Border country. It seemed the perfect choice.

Every hundred yards or so there'd be a sign by the road, which had buckled into little troughs, warning of the treacherous tides and quicksands.

The seaside town of Silloth was under water when I passed through, its wet cobbled streets no friend of the bicycle tyre. The houses were handsome, even grand, built around an orderly grid of streets, and the neat municipal gardens filling the space between the houses and the sea looked as if they were ready to receive coachloads of pensioners to doze on deckchairs while listening to a string quartet. But Silloth was empty of people, and carried the air of a place that had held a great party a long time ago. Maybe, I'd been able to find somebody to ask, I'd have been told that the locals liked it quiet. But Silloth seemed to resent its repose.

The road south ran right against the water, a storm-tossed, churning mass. Allonby, with precious little defences to speak of, looked as if it was in danger of being swallowed whole at any time by the Irish Sea. The grasses on the salt marsh were cowering. Great spumes of spray came over the road, drenching me further, coating my skin with a salty film. I went into a shop selling beach-fun paraphernalia and bought a large bag of wine gums. I stood outside sheltering under the awning for 20 minutes or so, munching away, the sugar of the sweets mixing with the salt on my lips. In that time I saw not a soul.

Maryport, Workington and Whitehaven came and went. They were all handsome enough, distinguished even – the Georgian grid-patterned streets of Whitehaven were reputedly used as a template for New York. But, like bigger versions of Silloth, they each carried an air of melancholy and doom, of having been forgotten. Once great centres of shipbuilding, coal-mining and steelworks that had built the railway lines for the world, they had, like so many of the former industrial areas I'd ridden through, their usefulness gone, been abandoned to their fate.

To ride through them, to see the decaying remnants of industry and the boarded-up little shops, felt like rubbernecking at an accident, intruding on private grief. If the world didn't need ships, coal or steel any more, if we were talking abacuses, or sextants, then maybe there'd be something to be learned. But the waste of all those skills and resources and people just seemed scandalous to me.

Highly visible in those three towns were the modern panaceas for industrial decline, the civic displays of bravado: the museums and street artwork celebrating their lost heritage, the aquariums, a flashy new conference centre in the shape of a wave, and, naturally, glittering new shopping palaces housing the multinational chains. Where once we made things to sell to the world, now we shop. And after we're done shopping, we can watch some fish swimming around. (Can anybody explain to me how that economic model works?)

I crested a hill and freewheeled down into lovely St Bees, thronged with already bedraggled hikers setting off on Wainwright's 190-mile coast-to-coast walk to Robin Hood's Bay and probably plotting their own revenge on John Kettley.

I found a B&B. The owner had one of the most curious accents I'd ever heard in Britain, a mixture of Geordie, Scots and Brummie. 'That's pure Cumbrian, that is,' he said. 'From Egremont, and proud of it.'

I asked him about the walkers doing the coast-to-coast.

'And cyclists. A godsend these days, what with everything. Big business it is. Numbers seem to grow every year. Poor sods out on a day like today, though. We had that Frank Skinner here. And the Director General of the BBC. My missus reckons he earns over £100,000.'

So business was okay then?

'It's getting tight. But we're lucky round here to have Sellafield just down the road. Employ thousands they do. We'd be fooked without it. They've got their own police force, you know. And there's always five of 'em staying here.'

I went up to my room to dry off, and then lay on the bed, exhausted from being battered by the weather, enjoying the rare opportunity to catch up with the national news on TV. I was always amazed at how quickly I'd lose track of what was going on in the world. But this only seemed to heighten my sense of how much I was enjoying the trip.

Huw Edwards ended the bulletin, as he always does, by saying 'and now for the news wherever you are'. That had always annoyed me when I was at home, because I was always on the same sofa. But now it was exciting, because I had to quickly think 'where am I?' before the channel cut to a studio, and there would be two unfamiliar faces with unfamiliar accents, who'd talk not of the latest strike planned for the Tube or Boris's latest gaffe, but of job cuts in Workington or Carlisle United's search for a new goalkeeper.

NCN72 took me along quiet lanes and across low rolling hills the next morning, my wheels in a constant slick of slurry. The fury of the previous day had blown itself out and all was still and silent except the rumbling murmurs of the sea against some unseen foreshore.

All was as you'd expect in a quiet corner of rural England, except the fact that many of the telegraph poles in fields had CCTV cameras attached to them.

The reason for the cameras was revealed as the unmistakable shape of Sellafield's nuclear reactor hove into view, surrounded by buildings so immense and numerous and just so plain dystopian-sci-fi-city weird that I wouldn't have been surprised to see squadrons of flying monkeys dispatched to repel me. Even if you had no idea what Sellafield was, you'd know, just by looking at it, that it harboured some fearsome power.

Route 72 went off-road, winding its ways across fields, crossing narrow cattle grids especially made for bicycles, which made me feel as if travelling by bike was a proper grown-up thing to do. I'd thought that there'd be some big exclusion area around the fences of Sellafield, but all of a sudden I was not 100 metres from the dome, so rusting and dilapidated-looking, so deathly quiet, so appallingly terrifying. My mobile phone buzzed into life, flashing urgently that I needed to insert my sim card and then, for the first time in the six years I'd had it, deciding to run a little demo film that I had no idea existed. I tried to turn the phone off but couldn't. So instead I just pedalled, really quite quickly, past the nuclear trains in the sidings loaded with flasks, and then along Route 72, sandwiched between the now-calm sea, the railway line and the cliffs. I rode surrounded by giant blooms of orange wildflowers and bushes bursting with blackberries that, to my fertile imagination, looked considerably bigger than any I'd ever seen before. For the first time on the trip, I wasn't remotely tempted to eat any.

Headlands hang like stalactites on the bottom of Cumbria, the map dotted with towns with Furness in the name – Askam-in-Furness, Dalton-in-Furness, Kirby-in-Furness and Broughton-in-Furness. Furness comes from the Norse words *futh* (bottom) and *nes* (headland) and so I could say, if I was feeling unkind, that I was in the arse end of nowhere.

I rode into Barrow-in-Furness. According to my guidebook, Barrow had grown hugely wealthy in the nineteenth century after large deposits of haematite had been found, leading to the opening of iron and steelworks which, for a time, made Barrow the largest producer of iron and steel in the world, a centre for engineering excellence and especially shipbuilding. The ironworks had closed in 1963, the steelworks in 1983. The shipyards, which as recently as the 1980s had 14,000 workers, now employed 5,000.

In 2008, the town had been named the most working-class place in Britain, based on a series of measures devised to evaulate lifestyles. The research found that Barrow had a fish and chip shop, a working-men's club and a bookies for every 2,917 people. Another survey found that Barrow was within the top 10 per cent most deprived districts in Britain and an unemployment blackspot. So make of that what you will.

Still, Barrow is one of those strange anachronisms in modern Britain: a town that's still actually making stuff. Okay, so every one of the factories, so gargantuan that I felt like Gulliver in Brobding-nag, has BAE Systems stamped on the side, and the 'stuff' now tends to be weapons of mass destruction, but hey, at least we still lead the way in something.

I cycled around the docks, past the nuclear submarines and the warships moored within a stone's throw of the main shopping centre, and past the Victorian red-brick tenement blocks. Then past the fabulously cocksure Gothic sandstone town hall, built in 1886 to proclaim loudly Barrow's place in the world, and then past the new retail parks. Then I headed straight out of town again.

A cyclist pulled alongside me and we rode together for a while up the Furness Peninsula. He was on his commute home from work. He was from Yorkshire originally, but had moved to Barrow as a young man.

'I'd never go back. I love it here. Great atmosphere, hardly any crime.'

Where did he work?

'BAE. I make guns, basically,' he said.

I said that war must be good business for Barrow and he replied that, funnily enough, it was the opposite, that countries always bought more weapons in peacetime.

'It's the possibility of war that keeps people nervous,' he said.

He told me how things in the town had changed in his lifetime.

'When I came here, the brightest left school on Friday and started at Vickers [the shipyard] on Monday. The rest went into the steelworks. Now, BAE only needs highly skilled workers, so young people with no qualifications have got nowhere to go.'

The decision on the renewal of Trident was key to Barrow's future, he said. If the government went ahead, Barrow would build four new submarines to replace the four Vanguard ones currently in service. It would guarantee work for the town's shipyards until 2030.

I told him that I would keep my eyes on the news.

I'd really liked Barrow. It had something special about it. But it would feel odd in the future to be rooting for a place whose very existence depended on the weapons that might mean annihilation for us all.

The man peeled off when we passed his village, after which the road rose gently. At the top of the hill I was greeted by one of the most astonishing and spectacular things I have ever seen. For below me was the seemingly infinite expanse of Morecambe Bay, 190 square miles of it which, when it was drained, as it was now, looked like a vast ocean of sand fringed by distant shores, the sheer scale of it impossible to process. Time and again, the road ducked into woodland, and each time it spat me out, I felt compelled to stop, staring at the scene before me as incredulously as if I were looking at Mars.

I followed the sweep of the bay, stopping off in Ulverston to have my photo taken next to a statue of the town's most famous son, Stan Laurel, cast grinning in bronzed perpetuity next to Olly. And then on to Carnforth, where I popped into the railway station to have a look at the clock made famous by Celia Johnson and Trevor Howard in David Lean's *Brief Encounter*. There was a young couple arguing under the clock, pointing accusing fingers at each other and swigging cider from cans. And they say that romance is dead.

I had done some big miles that day, clocking my first century of the trip just after Carnforth, a distance that would have seemed the stuff of fantasy to me when I'd set off from London. But after nearly 3,000 miles, my lungs were like bellows, my thighs like giant hams, seemingly willing to turn and turn as long as I stuffed enough food in my gob to fuel them. I felt as close as I'd ever done to seeing my body as the finely tuned machine of which athletes speak. Charles M. Schulz, the creator of Peanuts, once said, 'Life is like a 10-speed bicycle. Most of us have gears that we never use', and feeling my strength that afternoon, I could begin to understand where he was coming from.

The last 10 miles of the day were spent riding along the towpath of the Lancaster Canal. It was flat, obviously, and the surface under my wheels silky smooth, taking me though tunnels of trees and flying me high over the River Lune on a magnificent aqueduct into Lancaster.

A few miles later, and there in front of me was the reason I'd done such a big day: the art deco confection that is the Midland Hotel, Morecambe, curving simpatico with the promenade along the bay, barley-twist pillars flanking its entrance. It was a place I'd longed to visit since reading about its recent grand restoration and reopening. I'd called the day before and booked a room.

The Modernist masterpiece of architect Oliver Hill, with a central circular tower punctuating its three-storey white curve, was built in 1933, essentially to cater for the vacation needs of previously well-to-do people who, after being wiped out by the Great Depression, couldn't afford to travel abroad any more. It was known locally as Morecambe's Great White Hope.

That hope didn't last too long, and the hotel gradually declined until, at the start of the twenty-first century, it was derelict. The company Urban Splash took it on and, hey presto, £11 million and eight years later, it had been reborn. Designer Eric Gill's bas-relief, *Odysseus Welcomed from the Sea by Nausicaa*, stolen and eventually found in the back of a lorry, was back in place, as were his seahorse sculptures and ceiling medallion of Neptune and Triton. It was gloriously over the top.

'One would willingly climb its fairy spiral staircase till it reached to heaven,' *Country Life* had written back in the 1930s. One would have willingly climbed the staircase if one hadn't just cycled 120 miles, I thought, as I pressed the lift button.

My room was on the top floor and had unrestricted views over the whole of Morecambe Bay. The sun was gathering speed in its descent over Barrow. To my right the peaks of the Lake District were glowing fiery pinks and oranges like the angry tips of active volcanoes. The angel felt I should go and explore Morecambe, but from what I'd seen and felt on the ride in, the shuttered shops, the by-now familiar British seaside resort's weight of tired sadness, I thought I'd give it a miss. The devil agreed, and told me to order a gin and tonic from room service.

So, imbibed with the spirit of Gordon's, and also with the spirit of past guests, Edward VIII and Wallis Simpson and Noël Coward among them, I sat on my balcony high above the bay allowing the tiredness of the road to wash over me. As the sky darkened, I watched the desert flood with the speed of time-lapse photographic trickery.

The coastal plains of Lancashire were the widest and flattest piece of Britain I'd encountered since Lincolnshire, some 2,000 miles earlier. It felt slightly unnerving not to have the counterpoint of rising land on my left, or ahead, as if I was suddenly adrift in an ocean.

In the distance, I could see Blackpool Tower, acting as some kind of magical navigational beacon. The sight of it brought childhood memories flooding back. For it was to Blackpool for the illuminations and a day at the Pleasure Beach that my extended family headed every year in a convoy of cars from Birmingham. That was nearly 40 years ago, but to this day I can close my eyes and easily summon up the charged spirit of that journey, the willing of the miles to disappear. After passing Preston on the M6 and seeing the sign for the Blackpool exit, the frantic scanning of the horizon would begin.

'There it is!'

'No, that's a pylon.'

'Oh.'

'Is that it?'

'Where?'

'There.'

'It is. It is!'

I could have burst with happiness.

I took the little ferry across the River Wyre from Knott End-on-Sea to Fleetwood, then rode along the seafront on the smooth concrete between the tram tracks, tucking behind trams to benefit from the slipstream, peeling off to overtake when they pulled up at stops, then pulling back in rapidly to avoid the tram heading straight for me, bell clanking frantically. The sea was the colour of mushroom soup, slopping tiredly against the concrete defences and sending little spumes of spray onto the promenade. The grey, foaming sea, the trams. The years simply disappeared.

There are arguments for and against going back as an adult to the scene of some of your happiest childhood memories. Blackpool for me was preserved in a frame, filled with smiles and innocence and optimism.

I rode past the North Pier, right under the tower, and then found a B&B. That wasn't difficult. It's said that Blackpool has more beds than the whole of Portugal, and every guesthouse was flying a 'vacancies' sign in the window.

I went for a walk. If Blackpool had always been like the quintessential working-class British resort, but on steroids – bigger, brasher, ballsier – then what I saw made me feel instant regret for coming back. Everywhere were lap dancing and strip clubs, pound shops, tanning centres and bars advertising all you can drink for a tenner. There were teenage girls pushing prams, many clutching cans of lager, people so overweight they could hardly walk, and mobility scooters aplenty for those who no longer could. People looked ill, battered, careworn, like they were in the middle of some dreadful ordeal. It was only early afternoon, but lots of people looked drunk. Blackpool seemed to have got nastier since I was a child. The decline of the former manufacturing towns and cities that I'd ridden through, and Blackpool, the once-proud and garish resort where working-class people flocked and still do, appeared glaringly symbiotic. It all seemed so obvious: since the early 1980s, one structured, work-based culture has been deliberately lost with no sign or intention of it being replaced. A large slice of the working class, their opportunities curtailed, their jobs outsourced, is not so much in transition in Britain, but effectively in limbo, the truly horrendous price that they are paying for this economic experiment.

One of New Labour's solutions for the regeneration of working-class areas and resorts was, of course, super-casinos.

Blackpool had been red-hot favourite to seal the deal for the one in the north-west. Some argued it would be a magic bullet for the problems of the local economy, many others reckoned it would only worsen them. We'll never know what would have happened. The decision went Manchester's way and, shortly after, Gordon Brown replaced Tony Blair as prime minister and the whole super-casino business was quietly forgotten.

I pressed a buzzer.

'Yes,' said a woman's voice.

'Is Basil around?'

'Come up.' The door buzzed open.

I walked up some stairs into a reception area. Sitting on a sofa reading magazines were two gorgeous slender young men with lantern jaws and cheekbones you could cut glass with. They both glanced up from their reading and looked me up and down with puzzled expressions.

The woman behind the desk also looked me up and down.

'You're not here for the audition, are you?' she asked.

'Audition?'

'For the show.'

'Oh, no, I'm not.'

'Thank God for that,' she said, laughing.

She picked up the phone and spoke for a little while. On the walls of the office were lots of framed photographs of dancers from the drag revue show. I know I'd been on the road a long time, but they were all stunning.

'He's got a few minutes now. Just through that door.'

I walked into a large office. Basil Newby bounced across the room to shake my hand, motioned for me to sit down with a nod of the head and a theatrical sweep of the hand. I felt like I was in the presence of royalty. According to the guy in my B&B, in Blackpool terms I was. Basil was in his late fifties, but looked barely older than a teenager, with the energy to match. From scratch, he'd built a vast entertainment empire at whose core was Funny Girls, a high-end drag revue show now in its fifteenth year that had become a Blackpool institution, but also included many bars and nightclubs in the town's thriving gay quarter. He was reckoned to be one of the most powerful men in Blackpool.

'I wouldn't say I was that powerful. I just call it Basilpool now,' he laughed. 'I'd paint the tower pink given half the chance.'

'I think your receptionist thought I was here for an audition,' I said.

'That's hilarious,' Basil said.

'Right.'

'It reminds me of the other day when I was in Marks' and there was this tranny. She were like a lorry driver, with tattoos up her hairy arms. Just dreadful. Buying knickers she was. Some old couple were looking at her and then they saw me and said: "You're to blame for all this!" I said to them: "She's not on my books. She's definitely not one of ours!"'

I told Basil how I used to come to Blackpool as a kid, how it always seemed so alive back then, that now it looked as if it was struggling, tired.

'When I think of how it used to be and what it's come to, it's sad,' he said. 'It's a shame with Blackpool because it was the entertainment capital of the North and now it's gone downhill so much. The town is very good at reinventing itself, but I'm a bit scared that I'll be on a Zimmer frame when it manages it this time.

'Because I'm a Sandgrown'un [somebody born in Blackpool], I remember it in its heyday, when there used to be wakes weeks, when whole Lancashire towns would take their holidays en-masse and descend on Blackpool.

'I was born in a boarding house down by the North Prom and we used to have all the big-in-the-day theatre people staying: Shirley Bassey, Cliff Richard, Engelbert Humperdinck. They all did summer seasons here and they all stopped at our place. It was the height of their career. But now, if you do Blackpool, it's like panto, int it? People who can't get work anywhere else come and do Blackpool. I'm not slaggin' 'em off, but at one point it were trick or treat whether it was Cannon and Ball, or Little and Large, or the Grumbleweeds.'

Basil had been pinning a lot of hope on the casino coming to Blackpool. 'Losing that was a massive blow. Blackpool could have become like Las Vegas on heat. Things would have opened up around it. Trouble is that we've had a lot of bad publicity, especially around the hens and stags, which spreads quicker than good publicity. People think we're on the way down and are tacky and tired.'

I asked Basil about the rainbow flags I'd seen in Lord Street and about Blackpool's gay scene.

'We've got it good with the gay village around this area. Lord Street is practically all gay hotels. I think it's great that you can come to Blackpool and stop in the gay hotels and you're on the doorstep for our clubs and bars. The scene here is massive. The Pride march in May is mobbed. I think that's part of the buzz in Blackpool these days – it's so cosmopolitan. People are on holiday and they can see a couple of blokes walking down the street in leather holding hands, or a couple of drag queens.

'Blackpool is a lot more tolerant these days, and that's happened in my lifetime. With my first bar, the Flamingo, in the early eighties, I couldn't get a plumber to come and mend the toilet cos he was scared of getting Aids. It was horrendous. But young people these days are much more open and tolerant. They'll come in and we'll say "You know it's a gay club" and they'll say "Yeah, I'm trisexual. I'll try anything!"'

Basil laughed. He was in full flow now, the stories coming thick and fast. I felt like I was plugged into the mains.

'When I was trying to get a licence for the Flamingo, the magistrate said, whatever you do, don't tell the police you're gay. Because at that time you were considered an unfit and proper person to hold a licence if you were a homosexual. That was the law. So recently. Amazing, huh? The police used to come in and I'd give 'em a drink and they'd be saying "Come on, Basil, you're gay aren't ya?" and I'd say "No, I'm really good at acting."'

And now?

'Well, I think the police know now. Probably cos I've slept with half of them! Ha ha ha ha.'

We chatted some more. Basil hinted at some juicy gossip surrounding the gay clubs and Tory party conferences, but refused to elaborate. 'I'm like a doctor, me,' he said. 'Say nothing.'

And then he said he'd have to go, there were auditions to carry out and preparations for that night's performance at Funny Girls.

'Why don't you come?' Basil said. 'It's very West End, very professional, not tacky or anything like that. The guys as women are just amazing. Straight guys come in and dump their wives and girlfriends to go and wait by the stage door. It's really strange now cos the trannies know which ones they are and they'll say "Oh, he's a tranny shagger, and that one's a tranny shagger."'

I'd never been to a drag show before, tacky or otherwise. That was a big hole in my CV. Besides, it had become clear that I'd never get to appear in one.

'Great,' said Basil. 'You can have my box. You're very lucky. Not too many men these days get into my box.'

I now appeared to be playing a cameo in *Carry on Blackpool*.

Funny Girls was packed. Basil had told me that the show was booked solid at weekends for the next year.

I approached the bar. I could feel myself puff up my chest as I walked, trying to inject a little heterosexual swagger. The man dressed as a woman serving was absolutely stunning. I felt my heart flutter and when he asked me what I'd like, I felt my face redden just a bit. I've no idea what any of that meant, and at first it disturbed me enough to want to blurt out the words 'I'm no tranny shagger', but I just said 'A pint of lager, please' in as baritone a voice as I could muster.

I settled down in Basil's box feeling like an emperor and looked around the auditorium beneath me. The audience was mainly made up of straight-looking couples, some youngish, but mostly middle-aged and elderly, the scene full of spectacles and blue rinses. The

MC, a Lily Savage lookalike with a thick Scouse accent, invited a newly married young couple up on stage.

'Has he got a big cock?' the MC asked the woman, and then proceeded to grope the newlywed man's groin. The audience roared. The man blushed, and smiled.

The show group came on stage. The routines and costumes were fabulous, as slick and polished as Basil said they'd be. We had 'Thriller', as a homage to the late MJ, 'Putting on the Ritz', 'The Addams Family'. For a while, all I could think about was the fact that here were men dressed as women, with their penises sellotaped down, performing these routines to a largely straight, sell-out crowd, and trying to work out what the bigger picture was; why the great British obsession with cross-dressing seems to know no bounds. I got nowhere with that, apart from reaching the conclusion that sometimes trying to understand only gets in the way. After that I managed to love every minute.

I walked back through the darkened streets of Blackpool, slick with rain. Police sirens filled the night air. The bars were heaving. A woman was vomiting into a litter bin, her friends gathered around, rubbing her back. Bouncers were throwing a man out of a pub, his arm twisted behind him. I went onto the promenade in front of the tower, sat on a bench, and stared out to sea.

Of all the places I'd been through on my bike ride, it was Blackpool that seemed to be the most glaring microcosm of the changes that Britain had gone through in recent years; a place that refused to be beaten, that despite getting knocked down time and again, kept getting back up. It had heart. Guts. I was rooting for it. But it also felt that I was actually rooting for much, much more.

The flat plains of Lancashire continued the next day as I looped inland following the River Ribble, through Preston, and then back to the coast at Southport. The sun actually shone for an hour or two, but as the cranes of Liverpool appeared in the distance, the skies darkened and the rain returned.

I sat on the beach at Crosby and watched mesmerised as the incoming tide consumed some of the ghostly cast-iron figures that make up Antony Gormley's installation, *Another Place*. The 100 figures, six feet tall and dotted all over the sands, stare out to sea as if transfixed in some ancient ritual. Gradually, they disappear under the water, one by one. The official line is that the statues represent individual and universal sentiments associated with emigration, the sadness at leaving suffused with the hope of finding a new life in another place. Gormley himself has said: 'For some it might be about human evolution, for others it will be about death and where we go, where our bodies finally belong, do they belong to the earth and the elements?'

I couldn't even begin to fathom what it meant to me. But I did know it was one of the most moving things I had ever seen.

The road into Liverpool through Bootle was grim. Thick with traffic and potholed, it took me past yards with mountains of scrap metal, derelict warehouses with smashed windows, and an adult superstore. There were plenty of half-demolished houses, whose interiors, exposed to the world, showed the last owner's taste in paint colour and wallpaper, the nests, once decorated with love and dreams, now abandoned.

There was that big-city edginess to everything, a tension, a violence in the air, and especially in the way people drove, flying past me with inches to spare, casually indifferent to my safety. I'm sure that it was no more or less dangerous than cycling in London, but after so many weeks and months away from giant cities, it felt shocking.

I stopped at a petrol station to get a drink. The door to the shop was locked and the windows were behind bars. Through an intercom the man asked what I wanted and then asked for the money up front before he went off to get my drink.

At the ferry terminal in front of the Liver Building, a middle-aged man approached me. For the first time in ages, I felt myself watchful, protective, of all my stuff.

'You travelling on your own?' he asked.

'Yes,' I said. I wasn't really in the mood for long discourse.

'Must be awful.'

'It's not actually.'

'B&Bs I suppose. Soft option.'

'Camping mostly.'

'Bit old for that, aren't you?'

Oh, fuck. It was another member of the miserabilist tribe. There was only one way to beat those bastards, and that was with brute happiness.

'Suppose the weather's been bad.'

'Glorious. I've been very lucky.'

'Must have had some rain.'

'I love the rain, too.'

'People are horrible in this country.'

'I've met nothing but kindness.'

'I'd hate to do what you're doing.'

'It's the greatest thing I've ever done.'

On and on it went. My answers felt like red blood cells fighting infection.

'Why have you got that daft bell?' he asked, pointing at Winnie in his flying hat.

That was rich coming from Eeyore. The thought made me laugh. My laughing just seemed to annoy him more.

I looked over his shoulder. The Mersey ferry was docking.

'Nice meeting you,' I said. 'I've got to go.'

'The Wirral's a dump,' he said.

Chapter 17

'The bicycle had, and still has, a humane, almost classical moderation in the kind of pleasure it offers. It is the kind of machine that a Hellenistic Greek might have invented and ridden. It does no violence to our normal reactions: it does not pretend to free us from our normal environment.'

J.B. Jackson

The next few days passed by in a bit of a blur, with me getting some serious mileage in. I think this was partly because by that stage I was so fit that my body seemed to demand the exercise just to maintain itself. But there was something else, too. Up until that point, the distance to go to get back to London was always so immense that my brain could only process the journey in small daily steps. Each day's goal was always to be where I ended up. No more, no less. This had resulted in a blissful state of existing purely in the moment, concerned only with the need for food and a place to sleep and, for the times in between, breathing and pedalling. It was such an uncomplicated and happy life. The fact that my map consisted of ripped-out pages from a road atlas, like pieces of a jigsaw whose completed picture I never saw, only helped me keep my eyes on the piece of ground directly in front of me and not what was around the corner or over the next hill. It was liberating.

But after doing a quick tour of the Wirral and then, shortly afterwards, passing the 'Welcome to Wales' sign, I'd stopped at a garage in Connah's Quay to hoover up a packet of fig rolls. There, I'd idly picked up a magazine from the shelf and flicked through it, and then a road atlas. Looking at a map of the whole island for the first time since leaving home, I'd traced my route around the coast in its entirety, actually running my finger along the estuaries and across the bridges, around the headlands and out to the islands and back.

I couldn't believe how far I'd come, how much of the island's coast I'd travelled. But, instead of stopping my finger at Connah's Quay, I'd continued along the Welsh coast, over the Severn, down to Land's End and back along the South Coast to home. Home. Compared to what I'd already done, the distance to my front door looked so close.

I suddenly found myself thinking about my friends, my favourite pub, my colleagues at work, my flat, my books on the shelves, my bed, my clothes. And for the first time in over three months, I actually felt a longing for home.

The Victorians knew a thing or two about such things. They built tunnels with a slight kink at the ends, because horses tended to bolt towards the light when they saw it.

And that's why, for the next few days, although I didn't know it at the time, I was bolting for the light, eating up the miles, fixated by daily targets. And that change in mindset altered everything. I flew along the North Wales coast with barely a thought for the places I was passing through. I rode until sunset, largely oblivious to the seascapes and birds that had given me so much pleasure just days before, the peaks of Snowdonia to my left barely registering. I rode around the base of Great Ormes Head, and past the spectacular Conwy Castle. Very nice, thank you. I crossed the Menai Straits onto Anglesey and did a loop of the island, counting down the miles until I was back on the mainland again, seeing the hills no longer as an organic part of the journey, but as inconveniences, impediments to going faster, things to be ticked off, got out of the way. I camped mostly, but where I camped felt irrelevant, my tent was just a place to rest and recover, feeling indifferent to the other campers, not interested in swapping tales.

I rode out to the tip of the windswept and remote Lleyn Peninsula and stopped at the end just barely long enough to take a photograph of Bardsey Island across the sound. It was stunning, really stunning. But I can only say that by looking at the picture I took. I have no real recollection of being there, of actually seeing it. That wasn't the game any more. But, as I say, I didn't know it at the time. All I knew was that something felt different. Something had changed. I was now in a hurry to get somewhere else; I was under a spell. It would take a hurricane, a pigeon and a bright yellow diesel locomotive to break it. And that, I feel, requires some explanation.

No disrespect to Brians, but when you're getting battered by the tail end of a hurricane, with trees being flattened by 60mph gusts and comedy rain turning roads into rivers, you'd ideally want your nemesis to be called Zeus or Rambo. Not Brian. Hurricane Brian. That was just taking the piss.

South of Barmouth I crossed the Mawddach Estuary over the 113 spectacular but fragile-looking wooden spans of the railway bridge – which Brian was doing his best to demolish – and, shortly after, ducked, exhausted after another big-miles day, into a caravan site, where my brother had kindly put his van at my disposal.

I laid out my wet things to dry, got everything organised for a crack-of-dawn departure and then got out my various atlas pages and pieced them together, working out where I could be by the following night. My fingertips were numb from all those hours on the road, my palms tender and bruised. A hundred miles would get me to St David's. One hundred and twenty would take me to Pembroke. That would mean the day after I could easily be in Cardiff, or even, if I really got my head down, across the estuary and back in England. From there I could be in Land's End two days later, and home a week after that, or even sooner. Home.

I plugged my dongle into the laptop and called up the BBC's weather page. I wished I hadn't. The first thing I saw was 'Wales: Severe Weather Warning'. I clicked on the story. Brian, it said, would pick up in intensity over the next two days, bring south-westerly gusts of up to 80mph. Damage to property was likely. Police were warning motorists not to travel unless it was an emergency.

Bah! Nothing called Brian was going to stop me, I thought. Besides, they nearly always got the forecast wrong. I would still be leaving in the morning.

I opened the door and walked out of the caravan onto the little wooden deck that looked out over the grey pebble beach and the turbulent water of Cardigan Bay. I heard a train horn and turned around to see, through the gloom, a bright yellow locomotive, like something in a cartoon that would have eyes and a mouth, travelling

light, heading north on the Cambrian Coast line at the top of the
campsite.

I went to bed early and awoke at dawn. The van was being
rocked violently, the aluminium roof so pounded by the rain that
it sounded like somebody was dropping marbles on it. I got up,
put on my bike gear and went into the kitchen to make breakfast,
turning on the TV for the local news. The first thing I saw was
footage of a crushed car beneath the wheels of a bright yellow locomotive. The reporter said how the female driver had died instantly
when the train struck her car the previous evening at a remote level
crossing. The policeman they interviewed wasn't sure, but they
were investigating the possibility that the motorist had ignored the
warning signs.

It must have happened soon after it passed me. I recalled clearly
the sound of the horn, and thought how at that very moment somebody's life was entering its final few minutes, and just how fragile
everything was.

I turned off the TV, gathered up my stuff and opened the door.
It nearly blew off its hinges. I clipped my bags onto the bike. I saw
something move under the caravan. It was a pigeon, soaking wet,
exhausted-looking. I got down on my knees and could see that the
bird, tame as you like, had rings on its legs with a number on them.
Racing pigeon. I'd seen a few cats around the site and doubtless
there were plenty of foxes around too. I didn't fancy the bird's
chances.

I pulled out my laptop from the pannier, went back into the van
and googled 'what to do if find racing pigeon'. The first site up was
from the Royal Pigeon Racing Association. It said: 'Most lost or
exhausted birds will find their way home after a couple of days' rest.
You should provide it with water and food, preferably uncooked
rice or lentils, and try and house in a cardboard box if under threat
from predators. No need to report it. After 48 hours it should be
ready to continue its journey home.'

I unclipped my bags and put them back in the caravan. Then I
rode to the nearest village, where I bought some rice and lentils for
Brian (it seemed a more fitting name for a pigeon than a hurricane),
and a couple of days' worth of food and beer for me. The shopkeeper also gave me an empty cardboard crisp box.

I put Brian in his box under the van, served him his dinner of mixed rice and lentils with a glass of l'eau de Powys, closed the lid, poked in a couple of air holes and left him to convalesce. For the next two days, I topped up his bowls. Together we watched the clouds scud across the sky as we rested and chatted, although the conversation was pretty one-sided.

Whenever I'd been stuck somewhere on the trip previously, usually because of mechanical problems, I'd always felt a sense of claustrophobia, a frustration at being unable to move. But being in that caravan didn't feel like that at all. And I can only guess that having something that relied on me changed things utterly. Okay, it was only a pigeon, but that really wasn't the point.

On the third morning, I opened the caravan door to discover a stillness and a calm in the world, with a strange orange orb in the sky emitting warm rays. Had the British summer finally arrived, in September?

I took the pigeon his breakfast, but I'd hardly got the flaps of the box fully open before Brian had burst forth in a fury of wings, knocking the rice and lentils out of my hand. I watched him fly along the coast for a few hundred yards, then cut inland. I hoped he was heading home, but I felt a great sadness as the speck that was Brian faded to nothing.

I packed up my gear, loaded my bike and hit the road. I would be on the home stretch too, soon enough. But all thoughts of daily targets had now gone. I stopped to watch a kestrel hover over a field for a few minutes and, after it had abandoned its hunt, I just stared out across Cardigan Bay, as if seeing the sea for the first time.

It felt strange to be cycling with the sun on my back. I even had to break out the sun lotion. Just after Tywyn, I took a left onto a quiet lane, following the signs for NCN8, and found myself riding through a deep wooded gorge officially called Happy Valley. That struck me as a little odd. Abroad, and especially in Latin countries, it's common to come across places with beautiful or golden or happy or any number of positive adjectives in the name; in Britain, and much of northern Europe, we tend to be more prosaic and reserved, settling for more gloomy or literal titles to describe a place. I wondered what that said about us, and could only conclude that the naming of Happy Valley had the dabs of sun-soaked foreigners all over it.

I had a long detour inland to get around the Dovey Estuary and at the first available crossing point, in Machynlleth, a place light on vowels but, if pronounced properly, heavy on expectoration, I stopped for something to eat.

The high street was full of organic whole-food shops. The female shoppers walking up and down were all dressed in variations on a Laura Ashley theme. The men wore waistcoats and baggy trousers. Everybody seemed to be wearing some kind of hat, from woollen cloches to battered trilbies. Many of the dogs had bandanas tied around their necks. Drifting through the doorways of the cafés came the heady aromatic mixture of incense and camomile.

Tywyn, just a few miles behind me, had appeared to be a normal working-class seaside town. Machynlleth seemed to attract an altogether different tribe. As with the Aussies in Earl's Court, the Irish in Kilburn or the Bengalis in Tower Hamlets, it's a source of endless fascination to me how we always seem to find each other.

When I did finally decide on a café, I found myself ordering a salad with couscous and aduki beans, washed down with a mug of rosehip and ginseng tea. This was partly because, at heart, I'm desperate to fit in. But I was also beginning to get worried about the vicious hills of Devon and Cornwall not too many days away down the road, and thought a weight-loss regime might be prudent.

I finished my plate and sat there for a while waiting to feel full. The feeling never came. I decided that the hills of Devon and Cornwall couldn't be that bad, and went back to the counter and ordered three fried eggs with a double portion of chips and a can of Coke. The reaction of the two women behind the till made me feel like I was in a Bateman cartoon.

The A487 after Aberystwyth was the worst road of the trip yet: heavy, speeding traffic, two narrow lanes that climbed and plunged, twisted and turned, walled in by tall hedgerows so that the bends were blind. It was the most dangerous combination for a cyclist.

So at Llanfarian I headed inland, up and down the folds in the foothills of the Cambrian Mountains, climbing over 1,000 feet in the first six miles, regretting the chips. Overhead, two RAF Typhoons screamed, dancing, turning tight loops to reveal their sleek delta shapes, leaving the sky scruffy with contrails. It was like having my own private air show.

Many of the fences by the roadside now were made from slate, as were the headstones in the graveyards and the chalkboards left outside the infrequent houses and farms I passed advertising eggs or potatoes for sale.

I became lost in the labyrinth of back lanes and stopped in a tiny village at the bottom of a steep valley to ask for directions. It had a little post office that was still functioning. Maybe it was so isolated that the powers that be had forgotten it existed.

Inside, there were a few jars of sweets and dusty tins of food on shelves. It was as spartan as a Soviet shop. There was an old woman behind the counter chatting with a young mother and her little girl. I asked the old woman the best way to Cardigan and there was a pause for a while, not unlike those in the Outer Hebrides. Finally, she started reeling off directions, but then seemed to get stuck before turning to the young mother and saying something in Welsh.

'What was that?' I asked.

'Oh, she's trying to tell you to avoid the A487. But she doesn't know the English for "avoid",' the young mum told me. 'A lot of people round here don't really speak much English.'

And right at that moment, I felt so marvellously abroad in my own land.

Cardigan seemed to have more than a touch of the Machynlleths about it, with citizens in hats and dreadlocks and more dogs in bandanas. As soon as I rode down the high street, with its art shops and organic cafés, it felt like a nice place to be, brimming with good energy. Is it the place that attracts the people, or the people who create the place? Who knows? Back in Mull, my fellow round-Britain cyclist Nick Hand had described how places had a distinctive vibe, an energy, that was tangible when you rode through them. I'd agreed with him, but we'd both struggled to say exactly what created it, how to explain it to people. It was just there. Perhaps when you're effectively living outdoors all the time, part of the world in a way that's rare these days, then some ancient, long-dormant sensory system is activated. In any case, Cardigan just radiated goodness.

I popped into a bike shop to buy some spare tubes. There I met a man who asked me what I was up to and who introduced himself as Charles.

Charles was living up in the mountains in a caravan while he built a house. On his plot of land, he grew herbs to sell.

'Most of our herbs we import from Israel,' he said. 'That seems crazy when we can grow them perfectly well here.'

We swapped a few tales from the road. Charles told me he'd once set off from London to cycle to Edinburgh. He'd got lost near Carlisle and asked a woman for directions. She'd asked if he wanted to go in for a cup of tea.

'Aye, aye, I thought. Nookie,' he said.

But she'd started talking about how her son had recently died. 'She just poured her heart out. Really wept. I don't think she had anybody in the world. I was there for nearly three hours, listening. Afterwards, it felt like my journey was finished. I just cycled to Carlisle station and jumped on a train back to London.'

Outside the shop, I dialled a number Nick Hand had given me to call when I was passing through Cardigan.

'Oh, hi Mike,' a voice said at the other end. 'Nick told us about you. Pop in and see us.'

'Us', it transpired, were the people who ran the ethical clothing firm Howies, based in Cardigan. At their offices I was given the tour by Howies' founder David Hieatt, and afterwards a lovely merino wool cycling jersey. I felt like a visiting head of state.

'Your timing's good,' said David. 'The Do Lectures start today, out at the Fforest campsite. Do you want to go?'

'Love to,' I said and, wearing my smart new jersey and armed with directions, headed off for the camp up the Teifi Gorge, thinking about many things, the foremost of which was: what the hell are the Do Lectures?

'And you are…?' a woman with a clipboard asked me.

'Erm, Mike Carter,' I said. 'I won't be on your list though. David said I could come. I'm just passing through for the night.'

'You can sleep in the tent over there,' she said. 'Exciting isn't it?'

'What is?'

'The Do Lectures.'

'I suppose so, but I don't really—'

'First one starts at 3.30 this afternoon. See you there.'

I took my seat at the edge of a teepee holding around 80 people. A man in a beanie hat came on stage and started talking about branding and advertising. My heart sank. I wondered if I could sneak out and be on my way.

The lights dimmed. A film started. It was a compilation of old, jumpy home movie clips. There was always the same man in these clips. And he was always demonstrating a Heath Robinson device: there was a gadget that enabled the transfer of the toothpaste dregs from one tube to another; a pulley system that locked doors and put in place a draught excluder when you left the house; a bird scarer made from old margarine tubs; and many more.

The film stopped.

'That was my father,' the man said. 'He died three years ago. He never threw things away. Unlike me, he made things happen. People of that era knew how to do things. I worry that our generation is becoming useless.'

The man went on. 'All great inventions start off as play,' he said. 'The point is to allow yourself to make mistakes, to find joy in the doing. Do something you weren't going to do. Force yourself. Don't be scared of involving people, they are very giving. Don't worry about what others think. They'll support you, because the act of striving unites us all. Learn. Just try. Something very magical happens when you try.

On the seat next to me was a leaflet explaining the Do Lectures. *'Stories are important,'* it read. *'They have the power to change things. Stories are how we learn. They pass knowledge on. They explain things we don't fully understand. They inspire us.'*

The man on the stage was replaced by another speaker, a woman from the Welsh Assembly.

'Growth isn't the best model. We had a choice to question what could come next, but we missed it. We need to look at prosperity without growth. We need to say that the sustainability model is the best model. Waste has to become taboo. Communities must start talking to each other again. We must force this onto the mainstream agenda.'

I looked at the leaflet again.

'With each great story comes life's important lessons. About their determination, about what drove them, about trying to find a better way of doing something, about the struggles they met along the way.'

My heart was racing. What was this place I'd stumbled into? I felt like somebody who'd been scooped into a life raft from a raging sea.

The woman from the Welsh Assembly was replaced by a man called Alan from an organisation called Network World.

'There must be no more linear thinking. We have to get back to where we want to be as human beings,' he said. 'We make, you buy: people are profoundly uncomfortable with this, about being turned into mere units of production. The thing that made us fundamentally human in the old days was high levels of participation in society. We don't just want to be defined as consumers. We are in a spiritual crisis, we've lost our moral anchors. Even George Soros says that we're living in a closed society when we're only measured by our material wealth. Even he wants an "open society". An open society should not just satisfy us but inspire us.

'People embrace what they create: sport, music, Linux codes, friendships. We create context in our lives by telling stories. The professional media tell us that it's them that tell the stories and it's our job to consume them. But this model fails our basic needs as beings that need to communicate with each other.'

'People don't forget stories. They forget facts. That's why these stories act as the cat's eyes in the road, showing us the way forward… Stories are also important because they are about doing things. Stories need verbs. It's the verb in the stories that creates the action. And the word Do is all verb.'

I'd been sitting in my chair for about two hours. It felt like two minutes. I had always loved the saying that we read stories to discover that we're not alone. Well, I don't think I had ever felt less alone than at that moment. Here were people, not extremists, but ordinary people, speaking passionately about the very things that make us human, that make life a thing of richness and fulfilment – and they were all the very things that can never appear in a cost analysis, the only modern measure of man's worth.

The day's talks finished and I wandered out of the tent in a bit of a daze. Dinner was being served in a converted barn next door.

I sat at a large table and everybody introduced themselves. I was asked what I was doing, and when I told my story about cycling around Britain, everybody was wide-eyed. Nobody asked if I was doing it for charity.

At my table were people who worked in advertising, civil servants, farmers, housewives. They were all united by their sense of impotence about what was going on in the world, in particular the banking crisis, and had been drawn to the Do Lectures in search of clues as to how they might make a difference. A few of the people at the table were involved in Transition Towns. The dentist I was sitting next to told me he was keen to get a dialogue going in his industry about sustainability.

'Most of the people I see now are bankers wanting to look ten years younger,' he said. 'The recession has increased people's sense of insecurity, so they're willing to spend more on looking younger. How depressing is that? I keep asking myself: "How can I make a real difference?"'

A farmer talked about his role in the campaign against GM crops, a protest that was ultimately successful as the number of annual trials dropped from 134 to just one in 2003. He'd driven his tractor all the way to Westminster from Wales to join the protest. The journey had taken eight days. 'It was an immense, wonderful time,' he said in his soft Welsh lilt. 'If we allow GM to happen, then everybody should be able to choose. It would kill organic and we'd lose our choice. What are we condemning our grandchildren to eat?'

The farmer talked about trying to make a living as a farmer in modern Britain. 'In the 1970s, 30 per cent of the revenue in a basket went to the farmer. Now it's 3 per cent. How is water more expensive than milk? I'm hanging on by my fingernails to keep my farm. We need to value food, to pay the right price for it. Scrap the grants and give farmers a living wage. I'm dying to farm. I love farming. I want my son to farm. He wants to farm. But we're just glorified gardeners these days.'

Another farmer talked about localism. 'Food will dominate all of our lives in the near future,' he said. 'Wales could easily be self-sufficient in food, yet we import nearly everything, from meat to seeds to straw. It doesn't make sense to anybody but big business. And it makes all of us very vulnerable to the whims of the market. We have to create a movement from the ground up, engage with the public, say that this isn't just a "nice" thing to do, but is, in fact, vital. There needs to be a real commitment to buying local; a cultural shift of attitude to seeing food in its relationship to spiritual, economic and cultural health. We're in the biggest process of change since the Industrial Revolution and we have to get the message out there.'

After dinner, we all went outside and, amid much laughter, learned how to chop wood properly, build fires and identify which berries and mushrooms were edible and which were poisonous.

I was still there four days later, as speaker after speaker held the audience rapt. It was like being at a Bilderberg conference, except it was the good guys who were in charge. There was an architect who designed commercial structures using nature's closed-loop systems as a blueprint; a guy who, along with the indigenous people, was successfully fighting the oil companies' land grabs in the Amazon rain forest; an engineer who has drawn up an entirely feasible plan to return the Sahara to woodland by turning sea water to fresh water using nothing but solar energy and hot air.

During the slide show that accompanied a man whose American firm sold ethical cleaning products, there was a shot of his office. On the wall was a sign. It read simply: 'Assume Goodwill'. That hit me like a thunderbolt. For effectively, without any conscious awareness, that was exactly the mindset I had slipped into on this journey: approaching people assuming that they would be friendly, would want to help. And that's generally what had happened. It was the opposite of how I went about my daily life in London, where my default was to imagine a constant series of obstacles to be surmounted, a battle against people whose interests conflicted with my own. A small change in perception; an immense shift in reality.

And maybe it was the heady Welsh air, perhaps it was the copious amounts of beer we drank in the evenings while we all shared our stories and danced and laughed until our faces ached, but suddenly everything seemed possible.

I'd thought when I left London that this journey would change my life to some degree, as all good journeys must, but I never imagined it happening so profoundly in a teepee in a Welsh field.

When it finally came time for me to leave, the delegates and speakers all formed a tunnel to wave me off. I cycled through it, showboating a little, high-fiving, feeling the love.

Emerging from the tunnel, I turned around to give a valedictory wave. I felt my front wheel slip slightly on the gravel track. The next thing I knew, I was on the ground, panniers all over the place, handlebars bent, me flailing around like an upturned woodlouse, trapped under the bike. And all captured on dozens of cameras. It was the kind of total wipeout I believe American bikers call a yard sale.

The first flush of humiliation and shame started burning my cheeks. But then it stopped. For instead of berating myself for being a total bell end, I lay there thinking about everything I'd shared with those lovely people – challenging the notion of failure, and being prepared to make a fool of yourself, reconnecting with the child, the human need for stories. And as I shook my head and started giggling to myself, I looked up to see an ocean of smiling faces. Seconds later, the Welsh air was filled with laughter.

The torrential rain and headwinds were back the next day as I rode along the final flourish of Cardigan Bay. The Indian summer had lasted a week. My wrist throbbed from the crash at the Do Lectures. I hoped I hadn't fractured it.

A few miles past Fishguard, I heard an infernal racket on the road behind me and turned around to see a man on a bicycle closing fast. He pulled alongside, the noise now very loud, like a roller coaster being ratcheted up the first incline.

'How do,' he said.

'What's that noise?' I asked.

'Electric bike, see.'

I looked down. There was a motor the size of a hair dryer attached to his bottom bracket. The man was about my age, fairly fit-looking.

'It's quite noisy, isn't it?' I said.

'You get used to it.'

I'm not sure I could ever get used to that. Besides, there's something about electric bicycles that seems to me to completely negate the point of cycling: that is, the flats and the downhills are the rewards for the toil of climbing; tailwinds are only a pleasure if they're offset against the exertions of headwinds. If life were all downhills and tailwinds, as they are on an electric bike, then where would we be? Bicycles with motors seemed an inherent contradiction, but they take their place on the modern continuum that finds its ultimate expression in those virtual reality computer games that enable you to play tennis in your living room when there's a park with courts next door.

'I don't like headwinds, especially when I'm going for a pint,' he said.

'Wouldn't that make the pint taste even nicer?' I said.

'Not when I'm trying to get home after a dozen of the buggers,' he said.

Fair point.

The man was wearing a rugby shirt with St David's RFC on it.

As we chatted, we passed young children cycling the other way.

'Training tomorrow night, Jones, four p.m.'

'How's the club doing?'

'We lose our best players to Haverfordwest. Bigger club, see. Better standard. Mitchell, don't be late again, or I'll be speaking to your father.'

We were racing along now, 25mph into the wind. It was like being paced by a derny. I got the sense that the man was slightly stung by my suggestion, conveyed through my comment about the pint tasting nicer, that I thought he was cheating. And his electric charge down the road was his response. But I was determined not to show any weakness. I was representing the purity of cycling; he was representing the laziness of the modern world. I was puce in the face and blowing hard; he looked as happy as Larry. There was probably a lesson to be learned in there somewhere, but I was too busy trying not to be sick to look for it.

'You okay?' he asked.

'F... fine.'

'Oi, Hopkins. You might start on Saturday if you train well tomorrow. Think on it. Think on it.'

We came to a crossroads.

'I'm off here, the pub's just down this road. Cheerio,' he said, and with that he peeled away and clickety-clacked down the lane. When he was out of sight, I dismounted and sat at the side of the road for a good five minutes with my head between my knees.

A few miles on and the mist had come rolling in from the sea. Visibility was down to less than a hundred yards. The world had gone deathly quiet. A wraith-like figure emerged on a bicycle coming towards me. I instantly knew who it was and my heart was filled with joy.

'Jack!' I shouted.

For it was Jack Allen, the septuagenarian round-Britain cyclist whom I'd met at John O'Groats. I'd known, via texts from his daughter, that he was in this neck of the woods, but wasn't sure exactly where our paths would cross. And here we were, on a quiet back lane on the Pembrokeshire coast, passing again. I'd only spent a few hours with him in John O'Groats, but I couldn't have been happier to see him if he'd been Angelina Jolie, naked, bringing me beer and a Stornoway black-pudding bap.

We pulled alongside each other, front wheels facing in opposite directions, and hugged.

'So, how's it been?' I asked.

The two thousand-odd miles he'd covered since our last meeting had done nothing to diminish his enthusiasm for the road.

'Bloody fantastic,' he said, grinning that mischievous grin. He removed his helmet, and rubbed his close-cropped head.

'Just had a haircut and a shave in St David's. I was looking like Catweazle. Number 2 this time. I didn't ask the price. A tenner! Ten bloody pounds for haircut!'

We swapped tales of the road. Jack had popped into a couple of the bike shops I'd recommended, in Berwick and Skegness, and said hello from me. 'They remembered you,' Jack said. 'Said to say hello back when I next saw you.' It was like a bush telegraph, and gave me a nice warm feeling.

'Had a lovely supper the other night in my tent,' Jack said. 'Duck and chicken in a rich sauce. Delicious, it were. It was only after I finished that I looked at the pack more closely. Bloody dog food!'

I looked down at Jack's bike. It was showing signs of wear. The panniers were much more threadbare than I recalled back in Scotland, and his front tyre was worn through in places so bits of the tube showed through.

'You need a new tyre,' I said.

'I've only got to get to Liverpool and I'm done. Hopefully, it'll hold up.'

That was right. Jack was on the final leg now. A small part of me envied him for being near the end, but a bigger part of me didn't.

I asked Jack how he'd found the people along the ride.

'Fantastic. Kind,' he said, with a big smile on his face. I thought back to the sign I'd seen at the Do Lectures, 'Assume Goodwill', and imagined that Jack must find kindness wherever he goes. It's a rare gift.

'Mind, I had a hairy night when a bloke picked me up off the street in Norfolk and offered me a bed for the night. Flat were a terrible mess, needles all over floor. He were a drug addict! Said he'd come and stay with me in Stoke.'

He scratched his head at the memory, then let rip with a huge laugh.

I told him how I'd fallen off my bike in front of all those people in Cardigan, which brought another huge laugh. Then, bearing in mind the unwritten code between cyclists of understating the severity of hills, I asked him what the roads were like ahead of me.

'No way round it, Mike: Devon and Cornwall are brutal,' Jack said. 'Steepest, most soul-destroying hills I've ever ridden!'

'You can go off someone.'

Jack laughed.

'Maybe I should get an electric bike.'

'What would be the point of that?' Jack said.

Quite.

'Saw the weather on telly last night,' Jack said. 'They reckon the summer starts tomorrow. Supposed to be beautiful for the next few weeks.'

'Do you believe them?'

'No,' Jack said, smiling. 'It's been a shocker, ain't it?'

We were both getting cold now and the time was coming to move on. Jack ferreted around in his pocket, then reached over with something in his hand.

'It's a ticket for the Gosport ferry,' he said. 'They only sold returns. Rip-off. I've been keeping it for you.'

'Thanks.' I put it in my pocket.

'And put that bloody helmet on,' he said.

'I will,' I lied.

We hugged for the last time, and then I watched Jack pedal away along the lane, until the mist swallowed him and I was on my own once more. Just like had happened the last time I'd said good-bye to Jack, I felt a wave of loneliness wash over me.

They were right about the weather. I woke up in my tent the next morning feeling like I was being roasted alive.

I rode around the sweep of St Bride's Bay, up and down the steep little hills, past the stunning golden expanse of Newgale Beach, full that glorious day with kitesurfers, the blue above me full of bright canopies, like painted fingernails being tossed by the wind. Then I cut inland to follow the National Cycle Network's Route 4, which took me on a lovely off-road section on the Brunel Trail, a Beeching-axed railway line through deep woodland and along a deep valley that cuts through the Westfield Pill nature reserve.

I got onto the Pembroke Peninsula and shared the narrow road with a never-ending stream of articulated oil tankers that pumped their air brakes impatiently behind me until they could squeeze past. All the heavy traffic turned off at Rhoscrowther, where they headed for the refineries whose bright flames I could see burning in the distance. Peace reigned once more. I stopped by a field to take a photograph of the rows of supertankers queuing up to take their place at the pipe-lined piers that jutted out in Milford Haven Sound. When I'd finished, I looked around to see that the young bullocks in the field were all lined up at the fence. We had a chat. The usual stuff, which invariably involved me pledging never to eat meat again, a pledge that invariably lasted until I next set eyes on a menu.

Two middle-aged cyclists passed me on a tandem coming in the other direction.

'Very hilly, buddy,' the man on the front said in an American accent.

'Good luck,' the woman on the back shouted.

What was the point of that? Don't they have the cyclists' code in America? I spent the next few hours watching the landscape in the distance up the road carefully, expecting to see snow-capped peaks, but the hills never materialised. Maybe those folks came from the flatlands of the Midwest. They had a shock in store if they were heading up the Welsh coast, and I could only imagine what they'd say to cyclists then: 'Oh. Boy. Are. You. Screwed. Buddy.'

Tenby, standing on its cliff-top plateau, was as beautiful a town as I'd seen all trip, its tall houses in vibrant shades of blue and yellow and pink sandwiched together, so that from a distance as I approached, they looked like the spines of bright ring binders on a shelf. On the seaward side of the harbour wall, the lifeboat station stood high above the water, linked to the sea by the kind of steep chute you'd pay good money to go down at a funfair.

The children had returned to school, the holidaymakers largely gone, and Tenby had the feeling of a place recovering from its summer assault. I stopped at a coffee shop on the cliff-top, and supped a cappuccino on its little terrace, vertiginously high above the sea, looking south over to Caldey Island, and then east across Carmarthen Bay, following the coast I was soon to cycle, with the cliffs of the Gower Peninsula in the distance rising out of the blue. I felt at that moment as if my coffee had been spiked with ecstasy.

I rode along the seafront at Saundersfoot, feeling the hot sun warming the fabric on my back. The beach there was beautiful, with flat polished sands giving way to long eruptions of rock spines running down to the sea, looking like crocodiles half immersed in mud.

The footpath passed through a series of long, narrow tunnels cut through the base of the cliffs. They were long enough and dark enough for me to have to turn on my front light, which I switched to strobe just long enough to feel sick before switching it back to constant. Cold water dripped down my neck and along my spine.

I had a fantasy that these tunnels through the cliffs would last for miles, days even, and if Carlsberg made bike routes, they probably would have. But in the real world they stopped abruptly and I was soon huffing and puffing up a 25% hill to join the cliff-top path.

I rounded a corner. In the middle of the trail was a frail-looking elderly woman pushing a Zimmer frame on wheels. We were miles from anywhere. On top of a cliff. I stopped.

'How far are you going?' I asked.

'What's it to you?' she said.

'I was just—'

'I'll know when I get there,' she said. 'Not that it's any of your business. I'm ninety-six. I'll go where I bloody well like.'

And with that she was off. Clearly the Zimmer and bicycle communities had rapprochement work to do.

I was planning to stop for the night in Pendine. I popped into a shop just before and asked the woman behind the till whether there was a good place to camp. 'I'd kill myself if I had to live in Pendine,' she said, but didn't elaborate. So I carried on to Laugharne, home of Dylan Thomas, where I was guaranteed at least one laugh.

I found a campsite and caravan park at the far edge of town and followed the signs for tents, which led me to a sodden, deserted field. I pitched in the fast-fading light and went off in search of the camp shop and bar.

The shop was closed. The clubhouse, like the field, was deserted, save for John, the site's owner, cutting a lonely figure behind the bar.

I ordered a pint. My God, that first cold pint after a day in the saddle is like drinking beer for the first time.

'Got anything to eat?' I asked.

'Just crisps.'

I was famished. It was a few miles back to town. It had been stupid of me not to pick something up.

'Wait here,' John said.

He was gone 10 minutes, and returned with a couple of ham rolls. I could have kissed him.

'My wife knocked 'em up.'

'How much do I owe you?'

'Don't worry about it. Looked like you needed them.'

It was a lovely gesture, made even lovelier by the fact that I wasn't remotely surprised that he'd done it.

'Where is everybody?' I asked.

'Nobody comes to the bar any more,' he said. 'When I started running this place twenty years ago, everyone came to the bar in the evenings to meet other campers. Now they sit in their caravans, drinking six-packs they buy in the supermarket.'

'That's a shame.'

'We had a power cut a couple of years ago. Only place with electricity was the clubhouse, running off the emergency generator. I got my old table tennis table out. Everybody loved it. The kids were holding the bats like tennis racquets, and their dads were saying

"It's not a tennis racquet, it's table tennis. A more gentle game."
The mums and dads were wondering if they still had it from their
youth. It was like it used to be. The power came on next day and I
never saw them again.'

I ordered another pint. We sat and chatted. I told John that I'd
seen a lot of what he'd described on the trip. How people seemed
increasingly atomised, preferring the isolation of private spaces,
whether it's their car or caravan. The notion of shared space, of
communality, was something we were losing, but I wasn't sure why.

'People keep themselves to themselves more, that's for sure,'
John said.

I'd been pondering this on the trip, trying to work out why I'd
become much less of a misanthrope, far keener to engage with
people, strangers, than I would ever be in London. It wasn't forced.
It felt completely natural.

'It's weird,' I said, 'because for me the reverse seems to have
happened. Maybe because I'm living twenty-four hours a day in
"communal" space – eating, sleeping and cycling in the open – I've
lost all sense of what's mine and what isn't.'

I thought about those sentiments. At the Do Lectures, the
speaker talking about the Amazon Indians had explained how, for
them, the whole forest was sacred. The developers just saw wild and
uncultivated land not being used, and couldn't comprehend why
they shouldn't take it. But for the indigenous people, every tree,
every inch of forest, belonged to them, not in a deed-holding way,
but eternally, and they had a responsibility to protect it.

I'm not sure where my brain was going with that, and the
fourth pint and the road-tiredness was doubtless helping, but what
I really wanted to say to John in the fast-encroaching fug was that
the whole world now felt like it belonged to me. I had a deep
connection to it all, a responsibility towards it. I can't ever remember feeling that way before. All this I wanted to say to John, but I
didn't know how to start.

Chapter 18

'When I go biking I am mentally
far, far away from civilisation.
The world is breaking someone else's heart.'

Diane Ackerman

The sun was still shining the following morning. Two days in a row now. That, in British terms, constituted a summer as far as I was concerned. I rode along a footpath on the banks of the River Tâf, sparkling in the morning light, tinkling my bell and wishing a good morning to all the dog-walkers I passed. The trees and bushes looked fat and full, soaking up the rays, the world replenishing itself for another day. The air was dense with white butterflies, the brilliant azure of a kingfisher flashed across my bow and was gone. Up ahead, a buzzard was dissecting a vole by the side of the path, picking out its innards with its beak with the skill of a surgeon. As I approached, it lumbered into the air, the vole still clutched in its talons, entrails dangling behind like party streamers.

In the centre of Carmarthen there was a large concrete open-air velodrome with a sign warning 'Unauthorised use prohibited'. The devil kindly reminded me that I'd never been on a cycling track, and before I knew it I was doing my best Chris Hoy impression. Office workers sat on the grass with their sandwiches, seemingly fascinated by the sight of man carrying a house on a bicycle and ringing his bell trying to pedal fast enough not to slide down the steep banked track. As I completed each lap, I waved as I passed them. They waved back. I must have looked a complete tool, but did I care?

As I approached Kidwelly, nestled in a fold of land, its lovely castle showing itself for tantalising moments before disappearing behind trees, it struck me that travelling by bicycle must share some characteristics with our ancestors travelling the land by horse. Sitting high in a saddle, with the kind of views denied to car drivers, places revealed themselves gradually, like a burlesque show, creating a constant air of anticipation.

On the bridge over the River Tywi in the middle of Kidwelly, a class of primary school children were getting a history lesson from their teacher. I stopped to listen and after a while the teacher, a man with a tangled mop of black curls, asked where I'd come from. I told him, and his eyes acquired a wistful, misty sheen.

The children, however, were far more interested in my Winnie-the-Pooh bell.

'That is my dream,' he said.

'Diversion. Distraction. Fantasy. Change of fashion, food, love and landscape,' Bruce Chatwin wrote in *Anatomy of Restlessness*. 'We need them as the air we breathe. Without change our brains and bodies rot.'

Chatwin went on to quote a US survey that took encephalograph readings of travellers' minds. 'They found that changes of scenery and awareness of the passage of seasons through the year stimulated the rhythms of the brain, contributing to a sense of well-being and an active purpose in life.'

I've no idea what an encephalograph is, but I do know that this is the truth.

'Maybe one day,' I said to the teacher.

'I hope so.'

I rode through Pembrey Forest, on a quiet cycle lane between the pines, as dense and as dark as an enchanted forest, unseen woodpeckers tapping out Morse code. Then alongside the sea for miles on a smooth tarmac cycle path through the magnificent Millennium Coastal Park, with Llanelli in the distance, sitting on an enormous drained expanse of sand every bit as impressive as Morecambe Bay. The joggers and rollerbladers were out, plugged into iPods. Everybody looked healthy, happy, under the warm embrace of the sun. It wasn't too much of a stretch to imagine that I was in Venice Beach, or South Beach, Miami.

On the waterfront in Llanelli, a woman on a bicycle pulled alongside me. Her name was Maddy and she was just heading home on her nightly 11-mile commute back to her house on the Gower Peninsula, all on a bike lane which skirted fields fat with ripe corn and hugged the graceful sweep of the bay. What a commute! Who could resist the lure of the bicycle if the gods served you up a route like that?

We chatted. The miles disappeared. Maddy was a teacher at a school in Llanelli, her husband an environmentalist, the pair of them active campaigners for cycle routes. The bike lane came to an abrupt halt outside her front door.

'Hang on,' I said.

'Nothing to do with me!' she protested, laughing.

Maddy invited me to sleep at her house. This is such an intimate and generous thing to offer a stranger and I was always blown away when such offers were forthcoming. There are evenings when one is in the mood to be the 'turn' and, in exchange for dinner and a bed, regale people with your tales of the road. That's a fair transaction. But there are times when the lure of the solitude of a tent on a quiet beach is just too great. This was one of those evenings.

'Please don't think I'm being rude or ungrateful, but I just fancy being on my own this evening,' I said, feeling beyond rude. 'Looks like it might be an incredible sunset.'

'You're talking to a cycle tourist,' Maddy said. 'I understand.'

I rode along the top of the incomparably beautiful Gower Peninsula, passing a big line of racing cyclists, out for an evening ride. They all said hello. It was all right for them. They only had to say hello once. I had to say it 20 times.

I saw my first combine harvester of the year working a field, a line of excited children sitting on a stone wall watching it. The summer may have felt like it had only just begun, but here was a reminder that autumn was almost upon me.

I headed south and dropped down a steep, narrow lane to Port Eynon on the southernmost tip of the Gower, and headed for a spot on the edge of a field under the cliffs overlooking the Bristol Channel.

I pitched my tent, and distributed the contents of my panniers into their rightful places in my canvas world. I loved that nightly routine. Headtorch, book and water bottle in the left-hand pocket, camera, phone and wallet on the right; cycling clothes rolled into a stuff-sack for a pillow, cycling gear for the morning laid out on the right, pub clothes on the floor to the left of the Thermarest. In terms of pub clothes, all I had left was one T-shirt and one pair of trousers. It had been pared back to that. How to explain the joy of only owning one set of clothes!

I was deeply in love with my tent by then. It had come to represent so much more for me than simply being a place to sleep. I mentioned earlier about the bicycle as a transitional object, a powerful totem we treasure from early memories when such a gift arrives and suddenly our horizons are limited only by our legs and our imaginations.

Well, shrinks talk also of transitional objects as things young children cling to – the security blankets, the cuddly toys – to make them feel safe. They also have a theory that we retain the need for such objects throughout our lives, and adults channel this cathexis into things and sometimes other people. This could certainly help explain the way I felt towards my tent, my mobile house, my continuity. When I lay inside its flimsy nylon walls at night, zips fastened, I felt as safe and protected as if it were made from armour-plated steel.

I crawled back out. The sun was setting, turning the oleaginous water shades of pink and vermilion, through which giant tankers ghosted, lit up like Christmas trees. The light was amazing, ethereal, the visibility superb, as they say it always is when the north-easterly winds blow in these parts and bring an Indian summer. The glow of Swansea and Port Talbot to the east rose up to give the encroaching darkness a tungsten underbelly. For the first time I could see the bluffs of Devon, 20 miles away across the channel, monstrous slabs of rock rising vertically from the sea. I remembered what Jack had said about those hills. I would be there very shortly. I might have cycled over 3,500 miles, through Yorkshire, around Scotland, Cumbria and Wales, but looking at those cliffs across the water, I knew the hardest part of the trip was yet to come. My wrist didn't seem to be getting any better, either. I opened a can of Foster's and drained it in rapid fashion.

The cliffs of Somerset and Devon taunted me for most of the following day as I rode through Swansea, another handsome waterside city, with its coastal cycle path and gentrified docklands, past Port Talbot and the belching fumaroles of its steelworks, and around the Vale of Glamorgan. I tried to put the hills out of my mind, but every time I looked up, there they were, getting closer by the mile as the channel narrowed.

I'd wanted to enter Cardiff by taking the new bike path across the barrier that formed the southern side of the docks. But I got lost and ended up hitting town on a busy dual carriageway, before riding up a slipway and finding myself on the motorway. I had to ride back down the ramp against the traffic, much to the consternation and irritation of an endless succession of horn-happy motorists. Expect the footage on *Police! Camera! Moron!* some day soon.

To recover, I stopped at a café for a coffee. On the walls were pictures of flamenco dancers and posters advertising bullfights. The young woman behind the counter spoke in an accent that was half Welsh and half Spanish. It was either the loveliest or the worst accent I had ever heard, I couldn't decide. She was beautiful, and because I am a complete arse, I thought I'd impress her by telling her I spoke Spanish.

'OK,' she said. 'Order in Español.'

But when I opened my mouth and ordered my brain to go and retrieve the words, nothing came out. I stood there for a minute, pumping my mouth like a guppy, but there was nothing. I had forgotten everything. I had even long-forgotten those plans to spend evenings in my tent listening to my Spanish tapes on the iPod.

'*Usted no puede hablar Español,*' she said.

'What?' I replied.

On a busy inner-city street, I stopped at a red light. Nearby, a group of young people were pointing at me. They started to approach. They were all wearing matching green T-shirts, which convinced me they were either an incredibly well-coordinated gang of thugs or evangelical Christians. I wasn't sure which would be preferable.

'Can we tie this balloon to your bike?' one asked.

'Why?'

'It's a gift from God,' she said.

'Ah.'

She tied the balloon to my rear rack. The lights went green. I made to pedal off.

'Where have you cycled from?'

I stopped again and told her.

'Wow!' the green gang said in unison.

'How's the journey been so far?' said a young man.

The lights went red again.

I launched into my usual gushing monologue about the beautiful island we lived on, the lovely people I'd met. They looked impressed, but not really surprised. I guessed that had they not had faith in human nature, they'd be drinking bottles of strong cider down the park and not standing by the roadside handing out balloons.

'Now I'm off to the West Country.'

The lights went green.

'Big hills there,' said one of the young men.

'Thanks.'

'God's love will give you the strength to get up them.'

'Will it?'

'Of course, if you ask Him.'

The lights went red. I shook my wrist and grimaced. It was really hurting now.

'What's wrong?' asked the young woman.

I told them about falling off in Cardigan, about how I think I might have fractured my wrist.

'Would you let us pray for it?' she said, looking suddenly solemn.

Green.

'Sure.'

They all clustered around me in a tight little circle and, heads bowed, laid hands on my arm.

Red.

'God, we ask you to heal Mike's wrist and let him complete his journey,' said the woman. 'Fill him with your love and greatness.' Beyond my circle of God's young helpers, I could see that people in their cars were staring, thanking God, I'd wager, for their sealed little boxes and lockable doors.

The lights went green. We had a group hug and then I was off, waving, trailing a big yellow balloon in my wake. And the strangest thing was, I never felt another twinge from my wrist again.

Newport was a disappointment. Nothing personal about the town, though it had the familiar and depressing collection of boarded-up pubs and shops. Pound shops and hairdressers seemed to be proliferating, though, as in most of the places I'd passed through. And I reckon that would make a fascinating doctoral thesis about the state of the nation right there: shops full of cheap crap and a nice hairdo to make you feel better.

No, my disappointment with Newport was solely down to the fact that its transporter bridge was closed. There were sets that I was going to complete on the trip, like all the coastal nuclear power stations, the land-based points of the Shipping Forecast and the major bridges over estuaries. And I'd hoped that, consisting of only two, my bagging of Britain's transporter bridges, Middlesbrough and Newport, would be one of the easiest lists to tick off. But Newport's was closed.

I cycled away feeling resentful, a state of mind that lasted only for a few seconds, which was as long as it took for a lorry with Polish plates to squeeze past me with barely the width of a *kabanos* to separate us. Maybe that thesis could somehow stretch to include cycling accidents featuring left-hand drive lorries. I'd read it.

I climbed up onto the Severn Bridge. It was the last of the big bridges I'd cross and thus that particular list would be complete. Screw you, Newport. It was also the first time since John O'Groats that my journey had crossed the path of the Jogles or Lejogs. I wondered how long it would be before I bumped into somebody doing it.

I'd barely got onto the cycle track running across the bridge when two men cycling in the opposite direction stopped to say hello. They both had bright yellow T-shirts on advertising their chosen charity. I was guessing it was some kind of animal rescue centre, as they featured a picture of a donkey. Or perhaps they were fundraisers for the American Democratic party. I didn't ask.

'Hi there,' said the first man, whose name was Mike.

'Hello,' said the second, whose name was also Mike.

'Mike,' I said.

'That's easy,' said Mike.

'Really easy,' said the other Mike, who told me he was to be known as Michael for the duration of the trip to avoid confusion.

'You've got a lot of stuff,' said Mike. 'Can I feel your bike?'

We both dismounted. He lifted up my bike.

'Jesus,' he said.

I lifted his off the ground. Pretty light.

'We're not camping,' said Michael. 'B&Bs for us.'

Michael dismounted and lifted up my bike.

'Jesus.'

'You off to Land's End?' asked Mike.

'Yes.'

'Brutal hills,' said Michael. 'Oh, Jesus.'

'That bad?'

'Oh, Jesus,' said Mike.

'Porlock,' whispered Michael, as if reciting the name of a mythical beast that ate babies.

'Porlock,' Mike repeated, shaking his head.

'We only came down it,' said Michael. 'But that was bad enough. Could hardly stop. And you with all that weight.'

'Great,' I said.

'Still, you got the wind all the way now,' said Mike. 'We've been battling into it for two days now.'

The great British long-distance cyclists' courtship ritual: the weighing of the bikes and a discussion about wind and hills.

'It'll be worth it when you get there,' said Mike. 'When that money rolls in. What charity you doing it for?'

Okay. Pound shops, hairdressers, cycling accidents involving left-hand drive vehicles and the British passion for good charitable works. Discuss.

'Erm… local kids,' I said.

'It'll be worth it,' said Mike.

'Really worth it,' said Michael.

And with that they were off on their quest, which would end with happy donkeys/Democrats and Mike and Michael having their photographs taken by the most miserable man in Britain.

I took a self-timer shot of me standing underneath the 'Welcome to England' sign. I was back in England and it felt, very much, as if I was on my way home.

The flatlands and tailwinds on the south side of the Severn Estuary saw me barrelling along, skirting the topside of Bristol, and then through Weston-super-Mare and past the dunes of Brean Sands. Then it was on to Burnham-on-Sea, along the off-road NCN33, which twisted and turned, following the scoured-out trenches of the deep gullies in the mudflats, where boats lay flopped on their sides like fish on the slab. Across Bridgwater Bay, I could see Hinkley Point nuclear power station. Another tick.

There was no bridge over the River Parrett, so I had to follow the river south for 10 miles to the nearest crossing point, in Bridgwater. The sign on the outskirts of the town said 'Welcome to Bridgwater – The Home of Carnival', about which I'm sure Rio de Janeiro might have something to say. Underneath, somebody had scrawled in red paint: 'No it isn't.'

The hitherto flat estuarine landscape started to buckle slightly after Kilve. I was less than 20 miles from Porlock now. I knew from my conversations with Jack that Porlock marked the start of the relentless hills that would last for the next 600 miles, all the way until Poole. The idea of them had been in my head for so long, haunting me like a monster under the bed haunts a child. And yet, as I passed through Watchet and then Dunster, the pink crenellations of its lovely castle poking up out of the wooded hillside, and then along the seafront at Minehead, the land terrifyingly rearing up ahead before my very eyes, I had what I can only describe as an epiphany.

That epiphany involved the recitation to myself over and over of sentiments like 'pain is just weakness leaving the body' and 'when the going gets tough...' and any other self-help nonsense I could muster. Did Tour de France cyclists approach the Col du Galibier or Mont Ventoux thinking 'I hope I can get up this hill without having to get off and push'? No, they did not. Because they are hardened athletes, fuelled by the miles in their legs and an unquenchable appetite for suffering.

I had just ridden more than 3,500 miles – longer than Le Grande Boucle, thank you very much – up and over some of the biggest hills Britain could muster, with a shedload of luggage and not a hint of, ahem, 'assistance', unless you count Scotch eggs, Soreen and the love of God granted to me back in Cardiff. Was I not now a Grand Tourer, a road-hardened athlete? Could I not see myself in some small way as part of that club: Simpson, Merckx, Indurain, Pantani, Armstrong, Carter? Yes, I bloody well could. I would take on these hills and I would prevail, oh yes. I would not get off and push. I would rather die in the attempt. I mean, how hard could they be?

This was the dialogue running around in my deluded brain as I passed the sign saying 'Welcome to Porlock', followed shortly after by a sign warning 'Road not suitable for caravans or cyclists'.

'Yeeeesssss!' I said. 'Bring it on, baby, bring it on.'

Ten seconds later I was off the bike and pushing. About 20 seconds after that I was unable even to push, the bike and me having ground to a halt, forming an isosceles triangle with the road surface. I craned my neck up. I couldn't even see the top of the hill, just a wall of green and brown. There was a bin by the side of the road. Into it went my guidebook, first-aid kit, clothesline and pegs, wet wipes and worn-out sandals. That got me about five yards further. I started to think through what else I could dump. Could I cut down my socks below the ankles? What purpose did that bit of fabric serve? Did my laptop really need its casing? Did I need both ears?

I rolled back down the hill, thinking that I might have to live in Porlock for ever unless I could find a shop where I could buy a block and tackle. Then I noticed a private toll road. On it, in five miles and a little over an hour, I climbed from sea level to 1,400 feet. Halfway up, red-faced and convinced I was in the process of having a heart attack, I had to pay the toll of a pound, which I know would constitute a bargain in S&M circles. 'The Tour of Britain went from bottom to top in sixteen minutes,' the nice man taking the money told me. This, in the grand scheme of things, was not terribly welcome information.

I finally huffed and puffed my way to the top and rejoined the main road, which flew high along a narrow ridge. Exmoor, vast and wild, was below me on the left, the Bristol Channel, vast and wild, to my right, the visibility extraordinary, the distant chimneys of Port Talbot throwing out regular cotton-wool balls of smoke.

I had just about composed myself after the shock and exertions of Porlock when I came to a sign saying Countisbury Hill, beyond which the tarmac disappeared like the edge of an infinity pool. The road down into Lynmouth was ridiculous, a two-mile-long 25% descent hanging over the sea that had me clutching at the brakes, which squealed like banshees but did little to arrest my speed, my wrists aching, gravelled escape roads flashing by, my luggage pushing me ever faster, until I reached the river at the bottom, the Styx I think it was called, and then craned my neck up again to see another wall of tarmac going straight up the side of a cliff. I now understood why Jack had broken the sacred code.

There was no toll-road option out of Lynmouth, so I man-handled my bike and gear up the near-vertical slope to Lynton, where I arrived some considerable time later, half-dead and wearing the kind of expression familiar to anyone who's seen grainy footage of inmates in a Victorian lunatic asylum. I slumped by the roadside holding my head in my hands.

'Some hill, eh?' said a man out walking his dog.

I nodded, coughing and spluttering.

'With all that gear, too.'

The dog licked the salt off my knees and worked his way down my right calf. I could only watch him.

'Should have got the cliff railway,' the man said.

'Ccccclifffff rail…?' was all I could manage.

'Aye, grand it is. Bottom to top in a couple of minutes.'

My guidebook would have told me about the cliff railway. But that was now in a bin at the foot of Porlock Hill, along with my fantasies of being a decent cyclist.

'Thank you,' I said.

'Next time, eh?'

'Next time.'

I rode a little way outside Lynton and found a campsite beside a raging torrent that ensured I was up half the night going to the toilet. It was the same torrent that had carved Lynmouth's steep valley. That seemed doubly cruel. When I did manage to sleep, I dreamt of Sisyphus.

The next day was more of the same. Pushing up for half an hour, flat road for a couple of inches, then plunging down for 10 seconds. Those hills violated the cycling law that states that the effort expended on the ascent will be rewarded by the enjoyment of the freewheel down the other side. There was no enjoyment, only terror and a sense that death was always merely a snapped brake cable away. For Devon hills were not really hills in the conventional sense of the word. It was as if a giant had cleaved a series of notches in the cliffs with an axe. The roads on my map had more double chevrons than a whole army of corporals.

The scenery was perhaps the most spectacular I'd seen on the whole coast ride, though, tall wooded cliffs dropping vertically into the bluest of seas, every turn of the trail revealing another little scallop-shaped cove. Cloud shadows slipped and shape-shifted across the Bristol Channel like bubbles in a lava lamp.

The Valley of the Rocks, with its strange mesas, obelisks and herds of wild goats, looked not unlike a brilliant-green version of the Jebel Sahro in Morocco's Anti-Atlas mountains. Along with the usual hazard of sheep for passing cyclists, there were also now the wild Exmoor ponies, who strolled along the narrow roads, failing to indicate, responding to my imprecations and frantic bell-ringing with total indifference. Occasionally I'd elicit a shrug of the head and a whinny, which I suspected, had I been able to understand equine, wouldn't have been very polite.

The road dived steeply down to Hunter's Inn near Parracombe, an old, historic pub that sat in the fold of a valley so deep and heavily wooded that it felt like another Lost World. And then the long climb out again, the trees giving way to low scrub and then to bald moorland, the temperature dropping as the road rose, the exertion and the cooling sea air making it impossible to find the right combination of clothing.

After Ilfracombe – do I even need to mention that it sat at the bottom of a deep valley? – I rounded the headland at Bull Point, then swept around Morte Bay and Croyde Bay, followed by the vast and spectacular dunes of Saunton Sands, where dozens of grey landing craft deposited soldiers on the remote beach in a seaborne invasion drill. At least, I hoped that it was a drill. If it was a foreign invading force, they'd be needing their grappling hooks and climbing ropes or they'd be going nowhere.

In Barnstaple, I flicked through my bike computer. I'd covered 30 miles so far that day at an average speed of just over 5mph. I could almost have walked it quicker. I stopped at a bicycle shop to stock up on supplies. I bought some new brake blocks to replace mine that were now exposed to the metal and scraping on the rims. I'd ridden all around the coast of Britain, and last checked them in South Wales, when they'd seemed to have plenty of life left in them. Less than 50 miles of West Country hills had done them in. I picked up some new brake cables, too. I imagined they sold a lot of both items in that part of the world. I imagined brown cycling shorts were probably quite popular too.

On the shelves I noticed an inner tube whose USP was its self-healing properties, facilitated by the release of a green goo on puncturing that would automatically plug any hole. It sounded too good to be true. I grabbed one.

I took NCN Route 3 out of Barnstaple, along the banks of the River Taw, otherwise known as the Tarka Trail. This followed the track bed of the former railway line to Bideford – I had never felt so much love and affection for Dr Beeching! It looked as if I wasn't the only one. It was mobbed with cyclists, for whom, I'd be willing to bet my knackered brake blocks, the stunning estuarine landscape was of minor import compared, in that most creased of counties, to the trail's flatness.

After Bideford, the A39, the road nearest the coast, was busy and dangerous and fizzing with motorised menace, so I ducked inland a little, meandering along the narrow little lanes, through sleepy little postcard villages made up of thatched cottages, the tractors that I saw now pulling trailers full of hay and straw. Many of the roads were fully canopied by trees, still green and plump with no sign yet of autumn's gold. Pheasants, surely God's little self-indulgent jape, clucked and ran in panicked circles before my wheels when they had an entire county to escape to. The land was still rolling, but the valleys were nascent and much more agreeable to the thighs than the great cleaves of the coast. Those were indeed the happiest of miles.

A sign by the side of the lane advertised a gnome reserve. That sounded interesting. But not as interesting as the Devon cream teas it also advertised – for if, as stated before, the long-distant cyclist's commandments include 'thou shalt lifteth up each other's bikes', and 'thou shalt understate the severity of hills', then they also contain 'thou shalt not pass a vendor of sweet calorific things without popping in'.

'Would you like a gnome hat to wear?' the woman on the desk asked me. She was dressed as a gnome.

'No, thank you,' I said. 'I'm only here for some scones.'

'You should really go and see the gnomes. They like visitors. But if you don't wear a hat, they get embarrassed – big people without hats laughing at them. You can choose your own from the box over there.'

So I entered the reserve, my pink hat with black splotches worn at a jaunty angle to convey irony, hopefully, picking my way along the trail, through the beech wood. There were gnomes everywhere, over 2,000 in total, playing poker in a little cabin, sunbathing, on the dodgems at a little gnome fairground, blasting off at the gnome space centre. The banks of the stream running through the wood were busy, obviously. There were dozens of big people there, all wearing felt gnome hats, taking photographs.

'Magical, isn't it?' a woman said to me. And it really was, though I'd struggle to explain why.

A sign at The Circle of Imagination said: 'Sit on the seat and be whatever or wherever you like. Be a tree for a moment, a waterfall, a mountain, a subatomic particle, a kingfisher, a cow-pat, or a distant galaxy.' I sat on the seat and closed my eyes. I was whisked to a world where I was still a cyclist, but everything was made of scones.

The trail led to the wildflower garden, a rich profusion of cowslips, figwort, lavender, wild mint, thyme, evening primrose and over 200 other varieties of wildflowers, herbs and grasses. It was like walking through the perfume section of a department store. There were so many white butterflies flitting around it was like being in a blizzard.

An elderly couple with a clipboard walked passed.

'We're looking for fairies,' the man said.

'They must have wings to count, though,' said his wife. 'If you spot more than twelve, you get a badge.' And off they went, giggling.

Back at the house, filling my face with clotted cream, I spoke to the woman on the desk again. She was Ann Atkin, who'd founded the reserve back in 1979.

'Why gnomes?' I asked between mouthfuls.

'Well, I trained as a painter, at the Royal Academy, and painters are all a bit nutty, aren't they,' she laughed. 'Gnomes came into my consciousness and changed everything.'

She gestured behind me, where her acrylic paintings, featuring pixies and gnomes, filled the wall. 'My son Richard makes some of the gnomes that are in the wood. Where the rest come from, I have absolutely no idea.'

'No idea?'

'They just turn up.'

A family of four came in. Parents and children scrambled through the box for suitable hats.

'Once, a young boy came back from the wood, handed his hat back and looked rather sad. Then he said: "And now I'm just Jonathan again."'

The family found hats and walked off towards the reserve.

'We get people coming back who came here as children, now bringing their own kids. I love that.

'John Updike said that art should body forth the idyllic,' Ann continued. 'And I think it should, as a respite from all the cares and troubles of the world. It's more fashionable to make a song and dance about all the woes, but I don't agree with that. People come here and seem to find an inner energy to go and face the world again.'

The pensioner couple I'd seen earlier in the wildflower garden came in, still wearing their gnome hats. They presented their fairy-spotting quiz to Ann.

'Only eleven of these count,' she said to them. 'This one on the toadstool doesn't have any wings. Do you want to go back and see if you can find some more? Then you can go in the good pile.'

For a moment they looked crestfallen. And then they went again, shoving each other and giggling some more.

I passed the 'Welcome to Cornwall' sign near an ancient tiny stone bridge on the quietest of lanes. I loved crossing county borders, but this one had a special resonance. For this was the last county on the island before I would have to turn around and head for home.

I stopped in Bude for a pasty at a shop whose sign advertised, like seemingly every other pasty shop on the street, 'Award-Winning Pasties'. No hi-tech refuelling for me, just culinary clichés all the way. Haggis and black pudding had worked in Scotland, as had fish and chips in Blackpool, and cream teas in Devon.

I ordered an extra large steak pasty. My fingers were still covered in oil from slipping my chain a few miles earlier. The woman handed over the pasty and I clutched the indented crust with my filthy fingers, eating the pasty just as they were designed to be eaten, by tin miners underground with no access to water to wash.

'Look,' I said to the woman, holding up my oil-stained hands. 'This is how they're supposed to be eaten.'

I smiled at her, feeling pleased with myself.

'One pound fifty,' she said.

'Tin miners,' I said.

'Who's next?' she said.

It was back to the roads with the corporal's stripes after Bude. Up, down, up, down: Widemouth Bay, Milook, Crackington Haven. Boscastle's high street and buildings, despite the fact I'd never been there, looked so eerily familiar from the TV footage I'd watched of cars being pitchpoled down the River Valency like Matchbox toys in the flood of 2004.

Many of the gradient signs said 30%, but I reckon they were steeper. I spent most of the time pushing, grunting and sweating my way up. That pasty would have had to contain steroids to have helped me there. Where the lanes climbed through a tunnel of trees, the surface was blanketed in lichen and my feet slipped and spun like I was trying to walk up a glacier. So steep were they that I often ended up walking down as well, my new brakes as totally ineffectual as the old ones.

But the views more than made up for the toil, with the hazy millpond sea, and nothing out there between me and America. The sun was still shining, the winds were light, and when a man in a garage just outside Rock told me the worst of the hills on the north Cornish coast were behind me, it was all I could do to stop myself sticking my tongue down his throat.

In Rock, I just missed the little ferry that pootles across the estuary to Padstow and thought I could happily spend the three hours until the next one sitting in the sunshine outside a café drinking coffee and reading the paper. But if I'd passed through seaside towns that seemed firmly working class, and others that were magnets for bohemians and artists, Rock, with its rows of parked Porsches and Mercedes 4x4s, upmarket restaurants and the type of shops selling expensive sailing clothes for people who don't really sail, seemed to be frequented by the kind of upper-class London rahs I spend my life trying to avoid.

My uncharitable thoughts about posh rahs were interrupted by a hissing sound coming from my front tyre. And maybe that was a sign that I should be really lose the chips.

Now, ordinarily, such a hiss, followed shortly after by the feeling of metal rim bumping on road, induces a feeling of deflation in cyclists in all senses of the word. And I think I still carried the scarred memories of childhood when, on an early adventure, I'd unsuccessfully tried to mend a puncture 10 times, before my mum had had to come and rescue me and explain why it was a good idea to remove nails from the tyre before putting the tube back in.

But this was the first time I had ever been excited by a puncture. For in my bag was the miracle self-healing tube. I gently took it out of its box, held it for a moment as if it were a precious jewel, and then tucked it inside the tyre, with all the love, attention and sense of closure appropriate to marking the ending of a ritual. For punctures, on my front wheel at least, had gone the way of darning socks and the blue-and-cream Birmingham bus.

With joy in my heart and an indestructible inner tube on my wheel, I eschewed the ferry, said goodbye to the rahs and headed off inland around the estuary to Wadebridge, and thereafter found the delights of the Camel Trail to Padstow.

In St Ives, I saw my first road sign for Land's End, which, like the first one I'd seen for John O'Groats all those miles ago, brought a lump to my throat. I'd certainly done my Jogle the long way, not the regulation 874 miles, but 2,500.

I took the long hard climb out of St Ives and got on the B3306 heading towards Land's End. It was an absolute peach of a road to ride, the bleak moorland reminding me of the Scottish wilderness and giving it a real end-of-the-world feel. There were few trees to obscure the view of the vast Atlantic, above which I seemed to float. The skyline was punctuated by the chimneys of long-abandoned tin mines, whose ruins looked like churches.

A racing cyclist coming the other way said: 'Keep going. You're almost there.'

Then came the sound of hissing from my front tyre, and for the first time in my life I was beyond excited to be having a puncture. Such was the miracle of this technology that I didn't even need to stop. I leaned over the handlebars to watch the green goo work its magic. The luminous gunk spat out of the hole, like a scene from *The Exorcist*, ricocheting violently off the panniers and the mudguards, and ultimately splattering my face in slime. This fevered activity went on for about a minute. A final little dribble of goo farted out of the hole. Then the tyre went flat.

There was a convex mirror nearby adorning the top of a farm track with an awkward exit. I walked over and peered at my distorted self, all stretched and green. I looked like Shrek.

I dug in my pannier to find a conventional tube and then tucked my levers under the tyre wall. I should have been disappointed to be undertaking this ritual again so soon after consigning it to the cycling dustbin. But the truth was, I realised, I quite liked it. Things breaking down and needing mending to get you on your way again only added to the sense of achievement and satisfaction on arriving at your destination. Setbacks were an integral part of the journey. As with cycling, as with life.

After Pendeen, the road turned to head due south. I had run out of Britain again. I did a quick ride down a dead-end lane to visit Cape Cornwall. I did this not out of any real natural curiosity, but because Cape Cornwall and Cape Wrath are the only two capes in Britain, and my obsession with these tick-lists was knowing no bounds.

I passed the Last Inn in England and, shortly after, there it was: Land's End. I rolled over the start/finish line painted across the road, and pedalled through the various attractions designed to capture the essence of such a raw and elemental spot – Doctor Who Up Close, The West Country Shopping Village, The Last Labyrinth (which must really piss off all the country's other labyrinths) – beyond which was the dull business of mighty waves crashing against cliffs and the maelstrom of colliding seas.

At the famous signpost there was a queue of people waiting to have their picture taken by the official photographer (I could chalk off seeing Britain's two end-of-country official photographers, too. Boy, was I on a roll). For a party from Brisbane an extension was fitted to the direction arrow pointing down. Nice touch. A man from Horncastle (you can tell because they insert your town's name into the sign) posed proudly with his Mark I Ford Fiesta. Colin and Elaine from Wolverhampton were celebrating their third wedding anniversary. 'We came here on our honeymoon,' Elaine was telling the snapper. 'Since then, Colin's lost ten stone.' She wrapped her arms around his waist for the picture, a little more comfortably, I'd imagine, than the last time they were there. They are the last couple in England, I thought to myself. And I'm the last cyclist. And that litter bin over there, the last… I soon tired of that game, the last person to tire of a game and give up in England.

I looked at the gallery of pictures hanging on the wall of the photographer's hut. Most were of people either setting off on their Lejog or having just finished their Jogle. There were a few Elvises – or is it Elvi? – and Batmen, a Pink Panther, Snow White and her dwarves. There was a party of four people stark bollock naked save for rucksacks, boots and pith helmets. There were people on pogo sticks, unicycles, penny-farthings. I was still no nearer knowing what any of this said about Britons, but it perversely made me feel quite proud.

The photographer's name was Peter. He seemed a lot more cheery than his bookend at the top of the island. He'd been a wedding photographer, but preferred his job at Land's End. 'Look at this for an office,' he said, sweeping his arm across the 270 degrees of sea, the Longships lighthouse slap in the middle of the arc. 'How could you beat that? And you never know what or who is coming round the corner.'

He asked me if I'd like my picture taken with the sign. It would be £9.50 (the same as at John O'Groats, the same company runs both sites), but when I baulked at the cost, he said he'd take a pic with my camera for free. Nice man.

The man of a couple, both wearing rucksacks, said hello to me. I asked if he'd just finished or was just starting.

'We're not doing the John O'Groats,' he said, in a Yorkshire accent. 'We're walking around the South-West Coastal Path. Started in Bristol, we'll finish in Weymouth.'

'For charity?' I asked. I had caught the disease.

'No! People always bloody ask if we're doing it for charity. It makes me cross. We're doing it for ourselves. We walk everywhere.'

'Sorry.'

'Guess how old I am,' he said.

'Fifty-five, sixty?'

'Seventy-five.'

'Blimey.'

'I know. Look good, don't I?'

He did indeed.

'Ask me what's in my first-aid kit.'

It wouldn't have necessarily been my next question, but I was game.

'What's in your first-aid kit?'

'Bandages and a gun.'

'Okay.'

'Ask me why a gun.'

'Why a gun?'

'So when she gets injured, I can shoot her!'

'I don't know why I put up with it,' his wife said.

'We do everything together. That's the secret,' he said. 'Why watch telly? Life's too short.'

And with that they were off walking towards Weymouth, holding hands like a couple of love-struck teenagers.

I said goodbye to Peter and turned the Ridgeback around, wheels pointing east. As I rode back across the start/finish line and thus entered the home stretch, I felt a whole range of conflicting emotions: sad, elated, nervous, excited.

'Good luck,' a motorist said to me through his open window as he queued to get into the car park.

'Thank you,' I replied.

Chapter 19

'Wheel, kindly light, along life's cycle path,
Wheel Thou on me! The road is rough,
I have discerned Thy wrath, But wheel me on!'
Christian hymn

I pedalled up and down the steep, narrow lanes of the Land's End headland, through the lovely, quintessentially Cornish fishing village of Mousehole, where the wide sweep of Mount's Bay opened up before me. I pushed on through Newlyn, where the quayside sheds had 'Save Our Fish' spelled out in neon bulbs on the wall, and Penzance, where the giant helicopter that shuttled back and forth to the Isles of Scilly thundered low over my head, and past St Michael's Mount. Soon after, I was at Lizard Point, the southern-most tip of the British mainland. The vegetation was sparse, and the occasional gorse bushes of the remote Lizard were wind-bent towards the north-east in perpetuity, appearing as if in photographs taken in a fierce storm. They looked not unlike acacias. But they were in fact Cornish heath, endemic to the Lizard. The whole scene put me in mind of the African savannah.

Suddenly, a wet sea fog – what I believe the Cornish call a mizzle – made the world disappear, and I was alone with just my breathing and the sound of my tyres on the road. The winds eventually gathered to send the fog billowing and eddying, and the savannah had sprouted the vast satellite dishes of Goonhilly.

I dropped down into the tiny village of Porthoustock, and slipped and skidded my way up the slurry-covered 25% climb out the other side. At the top of the climb, Falmouth Bay lay below me, with rows of giant tankers silently at anchor at the mouth of the Helford River. I stopped to rest and drink in the view. It was so quiet, so immense. The hedgerows were bursting with blackberries, and I gathered some up, greedily shovelling great fistfuls into my mouth, the juice dribbling down my chin. Rabbits darted around the field in front of me. A kestrel hovered. My phone sounded its text alert. It was an automated message from the gym I'd left before setting off on the bike trip.

'We would love to welcome you back at a special rate of only £70 a month,' it said.

I thought about the low-ceilinged room, where rows of exercise bikes faced TV screens showing MTV or soaps. Then I looked again at the view in front of me and down at the bicycle beneath me. Modern life had never seemed so absurd as it did at that moment.

I rode around the dark and fantastically moody and muddy creeks of the Helford River, the landscape that had inspired Daphne Du Maurier's novel *Frenchman's Creek*, and finally into Falmouth. There I popped into a discount store to pick up a new ground sheet to replace mine which had perished, and afterwards rode down to the quayside. At a slipway, I watched a man row ashore in a small boat that looked as if it had been made from old fabric and twigs. The man tied it off and walked towards me.

'What's your boat?' I asked.

'It's a replica of a currach, the type of craft that carried the early Irish diaspora,' the man, whose name was Rory, said. 'St Piran, the patron saint of Cornwall, rowed here from Ireland in the sixth century in one just like it.'

Rory, who told me he was 53, was a lecturer in marine environmental management. He told me how, back in the 1980s, he'd read a book called Ancient Seacraft, all about the boats of the Polynesians and Inuits and Celts.

'It hit me like a thunderbolt – that was what I wanted to do with my life: build boats using ancient, intuitive design and try and figure out what voyages would have been possible using them.'

Rory explained how he went up the local creeks for four or five days at a time, bivvying on remote banks at night, making stews from the prawns and velvet crabs he caught and the marsh samphire he found. 'My God, those prawns are beautiful – really nutty, not like fish. For me, it's all about reconnecting with nature, history and self-reliance.'

Rory asked where I was staying for the night.

'You're more than welcome to stay at my flat. I'm going to be at my girlfriend's anyway.'

He fished in his pocket, threw me the keys and wrote down the address.

'And if you like, tomorrow I can row you across to St Mawes.'

'In that?' I said, maybe a little bit too incredulously and definitely too ungratefully.

'St Brendan rowed to Newfoundland in something similar, if you don't mind.'

'I'd love to.'

Rory's flat was beautiful, high over the town and full of the ephemera of a life lived closely connected to the sea: driftwood sculptures, ships' chronometers, books on ancient boat design. I sat in his living room, clutching a large glass of red wine, looking out of the window as the darkness fell on Falmouth Bay with the lights of the fishing vessels putting to sea fading into the black. Once again on this trip, I felt truly blessed.

The next morning, at the appointed time, Rory was waiting for me at the quayside. We unloaded the bike and placed the panniers into the currach, then I carried the bike down the slippery stone steps and handed it to Rory, who balanced it precariously on the bags.

Then we set off on the two-mile voyage across the Carrick Roads to St Mawes, me sitting on the stern transom in the manner of a Lycra-clad pharaoh, the gunwales just centimetres above the water.

As Rory pulled on the rough-hewn, plank-like oars, he told me about his plans for an upcoming protest. He was going to row up the river to Truro with some of his students and 'moor' the currach on the cathedral steps to represent where the sea levels could be soon unless we tackled global warming. 'The currach is a very important symbol of survival and resilience,' he said. 'And that's my message: self-reliance, pride, economy and, most importantly, local solutions for local problems.'

I told him about my time at Findhorn and the Do Lectures, and that I'd heard others talk about localism and community time and again on my journey.

'I'm not surprised,' he said. 'I think people are finally waking up to where globalisation is taking us, what happens to communities when the markets dictate everything. So many of the houses down here are holiday homes for rich people from London. Locals are priced out. Cornwall's got all this sea, rich farmland, ores, skills, yet it's one of the poorest areas in Britain. It doesn't make sense.'

I asked Rory about the tankers I'd seen anchored off the Helford River.

'They're all along the coast,' he said. 'It's the recession. Some of them are full of gas or coal, waiting for the price to go up. Others are just empty, sitting it out.'

What Rory would love to do one day, he said, was give up teaching and spend his days taking people up the creeks to reconnect them with nature. 'I've seen the effects a few nights out there has on my students. It's miraculous.'

About halfway across the Roads, I asked Rory about the currach. He'd built it using bent hazel rods for the frame and laths of larch.

'And the skin?' I asked, glancing nervously at the fragile-looking fabric.

'Artists' canvas, from Trago Mills in the high street. The Irish used to use shoelaces and ladies' underwear.'

'I bought a ground sheet from there,' I said. 'It cost 59p.'

'This fabric only cost 40p.'

'And how deep is this harbour?'

'Oh, it's one of the deepest natural harbours in the world,' said Rory, laughing, as he pulled hard towards St Mawes, ducking between the large dredgers and ferries ploughing up the Roads.

I spent the next day doing my best Sisyphus impression again. I knew that there were at least 200 miles of brutally hilly Cornish, Devon and Dorset coastline to go before the land started to flatten out, and it had begun to affect me both mentally and physically.

The physical battering was bad enough. My right knee was starting to ache more or less constantly, and I had developed a pain in the big toe of my right foot, which at times was so acute that I'd had to cycle with my heel. I wished I'd put in a request with God's children in Cardiff for a full-body policy. Convinced I'd got a stress fracture, the day before I'd googled 'toe pain', and minutes later, such is the danger of the Internet working in tandem with a fertile imagination, was convinced that I'd got a stress fracture, osteoporosis, Parkinson's, malaria or leprosy – or possibly a combination of all five.

But it was also the mental side of things that was really beginning to wear me down. I rode up the Roseland Peninsula, with its little white cottages draped in briar roses and ivy geraniums, and then around the bays Gerrans, Veryan and Mevagissey, where a profusion of rhododendron bushes and Cornish palm trees combined with the hot sun and azure seas to give it the look and feel of the Caribbean.

I should have been happy to be alive, as I had been for practically every second of every day since leaving London. But the relentless hills were breaking my spirit. They lurked around every corner, each one seemingly longer and steeper than the last. And the really weird thing was that there didn't seem to be any flat or downhill sections any longer. The only way was always up. It was like riding through an Escher picture.

Even the beautiful little Cornish fishing villages I passed through, such as Portscatho, Portloe and Mevagissey, failed to lift me. For every village on the coast in that part of Cornwall shares one characteristic: they all sit at the point where a deep, deep valley meets the sea. Bastards. I hated them all. The whole thing had suddenly become an ordeal. I may have covered over 4,000 miles, but here I was seriously considering giving up. I could throw my bike on a train and be back home in a few hours. To a stress fracture, osteoporosis, Parkinson's, malaria or leprosy, I could add lack of backbone, too.

For the next two days I pushed on as Fowey, Polperro and Looe came and went. All beautiful, but I was largely indifferent to them. Things were unravelling for me. Yes, I was in pain. Yes, the hills were killing me. But there was something else too. Every day for four months I'd been accompanied by the sea, always there on my right shoulder. And every day I had been surrounded by birdsong and vast skies. Each day I had looked at the sea as if seeing it for the first time. Every bird that flew alongside me was a miracle, every tree or cow I passed a work of art, every uphill just an integral part of the down.

I had been able to see beauty in everything, everyone. I had discovered a level of peace and happiness and balance I had long mislaid, and instead of it being a fleeting thing, it had been waiting for me every morning when I opened my eyes. It had transformed not just the way I related to the world, but the way the world related to me. And now I could feel it slipping away, was fixating on the future. The hiatus with Brian the pigeon had pulled me back for a while, but now I was racing ahead again. I had seen the light at the end of the tunnel and I was bolting.

Maybe the text message from the gym had brought it into sharp focus, with the harrowing thought of those exercise bikes facing the screens, the knowledge that in a few weeks' time I would be back in London and have to readjust.

I remembered something my mum used to say to us about holidays when we were young. The first couple of days of the break, she reckoned, were spent adjusting, shedding one's mind of quotidian worries. The next three were the glorious meat in the sandwich, the time when the return to normal life was far enough away to allow you to be fully immersed in the present. Onto the last two days were cast the dark shadows of re-entry.

And, as my brain whirred on those relentless hills, I thought that maybe endings had something to do with it. I'd never been good at endings, as I'd begun to work out on this trip. There was something about seeing something through that scared me to the core; something I'd always managed to avoid confronting by running away and starting again. Could this be the tension I could feel rising in me? The panic? The closing in?

In Cremyll, I took the little old ferry across Drake's Sound and entered Plymouth and, therefore, Devon. The traffic in Plymouth was terrible, and I found myself swearing at cars and buses belching black fumes that came too close. As a cycle commuter in London, I am all too used to heated confrontation with motorists, people travelling like tightly coiled springs ready to explode. But I hadn't really sensed much of that in four months. There had been many near misses and idiot motorists, obviously, but I'd always responded not with anger, but by laughing and thanking my good fortune for a lucky escape. Not now.

A blue Mondeo cut me up.

'Arsehole,' I shouted after him.

'Prick,' he shouted back at me at the traffic lights, his face puce, contorted with rage. 'You shouldn't even be on the fucking roads.'

I knew what was coming next. I'd heard it a million times in London.

'See that?' he said, jabbing his finger at his tax disc. 'I pay to be on the road. When you lot do, maybe you can mouth off.'

That old canard. Usually, in such a situation, I explain how the vast majority of the highways budget comes out of central taxes, not from vehicle excise duty, and that therefore cyclists, as taxpayers, contribute an enormous amount towards the maintenance of the roads. But I couldn't be arsed.

'Bollocks,' I said.

'Fuck off,' he replied.

I rode towards the South Hams on the busy A379, eschewing the quiet back lanes. My mood was turning the pedals at quite a lick. I wasn't really seeing anything, just riding to get somewhere, anywhere.

There were no pound shops or boarded-up pubs in Salcombe. Like Rock, it seemed to be set up exclusively for the posh London crowd. There were upmarket restaurants and delis aplenty, and coffee shops selling chocamochacinos for three quid. There were several well-heeled yacht clubs and plenty of shops selling sailing leisurewear and galleries flogging seascapes for eye-watering prices.

The narrow streets were choked with Range Rovers and Land Cruisers. I looked in the window of an estate agent's. Small one-bedroom flats were going for £300k, big family homes for up to £5 million. For £12,000 a week in high season you could rent a glorious house overlooking the water. Salcombe, I would discover, had the second-most expensive real estate in Britain outside London, after Sandbanks overlooking Poole Harbour. An estimated 50 per cent of all properties were second homes. Put a Martian on a bike and get him to cycle a loop of this island and he'd be convinced he'd travelled around two different planets, if not universes. Which, of course, in many ways he would have done.

There was a flight of steep and slippery stone steps, down which I manhandled the bike, managing to bang my shins several times to the sound of loud cursing.

At the bottom was the little open-decked foot ferry that went back and forth across the Kingsbridge Estuary to East Portlemouth on the other side. I loaded my bike onto it and took a seat.

The ferryman, a bloke in his early forties with a shaved head, collected the fare from me and the only other passenger, a man in his thirties with a salt-and-pepper beard wearing a small backpack.

'Come far?' the ferryman asked.

I wasn't really in the mood to talk about the trip or engage in conversation. I was still unsettled by my sudden change of attitude towards the whole thing. I told him just the bare bones, summarised in a short sentence, shouting to be heard above the engine.

'Sounds like fun,' he said.

'These hills are kinda killing the fun.' Boy, was I feeling sorry for myself.

'Tough, huh?' he said.

'You have no idea,' I replied. A wry smile crept across the ferryman's face.

'You should ask him about his trip,' the guy with the backpack said to me, pointing to the ferryman.

I really didn't want to hear about his Jogle or Lejog.

'Go on, ask him.'

'Guy says you've done a trip,' I said, without much enthusiasm.

The ferryman looked at the other passenger, as if to say 'I wish you wouldn't keep telling people', then turned to me and said something. I must have misheard over the noise of the engine, because it sounded like he said he had pedalled all the way to Hawaii.

'You pedalled where?' I asked.

'Hawaii,' he said, as the boat brushed against the landing jetty in East Portlemouth...

Chapter 20

'My legs and a silly something in me cry out for knocking the milestones down one by one and stopping at nothing. For years I have been telling myself that it's not the miles in the life that count, but the life in the miles. But still this silly restlessness hurries me on.'
Harold Elvin, *The Ride to Chandigarh*

'You pedalled to Hawaii!'

'If we're going to talk, you'll have to come back with me,' the ferryman said. 'Can't keep people waiting.'

So we headed back to Salcombe. The ferryman, whose name was Stevie Smith, told me how, in 1994, aged 27 and fed up with his desk job at the Organisation for Economic Cooperation and Development, he'd set off from Greenwich with his friend Jason to cycle to Lagos in southern Portugal. They planned to be the first people to go around the world by human power alone.

'Loads of people had cycled across continents and others had rowed across oceans,' he said. 'But no one had combined the two into a human-powered journey around the globe. We thought it was too good an idea not to act on.'

In Portugal, they hooked up with the boat they'd had specially made, a 26-foot-long glorified pedalo called *Moksha*, Sanskrit for 'freedom'.

There they'd partied till dawn with their mates and climbed into *Moksha* horribly hungover and pedalled off into the Atlantic.

'I turned to Jason, told him I had a confession, that I'd never spent a night at sea,' Stevie said. '"Don't worry, mate," Jason replied. "Neither have I."'

I sat there with my jaw on the floor.

For the next 111 days, the two men had been out in the Atlantic, taking shifts at the pedals between sleeping. They had hit huge storms that had tossed *Moksha* around like a toy in a bathtub and flung them into the ocean. They'd suffered terrible salt sores, had sharks encircle the boat and narrowly avoided being run down by supertankers. They'd gone badly off-course and run out of food, having to catch fish to survive, and slowly slipped into a madness so that the sea had started talking to them in the long, lonely hours at the pedals.

The ferry reached East Portlemouth again.

After 4,500 miles, Stevie and Jason finally arrived in Miami. Stevie set off on a bicycle heading for San Francisco, where he was to meet up again with Jason, who'd set off on rollerblades. Jason got hit by a car in Colorado and had both legs smashed to smithereens. It was three years before they could continue the journey. In 1998 they'd set off once more in *Moksha* to pedal across the Pacific.

On arrival in Hawaii, Stevie had had enough and quit the project. 'It had been five years all-in. I'd just lost the appetite for it.'

'I know just how you felt,' I wanted to say, but suddenly the hills of the West Country seemed to lack the adversarial qualities of being out in the world's biggest ocean in a pedalo. So I kept the thought to myself.

Jason had carried on alone, travelling by *Moksha* to Australia, then a combination of bike, kayak and walking to India, where he pedalled *Moksha* across the Indian Ocean to Africa and cycled back to Britain, finally arriving back in Greenwich in 2007 and thus finishing the world's first human-powered circumnavigation.

After drifting for a while in New Zealand and Australia, Stevie arrived home in Salcombe.

'Not long after I got back, my stepfather offered me a job as a ferryman,' he said. 'Strangely enough, it was a dream I harboured as a child.'

He's been ferrying people back and forth 300 metres across the Kingsbridge Estuary ever since.

'How do you cope with this, going back and forth over the same stretch of water, day in, day out, after your adventures?' I asked.

Stevie smiled again. 'I've an addictive personality. This is good discipline for me,' he said. 'It took me a while to settle when I got back, but then it dawned on me that there's no real difference between crossing the Atlantic and crossing this estuary. You can't rely on the attainment of goals or journeys, no matter how big or small, for your happiness, because the attainment of that goal will only bring a temporary gratification. If you want to be happy, then you must enjoy it all, at whatever point you are at, from the beginning to the end. Because ultimately happiness is the acceptance of the journey as it is now, not the promise of the other shore.'

We had arrived in Salcombe once more, and I had by now started going around the other passengers collecting the fares for Stevie. After I'd got the money, I joined him again at the stern. I was really struck about what he'd said about the vast ocean and the narrow estuary being fundamentally the same thing, and asked him about it again. It seemed important.

'I used to be very driven,' Stevie said. 'My life was a series of what I call "target practice", always targeting the next thing and the next. When I first started on the ferry, I was driven crazy by it.'

A yacht passed across our bow. Stevie waved at the guy at the helm.

'But actually, finding this job was a real gift for me. There is no promotion, no professional goals or advancement. It is just what it is: carrying people across the water. That was hard to come to terms with at first. It's easy to feel like a bit of a failure, especially as we're such social animals and prone to comparing ourselves to others. And of course Salcombe is a very wealthy place. It was difficult to maintain a sense of self-esteem in a job with no direction.

'As a ferryman you've got nowhere to go. You're either on one side or the other, or somewhere in the middle. It took me a while to realise that it didn't matter where I was in the estuary. Why should I get upset whether I was at one place or the other when I could only ever be in the place I was?'

We were approaching the shore again.

'It's a wonderful release when you find it,' Stevie said. 'When you discover that every step of the journey is the same. You can enjoy the first step and the last step and every step in between. They're all just as important. Crossing the line is euphoric, of course, but that's all there is. It's short-lived. After a couple of days you're back to taking single steps again.'

I asked Stevie what it was like to set foot on shore after so long out on the ocean.

'It was very, very difficult to deal with civilisation after all that time at sea: all that noise and frenetic pace. It was overwhelming, terrifying. I remember walking into a supermarket and seeing all that choice. All I wanted was something to eat, but I didn't know where to start. It was like a Stone Age man walking into Sainsbury's.

'If only I could appreciate now that first taste of fresh fruit, or tucking into a juicy hamburger, or that first cold drink sliding down my throat. If I could maintain that incredible joy I had for everything after months on the ocean, I'd be in a permanent state of ecstasy. The joy of finding miracles in the everyday,' he said.

We were back in East Portlemouth again. I started gathering my things together. I would be getting off this time and moving on.

Stevie tied off the boat and helped me put the bike and the bags back on dry land. We hugged.

'Two things, Mike,' said Stevie. 'First, just remember that finishing lines are good, but their most important role is to get you over the start line in the first place.'

'Thanks for that. And the second?'

'You owe me forty-six pounds.'

Chapter 21

'The bicycle is the most civilised conveyance known
to man. Other forms of transport grow daily more
nightmarish. Only the bicycle remains pure in heart.'

Iris Murdoch

I rounded Start Point and the coastline headed more or less due
north, with long uninterrupted views of Start Bay, backed by its
high cliffs. The sun was out, and people were walking their dogs on
the shingle beach. Half a dozen kites danced brightly against the
deep blue. It would have been difficult to imagine a more idyllic
British coastal scene. Only the incongruous presence of a black
Sherman tank in the car park at Torcross betrayed the fact that Slapton Sands had been, just 63 years earlier, witness to one of the worst
massacres on British soil in modern history.

For the gently sloping gravel beach, followed by a strip of land,
backed by a lake – a 180-acre freshwater lagoon – and then the cliffs,
not only make Slapton beautiful, but also almost identical-looking
to Utah Beach in Normandy. As a result, US commanders had
thought it the perfect place to mount a full-scale rehearsal in 1944
for the D-Day invasion. Operation Tiger had begun.

Early in the still-dark morning of 28 April 1944, 30,000 US
troops on board landing craft bobbed around in the waters of Lyme
Bay waiting for the signal to commence their mock beach landing.
Tragically, the flotilla of boats was being woefully protected by
just a single Royal Navy corvette. Tragically, because also bobbing
around in Lyme Bay that day were nine German E-boats who,
unable to believe their luck at finding such a soft target, opened fire
with a vengeance. Many of the servicemen jumped into the freezing
water. Unused to being at sea, many panicked and put on their
lifebelts incorrectly, so that when they jumped into the water, their
full combat packs flipped them onto their backs, pushing their heads
underwater and drowning them. In all, 638 US Army and Navy
personnel perished in the darkness of that spring morning.

When the remaining men made it to Slapton Sands, the blunders continued. General Eisenhower wanted his men to be battle-hardened and insisted that the beach be shelled with live ammunition, resulting in a further 308 men dying from friendly fire. Nearly 1,000 men died that day, compared to the 200 who died during the real invasion of Utah Beach a little over a month later.

After the war, perhaps embarrassed by the catalogue of cock-ups, the US and British military offered no support to recover remains or dedicate a memorial to the incident. For decades the truth was concealed. It took the efforts of a local man, Ken Small, who discovered evidence of the bloodbath while beachcombing in the early 1970s, to right this wrong. In 1974, he bought from the US government the rights to a submerged tank from the 70th Tank Battalion. In 1984, he finally raised the tank and created the memorial that now stood before me, all mud- and barnacle-encrusted. Small had spent the next 20 years of his life researching the debacle, writing a book about it, *The Forgotten Dead*. Nearly every day of those 20 years, he'd sat in his car next to the tank, selling his book and telling visitors of the atrocity, determined, despite the indifferent of the authorities, that those men's sacrifice would not be hushed up. Small died of cancer in March 2004, a few weeks before the 60th anniversary of Operation Tiger. His wonderful memorial and legacy remains.

I rode on. Blackpool Sands, a tiny crescent of shingle backed by a pine forest, entered my British Top 10 beaches list. Dartmouth, overlooked by its imposing Naval College high on a hill, basked in the sunshine, yachts moored at anchor on the River Dart. I took the little ferry across to Kingswear, with its pastel-painted cottages packed tightly on the steep hillside, and high above the town stopped to watch a train from the Paignton and Dartmouth Steam Railway chuff and puff its way down the Dart towards me, a rake of brown-and-cream coaches behind it, curls of smoke melting into the heavily wooded valley sides. The train passed right under me and I closed my eyes and inhaled. If there is a greater smell in the world than the coal smoke from a steam engine, I have yet to discover it.

Torquay, with its high-rise apartment blocks and huge villas overlooking the marina packed with luxury yachts, its giant palm trees and graceful Edwardian pavilion, could easily have doubled for Monaco. Grey-haired seniors in crisp whites played bowls by the waterfront, while other pensioners were out strolling or jogging along the prom. Not many mobility scooters in evidence here or, for that matter, thinking about it, in any of the wealthy resorts of the south-west.

I was tired after another day of climbing, and by seven o'clock I was losing the light. I stopped at a campsite just south of Teignmouth, high on a cliff overlooking Lyme Bay, where dozens of tankers and freighters lay at anchor a few miles off the beach, waiting to be scrapped or for the salvation of a cargo.

It was one of those campsites that had some pretension to offer the Butlins or Pontins experience. In the site office they advertised cabaret evenings and quizzes, and there were photographs showing small children cuddling up to the site's mascot, which was purple and may have been a dinosaur or a giant prune. It was difficult to tell. I assumed that at this late stage of the season – it was now getting on towards the end of September – such events had been mothballed until the following spring.

I pitched my tent and went to the clubhouse for some food and a pint. Sitting at a stool by the bar was the dinosaur/prune, looking as bored as a man/woman in a dinosaur/prune costume can look. A woman polished glasses behind the bar. At a table near the dance floor was a young couple with a little boy dressed in a leather jacket with gel-spiked hair. In the far corner sat an elderly couple, each doing a crossword. And that was it.

I bought a pint and took a seat. A poster on the wall advertised 'An evening of *Grease*'. I looked at the date. It was today's. The lights dimmed. The music started. The elderly couple folded away their newspapers and left. The curtains swept open to reveal a man and a woman, in their late teens or early twenties, dressed in a studded leather jacket and pink chiffon ensemble respectively, holding a pose. They started dancing, lip-synching along to 'Summer Lovin''. The little boy dressed as a rocker with gel-spiked hair took to the floor, jiggling away in that lovely unselfconscious-just-beginning-to-get-self-conscious way. His parents sat there, supping at their drinks. The two performers looked out to an empty room and shouted 'Now we're rocking, Teignmouth. Yeah!' They both looked like they wanted to die. The dinosaur/prune looked on impassively. I sat there for three numbers. Then I went to the bar and ordered a couple of cans to take back to the tent.

'Goodnight,' I said to the dinosaur/prune as I left.

'Goodnight,' said a muffled voice.

Chapter 22

'Socialism can only arrive by bicycle.'
Jose Antonio Viera Gallo

I took the little ferry across the River Exe from Starcross to Exmouth in bright sunshine. By the time I'd got to the other side, where the Jurassic Coast began, summer had ended – though I didn't know it at the time.

The Exmouth–Budleigh Salterton cycleway, running along the track bed of a railway line closed in 1967, was gorgeous, its tunnels of trees, now turning to gold, providing welcome sanctuary from the rain. At the top of the fearsome Peak Hill, just west of Sidmouth, I could see the coast stretching away: nothing but high cliffs as far as the eye could see. Just when I thought that the worst of the South-West's hills might be behind me, that cruel view was almost enough to make a grown man cry. But I had a new resolve now.

I thought about what else I might be able to dump from my luggage. I couldn't think of anything. I was down to the bare bones now.

I laboured long and hard that morning in the rain, my right big toe throbbing once more. I would have to get it checked out soon, because it seemed to be getting worse.

I looked at the map just after Lyme Regis, weighing up my options to make easterly progress. I could either follow the National Cycle Network's recommended route, which headed inland, zigzagging through Dorset's finest lung-bursting hills for mile upon mile upon unnecessary mile, and seemed to go in every direction apart from the one I wanted to go. Or I could just get on the attractively straight A35. I mean, how bad could it be?

D'oh! Forget the A487 outside Aberystwyth. I had found, definitely, the worst road for cycling on in Britain. Imagine the narrowest of two-lane highways, imprisoned in a canyon of 10-foot-high hedgerow walls, that dives and twists steeply down into valleys and up the other side, with blind sweeping bends, used by a never-ending stream of tailgating lorries and coaches who, if the carpet of broken glass and shattered wing mirrors was any indication, regularly clipped each other in passing. I got off and pushed, so dangerous was it. The hooting from the traffic stuck in a long line, unable to squeeze past me, and the constant stinging from the nettles I had to walk into to allow the said traffic to pass, seemed like just and divine punishment for my stupidity. My contributions to *Police! Camera! Moron!* were mounting up. Footage will doubtless emerge, at some stage, with that Mancunian bloke's voiceover saying: 'Tuesday morning. Just outside Bridport. CCTV operators are alerted to some geezer trying to cycle along the A35. Muppet.'

After Bridport, I got myself onto the relative sanity of the B3157, a strip of tarmac that rolled along open countryside high over the sea. There were strong and chilly westerlies blowing, up to 30mph, and the riding was effortless. I crested a hill, and there below me was the Jurassic Coast's World Heritage Site of Chesil Beach, the Fleet lagoon trapped behind its tombolo, running into the distance. It was like looking at an image on Google Earth. At the end of the tombolo was the extraordinary sight of Portland rising from the sea, its grey-marbled, sculptured cliffs looking like a set of molars that needed a good polish. Of all the coastal scenes of beauty and drama I'd witnessed those past five months, that view was right up there. I stopped to drink it all in. Whatever else can be said about the state of Britain at the moment, one thing is indubitable: we live on the most beautiful island on the planet.

There were plenty of red flags flying in the Purbeck Hills, but the barrier that closed the little road when the army was using its gunnery range was up, so I pedalled on, past the burnt-out wrecks of tanks and the large target boards with numbers on them, riddled with shell holes, that festooned the hillside. Up and up the chalk downs I laboured in my grovel gear, glancing north now and then to the distant huddles of soldiers and gun emplacements, waiting for the silent puff of smoke followed by the howling sound of incoming and another nomination for a Darwin Award.

At the top, I was moved to tears. For one thing, my big toe was throbbing in agony and I was again having to pedal with my heel. I would really have to get it seen to. But more importantly for me, as I ascended to the highest point of the Purbeck Hills and looked east, with uninterrupted views over the vast expanse of Poole Harbour and the green sward of the New Forest beyond, there were no more hills. Nothing. As flat as the proverbial pancake. The daily agonies and popping knee that had started some 600 miles before in Somerset were behind me. Sure, there were still some odd bits of climbing to go, but that moment felt like a true milestone. I felt like Moses gazing down from Nebo.

There was an island ahead, too, and it took me a moment to work out what it was. The Needles were the giveaway. I had cycled from London to the Isle of Wight on a day's ride in the past. The trip was coming to an end.

I freewheeled down a long hill, joy in my heart, singing loudly and badly. I rode through pretty Dorset villages of thatched cottages with roses around the door frames, and along a narrow wooded lane, over the end of which towered Corfe Castle, framed in the trees. From somewhere in the distance came the mournful whistle of a steam engine.

There was a rustle, and a young red deer leapt out of the trees and flew across the road, missing me by inches, before leaping through the hedge on the other side. I watched it race across the field like Road Runner, kicking up dust.

At the end of the Studland Peninsula, I took the clanking chain ferry across the narrow mouth of Poole Harbour, which paused to allow Brittany Ferries' giant Barfleur to glide by. I looked over the side of the little ferry, the tide race that drains the contents of Poole Harbour – the second largest natural one in the world after Sydney – churning against the hull like rapids. It didn't bear thinking about what would happen if that chain ever snapped.

The voyage across from Studland to Sandbanks may have been only a few hundred yards, but it linked two very different worlds. I cycled around the one-square-mile sand dune, the fourth most expensive real estate in the world. The Sandbanks phenomenon had started in 2001, when a local estate agent sold a 1,200 square foot apartment on the peninsula for £1 million. He worked out that this made it globally only behind Hong Kong, Tokyo and Belgravia in terms of price per square foot, and got it formally ranked as such. Of course, once it had been officially ranked as the kind of place only the über-wealthy could afford, the über-wealthy dutifully showed up. Prices had been skyrocketing ever since.

As I rode, I saw women of indeterminate age, thick of lip and thin of waist, parading around in huge sunglasses, walking ugly little dogs. Teak-hued men emerged from Bond-villain houses surrounded by huge fences and security cameras in the sort of blingtastic cars with chrome spinning hubcaps and tinted windows that always left me unsure whether I wanted to laugh or cry. The cars growled past me, and what they seemed to be growling was 'Get out of my way, you sad, loser twat.'

I looked in the window of an estate agent's. The prices made Salcombe seem positively déclassé. For almost the cost of a campsite for the night, I bought a coffee and sat drinking it at an outside table. People walked past looking at my loaded bike and I prepared myself for the questions that always followed: come far? How heavy's all that gear? But nobody said anything, just looked at me suspiciously, as if I was some sad freak. It was bizarre, and for the first time on the trip, I really started feeling like a saddo. I couldn't help but wonder whether obscene amounts of money suck all the romance out of your soul.

The cycle path took me right along the esplanade lining Bournemouth seafront. Behind me, the Studland peninsula was illuminated by spears of golden light penetrating the low clouds. Kitesurfers launched into huge leaps, using the ramps of waves to take off, climbing so high and hanging in the air for so long it sometimes looked as if they'd never come down again.

At Hengistbury Head, I took the little passenger ferry across Christchurch harbour to Mudeford. A sign on the boat advertised the fares: £1.20 for adults; 60p for children; dogs, cats and parrots, free.

Early evening had barely begun, but I was already losing the light again. I followed some small lanes on the edge of the New Forest, heading for a little tent icon. But when I got there, the site had closed for the winter. Cycling now in the dark, the trees dripping fat splots onto my head, I came to a small town. I saw a sign for a B&B and knocked on the door. A man and a woman in their sixties opened it and ushered me inside.

My experience of the road had taught me that there were two distinct types of British B&B: those where quarters for guests and the owners were kept very separate, where communal space had been given an institutional feel, the décor neutral or themed, but always unequivocally chosen to communicate that here was a place of cold commerce; and then there were those B&Bs that had no such pretensions, such as the one I'd just arrived at, where you effectively stayed in somebody's spare room for the evening, the place retaining all the feel of a family home. The latter type was definitely my favourite, but I always had a slightly odd feeling when staying at them, a stranger violating a sacred space.

We sat in the living room. The man returned to his jigsaw while the woman asked me about my trip. A shelf ran around the entire room at dado height, filled with mugs celebrating a half-century of Royal occasions. On top of the TV and along the walls were black-and-white photographs of their younger selves, handsome and smiling, on holidays wearing swimming costumes, at weddings, sun-kissed with friends raising glasses towards the camera in some foreign taverna, a life in photographs. There were graduation photos of a young man and woman, and the same two people, a few years older, each standing next to a new face, being showered with confetti. And then there was a recent shot of the B&B woman, cuddling a baby, beaming at the camera, an intensity in her eyes, looking as if she'd just fallen in love for the first time.

I loved looking at the pictures, but it was bittersweet. There was a stillness to the house, a sense of emptiness: the presence of ghosts.

I handed the money over to the woman. This always felt like a grubby transaction in such a B&B. Then I went up to my room. I looked in the wardrobe, with its empty hangers, and sat at the dressing table staring at the reflection of an invader. On the walls were generic prints of seascapes. Over the years, I imagined, from those same hooks had hung pop stars or ponies, Ferraris or footballers. I lay on the single bed and wanted to go home.

Chapter 23

'The bicycle has a soul. If you succeed to love it,
it will give you emotions that you will never forget.'
Mario Cipollini, Italian former cycling World Champion

At Lymington, I just missed a ferry for the Isle of Wight. While I was waiting for the next one, I looked across the Solent. All I could see were cliffs and hills. And all I could feel was my right big toe throbbing. The angel and the devil popped up. I hadn't heard from them for a while.

'I thought after Scotland you had decided to go around all the islands,' reasoned the angel.

'Ignore her. Just look at those hills!' said the devil. 'Don't you think you've done enough climbing?'

'This is the last island of the trip. Why blow it now?'

'Who cares? Besides, you need to get that toe looked at. It's getting worse by the day, might even be leprosy. You can be at the hospital in Portsmouth in a couple of hours.'

'They do have hospitals on the Isle of Wight.'

'They've also got huge hills to climb before you get there. It's all flat on the mainland.'

The next ferry came in. I watched the cars load and the stern ramp crank closed. Then I turned my bike around and headed back into the New Forest.

'Arsehole,' said the angel.

'Charming,' said the devil.

That Sunday morning, the forest was rammed with cyclists going in the opposite direction to me. All of them had a large sunflower on their chest or attached to their handlebars, the symbol of the local hospice they were cycling 30 miles to raise funds for. 'Morning,' each cyclist said as they passed.

'Morning,' I replied, at least 300 times.

The forest was spectacular in its autumnal finery, a richly woven tapestry of golds and russets that looked about as realistic as stage scenery. The bracken by the side of the road had turned the colour of chocolate.

In lovely Beaulieu, where donkeys replaced ponies as the roaming hazard, I stopped at the Queensmead Village Shop, for now and for all time quite simply the best sweet shop in the world. Aisle after aisle of shelves was stacked with jars and boxes containing all the sweets you've forgotten existed and many more you've never heard of. I'd been there before, while passing through by car, and always, mindful of my expanding middle-aged girth, and the hours I'd need to spend in the gym to compensate, had managed to show restraint. Not now. It felt like staring at all those selection boxes on Christmas morning and knowing your mum, for one day only, wasn't going to impose rationing.

I walked along the aisles, examining the jars with their precious vibrantly coloured contents of twists and squares and ovals, with as much hushed reverence as if I were in an art gallery. There were Summer Creams, Brandy Balls, Tom Thumb Drops, Rhubarb Rock, Stem Ginger and Mums & Dads. I looked at the other people in the shop. There were no children, just adults, staring in wonder.

In the next aisle were Raspberry Ruffles, Clove Drops, Army & Navy, ABC Letters, Fried Eggs, Space Dust and Bonbons of every imaginable hue. I opted for some Barley Twists, Iced Caramels, Liquorice Gums, Fruit Pastilles and Butter Toffee, and carried the five jars to the counter. The woman weighed them out, and slid them into little white paper bags, turning and twisting the bags to seal them.

'Just a second,' I said, and disappeared once more, returning with the jar of Rhubarb & Custard.

'And those, too, please.'

From behind me, I heard a woman's voice: 'Look, Frank, they've got Marry Me Quicks! Remember those?' I turned around to see an elderly couple pointing at a jar and smiling. The look on their faces reminded me of something, but I couldn't quite put my finger on it. Then I remembered: it was the pensioners looking for fairies at the gnome reserve.

I rounded the point at Lepe, the Isle of Wight just over a mile away across the Solent, taunting me for my broken promises, then headed up along Southampton Water, the giant brown towers of Fawley Oil Refinery appearing through the trees like denuded sequoias. At Hythe, I discovered the world's oldest pier railway, dating from 1922, and on it rattled along to the end, where I caught the foot ferry across Southampton Water.

We slipped between the giant container ships putting out to sea with Chinese script on their sterns, and past the floating pleasure palace that was *The Arcadia*, a cruise ship the size of a housing estate. On the quayside were multi-storey car parks, full of new vehicles awaiting distribution.

At Lee-on-the-Solent, on an otherwise deserted beach, a young blonde of the type *Private Eye* would describe as 'fruity' raced towards the water, whooping, ripping off her clothes and casting them behind her as she went. I could have cycled on, but felt compelled to stop and watch. This, obviously, was because I didn't want her to come to any harm. Just before the water's edge, she threw off her top and bra and then, just in her knickers, splashed knee-deep into the Solent, spinning, whooping, prancing and frolicking. The performance lasted a good five minutes, during which time I worked my way through most of my Iced Caramels. Whooped out, she calmly made her way out of the sea, got dressed, went to her car and drove off. I've no idea what that was all about, but if you ever happen to read this, young lady, I'd just like to say one thing: 'Thank you.'

At Gosport, I boarded the little ferry. A man came to collect my money, and I was just about to hand it over when I remembered the ticket Jack had given me back in St David's. I fished around in my bar bag, found it and handed it over. He'd have been home by then, and I wondered how he was adjusting back to Stoke-on-Trent after his epic ride around the coast. I smiled. Whenever I thought of Jack, I couldn't help but smile.

We pootled across the narrow mouth of the harbour towards Portsmouth, a city I've long loved, its littoral landscape – of Martello towers and ramparts, the rigging of HMS *Victory* and HMS *Warrior* skewering the skyline – now embellished by the sinuous beauty of the 170m Spinnaker Tower.

'Address?' asked the triage nurse at Pompey's St Mary's Hospital.

'I'm travelling around. Camping mostly,' I said.

He wrote 'no fixed abode' in the box. I liked that.

'Butter Toffee?' I asked.

'No thanks. Now, what's the problem?'

I explained that I probably had a stress fracture in my toe, seeing as how I'd just ridden 4,000 miles. I'd decided that a stress fracture was a suitably heroic injury. I was about to regale him with my Homeric story, but he just scribbled something down and moved on to my neighbour, a 'part-time professional wrestler' in a beanie hat called Wade, who'd hurt his arm in a bad wrestling fall the night before. Wade started to explain the manoeuvre he'd been attempting, but the nurse had moved on to two sheepish-looking teenage girls who'd been holding hands tightly ever since they'd walked in.

'No need to be nervous,' the nurse said kindly.

'We ain't nervous,' said one girl. 'We're superglued together.'

I nearly choked on my sweet.

After an hour, my name was called through to go and see the doctor.

'Butter Toffee?'

'No thanks,' she said.

'Rhubarb and Custard?

'I'm fine.'

The doctor tweaked and pulled away at my swollen toe and then sent me off for an X-ray.

'Probably a stress fracture,' I said, with some authority, as I sat back in front of her. She examined the plates.

'You see, I've just cycled all the—'

'Gout,' she said.

'Gout,' I said. 'Are you sure?'

'Quite sure.'

'That's not... well...'

'What?' she said.

'... not very heroic.'

'I'm sorry,' she said.

With my gouty foot and my prescription for Voltarol, I waited in the rain at the eastern end of Portsea Island for the foot ferry that would take me across Langstone Harbour to Hayling Island. Who knew we had so many ferries on the South Coast? This one would make at least a dozen I'd taken since leaving Land's End.

The ferry was operating its winter timetable, which meant departures on the hour. I'd just missed one. There was an information board by the slipway that told how four of the caissons built for one of the floating Mulberry Harbours that would enable supply ships to dock during the Normandy landings had been built in Langstone Harbour. If you looked straight ahead, the sign read, you could see the remains of one. And so I could, an angular slab of concrete sticking out of the water. That killed a few minutes.

I sat on the ground beside my bike in the rain, the hood of my jacket pulled tightly over my head, the rain drumming on my skull. It was a desolate, windswept spot with no cover. I decided to count all the blue boats I could see, then all the red ones. Afterwards, convinced this game had consumed a good slice of the wait, I looked at my watch. I tapped it to check it hadn't stopped. Then I went back to the board and reread, slowly, the information about the Mulberry Harbour. Four caissons, huh? Interesting. And just look at it over there, all concrete and sticking out of the water. Fascinating. I discovered that you can make the following anagrams from Mulberry Harbour: harbour blurry me; rural robbery hum; a humbly rub error. And then I started to try and make anagrams out of Normandy landings, but couldn't be arsed.

Finally, a little boat chugged into view. I loaded my bike and sat in the open bow, the only passenger. Still the rain fell relentlessly.

'Come and sit in the wheelhouse,' said the ferryman, who was wearing a fisherman's cap and a smile that lit up the gloom. 'Nice and warm in here.'

We cast off.

'See that,' he said. 'That's part of the Mulberry Harbour.'

'Is it?'

'They built four sections here?'

'Did they?'

His name was Mike, and he was a retired chartered engineer.

'Got bored sitting around doing nothing, then this job came up. I love it. Meet such great people.'

I told him about Stevie in Salcombe, and how, instead of going crazy shuttling back and forth across the same stretch of water, he'd managed to rid himself of the continual search for the next goal by realising that there was no end, only process, and that ultimately, this was just fine. Mike nodded at this ferryman philosophy. 'Sounds like a wise man,' he said. 'Across the Atlantic or across Langstone Harbour, it's no different really. The miracles are always found in the stuff of daily life if you have your eyes open.'

There must be something about being a ferryman that sits very well with the human condition.

'I'd find it very hard to live without the sea now. It gets into here,' Mike said, pointing to his heart. 'Coffee?'

He poured me out a cup from his flask. The little flat-bottomed boat rolled on the swell. Outside, whitecaps frothed up grey water, the rain beating against the windows of the little wheelhouse, winning the battle against the stuttering wipers.

'Met a guy a few months back who was doing the same thing as you,' Mike said.

'Older guy?'

'Yes.'

'That was Jack.'

'Full of the joys of life. Can't imagine much getting him down.'

'Amazing, isn't he?'

'A great advert for getting older.'

'How about those bankers?' said Mike, holding up his newspaper and pointing to the lead story. It told how, despite the huge taxpayer bailout and all the talk of savage spending cuts to reduce the deficit, champagne sales were rocketing in the City, and how the upcoming Christmas bonuses would be bigger than ever.

'Can't bear to think about it,' I said. And I really couldn't.

The strong westerlies blew me along the South Coast in heavy rain under a leaden sky, so effortlessly that I could have been on a moped. The land was still pancake-flat, and despite the fact that only a few days earlier I had almost burst into tears of joy at the thought of no more hills, I was now missing the exertions and the sense of achievement and the 'earning of the miles' that toiling up and down hills brought.

Bognor Regis, Littlehampton and Worthing all came and went in more or less one long continuous sprawl, a sign at the roadside the only way of telling that you were leaving one and entering the next. These were towns with the reputation of being where people go to die, and the glassed-in terraces of the seafront hotels full of dozing pensioners wrapped in blankets, with a wheelchair lift up the front steps of each establishment, did little to challenge that. With the grey sea churning against the sea wall, and hardly anybody on the streets braving the elements, it was hard to imagine being anywhere more depressing.

The devil popped up again, telling me there were direct trains from all of these towns to London. The angel whispered Stevie's words in my ear – 'happiness is the acceptance of the journey as it is now, not the promise of the other shore' – but a grey and rain-swept Shoreham-on-Sea was pushing that mantra to the limit.

On and on I rode, through Brighton, Newhaven and Seaford. The white cliffs of the Seven Sisters came into view and I started to climb once more, my laboured breathing and the tension in my calves feeling deliciously good. I pulled off the road at Beachy Head, and wheeled my bike across the grass to the edge of the cliffs. On the ground was a little stone plaque. It read: 'God is always greater than all of our troubles.' Next to it was a sign saying 'The Samaritans are always here for you'.

There were no fences at Beachy Head, just an unguarded sheer drop 530ft to the swirling English Channel and rocks below. That there were no fences at Britain's most notorious suicide spot seemed to me the most civilised of things; the idea that one of the last acts of somebody determined to end their life should be to clamber over a fence was too undignified to contemplate.

The rain was now monsoon-like. A shrivelled bunch of flowers was tied to a bench, the words on the little card too smudged by rain to make out.

I propped my bike against the bench and sat down. My head was spinning. I really wanted to try and work out why the voice in my head calling for me to bail out of the trip before the end was getting louder and louder. The voice had been silent until Wales, when I'd seen the whole map of the country for the first time and seen how relatively little ground I had left to cover. Until then, I'd not thought of anything much, apart from what was in front of me. But ever since, I'd been enjoying it less, looking for excuses not to finish.

I sat on that bench thinking about my life, about all the perfectly good things I'd bailed out of prematurely, about the projects I would start but couldn't or wouldn't finish, the dreams and fantasises that came to nothing ultimately because I couldn't see them through. The idea was always the thing. And now I wanted to go and live on the other side of the world. Did I really think that the answers lay there? That looking in a mirror in Buenos Aires would somehow offer back a different reflection than one in London, a different or better me? Yet still the idea of actually finishing something whole, completing a circle, was somehow frightening. All I wanted to do at that moment was catch a train to London and get on a plane to Argentina as soon as I could.

Back at the ferry from Salcombe, Stevie had asked me what had inspired me to take off and ride a bike around the coast of Britain. I told him about the restlessness that I couldn't seem to shake, the constant feeling that I wanted to be somewhere else. Stevie told me about his own restlessness, how even after leaving his friend in Hawaii he'd felt driven to keep going, cycling around Australia and New Zealand. He told me about a brother that had died when he was eight, and how he felt that this constant drive was something to do with feeling like he had to do something extraordinary to make up for the fact that his brother wasn't alive.

Cycling along the South Coast, I had been thinking a lot about what Stevie had said. Sitting up there in the driving rain at Beachy Head, it all seemed to coalesce, finally make some sense. I knew that I had to finish this thing.

Chapter 24

'The hardest part of raising a child is teaching them to ride bicycles. A shaky child on a bicycle for the first time needs both support and freedom. The realisation that this is what the child will always need can hit hard.'

Sloan Wilson

There was a good lung-bursting climb after Hastings, and from the top of the cliffs at Fairlight, across Rye Bay, there in the distance was Dungeness B. The full set.

Past Rye, the ring road skirting underneath it, the medieval town sitting high above me on its rocky outcrop, and on to Walland Marsh. The rabbits were dozy now, sapped of their skittish summer energy, and dawdled across the road in front of my wheels with sluggish abandon. Languid bees pinged against my face. The fields had far fewer sheep in them. In the sky above me, a great mass of black-and-white birds, perhaps thousands, swarmed and pulsed in a pre-migratory ritual dance. The wind was howling across the exposed Lydd Peninsula, cutting through my skin and penetrating my bones. Outside the little local supermarkets were piles of pumpkins ready for Halloween. The year was winding down.

I rode across the flat, eerie landscape fringing Romney Marsh, very few houses in sight, the entire landscape covered in shingle, like a giant litter tray, with just the odd tuft of false oat-grass and fan of viper's bugloss hanging on for grim death. An army of pylons marched out of the nuclear station, two by two. I passed a caravan park, the entrance flanked by two white pillars topped by Greek statues, after which the road to the office went right through the legs of a pylon, humming noisily above. 'Do you want the quiet life?' read the sign at the gate.

The cycle track ran right along the fence to Dungeness B, which, close up, looked as if it was made of Lego. I stopped to take a photograph, grateful for digital technology: I could imagine, in this day and age, that a man taking so many photographs of nuclear power stations into Snappy Snaps might have some explaining to do.

I cycled around the tip of the peninsula, the skies above me infinite, where little fairy-tale wooden dwellings sat on the shingle, dotted around in a seemingly random fashion. Although far from abject, this cluster of old wooden houses on an isolated beach reminded me of shanty towns I'd seen while travelling in Africa and South America. It seemed so incongruous in modern Britain, a nation of strict compliance and order, like it was an exclave of some developing-world nation with lax planning rules.

I couldn't tell whether I liked Dungeness or not – about which, I'm sure, Dungeness wouldn't give a stuff and rightly so. But it was one of the weirdest places I'd ever been.

I rode up the east side of the peninsula, flanked by a wide, flat shingle beach on one side, where rusting winches that once hauled fishing boats out of the sea were dotted around, and on the other by single-storey houses, hunkered down, braced for the weather-battering that this exposed part of the coast must take in winter. From many windows glinted the lenses of telescopes on tripods, as if permanently on the lookout for invaders.

In the distance to my right I could see white cliffs. It took me a while to work out what they were, and then it came to me. I was looking at the bluffs of Cap Gris-Nez in France, sparkling on the horizon. I stopped to have a better look. I thought back to Stranraer, where Northern Ireland was so close it felt like I could hit it by skimming a stone, and of all the various islands and headlands that had revealed themselves to me as the coastline buckled and turned, all pieces of a fabulous jigsaw. And now there was France, just over the water. You can look at an atlas and see the shape of a nation, but only by actually travelling all the way around it can you truly understand the way it was formed, hold that whole picture together in your mind. And there was now something else for me, something really quite marvellous. It was almost as if I could feel my country in my bones.

Just the other side of Folkestone, looking for somewhere to stay the night, I followed a sign bearing a picture of a tent down a long, steep and narrow lane. At the end, tucked underneath the chalk cliffs, sheltered by the low trees encircling it, and overlooking a beach with rows of battered wooden groynes, was one of the most beautiful campsites of the trip.

The site was deserted save for a few motor caravans bearing Dutch and German plates.

'You're just in time,' the site manager said. 'We close for the winter after tonight.'

I found the perfect pitch, on a little raised platform of earth overlooking the beach, enclosed on three sides by bushes, the mellifluous sound of the waves below me. The sun was setting, turning the chalk cliffs pink then ochre. Over the other side of the English Channel, the cliffs of Cap Gris-Nez were going through the same light show. A constant procession of giant tankers and freighters ran parallel to the shore, heading through the Straits of Dover, the busiest shipping lane in the world. There was also a constant procession of ferries cutting perpendicularly across them, coming from or heading to France, the boats all managing somehow to manoeuvre around each other in the gloaming, like some waterborne ballet.

I was sliding the last of the three poles into my tent when I heard a crack. The connecting sleeve linking two sections had shattered. I wound some gaffer tape around the join and gingerly fed it back through the tent, hoping it would hold up for the night. I looked at the rest of the tent: at the rips that I'd sewn up, at the patches and the strips of gaffer tape, the fraying guy ropes, the hardened trails of silicone I'd run along the seams and the splatters of seagull shit. I'd spent probably a hundred nights in the tent over the past five months. It had sheltered me from torrential rain, hailstones and ferocious storms, protected me from mosquitoes, midges and missiles. In it, I had experienced a righteous, exhausted sleep, the depth of which I'd only previously known under general anaesthetic. I'd awoken to the kind of views normally only millionaires could afford to wake up to, accompanied by 'The Lark Ascending', original nature mix. But perhaps the greatest thing was always knowing it was with me, like a snail carrying its home: a secure base in a bag.

The tent had been through a lot, and was showing the scars. I knew that this was probably my last night of the trip under canvas.

I ran my hand along the top of it and said thank you, grateful for the seclusion of the bushes. I could imagine the conversation in the camper vans taking a Fawlty Towers turn.

'Vot is he doing now, Hans?'

'He is stroking his tent and talking to it!'

'Theeze English, zey are crazy.'

'However did zey vin ze war?'

There was a ferocious climb out of Folkestone the next morning, after which I rode along the cliff-tops into a stiff, cold headwind, fantastic views out to sea, the Channel looking restless and angry. I stopped at the memorial to the Battle of Britain pilots, where full-size replicas of Spitfires and Hurricanes sat by a wall honouring the names of the dead. At the edge of the cliff sat an airman, cast in concrete, staring up at the skies over the sea as if in a trance.

There was a steep dive down into Dover, a vile tangle of busy roads and roundabouts, full of lorries spewing out of the docks, and then straight back out the other side, up another huge climb. There I picked up the start of the National Cycle Network's Route 1, which runs from Dover all the way to the north coast of Scotland, where I'd last seen it. Route 1 had been my constant companion for the first part of my trip, and it felt good to see the white number on its little red square again, like being reunited with an old friend. I also knew that Route 1 would take me all the way to Blackfriars Bridge.

I sat on a bench at Langdon Cliffs, high above Dover's docks, and looked down at the ferries and giant catamarans waltzing and pirouetting around each other gracefully, before they passed between the harbour walls and arrowed towards the bluffs of France on the horizon. The evacuation procedure announcements, in English, French and German, drifted up the cliffs to find me, as loud and as clear as if I was standing next to the tannoy.

Route 1 took me along some glorious car-free sections, the track following the gentle undulations of the land, and then, suddenly, the trail dipped down to the sea to St Margaret's at Cliffe and South Foreland Point. I'd run out of Britain yet again. I could go no further east, was just looking out at the grey mass of the North Sea. Just like John O'Groats, Cape Wrath and Land's End before it, South Foreland, wild and windswept, looked and felt like a proper turning point.

I looked up along the coast. I could see the promontory of North Foreland, on the Isle of Thanet, some 15 miles in the distance. I scanned my map. North Foreland would be where I'd run out of Britain for the last time, where the Thames Estuary met the sea. I stared at it for a few minutes, drinking in the significance of it all. Then I pointed the bike north. A little over an hour later, I would be turning for home.

Chapter 25

*'Whoever invented the bicycle deserves
the thanks of humanity.'*
Lord Charles Beresford

I woke up on my last day on the road in a single bed with a lurid pink duvet in a Margate seafront hotel. It was first light, and I wanted to have an early start so I could get to London before nightfall. I lay there for a while, staring at the ceiling, thinking that the next time I woke up it would be in my own bed, that there would be no packing to be done, no pedals to turn.

I started putting my stuff into the panniers. This had become another one of the trip's delicious rituals, everything belonging in its rightful place. There was one last thing on the bedside table: a book I'd just finished reading. I picked it up. It was *Pedalling to Hawaii* by Stevie Smith. I flicked open the cover. On the first page were the scrawled words: 'To Mike. Enjoy the adventure!' Ordinarily, books I had finished would be left behind for someone else to pick up. I put it in my bar bag.

The hotel had 50 rooms, but I was the only guest in the large, echoey breakfast room. The radio was tuned to a local station. Two men had been beaten up by a masked gang in Sittingbourne; an off-licence robbed in Ramsgate. The annual grape harvest started that day in Kent.

The breakfast waiter was a stonemason who'd recently been laid off.

'Unemployed two weeks, then this job came up.'

He had a young baby.

'Got to do what you've got to do, haven't you,' he said. 'Hopefully won't be for long. Where you headed?'

'London.'

'On a bike!'

Five months earlier, I'd have reacted the same way. But it all seemed so normal to me now. But I was constantly surprised by the surprise.

I left Margate and got on to the Viking Trail, the coastal cycle path running along the base of the low chalk cliffs of Minnis Bay, like I was riding under the ramparts of a giant alabaster castle. The twin towers of Reculver's ruined twelfth-century church, St Mary's came and went.

'Where's that?' I asked a man in Herne Bay, pointing to some land way off in the distance across the water.

'Essex.'

'Essex,' I said, in whispered awe, in much the same way I imagine Columbus did upon sighting the New World. 'I was there five months ago. Can you believe it?'

The man, without the benefit of context, and with not the foggiest idea what I was talking about, seemed to be able to believe it quite easily.

My phone buzzed a text message. It was my friend Simon.

'Where are you?' it read.

I'd not been in touch with any of my friends in the past few days, hadn't planned to let anybody know I was arriving home that day. I'd slipped away quietly, and imagined I'd slip back in under the radar. That was my way, usually. No fuss, no bother. But I couldn't lie.

'I'm in Herne Bay,' I texted back. 'Will hopefully make London later today.'

'Great. Will meet you at Tower Bridge,' came the reply. It surprised me, but it felt good that somebody would be waiting for me.

In Whitstable, with its lovely pastel-coloured clapboard houses, I broke the no-seafood-while-cycling-in-case-it-gives-you-the-shits rule. I figured that as black pudding was to Stornoway, clotted cream to Devon and pasties to Cornwall, so oysters were to Whitstable, so hell and be damned. At St Augustine's fish market overlooking the beautiful little harbour, I ordered half a dozen. The man behind the counter, on finding out what I was doing, insisted on making it a dozen, doused in lemon and Tabasco and pepper, and refused to take any money. Concerned that the oysters alone wouldn't provide the necessary energy, he then gave me a bun filled with smoked mackerel covered in sweet chilli sauce. Then another.

Then some winkles. My re-entry into London might yet prove to be an explosive affair.

Through lovely Faversham, with its ancient cobbled market square and Elizabethan riverside warehouses, the air a thick fug with the smell of boiling hops from the Shepherd Neame brewery. And then out into the fields and orchards, the quiet lanes flanked by trees groaning with ripe feral pears, damsons, mirabelles and greengages. I shovelled a few into my mouth, the juices running down my chin, then filled my bar bag. As with the blackberries I'd been eating all around the coast, it felt sublime to be refuelling from Britain's free larder. And still no sign of trouble from the seafood.

I cycled on, to the marshland village of Conyer, and then along the levees, floating across the sunken, drowned landscape, past the ribs of eviscerated boats sticking out of the mud like dinosaur carcasses, the crows in full voice, Magwitch haunting every creek.

Gillingham, Chatham, Rochester. A sign read London 30 miles. Time seemed to be accelerating now.

A little boy, maybe seven or eight years old, was riding his bike along the pavement and kept up with me for a while.

'Where you going?' he asked.

I told him London.

'Blimey! That's far,' he said, and his eyes couldn't have contained more wonder than if I'd told him I was riding to the moon.

At Gravesend, the Thames reappeared, not wide and majestic, as it had been the last time I'd seen it at Whitstable, before the Isles of Sheppey and Grain had obscured it, but imprisoned by concrete banks, so narrow I could easily read the names of the ships moored on the far bank.

I felt a little sick. But I knew it wasn't the oysters. It was a rising sense of being hemmed in, claustrophobic, flushed with a feeling of loss for the absent vastness of the sea, my constant companion for almost half a year, filling the right-hand side of my world. It had disappeared abruptly, and I was already grieving.

I passed the gigantic Bluewater Shopping Centre, buried in its chalk pit, a traffic jam of cars queuing back for maybe a mile waiting to get in its car park. I didn't know who looked more miserable at that point: the motorists going nowhere or me going somewhere I wasn't sure I wanted to be. Under the Dartford Bridge and I was back inside the M25, and then Erith. I was being sucked into London and I wanted the world to stop.

The traffic was heavy now, aggressive too. At Thamesmead Estate, on a dual carriageway, a car swerving between lanes to cut through the slow-moving traffic came so close to me he almost grazed my panniers. I clutched the handlebars so tightly my knuckles started hurting. My breathing was rapid and shallow.

I rounded the curve of the river and there, beyond the Thames barrier at Woolwich, were the towers of Canary Wharf, monstrous great things, much bigger and more numerous than I remembered them. Everything was grey, like the dimmer switch had been turned down. The Woolwich ferry shuttled back and forth across the river and for a second I seriously considered jumping on it and going around for another lap.

Greenwich, New Cross. Red buses (at least they hadn't changed). Sirens. Irritation. Familiar streets now, that looked utterly unfamiliar. My city. Not my city. I stopped at a red light and looked down at my bike. I raced through in my head the places it had taken me to – across the bouncing bridges suspended in the sky, past the castles of Northumberland, to wild Cape Wrath, through the Assynt mountains, the lonely, windswept Outer Hebrides, around the majestic sweep of Morecambe Bay, the Gower Peninsula, up and down the murderous hills of Devon and Cornwall, to Land's End and, finally, Bermondsey. The speedo read 4,625 miles. I would work out later that I'd climbed 232,000 feet in total, eight times the height of Everest. It seemed impossible to me that this piece of cobalt-blue steel could have carried me through and up all of that. I thought about my Colnago at home. My bedroom was going to be a little bit more crowded in the future, for how could I ever put the Ridgeback in the shed after all this?

A commuter on a bike pulled alongside.

'Hello,' I said. I would have to relearn the conventions of the big city, where talking to strangers at traffic lights was just unacceptable.

He looked at me for a second, an expression of confusion and fear on his face. Then he smiled.

Clocking my load, he asked: 'Going far?'

'Only just up the road,' I said, and for the second time in the space of a few hours I felt a great sense of loss.

*

Simon was waiting for me at Tower Bridge in the fast-encroaching dark. He shook my hand in the formal manner appropriate for the completion of a grand adventure. 'You did it,' he said. 'Amazing.'

I opened my bar bag and fished out a couple of pears and a damson.

'Here you go, present from Kent.'

We walked along the South Bank, Simon munching his fruit. After a while, we stopped at a riverside pub and sat on the terrace overlooking the water. He asked me how the trip had been, but I was struggling to remember much detail at that moment, like it hadn't been real. Sitting there, opposite the place I'd set off from five months earlier, it all seemed like a dream, fast-receding into the ether.

Two young men were fussing around my bike, their girlfriends standing alongside looking bored. One of the men said something in Spanish to his girlfriend.

'He wants to know where you just come from.'

I told her about the trip, and she translated the information. The young man said something to her.

'What did he say?' I asked.

'He said that when he grows up, he wants to be you.'

We finished our pints and carried on walking towards Blackfriars Bridge.

'So,' said Simon. 'Still going to Argentina?'

'I think I just want to go home for a while.'

'You can always go next year.'

'Maybe.'

We were at the south side of Blackfriars Bridge. All I had to do was ride across the Thames and the circle of Britain was complete. It was dark now, and the rain had started to fall gently. I felt reluctant to cross, as if this had been the best book I'd ever read and this was the last precious page.

I switched on my lights, said farewell to Simon and pedalled across the bridge, my last water crossing, the Thames below me black and oily and bubbling. How much water had flowed down it in my five months away; yet it would always be the same river. At the far end, I looked across to the road that went off to the east. Queen Victoria Street, my magic portal, the place I'd passed through to start the most extraordinary adventure of my life.

Then, as the rain grew heavier, I turned left and headed for home.

Acknowledgements

Thanks, first of all, to Andrew Goodfellow at Ebury, for his continued support, sage advice and unshakeable conviction that things will always turn out okay in the end. Thanks also to my editors, Liz Marvin and Ali Nightingale, for their patience, encouragement and help, to Jonathan Baker, the book's designer for what, I think, is a lovely job, and to the copyeditor Justine Taylor. For his efforts above and beyond, I'd like to say a huge thank you to Rory Foster, and also to my great friends Wendy Swan and Simon Shore for their input and guidance. I'd like also to mention the banana sellers and flapjack makers of Britain, and the producers of Stornoway black pudding, for their help in enabling me to complete my journey. I owe much to the people I met on my trip, who were always kind, generous, funny and hospitable to this stranger. Never let anybody say that Britain is broken. And finally, I'd like to say thank you to my bicycle. I love you, but not in that weird way that can get you arrested. I'm sure that anybody who loves their bike will understand what I mean.

About the Author

Mike Carter grew up in Birmingham and now lives in south-west London. He works for the *Guardian* as a travel writer and subeditor, although he considers his spell as a dancer at the Halikarnas nightclub in Bodrum, Turkey, to have been the peak of his career. He is the author of *One Man and his Bike* and *Uneasy Rider, Travels Through a Midlife Crisis*, his story of a 20,000-mile trip to the four corners of Europe on a motorbike.

http://authorsplace.co.uk/mike-carter/